130

New Jersey Dreaming

Sherry B. Ortner

New Jersey Dreaming

Capital, Culture, and the Class of '58

Duke University Press Durham and London 2003

Second printing, 2006

© 2003 Duke University Press All rights reserved Printed in the United States

of America on acid-free paper ∞ Designed by C. H. Westmoreland Typeset by

Tseng Information Systems, Inc. Library of Congress Cataloging-in-Publication

Data appear on the last printed page of this book

To my father,

Samuel Ortner,

in memoriam

To Gwen, as always

To Tim, for everything

With love to all

Contents

WHAT THE CLASS OF '58 MADE

List of Tables and Map

Acknowledgments

My first debt goes to the Class of '58 of Weequahic High School, most of whom filled out questionnaires, many of whom submitted to interviews, and most of whom waited patiently (even if they couldn't resist a little teasing) for a book that took more than a decade to complete. A big collective thank-you to the Class.

Second, for money: For financial support of this project, I thank the John D. and Catherine T. MacArthur Foundation, the Wenner-Gren Foundation for Anthropological Research, several research offices at the University of Michigan (the Literature, Science, and the Arts Faculty Assistance Fund, the Rackham School of Graduate Studies, and the Office of the Vice President for Research), and the National Humanities Center of Research Triangle Park, North Carolina. This project literally could not have been done without the released time provided by the MacArthur Fellowship, the research expense funds provided by Wenner-Gren and the University of Michigan, and the funded write-up time provided by the National Humanities Center. A final semester of write-up time came from the generous Columbia University Tenured Faculty Research Assistance Program.

Third, to people who helped me do the actual research: For ingenuity, energy, and tenaciousness in locating members of the Class of '58 (as well as hospitality and friendship—see below), I owe a great debt of thanks to classmate Judith Epstein Rothbard. Classmate David Wheeler, with great warmth and good nature, helped me find several of the African American members of the class, and also in some cases facilitated the interview process with these classmates. Sue Ellen Platnick Boff, Helene Rosenblatt Portnoy, and Barry Wiernik also shared address lists and other memorabilia from earlier reunions.

For their generous and open-hearted hospitality, without which I could not have afforded to do the project, I thank all the people I stayed with during the fieldwork: George and Judy Rothbard in New Jersey and Florida; Julian and Ethel Decter in New Jersey; Neal and Karin Goldman in Brooklyn; John and Betsy Canaday in Boston; Margie and Howard Drubner in Connecticut; Nancy Lutkehaus in Los Angeles;

and my cousins: Sheila and Frank Tretter in Southhampton, Long Island, Norman and JoAnn Panitch in Los Angeles, and Anita Auerbach in the Washington, D.C., area. All of these folks not only housed me and fed me, but often started me on my way in the mornings with directions and good cheer, and listened patiently to the accounts of my adventures and misadventures when I got home in the evenings.

Fourth, to fabulously intelligent, energetic, and willing research assistants and helpers in several institutions: At the University of Michigan, to Lynn Fisher for all her help with mailings, database organization, and coordination of transcribers; it was Lynn who helped me get control of this project in its initial stages. Gary Rothbard (son of classmates George and Judy), then an undergraduate at the University of Michigan and an all-around smart and organized person, took over the job after Lynn went off to the field. At the University of California, Berkeley, Rafael Reyes took a lot of time to introduce me to his new field-data text-management program, "InterView," and Allison Pugh spent hours coding the texts to work within that program. (With apologies to Rafael and Allison, I confess that in the end I did not use this program. Microsoft Windows's "Find" function actually did everything I needed in terms of locating relevant passages in interview transcripts and field notes.) At both Michigan and U.C. Berkeley an army of students, both undergraduate and graduate, transcribed interview manuscripts for me; unfortunately, their names are by now lost in the mists. My thanks to all. At the National Humanities Center in Durham, North Carolina, Brooke Nixon was the only brave person to answer an ad for an all-purpose research assistant for the year, and was both a great help and a pleasure to work with. At Columbia University, Chauncy Lennon again helped with the endless mysteries of text-data management (it was Chauncy who said you can do everything with Windows, and he was right), and Jennifer DeWan combed through the manuscript, redid all the tables, and generally cleaned everything up with patience and ingenuity.

I also wish to thank here some colleagues who provided smaller, but essential, pieces of the puzzle, especially Tom Fricke, who helped me work out the significance of the divorce statistics; and Barbara Rous Harris, who provided me with information about her mother, beloved Weequahic teacher and upholder of social justice, Mrs. Sadie Rous.

Fifth, deepest thanks to colleagues and friends who heard or read earlier drafts of chapters or chapter-papers of this manuscript and took the trouble to provide thoughtful and helpful feedback: Frank Cancian, Fernando Coronil, Enid Kesselman Gort, Webb Keane, Timothy Lensmire, Jo Anne Meyerowitz, James Morgan, Michael Peletz, Peter Redfield, Judy Rothbard, Lee Schlesinger, Nancy Tomes, Loïc Wacquant, Paul Willis, Ken Wissoker, and Kevin A. Yelvington. There were also excellent questions from audiences at the anthropology departments of the City University of New York Graduate Center; the University of Colorado, Boulder; Duke University; and the University of North Carolina, as well as from general audiences at the National Humanities Center, the Retzius Lecture (Stockholm), and the Social History Workshop of the University of Pennsylvania.

Finally, profoundest thanks to friends and colleagues who read the entire manuscript and provided detailed comments: Faye Ginsburg, George Marcus, Mary Murrell, Judy Rothbard, Abby Stewart, Timothy Taylor, Sylvia Yanagisako, and several anonymous press reviewers. As someone once remarked, detailed comments are among the most valuable commodities (or gifts) in academia. I take them very seriously and am truly grateful to those who take the time to make them.

At the level of personal support, thanks and love as always to my brother Mel Ortner and my sister-in-law Janine Simonell, who among other things try to teach and persuade me to relax, and sometimes succeed. And last but never least, thanks to Timothy D. Taylor for love and support, and for sharing with me a world in which good music, good food, and intellectual stimulation are all part of everyday life.

Some corrections have been made for the paperback edition. I am grateful to the many careful readers who spotted errors in the hardcover edition of this book. Unfortunately I did not keep a complete list of who pointed out which mistake, so let me just say a collective thank you to all. However I must single out Joseph Illick, who spotted the fact that I misinterpreted the numbers in Table 12, and to Bill Sewell who generously agreed to read through my revised paragraphs surrounding the table and offered extremely useful suggestions for their improvement.

Letter to the Class of '58

A few words about who got "chosen" to be represented in this book. Everyone I could find was contacted for a questionnaire by mail and/or by phone. If you sent yours back or if you allowed me to fill one out for you over the telephone, you are in this book, if only in the statistics.

I interviewed about one hundred people in depth. They were more or less chosen at random—not in the scientific sense (though I did try to get a broadly representative sample of the different groups in the class) but in the accidental sense. Of course, some people did not want to be interviewed, but they are probably not reading this letter. Beyond that, if you were not interviewed it was a fluke of geography, demography, or whether you happened to be home to answer your phone when I called. Please do not take it personally.

About kids. I interviewed about fifty of the children of the Class of '58. If your child was not chosen, it was for even more random reasons. In any event, this book got too long and a discussion of the kids is not included. I have not yet decided what, if anything, I will go on to do concerning the children of the Class of '58. I will say here that it was an incredible pleasure to interview those fifty young people, a breath of fresh air, a glimpse of the future.

About names. I promised everyone who was interviewed confidentiality; however, I soon realized that people who did something good or noteworthy wanted their real names used, at least in the context of their good deeds or great successes, while others who did not do so well or who said something mean or embarrassing did not want their names used, at least in those contexts. After both searching my own soul and consulting wise colleagues, I have decided to maintain the policy of total confidentiality. Thus all names have been changed except for a few cases (marked by an asterisk), which mostly had to do with the logistics, rather than the substance, of the project.

My strategy for inventing pseudonyms was to juggle and recombine the first and last names of all the members of the class while staying within relevant race/ethnic groups. At first I gave a single individual a single pseudonym and used it consistently throughout the book. Then

I realized—or at least feared—that this did not provide enough protection from the really assiduous classmate identifier. I therefore changed pseudonyms more frequently, so that the same person no longer consistently has the same pseudonym.

Finally, this is an academic book. Many of you may have hoped for something lighter and more readable. What can I say? I hope you are pleased anyway, if only for the fact that it exists and memorializes for all time the remarkable Class of (June) '58 of Weequahic High School.

A Note on Style

Quotations from verbatim transcripts of interviews are always marked with quotation marks. Quotations from my field notes (my own observations, summaries of what others have said, etc.) are not marked with quotation marks and are always preceded or ended with [from the field notes].

chapter 1

Introduction

On June 18, 1958, 304 classmates, including this ethnographer, marched down the aisle of the auditorium of Weequahic High School in Newark, New Jersey, to receive their high school diplomas.[1] This book is an account of how the Class of June '58 got from its modest, largely working- and middle-class origins in the late 1950s to a situation in which there is virtually no recognizable working class left, and in which close to 60 percent of the members of the class would now easily be described as part of America's wealthy "white overclass" (Lind 1995). In order to understand how this happened, I follow the Class of '58 from its childhood to the present. I attempt to tease out the incredibly complex interplay between the circumstances (class, race/ethnicity, gender) into which people were born and, in high school, "tracked"; their own imaginings and practices in relation to cultural conceptions of "success"; and the conditions of a larger American history, particularly a series of social movements, during the lifetime of the Class.

But the amount of mobility experienced by the Class of '58 was not unique for its time, nor are many of the other changes (e.g., in the divorce rate) between the Class and its parents. Thus the other major purpose of the book is to show the ways in which the upward mobility and other patterns of social change experienced by the Class of '58 fit into a picture of wider, and quite momentous, social transformations in the United States in the second half of the twentieth century. These changes, summarized under the rubric of the shift to "late capitalism," have often appeared as a sudden break with the past, starting in the 1970s. (David Harvey [1989] has actually pegged them to a particular year, 1972.) Yet it is possible to see many of the seeds of these late capitalist transformations in the slow evolution of the Class of '58 over the past fifty or so years.

My decision to shift my research to the United States was a long time in the making. I spent the first half of my career working with the Sherpas of Nepal, including four stints of fieldwork and the publication of three books. But I was increasingly coming to feel that anthropology has to be a two-way street, and that it was important to focus my anthropological and critical skills equally on my own culture. Contrary to popular notions, there is a long tradition of significant work by anthropologists in the United States, not only with Native American groups but on the dominant white culture as well.[2] Yet, by and large, it is fair to say that anthropology as a field has been largely identified with the study of other cultures, and that the otherness of those cultures— "primitive," premodern, "Oriental," exotic—has often been seen (despite good intentions to the contrary) as diametrically opposed to "us." Over the last twenty years or so, however, the field has radically questioned and reconstructed many of its own premises, including especially this one (starting with Clifford and Marcus 1986; see also Ortner 2000, 2002a). On the one hand, the attempt to understand the perspectives of other people(s) in other places, while still central to anthropology, is no longer construed as a study of exoticness and difference. On the other hand, and this is the flip side of the same point, there is an understanding that the very idea of exoticness—of difference that is "interesting" and titillating—can take shape only in cultures with histories of power and dominance against "others," including, of course, the United States.

I think of my last book on the Sherpas (1999a) as transitional and as embodying these changes in the field. Thus, instead of looking at the Sherpas alone, as if their culture were just another specimen of cultural difference, I looked at the long history of Sherpa involvement with Himalayan moutaineering and the ways in which Sherpas and Western climbers (and later "Eastern" climbers as well) shaped one another, and shaped as well this exotic (yes) subculture of mountaineering, with ripples and reverberations back into the respective lives and worlds of both sides. That book represented for me the shift noted above, but coming from the Sherpa side. On the surface, the present book moves fully to the Western side, and might seem to ignore the ways in which the Class of '58 is part of a larger world. Yet the base of this book is precisely the immigration of its constituent ethnic groups to the United States in the late nineteenth century, as well as the forced immigration of African Americans long before that. The cultures of striving and mobility, and of snobbery and discrimination, discussed in this book are grounded in part in those earlier moments of global "flows."

Newark, New Jersey, the originary site of this study, is a commercial and port city across the Hudson River from New York City (see map). In the 1950s it had a population of about 500,000, mostly middle and working class. It was very mixed in racial and ethnic terms, with just about every immigrant ethnic group one could imagine as well as a growing population of African American families moving up from the South to work. I note before going on that Newark and New Jersey have long been considered by outsiders—and by many insiders as well—to be ugly places.[3] Hence the irony of the title of this book, for many people dreamed of getting out of New Jersey rather than—as in the famous Mamas and Papas song about California—getting in.[4]

Newark in the 1950s had seven public high schools located in different neighborhoods. Weequahic High School, the point of departure for this study, is located in the southwest corner of the city (see map). The name, pronounced *Wee-QUAY-ic*, or, when spoken rapidly, *Week-wake*, is taken from the Native American group called Weequahic that inhabited the area when the first settlers arrived, part of the larger Lenape tribal group that occupied parts of New York and Pennsylvania as well (Kraft 1986). The name of the high school sport teams is, not surprisingly, the Weequahic Indians.

The high school opened in 1932 and was key to the expansion of the so-called Weequahic section of the city. Starting in the 1920s, and accelerating in the 1940s and 1950s, the section attracted a growing population of middle-class Jewish families. The "Gentiles," as Jewish folks called them, fled westward, and Weequahic became known as a predominantly Jewish neighborhood. The Class of '58 was still 83 percent Jewish at the time of graduation. The school was considered an excellent academic high school at the time (Cunningham 1988, Helmreich 1999, *Newark Evening News* 1959a, 1959b).[5]

The most famous graduate of Weequahic High School is Philip Roth, who has written with great ethnographic acumen about the school and the neighborhood in many of his novels (starting with the collection of short stories, *Goodbye, Columbus*).[6] Other graduates of the school, well known in other circles, include the former basketball star and coach Alvin Attles, a highly placed economist in the Reagan administration named Robert Ortner (no relation, as far as I know), feminist philosopher Susan Bordo, and urban sociologist Janet Abu-Lughod (who also happens to be the mother of anthropologist Lila Abu-Lughod). The poet Allen Ginsberg grew up in the Weequahic neighborhood, and his aunt, Hannah Ginsberg Litzky, taught at the high school, but "A.G."

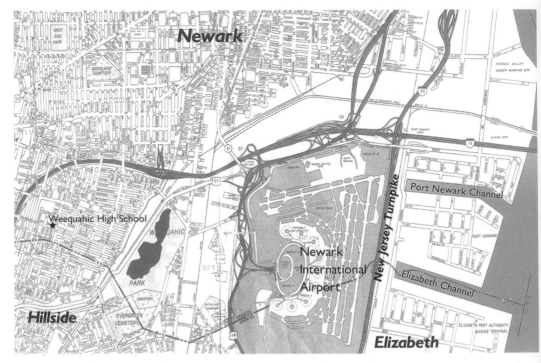

Southwest Newark, New Jersey. Map shows Weequahic High School between the
Hillside border and the Newark airport. The New Jersey turnpike and Port Newark
are to the east of the airport; New York City is to the northeast.
Map by James Colman.

and his family moved to Paterson, New Jersey, before he started high
school. In addition, Weequahic graduates are everywhere in academia,
and I rarely give a talk at an academic institution without someone
standing up and saying that he or she or his or her parent went to
Weequahic.

Newark began to change racially in the 1960s, as did the race/ethnic
mix of Weequahic High School. There were already some African
American families in the Weequahic neighborhood and a handful of
African American classmates in the Class of '58. Up until 1967, the
movement of Black families into the neighborhood was basically a
middle-class movement. But after the race riots/insurrection of 1967,
which left twenty-six people dead and more than fifteen hundred
wounded (Cunningham 1988:325), white flight accelerated dramati-

cally, and within a few years both the neighborhood and the high school were all nonwhite and largely poor.[7]

For the present study, however, I do not follow the fate of the high school and the neighborhood. Rather I follow the fate of a specific cohort, the graduating class of June 1958.[8] As already noted, the Class of '58 has been, for the most part, very "successful." This means that many of them have risen up beyond their origins, made a lot of money, and/or achieved positions of high prestige. Cultural and personal notions of success will be explored at length in this book. Here, however, it is important to note a particular point: success is always comparative. One is more or less successful compared with other people. But even more important, at least in the context of American ideology, one is more or less successful compared with where one started — one's family background, one's experiences growing up, opportunities seized or not. One classmate, for example, who by most accounts would be seen as quite successful,

> felt embarrassed to see people from high school, because "she didn't live up to her potential." She came back to this at the end [of the interview], when I asked if there was anything important to her that I hadn't asked about or that she would like to talk about. She said she just didn't become what people would have expected her to be, having been so highly ranked in the class. She thought her high school boyfriend was living nearby but she wouldn't look him up because she was ashamed of her lack of success. [from the field notes][9]

If success is relative to expectations for a past self, then a study of the success of the Class of '58 based on interviews conducted in the 1990s is necessarily retrospective, and I need to say a few words first about the methodological issues of this kind of work.

A Genealogy of the Present

The social and cultural genealogy of the present Class of '58 is pursued on several levels. The first is memory. Much of what came out in the interviews were memories in one form or another. That is, they were stories about the self in the past meant to illuminate the self in the present. But "memory" is a concept that goes off in an almost infinite number of directions.[10] Here let me specify briefly the ways in which it will play into the present work.

First, "memory" always raises simple questions of truth and accuracy. People forget things. People distort things. People lie. Most of this does not matter to the present project, or indeed to most ethnographic projects. The ethnographer is not dependent on the truthful and accurate memory of a single informant, but seeks instead the overlaps and/or contradictions between many people's memories or, more accurately, their accounts of their memories. As anthropologists (and probably psychiatrists) are fond of saying, everything is data, even the lies.

More relevant perhaps to the present project, on this point of distortion and lies, is the question of whether people would have reasons to withhold or change their stories in ways that are systematically related to me as their interlocutor—because of certain perceptions of me, and/or because there are still networks of relationships among former classmates along which information told to me might (it is feared) then travel further. There was almost certainly some of this going on, and I do try to note it or take it into account where relevant.

But there are larger questions of remembering and forgetting that must be addressed. People told me stories, and these stories, recorded and transcribed, form texts that could be more profoundly interpreted and interrogated for underlying ideologies, missing meanings, hidden patterns, systematic lacunae, emotional overtones—all the things that attract the attention of the interpretive anthropologist, the textual critic, or the psychoanalyst. The point here is not simply distortion or omission as creating problems of accuracy. The point is that the text always can be shown to say much more than it seems to say on the surface. This kind of textual analysis, whether Freudian, poststructuralist, or cultural-interpretive, can be very powerful indeed, and most of my other work relies on some versions of it quite strongly.

But such work is part of quite a different project from the one undertaken here. Thus at no point do I engage in close interpretation of a single informant's memory/story/text.[11] Indeed, I resisted what in some cases was a temptation to do so. I do, however, engage in a certain amount of cultural interpretation. Thus I bring out certain patterns across a number of texts, patterns that amount to a cultural discourse, or the echoes of a cultural discourse within individual stories. This is particularly true for the ways in which people talk about "success." There are striking patterns in success-talk that people generate individually but that are so consistent across informants as to amount to a cultural "tape." Here, then, the texts are interpreted for their underlying structures of culture/ideology.

Beyond this, however, memories/stories are used almost counter-interpretively. Rather than being treated as rich repositories of hidden personal truths or cultural anxieties, they are used to do other kinds of work. First, they are treated as pieces of a larger puzzle which, when fitted together, allow me to construct a narrative of the 304 members of the Class of '58 moving diversely through time and space, and becoming what they have become. And, second, they are used to convey the contours of people's quite conscious feelings in the course of this movement. Indeed the texts of memories/stories are rarely quoted for their "facts," which are narratively organized by me. Rather the texts are quoted to bring to the reader the powerful feelings of pain, pleasure, shame, pride, anger, humor, irony, and more that are always part of both living life and remembering it.

The other register in which a genealogy of the present is pursued is the register of "history." Like "memory," the word is enormously polysemic. But as I am using it here, "history" is the collection of (representations of) events in the world constructed by others (anthropologists, historians, journalists, and more) outside of, but intersecting with, the memories of informants. It is meant to be relatively "objective," although I wish to be careful here not to contrast memory as wholly subjective with history as wholly objective. Memory is full of historical truth, while history is full of selection, omission, and interpretation. Neither is wholly true or wholly false. They are nonetheless different kinds of knowledge-making, and they tell us more together than each alone.

History is itself used in at least three ways. There is first of all the notion of history as periods, usually decades, with their own social, economic, and cultural configurations: "the Fifties" with its associations of prosperity, stability, and repression; "the Sixties" with its associations of social and cultural upheaval; and so forth. These will be especially important in the first part of the book, as I try to play my informants' memories off against a larger world that they embodied, enacted, or in some cases resisted. The second kind of history, more relevant to the later part of the book, is the history of social movements. Again it is a question of putting memory in counterpoint with things known about in other ways. Thus Americans are culturally encouraged to imagine that "success" is a matter of personal effort, and of course that is true to some extent. But I argue in the later chapters that personal success must be seen in the context of social movements on which people were, often unwittingly, capitalizing. Thus for the Jewish members of the Class of '58 there had been a long history of collective struggle against anti-Semitism; for the African American classmates there were various movements of Black liberation; for the women of the Class there was feminism. The bootstrapping that moved so many members of the Class of '58 up the ladder cannot be understood except in the context of those histories.

And finally there is as it were Big History, the history of social transformation, to which I have already alluded. The past two decades have seen a spate of academic and popular arguments to the effect that we inhabit a whole new world, that there has been a massive historical shift from the modern, industrialized world of mid-century, nation-bound, classic capitalism, to the postmodern, postindustrial world of turn-of-the-millennium, global, late capitalism. While I have a certain resistance to this kind of apocalyptic characterization of world transformation, it is nonetheless clear that there have been major changes between the 1950s and the present. It is equally clear that, since they were not brought about by acts of God or acts of nature, they must be the product in some sense of human action—that is, of the interplay between people's lives, the formations that made them, and the formations that, willy-nilly, they played a role in reproducing or changing. Thus in the final chapter of the book I pull together the ways in which the Class of '58 of Weequahic High School—along, of course, with millions of other Americans—participated, through the many imaginings and practices of their lives, in bringing about some of these transformations.

The Class of '58 and the Question of Class

I count as the Class of '58 (hereafter sometimes C58) everyone who appeared in the Class graduation yearbook, plus one individual who finished early and whose picture did not appear. This is a total of 304 people.

Although 100 percent (known N = 246) of them have moved from their high school addresses,[12] more than half of the Class still lives in New Jersey (144 people, or 59 percent), and another 23 people, or 9 percent, live in New York State (most in the greater New York City metropolitan area), putting approximately 68 percent of the Class not very far from the original scene. The other two big clusters of graduates are in Florida (20 people, or 8 percent) and California (19 people, or 8 percent). The rest are scattered by ones and twos in twenty-two states around the country.

The gender composition of the Class at graduation was 146 men (48 percent) and 158 women (52 percent).

The race/ethnic composition of the Class at graduation was 83 percent white/Jewish (252 individuals), 6 percent African American (19 individuals), and 11 percent from all other ethnic groups (33 individuals, including 1 uncertain).[13] The striking thing about these numbers is, of course, the radical ethnic imbalance. Weequahic appears to all intents and purposes to have been a "Jewish school," and this immediately raises the question of the representativeness of this study. It depends, of course, on what one means by "representative." In any event, in chapter 5 I will present a detailed argument as to why Weequahic is just as "representative" as any other school/neighborhood for purposes of understanding certain patterns of American history and of American cultural thought.

And finally, there is class. The social class composition of the Class of '58 in the high school years would be described by most ordinary Americans as basically "middle class." There were few very wealthy families (most of those had already moved to the suburbs) and few very poor families. At the same time, there were significant divisions within this seemingly undifferentiated "middle-class" group—differences of occupation, material resources, and cultural capital. The question of how to demarcate these divisions, like the question of how to demarcate divisions within the class structure as a whole, is a matter of some contention, including whether one should represent it as a two-part scheme (owners/workers, haves/have-nots) or the more common folk tripartite scheme (upper/middle/lower). Sidestepping several cans of worms for purposes of providing a simple baseline, I will use the tripartite scheme for now. Using fathers' occupations (or mothers', if the father was absent) as the indicators, we arrive at a distribution of classmates roughly in the shape of a top: a small business/professional, or upper-middle, class at the top (27 percent), a larger middle-middle class in the middle (45 percent), and a smaller working and/or lower-middle class at the bottom (28 percent). It will be relevant for future discussions that the middle class at this point in time was nearly twice as large as either the upper-middle or the lower-middle/working class.

This project actually began from my sense that class in the United States is under-recognized as a factor in American social and cultural life. It was not originally a "study of a high school graduating class," but rather a study of the complex and amorphous phenomenon of social class for which my high school graduating class seemed to be as good a subject population as any.

One of the things that drew my interest to class is its extraordinary elusiveness. It seems to exist and not exist, to be everywhere and nowhere, to have a kind of now-you-see-it, now-you-don't existence (Lewis 1978, Vanneman and Cannon 1987, De Mott 1990). There is, in fact, a very marked discourse of visibility and invisibility surrounding class in America. One need only look at some titles: *The Hidden Injuries of Class* (Sennett and Cobb 1972), *Class Acts: America's Last Dirty Secret* (Eisler 1983), and "Identities: The Hidden Life of Class" (Ortner 1998a).

There are two senses in which class is "hidden" in American social and cultural life. One is personal embarrassment about talking about money—about personal income, family resources, or both. It has been said that most Americans would sooner discuss their sex lives than their incomes. American children learn early not to talk about their family's resources, high or low. For high-income people, there are cultural taboos on ostentatiousness. As one classmate said, "I just assumed we were somewhere in the middle [economically]. It wasn't quite frankly until my dad died that I realized . . . we were way up there. . . . Money was never discussed, period. Not in my presence." For low-income people, on the other hand, there are feelings of shame and failure. I have had students burst into tears and/or erupt with rage when they revealed poor or working-class or "white trash" backgrounds in the context of a college seminar composed mostly of middle- to upper-middle-class students. The experience of revealing this hidden truth about their socioeconomic selves was for many akin to "coming out" about a hidden sexual orientation.

The other sense in which class is hidden has to do with the changing place of the idea of class in American public discourse. In the early part of the twentieth century, the idea of class was largely embedded in a Marxist framework. By "class" Marx meant positions created by the mode of production of capitalism. In the classic Marxist perspective, there were fundamentally two classes: the owners of the means of production and the workers (Marx 1967). The relationship between owners and workers was fundamentally contradictory and carried the ever-present potential for class warfare and ultimately revolution. The radical notion of class in this sense drew increasing support in the United States in the 1930s (my most recent reminder of this was the film *The Cradle Will Rock* [1999]). But it was damped down by the ending of the Great Depression, the national pulling together of World War II, and the economic prosperity that followed the war. And it was given its death blow by McCarthyism and the Cold War in the 1950s, when it was equated with communism and everything antithetical to the American way of life. The story of the Class of '58 of Weequahic High School begins precisely in this era. The war, the postwar prosperity, the McCarthy era, and the Cold War basically mapped C58 lives from birth through high school.

The literature on class (mostly from history, sociology, and economics) is enormous and contentious. My own assumptions, which I will present very briefly here, are based on three areas of recent work about class that I find particularly useful.

First, I take it as fundamental that class is not some natural object lying around in the world but is culturally or discursively constructed (see Stedman Jones 1983, Scott 1988, Dirks et al. 1994). To say that class is "discursively constructed" is not to say that there is nothing "out there." On the contrary, there are real material and cultural resources out there, and they are profoundly unequally distributed. There is also a deeply entrenched capitalist order with its panoply of institutions for the production of profit. But the view of class as a discursive construction argues that different rhetorics of class do different things for different purposes. For Marx's purpose of trying to galvanize a revolutionary working class, it made sense to divide the world between owners and workers, with an emphasis on the exploitation of the working class and a call to class struggle. My own purposes here are more modest. Without denying the serious political issues raised by Marx, I am interested in understanding the workings of class in ordinary lives and in ordinary times. Specifically, I pursue two questions broadly related to the two forms of class invisibility just discussed. First, I am interested in the ways in which "class" as the general socioeconomic structure of U.S. society has undergone several massive shape-changes since World War II, including specifically the vast enlargement of the middle class after the war and its almost equally massive shrinkage in the last few decades.[14] And, second, I am interested in class as a component of personal identity like race or gender, though always less visible than those two. In taking the two questions together I treat class as something like what Bourdieu (1978, 1990) has called a "habitus," an external world of cultural assumptions and social institutions that ordinary people inhabit without thinking very much about them, and an internalized version of that world that becomes part of people's identities, generating dispositions to feel/think/judge/act in certain ways. One of the few, but very pervasive, American folk assumptions about class captures this outside-inside relationship: "You can take the person out of the class, but you can't take the class out of the person."

My second basic assumption is that class, at least in its American form, is always closely entwined with race and ethnicity. Much of the work on this point has grown out of race and/or ethnicity studies rather than class studies as such (e.g., Hall 1989, Brodkin 1989, 1999, Kelley 1997, Gregory 1998; see also Ortner 1998a). There is also a growing body of work theorizing the relationship between class-based politics and "new social movements"—the environmental or "green" movement, and the "identity movements" of feminism and race/ethnic liberation (Cohen 1982, West 1990, Aronowitz 1991, Eder 1993). In both of these bodies of literature there is an argument, with which I agree, that class still matters very much, and that making a case for the importance of other axes of inequality and/or other social movements does not obviate the necessity for paying attention to class issues. At the same time, the new social movements represent the ways in which important forms of contemporary political thought and action take place. Some of these have been very destructive, especially ethnic and religious nationalisms. But others have been powerful positive forces for change. Their relationship to class issues and class politics may be fuzzy and/or problematic, but it is precisely the challenge to both theory and practice to highlight and clarify that relationship (see especially Laclau and Mouffe 1985, Hall 1989).

Third, I assume a two-way relationship, fully active in both directions, between actors' perceptions/imaginings and objective locations. That is, at one level I subscribe to the classic position—traceable from the earliest to the most recent forms of class theorizing—that one's class location shapes one's sense of self, one's tastes, one's picture of the world and its possibilities (see, again, Bourdieu's brilliant *Distinction* on this point). At the same time, I depart from Bourdieu and others in emphasizing the degree to which the imagination, at both the level of the individual and the level of public culture, can always exceed the limits of any given position. People are never wholly constructed by their class position, or indeed by any other single aspect of their identity. These wider imaginings may take many forms, including radically oppositional forms. But even staying within the system one can always, as the saying goes, dream. Thus, for both American cultural ideology and for most of the members of the Class of '58, there is always the dream of "success," of rising above where one started. Whatever one may think of it politically, it is clearly the idea that drives most of the practices and judgments discussed in this book.

The idea that Americans are always meant to be striving upward, both for themselves and for their children, in turn suggests an important way of reframing some of the ways one might talk about class. Here I adopt the valuable concept from Sartre (1963) of the "project." If class is always an object of desire (or repulsion), whether historically or in the present, then it seems more useful to think of people, groups, policy makers, culture makers, and so on, as engaged in "class projects" rather than, or in addition to, being occupants of particular classes-as-locations. This book is thus framed partly in terms of class projects and related ideas (e.g., class "games"), and partly in terms of a processualization of class: "classing." We may think of class as something people are or have or possess, or as a place in which people find themselves or are assigned, but we may also think of it as a project, as something that is always being made or kept or defended, feared or desired.

The Research

The research for this project consisted of (1) finding the members of the Class of '58, (2) collecting basic information from them in a mailed questionnaire, and (3) traveling around the country interviewing class-mates. The process of finding people was fascinating and is still not complete; I am still locating new people while losing some I found earlier. I enlisted the aid of classmate Judith Epstein Rothbard, who had kept in much closer touch with the old Weequahic community than I had. She has written up some of her ingenious people-finding techniques, which appear in appendix 1. Twelve people were known to be dead at the beginning of the project, leaving a total of 292 people to be found.[15] Of these, we found all but 44.[16] These 248 people were subjected to questionnaires and/or interviews. In the end I got at least basic demographic and personal data for virtually all of them. For ex-ample, I have current occupations for 244 classmates.

I then interviewed about 100 of the found people in depth (and spoke to most of the rest on the phone). I visited about eighty cities and towns of the United States and drove over several thousand miles of American freeways.[17] The project was conducted intermittently over a four-year period (roughly, 1990–94), with the most intensive work done in the period 1992–94, during which I traveled for about a week of every month.

The fieldwork consisted of interviewing people wherever they hap-pened to be, at any site of their choosing. The interviews took the form of loose life histories: "So, tell me about your life since Weequahic."[18] Most of them were taped, although there were occasional technologi-cal failures and ethnographer's errors along the way. Untaped inter-views were written up as soon afterward as possible. All interviews, whether taped or not, were also summarized in field notes.

Interview-based (or interview-driven) fieldwork is becoming in-creasingly common in anthropology, and it is thus worth spending a bit of time discussing it here. Much of so-called qualitative research outside of anthropology takes this form, and as a dyed-in-the-wool participant-observer, I have long felt that research based largely on "talking heads," and especially unrelated talking heads, has severe limitations (see, e.g., *Habits of the Heart* [Bellah et al. 1996], however insightful it is in many other ways), because it loses much of the richness and depth produced by full-scale participant observation. Yet the critique needs to be refined. The growth of interview-based fieldwork is related to two important developments within anthropology: the concern with history—that is, with longer stretches of time than would be covered in classic fieldwork—and the concern with larger areas of space (the region, the nation, the globe) than can be covered in classic fieldwork (Gupta and Ferguson 1997). In both cases fieldwork is "delocalized" (Marcus 1998), and the standard practices of ethnographic fieldwork—long-term, whole-self, participant observation—are often severely curtailed. This in turn raises two questions: first, whether the kinds of data collected in this way can provide the fine-grained and experience-near accounts that ethnographic data (or perhaps one should say ideal ethnographic data) can provide; and second, whether the kinds of data collected this way should be seen as at most a partial form of data that must be articulated with other forms of knowing, including archival research, historical studies, the interpretation of public cultural forms, and so on.[19]

In response to such concerns, I pursued two different strategies. The first was to maximize whatever participant/observer potential I could in the project. This included drawing on my own long-term membership in the broader culture and in the Class of '58 itself (more on this below) as well as paying close attention to the details and textures of the sites in which the interviews were conducted. The sites were numerous and quite diverse, and included homes, with and without other family members around; restaurants (from the very expensive to the very cheap, including many of those great East Coast institutions, "diners"); bars; shopping malls; brokerage houses; law offices; medical offices; business offices; a schoolteachers' lounge; a principal's office; a country club; a nightclub where a classmate was performing; an examining room in a hospital; a law library; a social worker's office; the Newark Police Department; reunions (two) in catering establishments; synagogues; hotel lobbies; and a Hollywood television studio.[20] Most important, I drew enormous ethnographic benefit from the fact that these 304 people had once constituted a face-to-face community, and for many a very intensely experienced one at that. Many people were thus interested in hearing and gossiping about one another, thereby producing a kind of overlap and interlinkage between the interviews that approximated, at least at the level of talk, some of the experience of participant observation.[21] While not all researchers doing delocalized fieldwork can expect to work with a historically connected group like this, the point is that some kinds of social linkages between informants, whether of kinship, institutional connections, or shared projects—the possibilities are open to much creative construction—seem crucial in order to avoid the problem of unrelated talking heads, that is, the production of highly individualized, socially decontextualized talk.

Yet while trying to "ethnographize" my data as much as possible, I was also committed to a second strategy: to recognizing that ethnographic data, if it is to avoid the sins of ahistoricity and excessive localization, must be conjoined with other forms of knowledge. Specifically, I have embedded the interviews in a variety of historical narratives, all related to the course of American life in the second half of the twentieth century. This has entailed a kind of representational balancing act: if the historical narratives are too richly drawn, then the interviews become mere illustration; but if the interviews are quoted too heavily, in the hope that they will "speak for themselves," then their larger meaning may be lost.[22] I think of the ideal balance here between interviews and larger cultural and historical narratives as something like the balance one sees in great documentary films, where images, music, and documents, on the one hand, and interviews with participants and commentators, on the other, are interlaced in such a way that every part reinforces the whole. On this point, then, I locate the representational style of the present book in the space created in different ways by some of the extraordinary documentary filmmakers of the last thirty or so years—Frederick Wiseman (e.g., *High School*), Craig Gilbert (The *An American Family* series), Michael Apted (*28 Up* and its sequels), and Ken Burns (e.g., *The Civil War* series).[23]

Overall, the book has a fairly simple narrative structure. The first part asks what went into the making of the Class of '58 as a specific set of historical subjects. This section covers class, race, ethnicity, neighborhood, gender, high school, and the historical era—the Fifties—in which all of these were embedded. The second part of the book takes the Class of '58 after graduation from high school and asks what they "made": what kinds of lives and identities they forged for themselves, and how those lives and identities reproduced and/or transformed U.S. society in the second half of the twentieth century.[24]

The Native Ethnographer

There is one final piece to the question of the methodology of this project: my place in the whole thing. After all, I was not the unknown anthropologist showing up in another culture to—as we used to say—learn their customs. I was a member of the Class of '58, and the nature of my relationship to the people and the project necessarily differs in many ways from that in my work with Sherpas. Others have written usefully about the problems of the "native ethnographer." Kirin Narayan (1993) and Purnima Mankekar (1999), among others, have subtly examined the ways in which being "a native" among the people one studies makes the work both easier and more difficult, no more and no less complex than standard other-culture fieldwork, but certainly differently complex.[25] From a different point of view, George Marcus (1999) has written about a broader shift of fieldwork practices, in which the anthropologist, whether "native" to the culture studied or not, must be recognized as "complicit" with his or her interlocutors. This is to say that we all occupy subject positions that are meaningful, for better or for worse, to one another, and this cannot be ignored in the ethnographic project.

This is not the place to write an extended essay on the subject of either native ethnography or fieldwork in general, but let me say a few words here on the fieldwork and the writing for this project. I'll proceed in reverse order, talking a bit first about the writing. I am present in this book in several ways. First, of course, I am the writer, doing all the theoretical, methodological, and representational work discussed in this introduction. And second, I am an informant, a member of the Class taking the privacy of a pseudonym like everyone else. When treating myself as an informant, I sometimes use current memories, but I also draw from the texts of two interviews I gave (one to a journalist [Levine 1996] and one to a college classmate doing a project similar

to this one on our college graduating class),[26] which I take to objec-
tify my memories/representations in the same way as those of other
members of the Class of '58.

Concerning the fieldwork, I initially had a lot of trepidation about
doing the project. Like most Americans, I had very mixed feelings
about high school and the class/cultural milieu I felt I had escaped
from. Others must have felt the same trepidation, as they stood me up,
did not return my calls, refused to be interviewed, or, in several cases,
refused to allow me to tape or use the interview material. For the most
part, however, people not only opened their lives to me, but were extraordinarily kind, gracious, and funny in the process. I became quite
addicted to finding and hearing the next interviewee, knowing that I
could never anticipate what was going to come out of people's mouths.

In the course of the interviews I often had a very strong sense that my
presence was putting people on their guard. The question was, why?
Was it something about me? Did it have to do with my past role in
high school (not very threatening) or my present status in the world
(college professors can seem rather impressive)? Was it the fact, noted
earlier, that I was going around and talking to a lot of people, thereby
possibly replicating the terrors of high school gossip-mongering? No
doubt all of these things played some role. Yet in the end I came to feel
that the anxieties produced by my presence were largely related to the
simple fact that, as an anthropologist, I was putting people behind a
microphone, asking them to put themselves on display and—though
I tried to say otherwise—be judged. Some people remained guarded
throughout the interview, but most seemed at some point to decide
what the hell, and to let most if not all of it hang out.

As a way of giving the reader more sense of the fieldwork, I have
interspersed excerpts from my field journals between the chapters of
the "real" text. The excerpts are selected from among entries in hundreds of pages of field notes/journals,[27] and are not meant to represent
everything I did and thought in the field. (I freely confess, for example,
that I left out my own negative reactions to many experiences and encounters; I also left out most of the negative comments that individuals made about other individuals.) Unlike the selections in the regular
chapters from the official interviews with the members of the Class,
which are always meant to be faithful to the entire sense of the interview, and, further, faithful to the relationship of the interview to the

larger project, the selections from the field journals are simply meant to communicate *some* of the everyday activities, experiences, mistakes, and reactions of a working ethnographer.

I include this material in the spirit of reflexivity, not so much about me personally—indeed, I have reservations about how much of that is relevant—as about the process of fieldwork itself, which I do think can use some demystification. Further, fieldwork is notoriously difficult to teach or explain to a person who has not already experienced it. It did seem to me, however, that actual field notes/journals might convey more than didactic statements about the fieldwork process in the abstract, or in general (see also Sanjek 1990). In addition, the fieldwork for this project seems to have been a matter of particular fascination for others because many people have rather intense fantasies about reconnecting with their high school experience (see chapter 4). The field journal entries thus have the double function of opening some of the fieldwork itself to fresh air and of satisfying at least to some extent people's curiosity about how I did it, and how it felt.

Before getting to the young Class of '58, then, we turn to the first set of "project journals."

Project Journal 1: Getting Started

[A few notes to make sense of what follows. (1) Although I grew up in New Jersey, I was teaching at the University of Michigan at the time of the project, and indeed had lived in Michigan for about fifteen years at that point. Thus I discovered, quite to my surprise, that my perspective on the various regional cultures of the United States, including New Jersey, was largely a midwestern one. (2) On virtually all interviewing trips I stayed with classmates or cousins, to whom I am enormously grateful. They are thanked by name in the acknowledgments and also appear in many of the project journal entries. (3) Given the preponderance of Jewish people in the Class of '58, individuals mentioned can be assumed to be Jewish unless otherwise noted. (4) Real names are marked with an asterisk*.]

9/20/89 Spoke to [reunion co-organizer] Sue Ellen Platnick Boff* yesterday. She still has all the addresses and will be happy to share them with me. She also did a questionnaire at the time of the 20th reunion and will be happy to share that too. I'm off and running!

9/21/89 It's hard to remember to turn things into "data." Gloria [not a member of the Class of '58] said she's a good friend of Louis and remains in pretty close touch with him. This seemed like "general/normal/background" conversation—not something to write down. But then I realized it's fodder for my "less geographic mobility than you think, more maintenance of social networks than you think" thesis.

9/23/89 On the difficulty of making one's own culture into "data"—this is what novelists do. (I've been reading Saul Bellow's *Humboldt's Gift*. It says in the blurb that he was an anthropology major in college. It's full of anthropology references, both cross-cultural and physical. But it's also powerfully ethnographic, at least in places.) Novelists, or good ones anyway, are the traditional ethnographers of their own cultures.

9/29/89 At the beginning, Gloria said, so what is your project all about, which was my opening to try out my speech. I sort of stumbled around—I don't even know what I said, but it seems best to introduce it as a sort of debate: Some people think "class" is a real factor [in social life] and others don't . . . she interpreted the question in terms of the impact of class on individual success. I realize I have two different ideas in the question—one is the one she answered, and the other is the main factors of division in American society. I have to sort that out in my opening spiel.

12/21/89 [Interview with a professional woman.] She asked what the project was about. I said it wasn't fully articulated yet—that seems like a better strategy all around, especially since it's true, but also because it seems more open to a wide range of responses/information. I said there were two general areas, and I'm not sure how they link up: the general question of "success" or lack of same, both in reality and in people's perceptions; and the general question of social divisions and differences—class, race, etc., both in high school, and later. On the last point I said some people may feel that there weren't many divisions in our class, that it was very homogeneous, and she said, well "in broad sociological terms" it would appear that way, but obviously there were subtle differences. For example, "of course [she] wouldn't associate with Carol X or Harry Y."

1/11/90 [Same woman.] First of all she called to change the interview. I was supposed to go to her house but she had an appointment here in town and suggested we go to a restaurant. I should simply have said yes, but I was afraid it would be too social and I wouldn't be able to really do the interview, so I struggled and got her to come here. At one point her voice went rather sharp ("Well I don't really care where we eat lunch"); I wonder about the pattern of letting this sharpness show—[another woman] did it too. . . . Anyway I wish I hadn't struggled over the location—just say yes, whatever people want.

The interviews are inevitably going to have this social quality—I can see that now. After she started talking, I said I'd like to take notes, and she looked a bit startled, and it seemed like it would destroy the tone, so I never did it. I suppose I have to acknowledge that I am quite specifically drawing on pre-sumptions of friendship (in some sense) and of a shared social world and I can't have things both ways. I can't have the benefits of using these presumptions to get people to open up, and then for my part play the formal anthropologist with the notes and the tape recorder, and expect them not to clam up again. [After a few experimental interviews like this one, without a tape recorder, I switched to taping anyway, unless someone absolutely refused to be taped—and some did.]

3/19/90 [Interview with a middle-class man.] We sat in the kitchen—a pleas-ant middle-class kitchen with the usual things on the fridge—Camp [X], B'nai Brith, Trash Recycling schedule. [I was struck with the similarities of our re-frigerator magnet bulletin boards. I had been trying to exoticize the Class of '58, but there was no question, as Steve Barnett* once said, that "we are all natives."]

3/20/90 The interview format [is a problem]. There is something so flat about sitting at a table and just having someone tell you about their life. Without participant observation, there is no depth to this kind of reporting.

3/27/90 [After a formal interview with a professional man and his (also pro-fessional) wife, they invited me to stay for dinner, and a lot of interesting things emerged during the dinner conversation that had not emerged in the inter-view.] All of this just goes to show how one can't simply do questionnaires. All the good stuff happens when you close the notebook or turn off the tape recorder.

4/8/90 [Interview with a businessman. Somewhere along the line, he made a somewhat vulgar comment.] I actually didn't write down that last line in my notebook and Gary said, why don't you write that down, and I sort of hemmed and hawed, and then he started telling dirty jokes, and I said OK, I'll write these down. First, along the lines of his comments about how Jewish women push their husbands around, I [tried to be a good sport and] said I heard a Henny Youngman joke in a movie (*Amazon Women on the Moon*): "Why do Jewish men die before their wives?" and Gary knew the punch line and said it along with me:

"Because they want to." Then he told some more. One was about a husband and wife who had been married a long time. The husband wanted to spice up their sex life and he suggested oral sex to his wife. And she said, I don't know how to do it. And he said, here, take this ketchup bottle and go in the kitchen and practice, and come back when you're ready. And she came back and said, I think I've got it. So they get into bed and (the rest is done as a visual joke): she grabs his penis and bangs the end with the flat of her hand as if she is trying to get ketchup out of a bottle. Another one: "Jewish wives think Sucking and Fucking are two cities in China." And there were some more but I just wrote down a word or two and I can't remember them now.

6/15/90 [Todd Behling* wrote an undergraduate honors thesis at the University of Michigan on a Black church in the Weequahic section in the early 1990s. His data revealed a lot of hostility on the part of the present, mostly African American, residents of the Weequahic section vis-à-vis the former, mostly Jewish, residents. He and I took a trip back to Weequahic High School together.] First, it was almost impossible to get a cab to go to the neighborhood [all the regular commercial cab companies refused, and finally someone told us to call a private cab company that operates in that area]. Second, [once we got there] the secretary at the school was fairly hostile when I explained [that I was a former graduate]. She softened up later as I stood around and looked forlorn, and I took her hostility as generic, but Todd's information [about continuing Black resentment over Jewish flight] recontextualizes that somewhat. I didn't get past the front office: it was late in the day, the principal was tied up with some sort of "workshop," etc. She gave me the name and number of the librarian and said to contact her directly. I got the impression that the principal would have no interest in or time for me.

Todd and I then walked from the high school to Beth Israel Hospital. I pointed out to him all the former temples along the way. I was struck by how the Jewishness of the neighborhood was literally graven in stone. It was like doing surface archaeology — you could see the past right on the buildings. This is what the minister [one of Todd's informants] was complaining about. Todd was struck by the different tones on my tour and the minister's. He said mine was "nostalgic" and I suppose it was; the minister's was negative.

9/12/91 Got the questionnaires mailed out about a week ago. I thought it would be a magic data manufacturing machine — just making data with no human intervention. Probably in most cases it is, but obviously not with this project. People are calling.

...... I'm overwhelmed by the fact that my whole culture has become my text, my ethnography. I can't read a newspaper, see a movie, watch television, without it being part of my fieldwork. No escape.

11/16/91 Just a note on Judy Rothbard's* incredible energy about locating the unknowns. All in all she turned up 30 new addresses in a very short time. Fantastic!

1/17/92 I spoke to Helene Rosenblatt* on the phone and she was quite helpful. She offered to send me the biographies that people wrote for the Maple Ave. [grammar school] reunion, and she did, along with photos. Great!

The Making of the Class of '58

chapter 2

Reading Class

The Weequahic neighborhood in the fifties was the proverbially quiet and peaceful place, with clean, tree-lined, and above all, safe streets. Kids walked everywhere. They also played outdoors (in yards and driveways, in the school playground, in Weequahic Park, and, after a certain age, at the Dairy Queen) until late at night most of the year. There were several larger shopping streets, but most of the neighborhood was residential. The "better" streets had one-family houses with well-tended lawns and pretty flower beds in the spring. The "middle"-level streets had mostly two-family houses. In some cases the two families were unrelated, with one owning the house and the other renting. In many cases, however, the house was occupied by two related families—for example, the grandparents on one floor and the family of a married son or daughter on another. Finally, some streets were lined with apartment houses. Poorer families often started in these until they could—if ever—afford to move up to a house. Many people remember loving the neighborhood, as we shall see later, but the social distinctions lurking in these three kinds of streets became increasingly salient to the Class of '58 as they grew up.

Families and Class

When the parents of the Class of '58 began their own lives they were almost entirely working class and/or poor. A few were immigrants themselves; the majority were first-generation children of immigrants. They were born in the first decades of the twentieth century and came to adulthood during the Great Depression. I note this for several reasons. One is that it is fairly clear that the Great Depression shaped the work ethic—which is to say the ethic of working very hard—of many C58 parents. Another is that, when I reach the point of showing the class distribution of the parents—a distribution that will form the baseline for understanding the life and class trajectories of the Class of '58—it will be important to recall that the parental class distribution at that point was the (unfinished) outcome of the parents' own "class projects," and represented significant class mobility for many of them.[1]

The Class of '58 was born just before the United States entered World War II, in 1940, give or take a year on either side. The Class entered the school system just as the war was ending and the U.S. economy was beginning to return to relative normalcy. And it was at that point that the government launched (or many would say resumed from the Roosevelt era) what we may think of as a national project: the middle-classing of (white) America. This involved improving the lives of the working classes through the GI Bill and other programs that allowed them to buy into the middle class via homes, cars, and a vast array of consumer goods.[2] Part of the rationale for the middle-classing of America was the defense of capitalism against the Communist "threat," a threat that produced the horrors of the McCarthy hearings and the other forms of Commie hunting in that era. In addition, the terrifying rallies and unspeakable practices of National Socialism had brought home fears of an uneducated "mass" that would, like the Germans under the Nazis, be vulnerable to ideologues of all stripes. There was thus also a move to improve both the minds and the skills of the working class, again through the GI Bill and other programs that facilitated skills training or higher education for those who desired it (Ross 1989). The middle-classing of America was thus at once an economic, political, and cultural project creating a world of consumers with the means and the desire to buy goods, staving off the class consciousness and incipient class warfare that had been taking shape during the Depression years of the 1930s, and elevating the working classes to at least a certain level of culture and further aspirations.

All of this went a long way toward middle-classing large sectors of the former working class and obscuring the older middle-class/working-class boundary, especially among white people (see, e.g., Parker 1972, Baritz 1982). *Class* became a kind of dirty word (Paul Blumberg called it "America's forbidden thought" [in Fussell 1983:15]); the class boundary was largely replaced with a race boundary; and everyone white—with a few virtually invisible "exceptions" at both ends—became, or imagined themselves to have become, middle class.

Eventually the generation of the parents of the Class of '58 came to be known as "the wealthiest generation in the history of America, maybe the world" (Howe and Strauss 1993:39). The period of the childhood

Table 1. Median Family Income, 1950–1990

Year	Income	$ increase	% increase
1950	$18,305	—	—
1960	$25,220	$6,915	37.8
1970	$34,523	$9,303	36.9
By contrast:			
1980	$36,912	$2,389	6.9
1990	$39,086	$2,174	5.9

Source: Slightly modified from Samuelson 1995:70.

and adolescence of the Class of '58 was a period of enormous economic growth in the United States. The number of low-income families fell from 46 percent to 20 percent between 1946 and 1959, while the number of high-income families rose in that same period from 5 percent to 20 percent (Baritz 1982:184).[3] Table 1 supplies another angle on this extraordinary postwar boom.

Of course, not everyone shared equally in this prosperity, and I will come back to important differences later. The picture I want to emphasize here, however, is the degree to which the C58 parents' Depression-inspired hard work, in the context of the national "middle-classing" project, on the one hand, and the great economic prosperity, on the other, produced a particular class profile as the Class of '58 was getting launched in life.[4] This is a profile in which at least some parents had already pulled themselves up significantly from their origins, and in which many were still on the rise.

Table 2 presents a first way of reading the class distribution of the members of the Class of '58 in the period when the Class was growing up. It is basically "objectivist"; that is, it is constructed using fairly standard criteria of how different occupational categories are ranked in this culture. I need to begin, however, with several disclaimers. First, my classification is based solely on occupational categories. There are well-known debates over using occupational categories to represent class differences (see, e.g., Bendix and Lipset 1967). From some points of view, rankings by occupations are too "soft"; occupations (unlike income or years of education) are not measurable, and they embody a large measure of "subjective" cultural prestige assumptions (e.g.,

Table 2. Class Distribution of the Natal Families of the Class of '58, Based on the Breadwinner Parent's (Usually the Father's) Occupation (N = 207)

Business/professional class: 55 (27%)[a]

Middle class: 92 (44%)[b]

Working class: 60 (29%)[c]

---

[a] The BPC: 21 owners of relatively large businesses (manufacturing, wholesale, or large retail), 13 attorneys, 3 dentists, 3 pharmacists, 2 physicians, 2 businessmen, 2 CPAs, 2 engineers, 1 chemist, 1 contractor, 1 director of a social service agency, 1 executive director, 1 musician, 1 psychologist, 1 rabbi.
[b] The middle class: 47 owners of small businesses, 11 salesmen, 11 workers/managers in retail businesses, 5 managers (middle level) in industry, 4 insurance salesmen, 2 teachers, 2 accountants, 2 bookkeepers (mothers; father gone), 2 furriers, 1 advertising editor, 1 real estate saleswoman (father absent), 1 deputy chief of police, 1 office manager, 1 navy employee (civilian), 1 supermarket manager.
[c] The working class: 10 industrial workers, 3 butchers, 3 house painters, 2 brewery workers, 2 cab drivers, 2 longshoremen, 2 postal workers, 2 truck drivers, 2 wallpaper hangers, 2 worked in supermarkets, 1 baker, 1 cabinetmaker (worked for others), 1 construction worker, 1 delivery truck driver, 1 drape hanger/upholsterer, 1 factory foreman, 1 fruit peddler, 1 furniture maker, 1 garment worker, 1 glassworker, 1 jewelry maker (worked for others), 1 longshoremen boss, 1 maintenance man, 1 milkman, 1 movie projectionist, 1 plumber, 1 policeman, 1 railroad laborer, 1 refrigerator mechanic, 1 shipping clerk, 1 tailor, 1 worked in junkyard office, 1 worked in laundry room, 1 office worker (mother; father gone), 1 store section manager (mother; father gone), 1 health care worker (mother; father gone), 1 worked in shop (mother; father died), 1 took in typing (mother; father gone).

plumbers are culturally seen as "lower" than teachers, though they may make more money). From other points of view, class rankings by occupations are too "hard." They rank people by a single variable—the kind of work they do—and ignore features of education, income, and lifestyle. From my own point of view, and bearing in mind my earlier discussion to the effect that "class" is not a thing but a discursive construction, the mixture of cultural factors (prestige notions about different kinds of work) and Marxist assumptions (about the importance of position within a mode of production) renders occupation a reasonable mode of defining and ordering class positions, at least for present purposes.

Second, and by the same reasoning, I will use for now the standard American notion of class divisions, a tripartite scheme of upper, middle, and lower. I had originally followed a variant of the classic two-part Marxist scheme (bourgeoisie/workers), dividing the parents of the Class of '58 into a relatively privileged "business/professional class" and "everybody else." But that binary division—with the large undifferentiated "everybody else" including everyone from teachers and shop owners to brewery workers and wallpaper hangers—seemed to violate the cultural common sense of many who heard earlier versions of this chapter. In addition, it seemed to me that the middle class is far too important historically, and far too central to this project, to remain unmarked. I have thus divided the parents of the Class of '58 into a business/professional class (BPC) (doctors, lawyers, owners of larger and/or wholesale businesses, etc.), a middle class (teachers, salesmen, bookkeepers, owners of small and/or retail businesses, etc.), and a working class (painters, plumbers, longshoremen, etc.).

Third, I must emphasize how very rough table 2 really is. It is based on coding or classifying—putting people/families/occupations into categories—which is itself a subjective and imprecise process. Readers will surely differ regarding which occupations should go in which class locations. Is a musician, or a pharmacist, or a rabbi really a member of the BPC? There is no final answer, because it is a cultural system on which different people have different readings. I have tried to approximate what I take to be the standard or dominant view. In any event, I show my work in the footnotes to table 2. The coding, moreover, is based on the often very fuzzy occupational categories that people gave me when I asked for fathers' or parents' occupations. "My father owned a grocery store" tells us nothing about the size and prosperity of the business. I had enough information for the most part to separate out the larger businesses. Some of the "small businesses" were truly tiny, and by income the family was probably "working class," but I had no way of drawing the line and left all of them in the middle class. And finally, people were often intentionally vague, either because of modesty, at the high end, or shame, at the low end.

Some notes on the terminology. The label *middle class* probably speaks for itself, in the sense that most people would both understand it without explanation and accept it as a reasonable description of their class position. As for the term "working class," some people may be offended by having it applied to their families. As noted earlier, at least some of the working-class families owned homes, and probably most of the people in this category considered themselves (lower-) middle class in terms of consumption patterns, behavioral styles, and so on. But I chose this term because, for reasons explained above, the classification here is based on occupations—what kinds of work people, mostly fathers, actually did—and what "working-class fathers" did for the most part was industrial and/or manual labor.

Finally, I coined the term *business/professional class*, or BPC, for the upper-middle-class set, and this needs some explanation too. Like *working class*, the term is descriptive of the actual kinds of work represented in the category, with the largest group owning businesses, plus a handful of professionals and managers. In addition, I invented this term to parallel John and Barbara Ehrenreich's term *professional/ managerial class*, or PMC, coined in the 1970s (Ehrenreich and Ehrenreich 1979). The relevance of this will be clear later, when I consider the implications of the widespread success of the Class of '58 and the transformation of the BPC of the parents into the PMC of the Class.

Terminology aside, table 2 performs several functions. First and foremost, it gives us a baseline, however crude, for the Class of '58 itself. On the one hand, some parents had begun to pull themselves up, and there is a modest (27 percent) business/professional class among the parents. On the other hand, nearly three quarters of the Class were of the middle or working class, a picture they radically changed over the course of their lives.

The table is also a fairly accurate reflection of the shape of the larger U.S. class structure by the mid-1950s, a structure in which the middle had been significantly enlarged by the national middle-classing project discussed earlier. Note, for example, that the Weequahic numbers parallel reasonably closely the national numbers presented by Baritz (above), in which the low-income families had fallen (from almost half the population) to 20 percent in 1959, while the high-income families had risen (from a tiny percentage) to 20 percent by that time; this would put about 60 percent in the middle. The Weequahic numbers are not quite so extreme; the top and bottom are a little larger, the middle a little smaller, but the general pattern—the bulging middle— is the same. This is one of several reasons why Weequahic, despite its distinctive ethnic composition, can be considered reasonably "representative" of larger American patterns.

The class differences among Weequahic families were—as would be expected from my earlier discussion—both seen and not seen by the young Class of '58. Before getting to that, however, we need to look at another area of childhood experience, the question of family relational and emotional "quality." Family quality was, for many classmates, much more salient in their memories, and much more salient in their understandings of the trajectories of their lives, than things related to "class." Yet in the end the two aspects of family life—its class position and its emotional quality—turn out to be closely related.

Behind Closed Doors

As I talked to people about their lives, many of them poured out, with no prompting from me at all, quite unhappy stories of early family life. The informants often implied or stated that if these things had not happened, they might have achieved much more in life. One must immediately raise the question of memory: whether these stories should be taken at face value. As I have already discussed, whether the stories are perfectly true and accurate is irrelevant. I accept them in all cases as reasonably true accounts of things that really did happen, or at the very least, that really were experienced as told. The significant memory question here is the linkages: the fact that these stories were told in a particular discursive context, namely, as explaining later success and failure. There was no question that my informants felt that their family situations—the amounts and kinds of emotional support, on the one hand, and the amounts and kinds of social and psychological disruptions, on the other—made an enormous difference in their lives.

Once again the discussion must be set in the context of a historically specific national project: the (re-)normalization of the American family in the 1950s. The normalization of the family was at one level part of the project of the middle-classing of America, since the family was constructed in that era as the primary unit of consumption; but it was also very much a distinct enterprise. One aspect of family normalization was the reestablishment of "normal" hierarchies of gender and generation. Families had been enormously disrupted during the war. Men had gone away, and many had been killed or disabled. (As far as I know, no fathers of the Class of '58 of Weequahic High School were killed or disabled while fighting in World War II. The discussion here refers to patterns at the national level.) Most of those who returned were eager to resume "normal" family lives. Yet "the family" was not the same social and cultural entity they had left. In particular, women had gone to work in great numbers during the war, supporting and heading their families. Men returning from the war needed those jobs, both to make money and to regain their "proper" roles as family breadwinners. As a large amount of very detailed and very convincing feminist scholarship has shown, women were thus strongly encouraged to go back to their "proper" roles as wives and mothers, and were moved out of the workforce (or at least out of the more lucrative and/or "masculine" jobs) whether they wanted to go or not.[5]

At the same time, children had to relearn the proper hierarchies of respect, especially for fathers who had either been entirely missing from their early lives because of the war or who were still largely absent because they worked so long and hard when they came back (see especially Katz 1992; see also the hard-working father in *Portnoy's Complaint* [Roth 1969]). Some of the most influential family sitcoms of the Fifties (e.g., *Father Knows Best, Leave It to Beaver*), with their wise dads, loving moms, and cheerfully respectful children, have come to be seen as the ideological constructions that they were, denormalizing all kinds of family variation and hiding all kinds of family dysfunction. But they were clearly meant to play the enormously important role of providing models for the family normalization project (see, among others, Jezer 1982).

The family normalization project and the saccharine TV sitcoms that modeled it did not stand uncontested. The impact of movies like *Rebel without a Cause* (1955) and novels like *Peyton Place* (1956), both full of dysfunctional families, individuals flirting with violations of gender roles, and complicated class situations, provided an important counterpoint. Their very popularity tells us that they spoke either to real but hidden experiences or to real but hidden desires.

These films and novels bring up another piece of relevant cultural history from the Fifties (and on into the Sixties): the rampant Freudianism of the era (Hale 1995, Herman 1995, Rabkin 1998, Gabbard and Gabbard 1999). The middle class flocked to psychoanalysts in great numbers. All of *Portnoy's Complaint* is told from the point of view of the protagonist lying on the couch talking to his psychiatrist.[6] Further, popular culture was shot through with (simplified) psychoanalytic assumptions. To take just a few examples, Jules Feiffer cartoons often had characters bemoaning their Freudian hangups. In *Rebel without a Cause*, the James Dean character is messed up not only because he is the new kid in town, but also because his father is a weakling who never stands up to his domineering mother. In *Peyton Place,* there is a key character whose father is dead, whose mother gives him enemas every night, and who (the word "therefore" is clearly implied) becomes gay (Metalious 1956). And in *Forbidden Planet* (1956), an outlandish science fiction film from the era, a scientist lives with his daughter on a planet where an invisible monster runs loose at night and kills any newcomers; the "monster" turns out to be none other than the id (and the specific term is used) of the scientist himself. It is hard to open almost any piece of popular culture from the Fifties without finding some kind of clearly indicated Freudian subtext.

The cultural idealization of the "normal" family guaranteed that family problems were kept heavily under wraps. The diffuse Freudianism guaranteed that family problems were seen as the root of virtually every kind of "failure," from lack of popularity in high school to lack of success and/or happiness as an adult. This combination underwrites the pattern that emerged in the fieldwork concerning family problems: first, that people were eager to tell stories of family disruption in childhood (and the interviews sometimes had the feeling of a psychoanalytic session); and, second, that these stories were parts of larger narratives of success or unsuccess—whether they told of having been damaged by bad family experiences and therefore not having achieved as much as one might have otherwise, or of having overcome these bad experiences and risen up against the odds.

Let us turn, then, to the family memories/stories of the Class of '58. Some people felt very lucky to have had warm, supportive parents who also had enough cultural capital (whether formal education or general cultural competence) to provide good guidance about life. Most people had what psychologists call "good-enough" families—not quite as wonderful as the first group, but still providing the child with enough love and support to not be a negative factor. Retrospectively, there was often a sense that good or good-enough family life mitigated the raw effects of class. Many classmates said that they realized later in life that their families must have been poor, but they did not know it at the time because their parents made them feel that there was always enough, especially if they had each other. As one woman said, "I was brought up by this father who says, 'I'm the richest person on earth because I have all of you [her mother, her sister, and herself] in my life!' "

But a significant number of families among the Class of '58 were seriously disrupted, that is, disrupted to a degree that impinged on the child's life and consciousness. Within serious family disruption I include the following factors: long illness of a parent, death of a parent, high conflict levels or divorce of parents, parental financial or legal disaster, parental desertion or estrangement, presence of a problematic stepparent.[7] A little over a quarter of the (known) Class of '58 came from families that suffered one or another of these serious forms of disruption. I have to say I was stunned by these numbers; except for the deaths of parents, family problems were almost completely invisible when the Class of '58 was in high school. Moreover, the stories violated all my stereotypes about the stability of families in the parental generation, and specifically in a mostly Jewish and mostly middle-class group. Even when I began this project and sent around questionnaires, my classmates rarely wrote down things that indicated family disruption. Thus, for example, in the slot for "father's occupation" on the questionnaire, some people filled in the father's occupation with no comment, even though the father had died or deserted the family. In the interviews, however, much of this came out. I have a large number of quite detailed memory-stories and I will tell some of them here.

First, a significant number of families did not have fathers or did not have fully functional fathers. In an era when divorce was extremely stigmatized, and also—as it still is—very costly, some fathers just walked out on their families:

> *Murray Kurzrock:* "My family consisted of my mother, my sister, and I; my father kind of abandoned us when I was six years old, so I really grew up without a father in a sense."
> *Neil Rosenberg:* "So my dad left. . . . He took off and I saw him, I think, a little part of the rest of that year and then he was gone, and I didn't know where he was or anything. . . . I remember I was probably the only kid in the school, you know, in that era, I was like the only person I can remember that didn't have a father, who didn't have two parents. I mean, nobody got divorced in those days."
> *Marcia Schaefer:* "It was what I explained to you before, about losing my

father when I was very young. He was very, very successful, we had a beautiful house, and everything was terrific. Then when he left, the source of income stopped. My mother tried to run the business and couldn't, and so she rented it out, so our economic situation changed."

Other fathers remained home, but their presence was highly problematic. One woman's father was devastated by the deaths of his family in the Holocaust, and was apparently an emotional shell. One man described his father as "totally absent as a father, except to be destructive and negative." Another man's father had a serious illness that kept the family at a low financial level. Irving Taubman's father also had major financial reverses, which produced tremendous conflict between his parents:

[from the field notes] His father owned a wholesale flower business and had done very well, but he was a compulsive gambler and lost everything, went bankrupt in the late '40s. Irving remembers this. He remembers being very poor at this time, having to borrow coal from his aunt who lived upstairs for the furnace. He remembers they lost their car, but a cousin went to the auction and bought the car and gave it back to them. His father took to his bed for a long time and was said to be "sick," but Irving learned afterward that he was severely depressed and even suicidal. His mother was very down on his father for all this, and his parents' marriage was very bad. They stayed married but there was a lot of screaming and yelling.

There are even more stories of absent or ruined fathers. A successful lawyer and a successful business manager were both accused of theft and ruined as a result, though neither was tried or convicted; and a seemingly respectable businessman was reputed to have been murdered by the mob.

Turning now to mothers, several classmates expressed a sense of deprivation because their mothers had to work during their childhoods. Although I have skipped over this point in the interest of space, almost half the mothers of the Class of '58 worked outside the home, even when the children were small. There are several points worth noting here. First, this work was largely invisible, thus feeding the mythology that the vast majority of mothers in the 1950s were housewives (see especially Meyerowitz 1994 in countering this mythology). Second, although women from all classes worked, the largest percentage of work-

Table 3. Mothers of the Class of '58 Working Outside the Home, by Class (*N* = 189)

Class position	Housewives	Working outside the home
Business/professional class (*N* = 52)	31 (60%)	· 21 (40%)
Middle class (*N* = 88)	40 (45%)	48 (55%)
Working class (*N* = 49)	27 (55%)	22 (45%)

ing mothers in the Class of '58 came from the middle class, which suggests that they worked not simply for family survival, but as part of postwar families' efforts to pull themselves up (see table 3). Working mothers, then as now, provoked complaints of neglect from their children. I did not actually count them in the figures on "disrupted families," but I mention them here as representing the most minor form of (perceived) less than fully adequate mothering.

Much more serious for the Class were mothers who were critically ill for extended periods and/or mothers who died while the children were still young. Sondra Novick's mother died when she was twelve; her father tried to hold the family together, but then he too died when she was a senior in high school. Susan Wolkstein's mother was sick throughout Susan's high school years and died before graduation:

"And it's hard, I mean, my mother never wanted to die in the hospital, so my father brought her home. And I helped take care of her. That's a hard thing to do. And then it was even harder after she died because I had to come back to the same house that she had died in. . . . My mother, before she died, spoke with me, and she told me she was going to die. Now, that's a heavy thing to lay on a [kid], and I didn't believe it, I said, oh, you've always been sick, you'll get better. And she said, no this time I'm going to die. And I remember crying, and I said, what will I do without you? And my mother saying to me, well, she said, you'll have a choice. She said, you'll either pull yourself together—because she had lost her mother as a child—and you'll do fine, or you'll sink low, and she said you wouldn't want to do that."

Neither Susan's father nor Sondra's remarried, but most fathers who lost their wives did remarry, introducing stepmothers who were almost always felt to be highly problematic by the child. Robert Goldman's mother had died when he was six years old. His father remarried, and the father and stepmother fought constantly.

> "The problem was dissention between the two of them, the fighting, I mean it was constant fighting, constant bickering and everything else, and I just kept out of the house. . . . It was like an unfortunate [misunderstanding], you know what it was? The two of them, and I can look back now and see things, they each thought they each had money. That's funny, they each thought the other had the money. Neither one had it! [He laughed.] That's what it was."

Michael Stern's mother committed suicide when he was young, a devastating event in its own right, but then his father remarried, and Michael's relationship with his stepmother was very bad:

> [from the field notes] His mother had committed suicide when he was nine years old, and he never really recovered. . . . His father remarried and he hated the stepmother. So in general he was miserable, and he said later he used his schoolwork as the only thing that could get him some satisfaction, and some "recognition."

And finally, Edith Fromkin told a story of multiple family crises. Because she is funny, she told it in an often funny way. But the story obviously contains many wounds and many forms of pain:

> EF: "And so we moved up to the Weequahic section, my father [and I]. My mother had left [when I was six] and then seven years later they finally got a divorce. My father was always hoping, I think like I was hoping when my husband left, that she'd come back, which was insane. He used to tell me to tell everybody she was on vacation. For seven years I told people she was on vacation. I used to say, 'Dad, this is retarded, this is ridiculous. I'm a little girl and I know that it's ridiculous.' [But he said,] 'Do what I tell you.'"
> SBO: "Were you really upset? You must have been like crazy when [your mother] left [EF: no, not at all]. Or were you not very close?"
> EF: "Nothing, I didn't even cry. . . . And my father remarried. . . . She's an awful human being and I'm not hard to get along with and I very much wanted a mother. But she was just an exceptionally awful person."

These stories were often told, as I said earlier, in the context of explaining why the person had not been as successful—as popular, or

Table 4. Family Disruption by Class (known N = 207)

Business/professional class: 8/55 known, or 15%
Middle class: 23/92 known, or 25%
Working class: 25/60 known, or 42%

---

as rich, or as well educated—as he or she had hoped to be. I do not doubt this connection in many cases. I share the assumption that serious family problems can be damaging to vulnerable children, and I do not wish to undercut people's understandings of their own lives. At the same time, it is clear that these stories almost literally replace stories of class deprivation as possible explanations for later life experiences— lesser material success, depression and unhappiness, a diffuse sense of personal failure.

In fact, of course, the two are not mutually exclusive. Class comes to children through families, and the Class of '58 shows a quite dramatic correlation between class positioning and family disruption (table 4). Analytically, we may think of this correlation as both cause and effect. Thus, we may think of higher class positioning "protecting" people from family disruption, in the sense that having money can buy family stability, particularly with reference to divorce. In addition, money can buy better health care and can cushion the family financially in the case of prolonged illness and death. At the same time, we can turn the point around and see family disruption itself as a cause of lower class positioning. Any of the factors of disruption—parental illness, death, divorce, desertion, or father's loss of position—can radically pull down family income, and thus push the family downhill.

It is interesting, and in line with other discussions in this chapter, that people tended to recognize the second view more readily than the first. It was clear to many classmates, at least in retrospect (though if memories are to be trusted, it was clear even at the time), that major family disruption pulled family financial fortunes downhill. For example, Marcia Schaefer was well aware that her family suffered major financial decline after her father left, and Susan Wolkstein was well aware that her mother's extended illness consumed all of their insurance and ate into her father's income as well. But the first argument— that money and privilege might have protected people in higher class positions from family disruption—was virtually unrecognized in the interviews. All of which brings us back to the question of "seeing class."

Hiding in Plain Sight

I said earlier that there are always visibility issues concerning class in the United States. In many contexts class appears "hidden," "secret," "invisible." Americans do not talk about it, or they deny it or resist it. In his fine ethnography of a chemical plant in Elizabeth, New Jersey, David Halle said that his informants described themselves as "working men" or "working women" but resisted the idea that they were part of a "working class" (1984:202).

Yet at another level, Americans do recognize "class" in some form. Or rather I should say, *some* Americans recognize it, from a particular point of view. To forecast the general argument of this section, I will argue that "class" in American discourse is almost entirely a matter of economic gradations of goods and privilege, and is almost entirely embedded in narratives of snobbery and humiliation—what Sennett and Cobb (1972) unforgettably called "the hidden injuries of class." Not surprisingly, "class" is not embedded in a Marxist narrative of irreconcilable differences between owners and workers. Somewhat more surprising, it is not even embedded in narratives of personal success and failure. Virtually none of my informants attributed their own success or failure later in life to their class backgrounds. Rather questions of success and failure were embedded in the kinds of stories we have just heard: stories of the psychological impact of early family experience.

Who, then, sees, or acknowledges, class, and why? In general, the possibility of seeing class is unlikely to arise until the high school years, when people from different neighborhoods are brought together into a single social universe. For the following section, then, we move with the Class of '58 into the high school years.

By and large, people higher up on the ladder did not see class. One man from a high-end family said, "Money didn't mean anything in high school, everybody was equal." Another said, "None of us were rich . . . we all pretty much had the same economic standing, and I never thought about it at all. Not at all." When in another interview I raised the question of social classes in high school, the man said, "At

Weequahic High School? Were there many social classes at Weequahic High School?"[8]

On the other hand, some high-capital students recognized that there were differences/inequalities but insisted that these had no impact on social relations within the school. Louis Spiegel, for instance, said: "Obviously there were people [like himself] who had a high income, as opposed to people who lived in the other sections. . . . But in [school] class[es], I never felt that they felt any different toward me than they did to their own peers."

For many students, however, class in the form of invidious distinctions of money and privilege was both noticed and felt as significant all the time. One common factor that heightened the awareness of class came from either physically moving into the neighborhood from another place or from undergoing a decline of fortune:[9]

> *Claire Adelsohn:* [from the field notes] She said going to Weequahic was a huge shock, in the sense that although where she grew up everyone owned their own home and seemed to be comfortable, nonetheless when she got to Weequahic she definitely felt shut out, people had a lot more money and looked down their noses at her.
>
> *David Birnbaum:* [from the field notes] I think the reason [the economic differences implied by different grammar schools] was particularly meaningful to David was because he moved from one of those other grammar school districts to Chancellor in fifth grade or so.
>
> *Merle Rosen:* "I started out living on Chancellor Avenue, and started school at Maple [a high-end school]. And when I was in third grade moved to Bragaw [a school in a lower-income neighborhood]. . . . I remember very well walking down the street with Tamara Silberman . . . and somebody saying to her in front of my house, 'Are you slumming?' "

But most of those to whom class was not just visible but almost tangible were from the lower end of the economic spectrum. Looking up from below, class was often very visible indeed. Unlike the table constructed by the social scientist, however, class was rarely read through fathers' occupations, which indeed were often unknown to others. Class-by-occupation came up in the context of only one interview. The student was talking about Mrs. Rous's [her real name] American history class, in which Mrs. Rous was actually teaching about the class structure of the United States:

Franklin Bodnar [whose father was an auto mechanic]: "We were talking about socioeconomic things [in class] and that was one of the biggest turn-offs in high school. [SBO: "Somebody said something to you?"] Yes, in the class, as a comment. . . . Something about, 'Oh, blue collar?' And somebody said, 'Did [your father] ever get out of elementary school?' "

Instead of parents' often invisible occupations, one of the major, if not *the* major, markers of class difference among the Class of '58 was geographic location. There was first of all an awareness of the difference between the Class of '58, still in Newark, and those who had moved to the suburbs:

Susan Tureff: "The ones who went on to Maplewood and South Orange and those areas, and Columbia High School [in South Orange], there was a sudden outflux for me among [my] friends. . . . I think it was the period right after the war when people were making enormous economic leaps. . . . I was very aware of the differences."

Dorene Bressler: "The people at Columbia High School, which was in the suburbs where the people who had money lived, were of a different social class than I was, and I felt inferior to them. And I remember once in chem lab with Charles Rosenberg talking about how he went up to Columbia to date some girls and how much better they were than we were." [10]

And then there were the more local, but in some ways more regularly felt, variations—where one lived within the larger Weequahic neighborhood and what grammar school one went to. The neighborhood was not homogeneous. At the northern and eastern edges, where it blended into the larger city of Newark, it verged on poorer neighborhoods in which other racial and ethnic groups predominated. The grammar schools in that part of town—Peshine, Bragaw, and Avon (the latter feeding into Madison Junior High)—were more racially and ethnically mixed. In Peshine and Bragaw, the Jewish kids predominated, but they were often from the less affluent Jewish families. In Madison Junior High, the Jewish (but again, less affluent) kids were actually in the minority. In contrast, the southern and western parts of the neighborhood, where the high school is located, were considered the better parts of the section. The families who lived there had slightly more money, and the population was almost entirely white and Jewish. The

Table 5. Grammar School Origins of Class of '58 by Status of School
($N = 299$)

Higher status	Middle status	Lower status
Chancellor, 41 (14%)	Peshine, 36 (12%)	Madison Jr. High, 37 (12%)
Maple, 62 (21%)	Bragaw, 55 (18%)	Other, 62 (21%)[a]
	Ivy Jr. High, 6 (2%)	
Total 35%	Total 32%	Total 33%

[a] Includes transfers from other high schools.

two grammar schools in this area, Maple and Chancellor, were considered the premier grammar schools (see table 5).

The grammar schools were thus ranked by members of the Class of '58 using a tangle of class and race/ethnicity factors. I first realized the significance of these variations as ways of "reading class" in an early conversation with Edna Cohen and Ira Katz about doing this project. As I wrote in my notes:

> [from the field notes] I introduced the question of class [differences at Weequahic] (I think I said "money"). At first this didn't resonate with them at all, so I mentioned this interview with James Altschuler (I think it was) who had made some reference to "the Chancellor Avenue crowd" or something like that in terms of money differences. And then they both said well yeah, now that I mentioned it, they could see how some of the kids who went to Bragaw might have felt that way, although they said that they themselves never felt any differences. [But it was clear that] they tended to think of the differences in terms of geography—people living on this or that side of various street divides, and in various grammar school districts, none of which was meaningful to me.

Once I was alerted to this, however, I realized that the grammar schools and their related subneighborhoods formed an extensively used code for reading and expressing class differences within the Weequahic section. Some people talked about the feelings of "lowness" of coming from "lower" parts of the area:

> *Lynn Marans:* [from the field notes] First thing she said was how cliquey [pronounced *clicky*] high school was. She went to Bragaw and definitely felt left out of certain groups. . . . In retrospect she realized there was

an economic difference between the groups although at the time she wasn't aware of it.

Jerome Kriegsfeld: "I grew up actually where Clinton Hill is so it was out of [the core Weequahic] neighborhood. I always envied those that grew up there because that was the crème de la crème, and I wasn't really in that area. [SBO: Yeah, a lot of people had that feeling, like they were on the fringe.] I was on the fringe, yeah. All right, look, that's reality."

Gloria Traberman: [Gloria also grew up in the Clinton Hill section] "Well, it's real different when you come from the other side of the tracks."

Barry Sommer: "I grew up in Clinton Hill which was certainly not the right area to be in, [people] didn't even know where it was practically and you certainly wouldn't have gone to visit it."

Others emphasized the privilege/snobbery of those who came from the "higher" parts of the area:

Lynn Sommers: "The kids that came from Maple and Chancellor definitely were perceived as the 90210 [the posh section of Beverly Hills] of television. . . . When you said Lenore Goldman and Irv Tester, she is perceived in my mind forty years later as Chancellor and he is perceived a something else, a nice regular guy."

Linda Cherny: "There were them that has and them that didn't. . . . You know, there were the ones [that lived on certain better streets]. . . . I just found that they were the in-groups, and if you were of money at that time, I mean, there were ones that went and did, and other ones that couldn't."

Aaron Martin: "Coming from Bragaw you know we were always concerned about the other people, the people from Chancellor [Avenue School], Maple [Avenue School], etc. . . . I think as a group we were the quieter, more fearful . . . people. . . . We were just that much behind. . . . It took a lot of years to get past that."

The sense among these people that they were looked down on by those from "better" grammar schools and/or neighborhood locations was not entirely imagined. Although most people went out of their way not to appear snobbish in the interviews, one high-end woman was more candid:

[from the field notes] She kept referring to people who were just "not very fine." Even in grammar school she was very aware of "these people who were a little less fine." And then there was a real difference . . . between the kids who went to Maple/Chancellor and the kids who went to

the other grammar schools, she was very conscious of it when she went
to junior high school, where these other kids came in.

It is of interest to note that Philip Roth went to high-end Chancellor
Avenue School. In *Operation Shylock* (1993) he memorializes it by having
a character (the "other Philip Roth") show how much he knows about
the "real" Philip Roth by invoking Chancellor: "But it goes back, Philip,
all the way back to Chancellor Ave. School." The character then—to my
astonishment—sings the school song. And here I confess that I went
to Chancellor too.

The other major way of reading class worked with a code from consumer goods, especially clothes for girls and (somewhat later) cars for
boys. With respect to clothes, cashmere sweaters were virtually iconic
of wealth:

> *Edith Fromkin:* "It was hard to go to a school where they wore cashmere
> sweaters on a regular basis, instead of to a party or something."
> *Jacqueline Golum:* "Well, in Weequahic I certainly wasn't a 'have-not,' but
> certainly wasn't a 'have.' [And there were certain girls] and they always
> had cashmere sweaters and whatever."
> *Susan Kleinman:* "How much did I have in common with those kids? I
> wasn't interested in charm bracelets and cashmere sweaters."
> *Judith Gordon:* "There were a lot of rich people in Weequahic . . . yeah,
> somebody had more cashmere sweaters than [me, but] it never both-
> ered me." [11]

It is perhaps a triumph of some late 1940s or early 1950s marketing
campaign that the cashmere sweater appears to have been a virtually
national fetish of status and wealth for girls in the 1950s. It is not only
mentioned in quite a few of my interviews (more Weequahic "representativeness"), but it also shows up in C. W. Gordon's discussion of a
midwestern high school of the late 1940s: "Of course, everyone longs
for the cashmere sweater, but in case you can't afford that you'll have
to take wool" (1956:116). And, "Cashmere sweaters are now worn by
the right crowd" (ibid., 117).

But of course consumer goods like cashmere sweaters indexed something more basic: money. Some informants simply cut to the chase.
Dorene Bressler, for example, said, "There are a lot of definitions of
social class, maybe, . . . but growing up, it was how much money you
had." Davita Reingold thought Weequahic "was a very cliquish place

to be." When I asked if she felt it was cliquish in terms of money, she answered, "Oh, money! Money. Money was a big issue."

At issue consistently in all of the above quotes are memories of feeling small, low, humiliated, envious (or of fending off those feelings) in relation to those who had more goods, money, status. Most of these feelings derived from reading differences tacitly through the codes just discussed, especially grammar schools and consumer goods. People rarely put other people down directly, although it did happen. Remember Merle Rosen's friend who was accused of "slumming" because she walked Merle home in a "lower" neighborhood. And here is another bad memory of a near-direct put-down:

> *Harold Decter:* "[Roger and I] went in jointly on a [project] for [extra credit in a science class]. [But] it was getting to be nice weather and he decided, well, I [Harold] could buy all the equipment to build all this stuff. He left me alone in his basement and he said, 'Why don't you finish it up, Harold. I'll give you all the money.' And he came from a fairly well-to-do household, and to add insult to injury, one gal who I really always wanted to ask out for a date . . . is the one he took out in his brand new car at that time. And you know, I come to his house, the maid answered the door and she says, 'Oh, Roger's gone; he says go work in the basement.' "

Here, indeed, is an adolescent version of "the hidden injuries of class." [12]

We see, then, that any kind of political language of class, or even anything in terms of occupation, is virtually absent from the native discourse. Instead there is, as Bourdieu (1984) has stressed, a language of "distinction" that draws on codes from the everyday world: clothing, streets, neighborhoods, grammar schools, money. And the relevance of these distinctions is largely psychological. They make individuals with less resources feel bad, or force them to resist feeling bad, as they are starting out in life.

Looking back at this chapter, I realize that it has a certain schizophrenic quality. I began by showing that the parents of the Class of '58 were already doing fairly well, economically, during the time the Class was growing up. But then I veered off into some less cheerful discussions: the fact that many classmates turned out to have grown up in severely disrupted families, something that patterned out quite clearly by class; and the fact that class differences themselves were much more visible to, and much more hurtfully felt by, those in lower positions. In fact, the book as a whole will have this double quality. On the one hand it is a story of the tremendous "success" of the Class of '58. The underside of this success story, however, will be a story of the many, usually hidden, workings of class advantage and disadvantage as C58 collectively moved through life.

Project Journal 2: Florida

2/9/92 I'm sitting in the screen porch of the Rothbards'* home in Boynton Beach, Fla. Arrived yesterday for the first official field trip. Sitting outdoors in Florida and typing reminds me of "real" fieldwork, sitting in the garden of the Kathmandu Guest House in the balmy air, feeling very relaxed. Well, I suppose that's not real fieldwork either, it's not [the high mountain villages of Solu-Khumbu] and radical discomfort. But the association of work and being outdoors in some lovely place does it.

...... One thing I've noticed, it's hard to peg people's politics. Everyone is very cautious in expressing their views (including me). You sort of feel around conversationally, trying to get a line on it, and they'll say one thing that seems to go one way, and then something else that seems to go another.

...... Cindy Keselman had agreed to meet me in Fort Lauderdale airport after I landed, but never showed up and never returned my calls.

...... [At a small party of classmates.] These reunion-type events seem to have a high level of erotic charge; sex is a big topic in general—who was screwing whom in high school, or who has run off from his spouse, or who one had a crush on or fantasies about in high school. Everyone is projected back into adolescence to some degree.

...... I realize that one's field notes in this project are almost as incomplete as among the Sherpas. There it was the language problem. Here it is a question of not being able to take notes most of the time. The party is defined as a social occasion, and it would have been wildly inappropriate to jot things down. So while I hear more and understand more, I remember less, because I can't take notes. The net number of things I can write down—"DATA"—is probably about the same.

...... This fieldwork shit is hard work. Here it is 1:30 A.M. and I'm sitting and typing notes. But there's no way out. I'm doing two interviews tomorrow and if I don't type these notes tonight they'll be gone. They're almost entirely in my head, except that I did have a chance to jot down David Barna's name or I never would have remembered it.

2:00 A.M. I read back over the notes and filled some more stuff in. I'm going to bed. It may be Florida but it's still work.

2/10/92 Michael Rabstein just broke his appointment for tomorrow. I had a feeling that was coming. He's been elusive and his wife has been basically hostile. I'm relieved—I'd like to get some sun and this will be the only chance, if the sun does indeed come out.

2/12/92 Later this afternoon I went to Leo Mendelson's house. He's married to [the daughter of very wealthy parents who took him into their business]. He lives in an unbelievably rich huge house, beyond anything I've seen down here. He was all decked out in gold rings and chains. I mean, in terms of wealth he was beyond it. Like [some other classmates], he lives in one of these communities with guards at the gate. This seems to be a big thing down here. Also everyone had told me to lock my car at all times, including when I'm in it. Most people have elaborate burglar alarms. Is this just the mentality of the rich [or is it some local pattern]?

...... [Interview with a middle-class woman.] The reason [a particular point] is not on the tape was that she (like many others) was very aware of the tape, and didn't want to put certain things on it. So I would turn it off. There's a certain game played with the tape recorder—people would ask me to turn it off (or they'd say, I don't know whether to say this on the tape, so I would offer to turn it off) and then they would spill some revelation, or would spill it afterward, as if in some way it would not exist as data. Maybe I need to make it clearer that everything is data, although of course confidentiality is protected.

2/13/92 Last night Bernie Parness called back, and was apologetic about standing me up. . . . Meanwhile, Gary Fisher's secretary broke today's date, and Sylvia Zashin who was scheduled for the afternoon also disappeared, so I'm at the pool.

...... Bernie Parness said he still has the yearbook, as does virtually everyone else, and—like everyone else—not in the basement either, but right on the shelf in the living room. This is quite incredible, especially considering how much people have moved around, redecorated, etc.

2/16/92 I'm back home, having arrived with a terrible cold. I've discovered that Lewis Friedland's whole interview [in Florida] didn't take on the tape. Apparently the switch got pushed and the radio rather than the tape was on. Also by the end the batteries were dead—I don't know how long the radio was on. . . . [Grr.]

chapter 3

Drawing Boundaries

The fact that the Class of '58 was 83 percent Jewish seemed at first to get in the way of writing a book about "class," which appears as an ethnically neutral category, rather than "ethnicity," which seemed like the "natural" form for the book to take. I have argued elsewhere, however (Ortner 1998a), that race and ethnicity are not simply discourses of "natural" identities, but also function as sites of displacements of class, and as crypto-class discourses (see also Vanneman and Cannon 1987, Hall 1989, Baraka 1997, Segal 1998). This is not to say that race and ethnicity are not meaningful to actors in their own terms. Indeed, they are often overwhelmingly meaningful as deeply rooted cultural identities, and often are much more meaningful than "class." The trick, then, is to keep both dimensions in focus, to neither reduce race/ethnicity to class nor lose sight of the class implications of racial and ethnic categories.

There are several ways in which to consider the class/race/ethnicity nexus. One is to note that the race and ethnicity categories almost always carry a hidden class referent. Thus WASPs (White Anglo-Saxon Protestants) are almost always assumed, in casual American discourse, to be upper class. Jews, at least in this context, and to some extent in much of the United States since the 1950s or 1960s, have been seen as "middle class," even when, as I have already indicated, there was a substantial number of un-raised-up working-class Jewish families in the neighborhood. "Other ethnics," usually Catholic, were seen as "working class" even when they owned homes and were more prosperous than some of the working-class Jews. And African Americans were seen as "lower class" even though, like many of the "other ethnics," they were often solidly employed, owned homes, and in some cases had actually suffered downward mobility by moving from the South to the North.

Since ethnicity and race are the dominant discourses of social difference in the United States, these class associations generally remain in the background, although they never disappear entirely. Thus in ordinary conversation there is often a kind of slippage between the two discourses, as can be heard in some of the interview talk among the Class of '58. When I asked one (white, middle-class) man whether he remembered "class divisions" in high school, he answered, "Well, only between us and the Gentiles." A woman (white, lower middle class) from a poorer and more racially mixed edge of the Weequahic neighborhood said that she felt "underclass" in high school: "not as much as the Christian kids or black kids, but compared to the rich kids, I never even felt white." Another woman (white, business/professional class) talked about going away to an upscale college: "And then when I went to [X College] I was just struck by class. . . . I'd never seen an upper-class person, a plain WASP." In these kinds of statements, then, ideas of race, class, and ethnicity are virtually interchangeable.

A second way to think about the class/race/ethnicity linkage, and one more central to this chapter, is to consider the ways in which racial and ethnic groups represent to one another their own class desires and fears. Thus, for example, from the point of view of a group that has advanced itself in class terms, or is seeking to do so, lower-status groups may represent their own past, only recently and tenuously shed (see Ortner 1991). This often means in turn that boundaries must be drawn, literally and figuratively (see Lamont and Fournier 1992). Rising up is not only a matter of gaining positive goods—a better house, a nicer neighborhood, more possessions—but also drawing negative lines between one's own group and those below it. Such drawing of lines is quite irrational, invested with fears of social pollution and danger (Douglas 1970). But the irrationality and emotionality can be understood in part in relation to the anxieties of upward mobility itself: the fact that such mobility is economically tenuous, at least at the beginning; the fact that it carries ambivalent feelings about leaving kin, culture, and even pieces of the self behind; the fact that the uprisen self may feel out of place in the higher-class surroundings; and more.

In this and the next chapter, then, I look specifically at the ethnic and/or religious and/or racial categories through which the Weequahic neighborhood and the high school organized themselves: the Jews, the other white ethnic groups, and the African Americans. I will look at them briefly in terms of their own distinctive identities, as these are grounded in their distinctive historical experiences. But I will go on to argue that these ethnoracial groups were also to a significant extent class groups, and that the race/ethnic configuration of the neighborhood and the school was the historical product of what might be called "class projects," of groups trying to move up-class, and drawing boundaries between themselves and those below them, or—from the other direction—dealing with those boundaries.

In the present chapter I focus on the large Jewish majority.[1] I must warn the reader that I will make little attempt to present a "thick description" of Weequahic as a Jewish cultural and religious community.[2] This is not an ethnography of Jewish "culture," which, to the extent that one can say that it exists as some unitary object at all, is far too complex and contradictory to risk tackling without the most careful ethnographic and historical specificity. Instead, for the purposes of this book, I emphasize the ways in which Jews and other groups are most usefully seen as defining themselves vis-à-vis both other groups and their own recent pasts, all within a complex tangle of class, race, and ethnicity.

To Melt or Not?

The Jewish families of Weequahic were by and large rather middle-of-the-road in their Jewishness. There were some Orthodox families (many of them recent immigrants), and there were also some highly secularized families. But most families were somewhere in between.[3] Further, many were ambivalent about the place and degree and nature of their Jewishness within the 1950s American context. This was the era of the "melting pot" and "Americanization." One man said, "My grandparents were [religious] but my father wasn't, he threw a lot of it out of the window." Another woman said that her father "would sort of look to a more upper-class WASP-y lifestyle. And none of the very traditional Jewish foods or accent. . . . My father definitely did not like to think of this excessive Jewishness."

But most parents were more ambivalent.[4] They wanted to be Jewish but they also wanted to fit in. They wanted traditions but they also wanted to be "modern." One man talked about how his parents disagreed over whether or not he should have a Bar Mitzvah. Other parents began to cut corners on the question of keeping kosher dietary

practices. Joel Lipman and I joked during an interview about one manifestation of this:

> SBO: "I remember when I was growing up, it was a joke, I think, a lot of
> Jewish people ate in the Chinese restaurant. . . . Because, they knew
> there was pork in [the food]. And they wouldn't eat pork at home but
> they would pretend, you know."
> JL: [He asks a riddle:] "How do you tell a Jewish community? By the
> amount of Chinese restaurants in it." [We both laughed.]

Lest this be thought idiosyncratic to Weequahic, the scene is replayed,
with a somewhat different outcome, in a popular novel of the period,
Marjorie Morningstar (Wouk 1955). Marjorie (née Morgenstern), who
is trying very hard to act liberated from her parents' Old World Jewish ways, goes out with a friend to a Chinese restaurant and is presented with some food that she suspects of having pork in it. She tries
to eat around it but cannot; finding a questionable piece of meat in her
mouth, she surreptitiously spits it out and gives up on the meal (p. 63).
    Finally, one woman told a story of her father trying to have it all:

> "We didn't have a religious education, but we were like raised as Chris-
> tians, basically. . . . We ate our chicken dinner on Sunday afternoon. Like
> all the Christians did. And we had Christmas and Easter and we had Pass-
> over and Hanukkah also. . . . Have you done any reading about the Jews
> that came from Europe who wanted to be American, and being Ameri-
> can was being Christian, in a sense? . . . You see, my grandfather had that
> influence. He dressed up like Santa Claus. . . . And yet he did Passover
> and everything else. . . . They did everything."

The Jews of Weequahic were thus a mixed lot and should not be
thought of as homogeneous in their Jewishness, or in their religious-
ness, or indeed in their "culture." Nonetheless, there was clearly a
strong ethnic identification, and I will look at this in two ways: first, as
an almost natural kind of group bonding that led, among other things,
to a virtually all-Jewish neighborhood and high school; and, second, as
a process of class consolidation that led, among other things, to complex and emotionally fraught relationships with other ethnic and racial
groups in the area. I will argue that both kinds of stories—of ethnicity
and of class—are true, and that it is only by keeping them in tension
with one another (as I shall continue to do throughout this book) that

one can understand how "class" itself works in the lives of ordinary Americans.

The Ethnic Story

The time was the 1950s. Many Jewish individuals and families still had very strong memories of the Holocaust. Some of the Jewish parents were themselves survivors and/or refugees from mortally dangerous situations in Russia, Germany, and Eastern Europe before and during World War II. Not only was their immigrant experience traumatic; many of those immigrants left behind families that were wiped out, and they never got over that. One woman spoke of her father:

> "My father was not technically a [concentration camp] survivor, but he was in the sense that . . . [he] came from an upper-middle-class family in Lithuania. In 1916 he was sent out of the country because he was going to be [tape unclear—possibly "drafted"]. And the rest of his family stayed, because one brother was too old, one brother was at the equivalent of prep school, and my father was just at the age when they sent him out. So he lived in South America for a while, and then came up here. And he was always an exile. . . . Somewhere along the line, and I think it was because most of his family died . . . he just gave up, Sherry. He never became part of anything. . . . He was completely shattered, and completely withdrawn, and [had] completely given up on everything."

The majority of the parents of the Class of '58 were born in the United States; but most of them were born of immigrant parents, and some told similar stories.[5] One woman told the story of her grand-mother, who left Russia alone at the age of sixteen. The grandmother was smuggled out of her village under blankets and was hidden in basements by seemingly kindly Russian peasants, including one couple who tried to kill her. Memories like these formed the framework within which many Weequahic Jews (and probably most American Jews coming from that sort of background) were operating in the 1950s. Even if there was no specific trauma in the family background, there was a sense of wanting to find safety and solidarity among fellow Jews.

> *Marilyn Schwartz:* "So [my parents] bought a house in a very mixed neighborhood, they were concerned that there was a *schul* [synagogue] so

that I could go to Hebrew school and do all those things, but it was a mixed neighborhood [and] the smallest percentage of ethnicity there was Jewish. [SBO: That's probably why your parents wanted you to go to Weequahic High School.] I'm sure it was! . . . There were a lot of us who migrated to Weequahic, and it was to be in a . . . more Jewish environment."[6]

Thus one could think of the formation of a neighborhood like Weequahic as a kind of mini-Zionist movement, a drive to form a little homeland where it was OK to be Jewish and where Jews were not threatened.[7]

Many of the practices of Jewishness in the Weequahic section in the 1950s had to do in one way or another with simply instilling in the Jewish kids a sense of their own identities and histories. Going to Hebrew school, observing certain food taboos, being Bar Mitzvahed,[8] showing up at temple (even if one did not actually participate in the service) on the High Holidays—these were all components of a Jewish identity that were grounded in a very long-standing (even if constantly reconstructed) "tradition."

It is in the context of this ethnic/religious consolidation story that one can understand the degree to which the Weequahic Jews inscribed themselves quite literally into the neighborhood and made it their own. There were Jewish delicatessens, Jewish bakeries, kosher butchers. There were also innumerable temples, synagogues, and community centers scattered throughout the neighborhood, with the Star of David molded into the concrete, carved into the stones, and worked into the wrought iron railings. There was no mistaking the fact that this was a Jewish neighborhood. Between the physical marks of the landscape and the overwhelmingly Jewish population in most parts of the neighborhood, Jewishness was naturalized and normalized. This is the neighborhood memorialized by Philip Roth in his novels. One did not have to defend it. One did not have to explain it. It was just the way things were.

Many of the Class remembered the neighborhood with great nostalgia, as a self-contained and peaceful village. Francine Rosenblatt, for example, loved "the closeness. The people in our area knew everyone on every single block, who lived upstairs, who lived downstairs, who lived next door, whose aunts were cousins. I mean it was a family."

People remembered that the streets were safe, and that there was a sense that kids could operate quite independently within the neighborhood:

> *Walter Markowitz:* "Everybody lived in closer proximity and you could walk out of your house, leave your door unlocked, and go everywhere you wanted to go and not have to worry. . . . In our high school days we just about lived on the playground during summer vacations . . . it was fun, fun, fun."
>
> *Joan Kampf:* "It was great. . . . I loved it then. I mean, that was when you could walk around, you didn't have to spend money to do things and have fun, you know, you had friends, you could walk places. . . . I would love to do that again, that was one of the happiest times of my life."

Others remembered just a kind of diffuse pleasure:

> *Robert Weinstein:* "I loved growing up where we grew up, when we grew up. And I would not have wanted to grow up anywhere else, at any other time. We were really lucky. . . . At that time, I never really wanted to leave. I loved the neighborhood and the people. . . . We grew up in the best time in the best place."

These sentiments were echoed by the neighborhood's greatest native son, Philip Roth:

> If ever I had been called upon to express my love for my neighborhood in a single reverential act, I couldn't have done better than to get down on my hands and knees and kiss the ground behind home plate [in the playing field next to Chancellor Avenue School]. . . . [This was] the sacred heart of my inviolate homeland . . . as safe and peaceful a haven for me as his rural community would have been for an Indiana farm boy (Roth 1987:1).

One could call this situation a "Jewish hegemony." By this I mean not only that the neighborhood was full of Jewish people and Jewish places, but that its homogeneity was naturalized to the point that younger children often literally did not know there were any other kinds of people in the world but Jews:

> *Rita Weiss:* "I thought the whole world was Jewish until I left Weequahic."
>
> *Ellen Modell:* "I remember in grammar [school] that someone came up to me in fifth or sixth grade, so I was eleven or something. And as far

as I knew Jew equaled just human being, there was nothing else. And someone came up and said, Richard Miller isn't Jewish. And it was like, he was a Martian. I said, 'Well, what is he?' You know, there was just nothing else."

But others, particularly Jewish kids who came from the more mixed edges of the Weequahic neighborhood or transferred in from more mixed neighborhoods, were much more conscious of the abnormal lack of diversity even at the time.

Brenda Freling: "When I went to elementary school most of the people, there was a normal mixture. . . . One of the shocks to me in going to Weequahic, so many people were Jewish. It was like that was the whole world. . . . That was such a strange orientation when you think about the rest of the world."

This difference between the kids who lived at the center of the neighborhood and barely knew that there were non-Jews in the world, and those who lived on the edges, side by side with other groups, and had a rather more realistic sense of diversity, reintroduces one of the points I made in the last chapter: that there were class divisions among the Jews themselves, or at the very least, significant gradations of wealth and other resources. This brings us to the second, equally plausible, story of Weequahic/Jewish identity, a story of class formation and class mobility.

The Class Story

There were no groups socially higher than the Jews in the Weequahic section of Newark. There was a fairly simple reason for this: As Jews moved out of poor immigrant enclaves and into more middle-class neighborhoods and suburbs in the postwar period, the effects of their movements were not unlike those of African Americans in later decades. When the Jews moved in, the Gentiles moved out, leaving heavily or even all-Jewish neighborhoods—like Weequahic.[9] A WASP neighbor in my grown-up life in Ann Arbor told me the following anecdote about the encounter between Jews and WASPs in the town where she grew up in western New Jersey:

[from the field notes] Candy was asking me about my project, and I told her [my observation] about how when Jews move in WASPs move out, and she said yes, that happened in Westfield, and in fact her family had a summer home in Cape Cod and eventually moved there. She was talking about what it's like when the Jews move in, and she said quite unself-consciously, despite knowing that I'm Jewish, "Well, you know how it is, when the Jews move in they tend to be very vocal about what they don't like, for example, wanting to do away with some Christmas pageant that the town had only [here with a clear note of sarcasm] been doing for fifty years." She said that the locals and the Jews did share the same values of good education for their children, and that was a point they could come together on, but there's a real clash of style.[10]

WASPs aside, Newark had had its share of wealthy and relatively elite German Jews, part of an earlier wave of immigration described, for example, in *Our Crowd* (Birmingham 1967). Perhaps the most prominent of these were Louis Bamberger and his brother-in-law Felix Fuld. Bamberger and Fuld made their money largely from a department store in downtown Newark called Bamberger's, and went on to make major contributions to an astonishing array of institutions, including the Newark Public Library, the Newark Museum, the New Jersey Historical Society, the YMHA, and the Beth Israel Hospital. In addition, Bamberger and his sister, Caroline Bamberger Fuld, together donated five million dollars to found the Institute for Advanced Study in Princeton (Helmreich 1999:85); the main building there is still called Fuld Hall.

But the Jews of Weequahic were products of a later, much less elite (Eastern European as opposed to German), and much poorer immigration. These Jews originally moved into the poorer parts of Newark side by side (though not, apparently, intermingled) with other immigrant groups.[11] In time some of them did relatively well, and as they did they moved out of these poorer neighborhoods. Some successful Jews moved directly to the suburbs, but others moved to middle-class enclaves within the Newark city limits, and this was the movement that formed the Weequahic neighborhood, starting in the 1920s. In this context it is clear that the movement of Jews into this neighborhood was not just part of a project of ethnic solidarity, but of individual family middle-classing projects.

But upward mobility, as I said earlier, is always double-sided. It involves moving toward better things, but it always also involves moving away from what are seen as poorer things—poorer people, poorer neighborhoods, and so forth. This brings us to the relationships between Jews and the non-Jewish groups in the neighborhood.

There were two groups of "others" in the neighborhood: non-Jewish white ethnics and "Blacks" (as they were called at the time), or African Americans. Both groups were largely working class, and thus—despite a large working-class contingent within the Jewish community itself—were considered by many C58 parents as socially below the Jews. Let me address them separately.

Jews and African Americans

Many Jewish families are remembered, by their children, to have moved to Weequahic precisely to get away from African Americans:

> *Norman Salz:* "Part of the thing that [caused my parents to move was that] the area of Newark I grew up in was the one that changed rapidly when the block busting occurred. And I lived in an essentially Black neighborhood, right on the periphery, and it changed."
>
> *Rhoda Rosenberg:* "I was at Bergen Street School, I was living really with a friend. The neighborhood then turned completely Black at the time and there was not a [specific] problem, just the way it was, [but] I moved to Maple Avenue School in eighth grade."
>
> *Alan Kaduck:* "I did my first year of high school at [increasingly Black] South Side High. . . . My parents wanted me out of South Side. . . . I was with the people I'd been with in grammar school. . . . [SBO: Were the Jewish kids in a minority at that point?] Yeah, yeah, which is obviously why my parents wanted me out."
>
> *Barbara Cohen:* "I grew up on Johnson Avenue, right across the street from South Side High School. We moved to the Weequahic section when I was in fifth grade. By that time South Side was a heavily Black school and it is clear in retrospect that my parents were moving away from that."

Even after moving to the whitest part of the Weequahic neighborhood, parents were aware that there were some African American students in the high school, and here we see some of the more active boundary drawing:

Louis Balk: [from the field notes] He grew up in an open house. The door was always open, kids could always come over, play basketball in the driveway, come into the kitchen and help themselves to sodas in the fridge, etc. The only time anything happened was when he brought two Black kids home to play basketball and his father told him never to invite them again—"after all, your mother and sisters are here."

Michael Brown: "And my brother, suddenly he met a Black girl. . . . And eventually they did get married, and my parents were like, 'He's dead! . . . [The brother was a musician but] he can't have the piano . . . and doesn't get the car. Let him go.' " [12]

Murray Barnett: [He said he was asked out by one of the African American girls in the class. They used to walk home from school together and talk about race relations.] "And she asked me out. She said, 'I'd like to go out with you.' And then we said, well, we'll meet. I won't tell my mother. And then she said, 'We can't do that.' And so it never happened."

There are other examples of this sort of primitive racism. Some Jewish parents would reserve separate plates and glasses for the Black maids. At issue is what anthropologists call "pollution," in the social, not the environmental, sense. Fears of social pollution are different from fears of either physical violence or economic competition; they are irrational fears of being personally degraded and pulled down by bodily contact with a "lower" person. African Americans seemed to embody everything that the Jewish parents were trying to no longer be: poor, stigmatized, victimized. The only excuse—though of course there is no excuse—for the racism of some of the Jewish families was their own sense of vulnerability to degradation, to "lowering."

Yet it is impossible to disentangle the racism, as a bundle of irrational fears and antipathies, from economic and social issues also in play. For the white working class (Jewish and non-Jewish), racism was intertwined with competition for jobs. For the businesspeople (almost entirely Jewish in the Weequahic section), racism was one dimension of the sometimes brutal drive for economic success, for which the exploitation of cheap (unskilled, but also socially demeaned) labor was an essential ingredient.

Yet even in the context of the Jewish bid for middle-class status in the 1950s, the bid for what Brodkin (1999) has called "whiteness," some

Jewish families were quite actively antiracist, and it is important to tell those stories here as well.

> *Judith Graifer:* "I grew up knowing that it was so wrong about Black people. I don't know if you remember, when I was in the eighth grade, Evelyn Heistein [and I], we wrote this letter to the *Newark News* about Emmett Till.[13] . . . We wrote this letter, and my part of it was, if this is America, count me out, or something. So I mean, I grew up knowing this was absolutely deeply wrong."
>
> *Marilyn Greenwald:* "My mom . . . did teach superb values. . . . And nobody had to drink from a jelly glass. Do you remember how people [SBO: treated the maids?] Yeah. Drinking from separate glasses."
>
> *Ina Vice:* "I think there were financial reasons that it was cheaper to live where we were living [in an integrated neighborhood]. But I think that there were also socially conscious reasons for staying and not letting the realtors scare you and move."

I tell these stories not to negate the instances of racism, but to represent the mixture of views on and practices of race relations in Weequahic at that time.

All of the above—the attempts to move away from non-Jewish/working-class neighborhoods and to draw and police symbolic boundaries between Jews and "others"—applied not only to relations with African Americans, but also, in milder form, to relations with the "other ethnic groups" in the neighborhood as well.

Jews and Other Ethnic Groups

Like the African Americans, these groups were largely "working class" or tenuously "lower middle class," precisely what many of the Jews were trying to pull away from. Moreover, the Jewish bid for middle-class status and definitive "whiteness" was an ongoing project and was at that point (or maybe is always) incomplete. As already noted, there were still many poor and/or working-class Jewish families, including many within, but on the edges of, the Weequahic school district. Their kids went to Weequahic High School but formed a kind of lower class within the school, something that will be a major factor in the high school social system discussed in chapter 6.

It was in fact at this level, where working-class Jewish kids and working-class other kids found themselves together—first in the more ethnically mixed elementary schools on the edges of the Weequahic district, and later in the non–college prep tracks within the high school —that there were a lot more cross-ethnic friendships, and where ethnicity seemed less an absolute difference than a kind of inflection on a shared class culture. Thus, from some of the working-class Jewish kids:

> *Robert Goldman:* "The area I lived in . . . was not a Jewish area. It wasn't, it was a mix. We had everything in that area. You walked past Chancellor and then on the other side, it's virtually [all] Jewish, but not where I lived. . . . In fact, Catholics, Protestant, German, we were all friends there! [He laughed.] We had a very mixed group there. . . . It was like a little melting pot there, that street."
>
> *Judith Gordon:* [Judith is Jewish, talking about friendships with non-Jewish girls.] "I went all through grammar school with [Despina LaFon]. And we used to hang out—we used to go to her house to put up the Christmas tree, cause we didn't have Christmas trees [at home]. And that's what was nice about Weequahic then. I mean, [ethnic/religious differences] didn't matter."

And indeed, same-sex friendships between Jewish and non-Jewish kids were often tolerated by Jewish parents, although more at the working-class than at higher levels. Further, unlike African Americans, non-Jewish kids did enter Jewish houses, usually without consequence. One non-Jewish white woman, however, told a story that parallels the stories of the Black maids:

> "I can recall just one instance where I was dreadfully offended. . . . Once, we were at a party, . . . and we had gone to someone's house, and her parents weren't at home when we arrived. . . . Her parents came home [later], and her mother knew that Karen and I weren't Jewish, and she had a kosher home, and she took out a pot and she boiled the spoons or whatever it was that we ate off of. . . . And that was the only time that I was really offended."

And as with African Americans, there was a bottom line. The real issue with respect to boundary drawing had to do with Jewish kids dating (and not simply being friends with) non-Jewish persons. Dating non-Jewish persons, even white ones, was almost as strongly forbidden as dating Black persons.[14] One can see it as purely an ethnic solidarity or ethnic purity question, and for many Jewish parents it was:

Steven Mogelefsky: "One time [my sister] had a date with a non-Jewish guy. If you grew up in a Jewish household, and I had my grandmother living with us, I mean it's like the world erupted."

Melinda Mogelefsky [sitting in on her husband, Steven's, interview]: "I had been dating a Polish boy before I met Steven, and my grandmother just, I mean it was driving her absolutely crazy that I was seeing all these Gentiles, all these goys."

Many Jewish kids absorbed the idea that liaisons with non-Jewish others was unthinkable, even terrifying:

Robert Schimmer: "A shiksa [a non-Jewish girl/woman] was somebody, you know, in Weequahic, if a [shiksa] had a crush on you, I was afraid to death of her. I was, I was scared of her! Isn't that ridiculous? That's part of the ghetto upbringing . . . [the] old ethnic areas . . . [were] good, but bad because you think other people are different than you are."

Yet sometimes boundary markings rebound on their markers. Some Jewish girls viewed non-Jewish men not only as different (in a negative or lower way) but as interesting: sexy, attractive, mysterious.[15] Wini Breines has written compellingly of the fascination that "darker" men had for young, white (and often Jewish) women of the fifties (Breines 1992; see also Jones 1990). Given the general sexual repressiveness and gender inequality of the era (much more on this later), getting involved with a nonwhite or non-Jewish man was one way for a Jewish girl to express a certain kind of gender resistance. While none of the white/Jewish girls of the Class of '58 got involved with Black men, some did get involved with either non-Jewish white men or Jewish men who themselves acted out a "hoody" (working-class/outlaw), non-Jewish style:

Anita Schildkret: "[My first husband] was Jewish but he grew up in the Barringer neighborhood so he was ridiculed for being Jewish . . . he identified with the aggressor so he ran around with the bad boys to be accepted. . . . Then they moved next door to us when I was eleven and he was in jail [for drugs] and then he came out of jail and he was very, very charming, very charismatic guy, extremely handsome like a James Dean look and very un-Jewish."

Joan Rubin: "I was just sort of fascinated by the non-Jewish kids, the Italians and the Irish, and so on. And I was always attracted to the guys. I don't know why, you know. I had an Italian boyfriend and my parents didn't want me to see him."

Judith Cherny: "I don't know, I just didn't like Jewish boys. I need a man's man, and they didn't fill the bill. . . . I just don't get along with Jewish people. . . . Even when I went to Weequahic, I never hung out on Chancellor Avenue. I was down at the port in Elizabeth. I hung out down at [Port] Newark [a lower-class and mostly non-Jewish part of town]."

Lois Gordon: [from the field notes] Harriet also said that Lois was very "avant-garde"—dated all these non-Jewish men. She remembered that it got to a point where Lois's mother didn't even ask if the guy was Jewish, only if he was white. And of course finally the husband wasn't white.

But these examples bring us back to the central argument of this section. For what is noteworthy about these stories is that most of these sexy, non-Jewish men were not simply non-Jewish, they were in one way or another lower class. Anita Schildkret's boyfriend, who was actually Jewish but hung out with non-Jewish hoods and affected a non-Jewish style, had done jail time, the ultimate in downward class mobility; Joan Rubin's Irish and Italian boyfriends were from industrial working-class families; Judith Cherny sought out non-Jewish guys in a rough working-class part of Newark. In other words, breaking ethnic boundaries was, once again, a matter of breaking the less-articulated class boundaries as well.

I have been arguing that the formation of Weequahic/Jewish identity was at once an effect of ethnic consolidation and of upward class mobility, and that the two stories must be taken as equally true and mutually sustaining. Both forms of identity formation required a distancing from racial and ethnic others, in part because of the threat of those others to ethnic purity, but equally because they represented a lower-classness that the Jews were trying to leave behind. At the same time we have seen that it was impossible (as it inevitably is for any neighborhood) to keep the Weequahic section pure and homogeneous, whether in ethnic or in class terms, as C58 parents had hoped to do. Thus, where geography failed, the boundary between Jews and non-Jews was both socially policed and psychologically hegemonized. In the next chapter we will take up the view from the other side of those boundaries.

Project Journal 3: Los Angeles

3/8/92 I've been arranging LA interviews. . . . All the women (as well as all the men) are working, and it's a lot harder to schedule. [One of the professional women] in particular sounds virtually hysterical about her time and constantly says that she doesn't want "to commit." And she gets terribly edgy and this note of hysteria creeps into her voice at the slightest pressure. Nonetheless with people like her it is clear that I actually—against my "niceness" and agreeability instincts—have to put on some pressure. Otherwise people keep wanting to put me off.

...... [My doing the project had a definite Heisenberg effect; that is, the study itself changed the object of the study.] Susie Rosenblum said, "Your project has been the catalyst for quite a few mini reunions." All kinds of people are contacting one another and getting together who wouldn't otherwise have done so.

3/11/92 I'm realizing that the kinds of scheduling difficulties I'm experiencing with people is actually local culture. Although people vary in the extremeness of the pattern, there is this tendency not to "commit." [One Jewish professional man] is the extreme case. He simply will not make an appointment of any fixed sort. He'll set up some target (if you really push him) like, he may be able to do it Tuesday night, but he won't actually make an appointment, so you have to keep calling him to see if it's on, and then finally—and I read this all as a Goffmanesque "if I don't have anything better to do"—when he finds himself going home with nothing better to do, then it's on.

...... [One of the classmates] lives in Century City, which is a complex of highrise condos in LA, approached up a wide boulevard called "Avenue of the Stars," with fountains and colored lights—somehow like a movie set of a fantasy city of the future (from the thirties, i.e., with that dream of modernity and the modern city as beautiful and clean and not dirty and decayed). And of course all the buildings are high security, with gates and guardhouses, etc. [These observations were all made before I read Mike Davis's *City of Quartz*, which captures the fortress mentality of LA.]

...... As I tried to explain my project to [another professional man] and my interest in "class," the part of the explanation that he latched onto was the point that in many families with an upwardly mobile child, there's also a downwardly mobile one . . . , and this is the case between him and his brother. It's interesting which part of my "class" narrative people latch onto as making sense to them.

...... I'm exhausted. Did about 5 hours of total driving on freeways today. I feel like LA is both the most exhausting and the most dangerous fieldwork I've ever done. I'm a real white-knuckle driver here, gripping the steering wheel, my shoulders and neck hunched up, heart pounding all the way. The only redemption is that they've got a great oldies station here, which I listen to on the last leg of the driving, at night when there's not much traffic, and I more or less know where I'm going.

...... Don't forget to thank [my cousins] JoAnn and Norman Panitch,* for the hospitality, but also for JoAnn's incredible help with all the route planning, maps, etc. She sees me off every morning with a sheaf of excellent handwritten instructions for every leg of my journey.

...... Interviewed David Mandell this morning. He took me on a tour of the television studio where he works, and I saw them actually taping a soap opera. Also walked around a bunch of sets. Pretty interesting. When you look at the sets as sets, you realize what good ethnography goes into making them—pegging them to particular class styles, down to the tiniest knicknacks, knowing how to make a kid's room look like a messy kid's room, etc. Somebody's really got their eyes open in putting these things together.

3/12/92 Lunch today with [old friend] at an outdoor café on the beach at Venice. Ah California. Ah LA. Sun is shining, ocean is blue, breeze is caressing.

...... Conversations with [the wife of one of the professional men in the class]. She's into sheltering all her kids' future wealth from a possible second marriage by her husband. She says straightforwardly that she "doesn't trust men—they follow their penises." You know, the amount of feminism among nonfeminists is amazing. The women's movement has just somehow lost the ability to tap into all this.

chapter 4

Dealing with Boundaries

From the point of view of the Jewish hegemony, it must have seemed as if the lower others were fixed in their lowness. Yet of course that was no more true for those groups than for the Jews. Most of the non-Jews were engaged in "class projects" of their own. Given their different histories, these were somewhat different for the African Americans and the other ethnic groups, and somewhat different for both vis-à-vis the Jews, as I will discuss in this chapter. In general, however, there was a desire on the part of all for both material improvement and social acceptance, if not for full-blown social mobility. The very fact that these non-Jewish families were living in the Weequahic neighborhood and their kids were going to Weequahic High School betokened some of these aspirations.

Nonetheless, the Jews were in a sense ahead of these other groups. They generally had more money, they had gotten to the Weequahic section first, and they were in the majority. In addition, and this was the part that put them more on the ladder of "full-blown mobility" than the other groups at that time, they had more fully bought into— one could even say played a role in crafting—the middle-class ideal of higher education. And just as they looked back/down at the other groups as part of moving up, so the other groups in the neighborhood had to deal with the dominance of the Jews as part of their own class projects.

As we look at these other groups, I want to contemplate the meanings, experiences, and responses to being both outside and below the dominant group, to being literally "in the minority." I will first look at some of the kinds of boundary maintenance and exclusions that were practiced by the Jewish majority, here by the members of the Class of '58 themselves more than—as in the last chapter—by their parents. I will then consider the range of ways in which excluded students responded to those exclusions. Finally, I will consider that range of responses in terms of the future that was still to come, including, in the short term, the Newark riots of 1967, and, in the long term, the relative upward mobility of many of these excluded "others," who eventually managed to unburden themselves of these early limitations and move on.

The Others

First, the African Americans. A few preliminary historical notes are necessary to understand the African American students' point of view at that time. Many African Americans moved up from the South during and after World War II, primarily for work. Newark was an industrial and port city, and there were many jobs for unskilled and semiskilled workers. African American families also moved north to improve their social environment: to get away from segregation and make better lives for their children.[1] This then was their "class project," again a mixture of material and social improvement. As another of Newark's native sons, Amiri Baraka, said with respect to this mixture, "What you-all is doin' is class struggle of a sort, yeh, it's only that, translated as it has to be through the specifics of your life" (Baraka 1997:16).

The "other (white) ethnics" of the Class of '58 included a very mixed group of kids of hyphenated ethnic identities: Italian American, Irish American, German American, Greek American, Polish American, Portuguese American, Chinese American, Latin American, and some from even more complex mixtures. (To the contemporary sensibility there might be a tendency to see the Latin Americans and even the one Chinese American individual as being "of color," but that was not the thinking at the time.) There was something of a tendency to glamorize the Italian Americans, to see them as the type-case white ethnic group of New Jersey (think of the popularity of the television program *The Sopranos*), but in fact the non-Jews were an extremely mixed and diverse group.

Like the Jews, they were children or grandchildren of immigrants, and their elders had probably come to the United States at about the same time as the grandparents or parents of the Jewish kids. Most of the non-Jewish fathers got jobs as industrial laborers or on the docks, and this was one of the differences between the two groups: Most of the Jewish grandparents or parents, equally poor at that point, were probably either barred from those industrial or port jobs (which came to be "owned" by other ethnic groups and kin networks) or were culturally/historically more accustomed to petty (in many cases very petty—pushcarts and the like) private enterprise; or both. In the short run this divergence of economic practice may have been the difference that made a difference, the reason that the other white ethnics were somewhat behind the Jews in mobility in the 1950s, even though both had started out at more or less the same time and with the same lack of resources. For the manual and industrial working class did very well after the war, and perhaps felt less pressure than the Jewish families to push for more money and more security.

In any event, both the African Americans and the white ethnics were largely working class, although in both cases there were some exceptions. Several African American classmates came from educated and/or entrepreneurial families. One was the son of a teacher and a small craft business owner; one woman's father was a baker who later also owned a small restaurant, while her stepmother was a trained and licensed nurse.

Among the white ethnics, Rose Lorski's family had "fallen" from middle-class status but still saw themselves in middle-class terms. Rose's father had been a successful businessman and landowner in Europe. He lost everything when his land was expropriated during World War II, and wound up working as a butcher in the United States. In class terms this put Rose in the working class, yet her family's and her own self-image was clearly middle class. Or take Thomas Neeley, probably the closest thing to a real WASP (although he was Catholic [WASC] rather than Protestant) in the Class of '58. Thomas's stepfather was a college-educated scientist, and Thomas was thus of higher class than many of the Jewish kids in the Class of '58. All of these exceptions, among both Blacks and whites, were largely lost in the general racial and ethnic stereotyping that went on, in which "Gentiles" were coded as working/lower class, and African Americans were coded even lower.

Overt Racism

According to my somewhat limited data, most of the African Americans in the Class of '58 had moved into Newark and/or the neighborhood very recently, in some cases directly from the South. Although the South was still largely segregated, and although northerners tended to feel superior about the lack of formal segregation in the North, the fact is that in many parts of the South relations between Blacks and whites had settled into a certain courteous and civil mode of interaction, at least on the surface. One student, for example, came from a town in West Virginia where race relations were apparently very harmonious: "Even though the schools hadn't integrated down there, we did everything together in that town. When they did integrate, I understand it was one of the smoothest [in the region], no problems at all."

At the same time the racial ideology of the North was strongly integrationist. It is important to try to recapture the difference between the racial politics of the fifties and today. The ideas of Black nationalism and other kinds of identity politics with which we are familiar today were still in the future. Rather, the prevailing liberal view of the fifties was that there was a lot of racism, but that white people of good will and Black people of good will could overcome this ("We shall overco-o-ome"), and would bring others around to this position. All of this may seem very distant today, but integrationism was virtually hegemonic at the time.

Between the prior experience of at least superficially civil race relations in many parts of the South and the very rosy ideology of integration in the North, African American families coming to the North evidently expected a much more positive situation than they encountered. For one thing, they experienced de facto segregated housing, often in worse conditions and with fewer amenities than they had had back in the South. William Smallwood talked about this:

> "When we first got here we were in what they call a coldwater flat or a boxcar or whatever it is, and that was a new experience for us because we lived quite comfortably while we were in West Virginia. When we got here it was a whole new experience, all of us in a two-bedroom apartment, five boys and mother and father, that was new. . . . I come from a family that owned their own home and got here it was a different story."

In addition, in part perhaps because of the "integrated" schools, many African American kids were shocked to experience much more overt, and sometimes much more violent, racism from other students. William Smallwood's family had moved to Newark when he was a sophomore in high school because his father was looking for work and some relatives in Newark promised him a job. The family moved first into a mostly white working-class neighborhood, and William enrolled in Barringer High School. He was shocked by the overt racist violence:

> "It was a very bad experience for me, I couldn't believe it. . . . Everything that I heard that was bad in the South was what I saw in Barringer High School. [SBO: You mean there was a lot of racism at Barringer?] Oh, my God, I couldn't believe it. I was so glad to get out of there I didn't know what to do. . . . The only thing to say about me and Barringer was that I was in the band, good thing I like music, because when [other kids] had to run home from school, when they had the little small race riots, I was always at practice, so I was never involved in it. But I saw it. And that was more than I could take, because I [had] never seen anything like that *in my life.*"

At this point, I cannot resist a detour through Amiri Baraka's 1984 autobiography (Baraka 1997). Baraka was from a settled, lower-middle-class, African American family in Newark. He too went to Barringer High School, some seven years before William, and described his experience in virtually identical terms:

> I was totally unprepared for the McKinley [Junior High] and Barringer experience in which the whites ran the social and going to school/academic part of that institutional life. And I put up with many nigger callings and off the wall comments and intimidations, even gettin cussed out regularly in Italian. . . . I was [also] run home a few times from Barringer by the warring white boys. (Baraka 1997:41, 51)

For this and other reasons, Baraka (at that time LeRoi Jones) holds a rather different set of feelings about Newark than Philip Roth's warm nostalgia:

> Newark was iron grey for me then . . . in those days grey and steel were its thrusts into me, its dominant unwavering tone. And the strongest, the deepest, the basic constructional element of its design was the black of its bottom of the lives whose majority it held and spoke for. Such an ugly place, so hard so unyielding it seemed. (Baraka 1997:56)

Why was Barringer so much more overtly racist than Weequahic? This is not the place to get into a debate over whether the white working class (which was dominant at Barringer) is more racist than the white middle class (which was dominant at Weequahic). Positions have been taken on both sides. My own view is that the state of race relations in the working class very much depends on historical context. It is plausible in many contexts that the white working class would feel threatened by poor Blacks in many of the ways discussed earlier. In the case of Newark in the 1950s, as in the case discussed by Jonathan Rieder in *Canarsie* (1985), many white working-class families had inched up into the lower middle class. Most of the fathers in this group had working-class occupations, but most had also made enough money to buy a house, a car, and other trappings of settled, middle-class life. Working class in terms of production, middle class in terms of consumption, they inhabited that most unstable and insecure place in the American class structure, the lower middle class.

In this context, then, the kinds of class anxieties discussed for the Jews in chapter 3 would also apply to the other white ethnics making bids for a better life. Lines were drawn, and African Americans were seen as both "lower" and polluting in the sense discussed earlier. In addition, African Americans represented, or were feared to represent, direct competition for jobs. Kept out of the unions, and accustomed to a cheaper economy in the South in any event, they were assumed to be ready to accept lower pay and worse working conditions than the whites. All in all it was not a recipe for good race relations in that time and place.

Weequahic, however, was not primarily a working-class neighborhood. While, as we have already seen, it was not free of racism and other forms of boundary drawing, the practices of segregation and exclusion were, as one classmate put it, more "gentle," or at least more subtle.

Race and Ethnic Relations at Weequahic

Weequahic High School in the period under consideration (1954–58) did not have what would be described as "bad" race relations. Many white classmates remembered being friendly with individual Black students, or at least remembered having a positive and friendly attitude toward Black students. Some of this comes across today as rather thin; some of it may have been for the benefit of the interviewer or the tape; but some of it, at least, has the ring of authenticity:

Rhoda Rosenberg: [SBO: I wanted to ask you about race. What you remember about race in high school, whether you were friendly with any of the Black girls, that kind of thing.] "Oh yeah, I was. I think it was a very gentle time. . . . We had some wonderful Black people in our class . . . [SBO: Who were you friendly with?] Well I don't remember names of people; I remember very few names, white and Black, but I can tell you if I looked in my yearbook, there'd be lots of people that I thought were really nice people. Ah, I remember Eliza McCloud, remember her? . . . And a lot of guys that were just really nice guys."

Franklin Bodnar: [Franklin did some tutoring with Black kids.] "A couple of people I worked with had been in [the] Reading Readiness [program] and people I got close to were some of the Black kids. That's an interesting thing, especially the ones that came up from the South, seeing how different they were from the resident Blacks in the city. And I was at their homes [tutoring], I ate at their places, I met them, and learned a little different perspective than I think most of the kids in Weequahic."

Louis Spiegel: [SBO: Because you were on all the sports teams, you had more contact with the Black students, and with the non-Jewish white students, than most. . . . Anything you care to say about that I'd be interested to hear that.] "We were teammates. There were no conflicts." [He came to a full stop, so I said, oh I see, that's the answer, that you were teammates.] "Team, we were teammates. We were teammates. There was never anything about the color line. There was never any incident when I was in high school that dealt with the color line. [SBO: None at all?] . . . No."

Walter Markowitz: "I knew the Black guys mainly from sports . . . because I was in sports or baseball, I always got along with them fine . . . kibbitzing around with [he named some individuals]. No problems with the Blacks at all. With our [baseball] team we had one Black on the team [again he named an individual]. He was a star but he was treated the same as everybody else."

Linda Grossman: "The Black people who I wasn't friendly with, they weren't part of my clique, but I thought they were nice. You know, they were just another group, a different group in our high school."

These comments from white classmates are diverse, but they betray a kind of generalized good will and a sense that there was not a conflictual divide between Black and white in that era, at least not one that could not be overcome.

Yet in many ways, certain boundaries continued to be in effect. At the most innocent level, there was the problem of the Jewish holidays. When those holidays came around, all the Jewish kids stayed out of school while all the non-Jewish kids, both Black and white, found themselves rattling around the halls, clearly marked as outside the Jewish hegemony:

> *Marie Rio:* "Sometime when there was a Jewish holiday [she laughed], oh, I would be one of maybe ten in the whole school. . . . [And it seemed like] they had a holiday every month" [she laughed again].
>
> *Elaine Colecchio:* "And when I went to high school in Weequahic, and I guess it might have been the third Jewish holiday. When I saw that it was only me in school, and a couple of the Negro kids, who I loved, they were great, [then] I said, '. . . Somebody's going to be Jewish in my family. I have to work this out.' So I made my mother Jewish. I had one of my friends write a letter, and I lied: 'You have to excuse my daughter. While my husband is Italian, I must have her observe the Jewish holidays.' . . . That's a true story. I could hack anything, but I couldn't be there on Jewish holidays. I felt like, you know, *come on.*"
>
> *Thomas Neeley:* "Certainly some of the more memorable experiences of Weequahic High School would be in the high school during the Jewish holidays, when there were about six of us running around the hallways, saying, 'Hey! All of these guys get Christmas off, how come we don't get Rosh Hashanah off?'"

But the sense of "difference" was often more negative, involving more of a sense of active social exclusion and/or social inferiority. Again this came across in memories of both Black and white students, like this from one African American classmate, Anna Granger:

> "I had started high school in [another part of New Jersey] and we moved the first of the year that January so that was very, very traumatic for me. And I went into a school that was predominantly white and I had a very rough time there, I had a very rough time. My two older brothers were still in high school at the time [and] seemed to adjust a lot easier. . . . It was a lot easier for them making friends, that kind of thing. . . . I always felt apart from what was going on, I never felt included . . . and I kind of understood it because I knew that the kids there had all grown up together and they knew one another, but I guess I kind of felt they should have extended themselves a little bit. Those three and a half years I don't have too many happy memories about it. It was a deal, I went to school because I had to, I came home after school, you know, that was it."

Anna does not directly blame racism for her unhappy time at Weequahic, partly because high school students are often cruel to outsiders
(they had "all grown up together"), partly because her brothers' good
adjustment seemed to negate a racist interpretation. She did say, however, that her "rough time" related to coming into this "predominantly
white school." I will return to other cases of avoiding the racist explanation for social exclusion below.

The story of exclusion is somewhat different for the non-Jewish
white students. As noted earlier, many of the non-Jewish girls were
friendly with Jewish girls and specifically reported not having felt excluded. On the other hand, one non-Jewish girl did mention a girlfriend of hers who felt looked down on in Weequahic. She did not
name any names, but another woman told me that it was Rosemary
DeHagara who had felt that way: "Listening to Rosemary later on, I
find out that maybe [the non-Jewishness, or outsiderness] did matter.
That she had a harder time than she showed on the surface." Another
case was even more explicit. One (Jewish) woman talked about Maria
Figueroa, whom I never found for this study:

> "You wind up with the 20 percent who weren't Jewish, which in many
> instances considered themselves less of a person. When you look back I
> remember one person . . . Maria Figueroa. . . . She was extremely bril-
> liant but very subservient because she felt that she was not as good as the
> Jews. . . . She dressed different, she looked different, and we knew there
> was something different about her. She was not friends with anyone, she
> did not mainstream with anyone."

There were also boys who felt excluded because they were not Jewish. Derek Goethe, a German American, had a conversation at a reunion with Susan Wolkstein, which she recounted to me:

> "I [Susan] remember also saying to him, how did you like growing up in
> a . . . it must have been hard. . . . I thought the whole world was Jewish
> until I left Weequahic. . . . He said he really liked his high school days,
> but when kids found out he was German, they gave him a hard time in
> school."

Thomas Neeley went on at some length about how great Weequahic
(the school, the neighborhood, even Newark) was at that time, but at
the same time he felt it was very prejudiced against non-Jews:

"It was a very cliquey high school. . . . I remember—in fact, you mentioned Arthur Mayers, so—he belonged to a fraternity and they wouldn't take non-Jewish members. . . . So I couldn't join the fraternity, which was a real sore point. . . . It was very, sort of prejudiced that way."

Joseph Keefer also felt the prejudice but was less willing or able to get past it and enjoy himself as some of the others seem to have done:

"I hated high school. . . . I didn't like it, probably growing up in a very Jewish section of New Jersey at that time—I don't know what it's like now, but at that time it was very Jewish. And I did have some very good friends, but I wasn't 'part of' [it]. I was an outsider. And I always remained the outsider."

Finally, there were questions of academic abilities. Here white and/ or Jewish was equated with "smart," while nonwhite and/or not Jewish was equated with "dumb." Mostly these comments were put in terms of the school itself and how the very fact of being in that school made one feel stupid. From the point of view of African American students, the main point was that the school was northern and, as the woman quoted here said elsewhere, white:

"I was behind, I got behind, and I had to get a tutor, . . . it was quite devastating. I didn't realize how far behind the schools [in the South] were. . . . So I had to get a tutor for the first year. My grades just fell behind. . . . You know, in [the South] I was an A student, but when I came here, I was getting Ds, and Cs, and, oh, I was really [upset]."

But from the point of view of northerners aware of ethnic distinctions among whites, the main point was that it was "Jewish." One Italian American woman said she had "a lot of apprehension" about going to Weequahic. "You know, I wasn't as smart as a lot of the kids I hung out with. No, I wasn't." Elsewhere in the interview she made it clear that she meant the Jewish kids. The idea that Weequahic was academically tough because it was "Jewish" provoked anxieties even for (working-class) Jewish students who had coasted in schools in non-Jewish neighborhoods, and who now felt they were pushed much harder in middle-class/Jewish Weequahic:

Alan Kaduck: [Alan had started at South Side, which was becoming increasingly dominated by African American students when C58 was

growing up.] "I coasted, my first year [at South Side]. Got straight As
my first year. I wasn't really doing any work, it was easy, you know. . . .
[His parents moved him to Weequahic.] And so I went from that, to an
environment where there were a lot of smart kids. And you couldn't
coast. So my first year was horrendous."

William Balk: "I also had a lot of problems when I went into Peshine
[elementary school] because I then went into a predominantly Jewish
school where the kids were all very bright. I had to be tutored, I had a
couple of tough years in grade school from being the smartest to being
the dumbest, well, not being the dumbest but not . . ."

In sum, the Jewish hegemony at Weequahic did impose itself on
the non-Jewish students, and even on some working-class Jewish students who came from a more ethnically mixed milieu. The lines were
often invisible, yet suddenly they would make themselves felt: the halls
empty of Jews on the Jewish holidays, leaving the other students to
recognize their own minority-ness; the failures to extend a friendly
hand to some "others"; the superficial friendliness with some non-
Jewish whites that would suddenly reveal a limit, like the rules of admission to the fraternity; the academic toughness of the school, which
was equated with its high Jewish population, and which equated non-
Jewishness with less brains, or at least less motivation.

Internalizing Limits

Pierre Bourdieu has written about the ways in which subordinate
groups, including the working classes in capitalist society, often internalize the objective limits of their own position. That is, they either
scale down their aspirations in the first place, or they blame themselves
for failing to succeed when success was never really possible, or was at
least very unlikely. In a moving chapter of *Distinction* (1984), his brilliant work on class cultures, he calls this internalization "the choice
of the necessary." Elsewhere he discusses the psychological processes
in more detail, the ways in which the actor's experience of economic
necessity, social pressure, and cultural "common sense" are internalized as a *habitus* (a structure of dispositions) of low ambition and self-
blame:

Because the dispositions durably inculcated by objective conditions (which science apprehends through statistical regularities as the probabilities objectively attached to a group or class) engender aspirations and practices objectively compatible with those objective requirements, the most improbable practices are excluded, either totally without examination, as *unthinkable,* or at the cost of the *double negation* which inclines agents to make a virtue of necessity, that is, to refuse what is anyway refused and to love the inevitable. (1978:77; italics in original)[2]

Bourdieu's perspective was developed in the context of interpreting a relatively stable, relatively undifferentiated, precapitalist society, and he fully recognized that this kind of closed loop of objective conditions and subjective aspirations is more likely to be found in those kinds of cases (1978). Even when he got to modern, capitalist France, however, he argued that the working class tends to internalize its own subordination in similar ways, largely because they do not fully participate in the educational system, which would give them the tools to critique those objective conditions and their associated psychological structures (1984).

One certainly sees this kind of thinking among some members of the Class of '58, and I will discuss some examples here. Nonetheless I have argued elsewhere (Ortner 1996) that Bourdieu underestimated a whole variety of counterforces, even in "simple" societies, that would constantly threaten to disrupt these closed loops of social and cultural reproduction. Thus after I discuss some of the more classic Bourdieusian examples, I return to the wider range of responses to the Jewish/middle-class hegemony on the part of African American and white ethnic classmates. These responses, in the end, will allow us to understand how—despite certain classic working-class patterns, like a low level of participation in higher education—members of these groups nonetheless moved up the class ladder at almost the same rate as the rest of the Class. Indeed, when we get to the final chapter and the current class configuration of the Class of '58, we will find that there is virtually no working class left. A handful of relatively comfortable industrial workers aside, most of the working class of the Class of '58 has moved, at least occupationally, into the middle class or even higher.

But first I must report and briefly discuss a few cases in which the many social exclusions discussed above were felt as personal failures.

It is perhaps necessary to say that, for various reasons, some students may have been more vulnerable to these kinds of reactions than others. One non-Jewish white man, Richard Lawrence, came from a disrupted family background. He talked at length about how he did not do well academically in high school, and was also somewhat socially marginal, because he hung out with his "wise guy" friends. I asked if he felt excluded by others, but he denied that:

> "I think people are excluded, probably because they don't put enough effort into being included. I think if I really wanted to be included, if I didn't have this [other] social group I was involved with, I think I could have joined [certain in-groups]. . . . There's no reason why they wouldn't [include me]."

This man blamed himself for his poor grades (though at another point he did link them to his parents' problems), and also for his noninclusion in the Weequahic social networks. It is probably true that he in a sense segregated himself; we will see below that withdrawing into other social networks was one kind of adaptation to being on the downside of the Jewish hegemony at Weequahic. At the same time it is hard not to hear in his comments the Bourdieusian move noted above, "to refuse what is anyway refused," to not try to enter the networks that might have excluded him in the first place.

Another source of vulnerability is particular to the African American students. The move from the South to the North was evidently quite traumatic for some of them. Moving is always hard on kids (actually, according to stress studies, it is hard on everyone, nearly as high on the list of stressors as death of a parent and divorce), but it seems to be especially hard on adolescents.[3] Moreover, for virtually every one of the African American students, it seems to have been the first experience of being a minority on a day-to-day basis in a predominantly white environment.

Thus while there was always at some level a race issue, there was also a kind of culture shock. One can hear this quite clearly in Pearl Smith's story. Pearl had lived with her mother in the South, but her mother (tape unclear, maybe "remarried"), so she was sent up north to live with her father and stepmother. Thus there was a certain amount of family disruption and readjustment to begin with, although the family situation seems to have settled down after a while. In addition, however, Pearl found it strange and unsettling to go to school with white kids: "When I came here and gee, everybody goes to school together, everybody sits together, you know, Blacks and whites at school. And it was no big thing. But you were not used to sitting next to them . . . so you had a sense of being inferior. . . . I thought, I'm not equal." Pearl distinguished this experience from "racism," by which she seemed to mean formal segregation: "I don't think it's prejudice, not like in the South, because in the South you know there were times when we had to . . . go to the back of the store, as opposed to coming in the front." She also distinguished this experience from racism because there was at least a surface friendliness between whites and Blacks, and she felt it was her own shyness (related to not having been around whites much before) that held her back from closer relations with whites:

"I wouldn't say it was prejudice. I would say that I was not used to being around them, and me myself, I was like [an] introvert . . . because I was shy, you know, as to coming close and being friends with them. . . . I'm sure if I had come to them, because there were some I did speak with and . . . had conversations with. But I mean, [we were] usually never invited to each other's homes. But that I would not consider prejudice or racism, it was that [there were] things you didn't do!"

Pearl felt quite excluded, but she refused to blame this on "racism." In part this was relative to the South; she was clearly distinguishing between the direct humiliation of formal segregation and the harder-to-locate hurts of being ignored at Weequahic. At the same time she blamed her own shyness, saying she was "sure if she had come to them" she would have made some white friends. This is the first Bourdieusian displacement, but there is a deeper one yet to come: that Blacks were not invited into white homes, but this was not "racism," it was just that "there were things you didn't do!" Here, as Bourdieu nailed it, "the most improbable practices are excluded . . . as *unthinkable.*"

Survival Strategies

Although some non-Jewish students felt wounded by their exclusion, many did not (or at least did not remember/report it), and in any event all found ways to cope with it. I distinguish at least four different survival strategies in my data, although several of them overlap. The simplest strategy was disengagement from and/or avoidance of the scene. We have seen that Anna Granger gave up on trying to make friends: "It was a deal, I went to school because I had to, I came home after school, you know, that was it." Many of these working-class kids also worked after school, and had done so from an early age, and so had a reason/excuse for not hanging out with groups that might have excluded them. Others, like Richard Lawrence, maintained friendships outside of Weequahic, presumably with other non-Jewish, working-class kids with whom they had grown up.[4]

The second strategy was to try to ignore and overcome the boundaries. Thus many of the non-Jewish kids seemed to have successfully participated in the Weequahic scene in various ways that made it a satisfactory experience. Some of the boys, both Black and white, got involved in sports. I do not have any information on the white, non-Jewish boys who were on the sports teams, though they are visible in the yearbook. I did talk to two of the African American men who had been involved in sports, and both seemed to have had a fairly positive experience at Weequahic, and to have identified to some degree with the school and the Class. Herbert Graves commented that our class was a "good class to study." He said there are more "sad stories" in later generations, but "ours was in the heyday of prosperity." These comments (as well as an extremely warm reception when I contacted him, though I barely knew him personally in high school) suggest basically good feelings about that time and place. Al Walker also said in a fairly positive way that he had "some good times" at Weequahic.

Others simply managed to make friends across the color line. One was William Smallwood, who had such a bad time at Barringer but then moved to Weequahic:

> "Going to Weequahic was a unique experience, what I was looking for. It turned out to be exactly what I thought integration was supposed to be about. . . . I had very good relationships in Weequahic High School. Even though I didn't know my whole class, . . . some things in life you just like. There were a couple people in my class that no matter what happened, I will never forget who they are or how they treated me."

Another African American man who was friendly with whites was John Koonce (now deceased), whose mother talked to me about these friendships:

[from the field notes] I asked who John was friendly with in high school and she said, "Mostly white kids, yes, John liked his white friends." . . . She told a story of them all going swimming in Irvington Park, and John going out into deep water but not knowing how to swim . . . but his friends pulled him out and brought him home.

There were also two African American women who seem to have been/felt less left out than the women discussed earlier: Eleanor Willis and Eliza McCloud. I did not locate either of them, despite major efforts, so the following comes from other people's comments. Both of them seem to have been quite friendly with white students. Several people mentioned Eleanor in particular very warmly in their interviews. As for Eliza, two Jewish women of working-class families who had gone to the much more heavily African American junior high school, Madison, apparently knew her at Madison and considered her so closely connected with the white girls that they tried to remember whether she had been in one of the (all-white) girl clubs with them. They concluded that she had not been, but the discussion itself suggests close connections.

Many of the white, non-Jewish girls also seem to have become, or remained from grammar school, close with Jewish girls. I noted some instances of this in chapter 3, as part of saying that the boundaries were somewhat weaker between Jewish and non-Jewish whites, especially in terms of same-sex friendships. Here I will tell a few more stories of these friendships because they were clearly the condition for not experiencing a sense of exclusion. Marie Low, for example, was the daughter of immigrant parents who owned a tiny business. She was the only member of her ethnic group in the class, and I asked how she felt about being a minority of one:

"I don't really think much about it, because I was born here and I just grew up and just mingled. It didn't really affect me. Because look where I'm teaching [she is a teacher at an all Black and Hispanic high school]. I grew up to be a teacher and I'm teaching people that are not of my own ethnicity, right? And it really doesn't come into my thinking."

I wrote afterward in my field notes: "She [said she] never felt herself to be something terribly different, no problem being the only [member of that minority] in the class, she just 'mingled with everyone,' if she felt close to any group it was the Jews, after all [as she said] she grew up with them, babysat for them, etc." Elaine Cuomo also felt that she fit in socially: "I had the most wonderful high school years. And I was so accepted by all of the Jewish families. It was just unbelievable." Mary Lou Papa felt the same way:

> "I never had a problem. The people that I'm friendly with today still feel, or speak as though they are scarred from that. I never had a problem with it, it never bothered me. I never considered myself in a minority, I felt that I fit in. . . . My friends were all Jewish, and I never felt that I was any different from any of them. I mean, I don't know how Black people feel as being a minority, but I certainly didn't have any feelings of not belonging. You know?"

It is hard to overstate the importance of personal friendships for overcoming/ignoring social boundaries, avoiding a sense of injury and insult, and managing to enjoy life as a high school student. Virtually every person I interviewed talked about the value of their friendships at the time. In some cases (outside) friendships were what allowed one to withdraw from the potentially hurtful social scene, as in the case of Richard Lawrence, above. In other cases one had friends within the school, but very much within one's own race/class/ethnic group, that allowed one to ignore or redefine the ways in which one was excluded. And in yet other cases, like the ones I have been discussing here, people actually made friends across the various boundaries. This not only generated a sense that one was not in fact excluded, but represented some small successes for integrationist ideology.

A third strategy was to recognize that one was on the downside of the race/class/ethnic boundary, but to use Weequahic as a resource — to make it work for, rather than against, one's interests. My sense here is that the following patterns were not parts of conscious "strategies" at the time, but rather retrospective ways of people saying, to themselves and to the ethnographer, that despite the ways in which Jewish Weequahic drew hurtful boundaries, they were nevertheless able to get some value out of the experience. For example, some felt that Jewish prejudice spurred them to succeed; others said that Jewish "traits" furnished useful models for success. Harry Liscio said he felt that he was looked down on, but that dealing with this gave him a good start in life:

> [from the field notes] I asked Harry if he felt sentimental at all about Weequahic High School and he said oh yes, definitely. He said he thinks it

really got him started in life, having to overcome being looked down on. I said [in some surprise], did you feel looked down on at Weequahic? And he said, "Well, yeah, coming into a Jewish school like that, of course."

Pearl Smith expressed the idea that the academic difficulty of Weequahic High was a positive motivator:

SBO: [trying to suggest that the academic difficulties Pearl had when she first came into Weequahic were not her fault] "I think Weequahic was one of the harder high schools in Newark."
PS: "Yeah, it was, but in a way that was good, it kept me up."

Patricia Gandy felt similarly motivated by the academic challenge, but also suggested that "Jewish competitiveness" was a useful skill to learn:

"Weequahic was a struggle. You're [Jews] a very competitive people. And I think that's a great environment to be in. To be forced to be competitive, because it tests us. You know, I wasn't as smart as a lot of the kids I hung out with. No, I wasn't. But I was able to keep a certain pace. And I learned from the Jewish people. I really did. I really mean that sincerely."

And finally, Marlene Keefer highlighted another supposed Jewish ethnic trait that she felt gave her a boost in life: "materialism." As with academic competitiveness, this was not seen as entirely a bad thing.

"I'm more materialistic than my siblings, and my brother teases me and says that's because I'm a product of Weequahic High School, which doesn't bother me at all. Obviously it doesn't bother me. I raised my daughter to be very materialistic as well, hoping that she would want the better things in life, and find someone who could provide her with that."

A final strategy (along with withdrawal, integration/friendship, and recognition of strategic benefits) for dealing with the Jewish hegemony at Weequahic would have been some kind of strategy of resistance. As far as I can tell, and I certainly looked for it, there was none of this in the Class of '58. The reasons for its absence are no doubt diverse. For many non-Jewish whites, these would have included the prosperity of the era and the fact that their families were doing relatively well financially, as well as the fact that there was enough social acceptance among the kids to make it seem that class/ethnic barriers could be overcome, or at least equalized.

For some African Americans, too, it may have seemed that integration might work, at least on an individual level. People had experiences that seemed to indicate that racism on the part of whites could be overcome, and that whites might come to appreciate the equal humanity of African Americans. One white, Jewish, working-class man told a complex story along these lines about his father. He first described his father as "very bigoted" toward African Americans, but also said his father was always making exceptions for individuals. The father hired one such "exception" as a helper in his tiny business, and eventually helped the helper set up in business on his own. This man thus became "the first independent Black owner of a [similar] establishment." Later, the father became ill, had to close his business, and lost a lot of money. But the former helper returned the father's earlier support: "My father [got sick and had to close his business. Later he] went to work for [the former helper]. And this guy was the only guy who treated my father well toward the end of his life . . . [even] covered some of the bills." Here, then, personal support in both directions seemed to override both the father's bigotry and the helper's low origins.

Without undercutting the importance of these kinds of individual experiences, there is nonetheless a more political interpretation available for the lack of African American resistance to racism in that time and place. Specifically, the high rate of African American geographic mobility would have played at least some role in maintaining integrationist ideology. Since virtually every African American student in the Class moved into the neighborhood from somewhere else, either from distant southern states or areas closer to Newark, there was very little history between them, very little basis for social solidarity and mutual support to develop among these students. (Of nineteen African American students in the class, the grammar schools of three are unknown, but the rest were scattered over eleven different grammar or junior high schools.) While as far as I know, most Black students had friendly relations with one another, they did not have the kind of collective history that many of the white kids did, that would lead to strong personal ties and/or a cohesive social group—the bases for the development of a more political consciousness.

In fact, however, the forces that would undo the integrationist optimism of the fifties were already at work. Although some African American families succeeded in finding stable work at decent wages, many others were not experiencing the same kind of financial success as many white working-class families. Further, many African Americans quickly learned that the North was just as racist as the South, although in different ways. Which brings us back to the Class of '58. If there was no overt resistance, there were nonetheless some angry African American classmates: the woman, discussed earlier, who was still hurt and angry at being ignored; another man, not discussed, who felt discriminated against by the high school administration; and no doubt some among those who cannot be found or who refused to meet with me. They need to be mentioned here because in 1967, only nine years after graduation, Newark would erupt in devastating race riots. As far as I know, none of the members of the Class of '58 were directly involved. Nonetheless, those angry classmates at least remind us that the seeds of the Newark riots were already in place, even in the seemingly peaceful Weequahic area.

In this first set of chapters I have tried to lay out the social geography of the Weequahic neighborhood—the more visible dynamics of ethnicity and race, and the more hidden workings of class. I have tried to examine the ways in which these factors constructed the young Class of '58 as a diverse set of social subjects moving into the high school context. The next set of chapters is concerned with high school itself, that crucible of practice, consciousness, and memory that links one's childhood self and community to one's life as an adult in the "real world."

Project Journal 4: New Jersey

4/12/92 [Interview with one of the professional men in the class, recently married and with a new baby.] His wife is Italian and a practicing Catholic, today is Palm Sunday and she went off to church, leaving him with the twenty-month-old. He tried valiantly to talk to me while caring for this kid who of course was endlessly requiring attention—I felt sorry for him.
4/13/92 [Staying at the Rothbards' again.] Last night we watched a video of George [Rothbard's]* fiftieth birthday party—huge blast at a 1950s-type diner. Friends, neighbors, relatives. Lots of family togetherness. The kids, along with a batch of their cousins, wrote a rap song, "The Rothbard Rap," which was really

very well done. The kind of community stuff that I guess still exists in America but you have to go and find it. An anthropologist from another culture looking for "rituals" would have been thrilled to see this event.

...... I walked over to [a classmate's medical] office the other day. He wasn't in. However I was struck by the New Jerseyness of the situation in the waiting room—very crowded, people waiting for hours, one lady complaining that six people who had come in after her were taken while she was still sitting there. I guess part of the culture that strikes me both here and on the West Coast is the sheer overpopulation, compared to Ann Arbor. Waiting for everything, sitting in traffic. The thinness of the traffic on, say, I-94 compared to the LA freeways or the Long Island Expressway.

...... I was talking to Jack Rosenberg about the public culture here. Maybe it's really quite obvious, but somehow I never put the pieces together quite like this: in the Midwest you get great (and genuine) civility, but what people lack is a sense of the irony of life. The rudeness in NY often takes the form of sarcasm (Jack told a story of asking someone in a store if she worked there, and she said no I'm just here to hold down this desk), which has to do with this ironic view of the world—and themselves. This is what you trade off for the civility, the "politeness" and "friendliness" of the Midwest.

...... [Dinner at a restaurant with a classmate of working-class origin.] I forgot the tape recorder, forgot the whole work bag, somehow was just thinking of it as a dinner. In a way I think it would have been difficult to tape—I never could move her toward anything resembling a formal interview anyway, partly because it was a social [event], partly because of her rambly style, partly because of the class "thing" in some sense—I had to work to just be an ordinary person, not high status, about which she almost definitely felt insecure, or so I felt/feared. If I had pulled out the tape recorder, she would have gone all formal, and her husband would have moved into the Uncle Gerry hostile teasing mode.

4/14/92 [Waiting for an interview with a schoolteacher, at her school.] I waited for her for about an hour in the teachers' lounge and that was a bit of participant observation. There seemed to be many more white teachers than Black, even though this was an all-Black school. The basic mode of conversation was complaining—I guess we all do that with our friends and colleagues, but somehow it seems more pronounced in New Jersey. One of the white teachers kept going on and on, and one of the Black women finally told her, quite angrily, to shut up, she was sick and tired of hearing her complaining about everything, to just keep her mouth shut. It's one of those things people don't usually do— if you can't stand someone you just drift away from them, so this created a real silence, and then the white woman tried to start talking again in a way that she obviously hoped would be more acceptable, but the other woman told her to shut up again. Others then tried to track the conversation in other directions. There were a few male teachers, and they tended to silently eat their lunch and stay out of the whole thing. Then some assistant principal (white, male) came in and started dickering with the teachers about who would do auditorium duty, and all of them were damned if they were going to give up their "prep" (free period), and while they were reasonably deferential to him, you could hear the "don't mess with me" edge in the whole thing. Sort of the foreman/worker interaction, the little intraclass hierarchies of life.

...... [Interview with a professional/managerial class classmate.] It was weird looking into Brenda's present face and seeing her original face. I mean, we go back so far, virtually the whole fifty years, and when I look at her I can see this fifty-year-old woman—I mean, individuals may look better or worse individually, but collectively we do really look fifty years old, and we all look like the grownups I remember from my childhood, sort of pouchy—pouchy in the face, in the body, etc. But then inside those faces I can see the younger faces that I knew, and there's some strange time thing that happens, where I feel like I'm seeing the past shimmering under the water of the present like Atlantis.

4/15/92 [After an interview with a working-class African American classmate in a restaurant.] I took him back to a bar a few blocks away, where he switched to the car of one of his relatives, and they led me through the nightmares of Port Newark at rush hour—huge trucks barreling along on little skinny roads, crisscrossing all sorts of spaghetti highway where you enter on the left and need to cross four lanes in ten seconds to get where you're going, back to 78 West. We waved good-bye as I headed west and they headed for New York to play the lottery.

chapter 5

American High Schools

I began drafting this chapter four months after the 1999 shootings at Columbine High School in Littleton, Colorado. The shootings left one teacher and fourteen students dead, including the seventeen-year-old gunmen, Dylan Klebold and Eric Harris, who committed suicide. The tragedy set off a spate of searching questions regarding the easy availability of guns, the responsibility of parents to know what their children are doing, the security systems of schools, and the role of the Internet in fueling homicidal fantasies. But there was one more theme that is specifically relevant to the task at hand. It was captured best in a story in the *New York Times* that was entitled "Two Words behind the Massacre." The two words were *high school*.

It is hard to overstate the significance of high school for the American cultural imagination. Peter Applebome, who wrote the *Times* piece, called it "something that is burned like a tattoo into the memory bank of most adults" (1999:1). David Denby, writing shortly afterward in the *New Yorker* about teen movies, called the leading social figures of the American high school scene "a common memory, a collective trauma, or at least a social and erotic fantasy" (1999:94). Camille Paglia described clique formation in high school as "a pitiless process" (quoted in Applebome 1999:4). Japanese ethnographer Keiko Ikeda wrote of the "hell of the critical gaze" of students vis-à-vis their peers, and quoted among others Frank Zappa and Kurt Vonnegut Jr. on the power of high school in the imagination. The Vonnegut quote is worth repeating in full:

> High school is closer to the core of American experience than anything else I can think of. . . . We have all been there. While there we saw nearly every form of justice and injustice, kindness and meanness, intelligence and stupidity, which we were likely to encounter in later life. Richard Nixon is a familiar type from high school. . . . So is J. Edgar Hoover. . . . So is everybody. (quoted in Ikeda 1998:15)

To all these I can add a few more, picked up in the course of working on this chapter. Amiri Baraka said, "The life of emotion, which is historical, like anything else, gets warped in high school I'm certain now" (Baraka 1997:41). And Anna Quindlen, writing about the TV show *Survivor,* said, "The whole thing sounds . . . no scarier than high school. (Although in the last analysis, nothing is scarier than high school.)" (2001:74)[1]

Why is the high school experience "tattooed" into the memories of so many Americans? My key point here is that high schools as social systems attempt to "force" identities—to, as Foucault put it, "pin people" to particular types and categories; or, as Bourdieu put it, to create the conditions in which people ideally both inhabit those categories and are inhabited by them. Moreover, those identities are not innocent functional categories (e.g., student/teacher), but social types based on seemingly natural, and thus seemingly randomly distributed, characteristics (beauty, "personality," athletic prowess) which are neither natural nor random, and which always carry, I will argue, a heavy load of class baggage. Put in other words, I will retrieve the class issues of chapter 2 and consider the ways in which all those class things—family income, family quality (the question of emotional support or disruption), and family cultural capital (parents' education and/or knowledge of the workings of the dominant culture)—are codified in unrecognizable ways into high school identities, identities people are hailed to inhabit, whether they like it or not.

I need to say at the outset, and will repeat several times as we go along, that this system is not always successful in imposing itself on every student, and I will devote the entire next chapter to the ways in which some students escape these identities. For them, indeed perhaps for the majority of students in any given high school, the relationship between one's own relatively (at that point) inchoate personal identity and the identities being promoted by the social system is often felt as a painful struggle. But "the system" is powerful and durable, and we have to understand its power and appeal before we can think about the many ways in which most people are never fully caught by it.

In order to pursue this more general analysis of high school social systems, I need to step back from the Class of '58 of Weequahic High School and consider the place of high schools in general in the American cultural imaginary. Virtually every high school in America has a set of evaluative social categories. The labels for the categories vary from school to school and from era to era, but the basic types remain amazingly constant. There are the popular kids, often the class officers; there are the athletic stars, or "jocks"; there are the cheerleaders and twirlers who perform at the sporting events and are the female counterparts of the jocks; there are the "nerds," "geeks," and "eggheads," terms for socially awkward (but sometimes very smart) students; there are the "hoods," "druggies," and "burnouts"—the most alienated students; there are the "prom queens" (beautiful/popular girls), on the one hand, and the "sluts" (supposedly sexually promiscuous girls), on the other; there are the "average citizens" and the "nobodies," whose main distinction is that they do not fit into the other categories and are rarely noticed by those above them (Palonsky 1975, Schwartz and Merten 1975, Varenne 1982, Canaan 1986, Eckert 1989, Chang 1992).

This system has been extraordinarily durable. It seems to have begun taking shape early in the twentieth century and remained remarkably consistent throughout the century for different parts of the country and different ethnic mixes.[2] And although U.S. public high schools have gone through major transformations and continue to do so in relation to changes in larger American configurations of class and race, some version of this often cruel system of categories is still in operation in many schools in many parts of the country. The high school jocks and freaks, the cheerleaders and sluts, the popular kids and the nobodies keep coming, year after year.

In another paper I emphasized the long-term durability of the system and focused on trying to account for that (Ortner 2002c). Here, however, I wish to emphasize the fact that, for all its earlier antecedents, the system seems to have congealed in much stronger form, and gained much more public visibility, in the postwar era, the era commonly shorthanded as "the Fifties."[3] The hyperarticulation of the high school social system in the fifties was one part of a broader coming together of a so-called youth culture with its own self-awareness; its own (heavily marketed) styles of clothing; and its own "public culture" of music, movies, and television.[4]

There had, of course, been other "youth cultures" before, notably in the 1910s (Ueda 1987) and 1920s (Fass 1977). But these earlier formations tended to be much more elite. The fifties youth culture, in contrast, was based largely in the middle class and had important, if ambiguous, links to the working class. Indeed, its class shape and tone precisely reflected the postwar class changes with which I started this book: the enlargement of the middle class as a result of both the high level of general prosperity, and the government social engineering that contributed to lifting a large chunk of the former working class (tenuously) into the middle class.

It is important to note, however, that there was (and is) no single fifties "youth culture." The most visible strand was the romanticization of rebellious youth, as captured, for example, in the film *Rebel without a Cause* (1955). But at the same time a kind of serious, educationally committed youth was also interpellated or "hailed" (Althusser 1971) by politicians in the wake of the Russian launch of Sputnik in 1957, inspiring the need for more scientists to make the United States competitive. And perhaps most important, increasingly affluent youth were also identified and targeted by the advertising industry as consumer markets expanded dramatically in the extraordinary affluence of the period.[5] It is not difficult to see how these variations in youth culture can be mapped onto some of the high school categories: advertising/consumerism and the wealthier, popular kids; Sputnik and the "nerds"; James Dean and the "hoods."

In addition, the emergence in the fifties of a distinctive (if very diverse) youth culture, both from the point of view of adults and from the self-perceptions of young people themselves, no doubt added fuel to the high emotional charge of the high school experience with which I began this chapter. As both cause and effect, the emerging youth culture intensified the construction of the high school as a relatively autonomous social space. The emphasis shifted, to some extent, away from the high school's educational functions, and away from its function of preparing young people for adult life, and toward treating it as a kind of social world unto itself. Or, to turn the point around, one could think of the kind of social world operating in high schools as the institutional base—the base in real, everyday practice—for the emergence and persistence of the "youth culture" itself.

Memories and Categories

I have indicated already that the American high school is represented in the popular culture as an experience that leaves very deep marks on people's souls. Before considering why and how this might be the case, I will introduce a little Weequahic ethnography to support this generalization. One of my stock questions in the interviews was how people "felt about Weequahic." A few people could not remember having strong feelings one way or the other. Some expressed ambivalence. But the vast majority of classmates had very clear and unambiguous memories, pro or con. I will start with the negatives. In some of the milder statements, people simply said they "didn't like Weequahic," "had not such great feelings about high school," had "a lot of negative feelings from Weequahic," "did not have a great time there," "never found it an easy time"; they were not "comfortable there," and "it was not a great experience." But many people had much stronger negative memories than these:

> *Susan Kleinman:* "I hated it, simple, I hated it. I couldn't get away from it fast enough."
> *Steven DeLeon:* "I hated school."
> *Lila Lohman:* "I had a lot of difficulties in Weequahic because I was made fun of because I was so heavy. . . . Terrible, terrible experiences."[6]
> *Michael Feldman:* "I think it was one of the most painful times of my life. . . . I felt socially isolated, well, except when I was doing sports, but I felt out of it, inferior, and it was a horrible, horrible time."
> *Janet Cooper:* "It was awful. I never have known [such] a bunch of snobs in my entire life."
> *Linda Kirschner:* "I count those three years as the worst of my life."
> *Stuart Marcus:* "I am really glad you are doing this [study] since I had such a crappy existence in high school."
> *Eric Tasco:* [from the field notes] He said he emphatically does not want to participate in the project, he feels no connection to Weequahic, he went to a reunion and it was "all the same bullshit," all the cliques, making him feel uncomfortable.

But even more people ranged from quite positive about their high school experience to totally ecstatic. Again I will start with some of the milder statements. People said that they "really enjoyed" high school, that they had good memories because they "found companionship and learning and friendship," that they "really thought it was great," that they have "wonderful memories," that they were "very happy in high school," that it was "a good four years," and that they looked back "fondly" on the Weequahic experience. But many had much more positive feelings/memories than those:

William Smallwood: "Weequahic was the best thing that ever happened to me."

Sue Ellen Schanerman: "I thought it was probably the best high school to go to in America."

Paula Bank: "I think it was so terrific and so complete that everybody took it for granted."

Arthur Mayers: "Weequahic was an experience that probably most people will never be able to understand what we had when we had it. . . . The remembrance of high school for me was fantastic. I just think it's something that can never be duplicated again."

Robert Schimmer: "I look back on it now as the greatest time in my life."

Judith Gordon. "I loved Weequahic. Yeah, I had a great high school era."

Larry Kuperman: "My high school years were fantastic. Absolutely fantastic."

Beverly Rothman: "Weequahic High School was wonderful for me. . . . Weequahic was a family, it wasn't a school. . . . Weequahic was a state of mind; it was not a school. . . . Did I love Weequahic? Yes."

Needless to say, these kinds of strong feelings are not randomly distributed. Rather they can be seen as partly (though not, as I will discuss later, entirely) tied to the person's position in the high school social system; that is, to whether one was "popular" or at least had plenty of friends or, alternatively, whether one was classified as a nerd or a nobody or simply felt friendless and left out of the whole system. This brings us back to the system of social categories (popular kids, jocks, nerds, hoods, etc.) through which the system of social judgment operates. These may be thought of, as I said earlier, as "identities" being offered to/foist upon students, as ways of both placing them socially and characterizing their supposedly personal "essences." But what kinds of identities are they?

Deconstructing High School

The time has come to try to understand both the power and the durability of the high school social categories. I will suggest that the system is built on a "structure" in the more or less old-fashioned Lévi-Straussian (e.g., 1966) sense. This is to say, it is based on an underlying logic that, however much the visible shapes of social life have changed in the past century, and especially since World War II, nonetheless continues and endures like the underlying grammar of a language. The structure is composed of two intersecting axes, one a version of "class" (including a variety of kinds of capital), the other a version of qualities related to the "individual."[7]

While the students tend to think that the categories are based primarily on individual traits and qualities (looks, personality, athletic abilities, and so on, or their lack), a number of social scientists (e.g., Hollingshead 1949, C. W. Gordon 1957, Eckert 1989) have argued that they are primarily based on social class. I will argue instead that they cannot be reduced to either the folk emphasis on individual qualities or the objectivist emphasis on class; they arise at the intersection between the two axes of difference.[8] At the same time the two axes do not have equal weight, or perhaps better said, visibility; "class" is as usual more hidden, while personal qualities are highly visible and are indeed thought to carry most of the weight. A few words about each axis.

"Class" is the basis of the vertical axis of the table of high school social categories. By "class," I mean in this context an amalgam of all those conditions of *social* background discussed earlier: the family's place on the socioeconomic ladder, the family's cultural capital in the Bourdieusian sense (education, cultural know-how), and the emotional/psychological quality of family life. I will treat "class" in this compounded sense, and for these purposes, as a simple binary opposition that I will label "high capital" and "low capital." This binary treatment of class is not without both theoretical and ethnographic basis. I said earlier that a binary model (like Marx's, although I am not using his version here) is useful for certain purposes, and this is one of them. When one sorts people into class categories in the United States, or when one asks people to place themselves, they almost invariably use the three-part model (upper/middle/lower), and indeed almost invariably place themselves in the middle. Yet if one listens to other kinds of class talk, one hears people using a binary model all the time. The discussion of how the members of the Class of '58 "read class" contains numerous instances of binary categorization: "the haves and have-nots," "them that went and did and others that couldn't," or— when translated into ethnicity—"us and the Gentiles." Even the grammar school code tended to operate in a binary manner: the Chancellor/Maple crowd and everyone else.

The top axis of the table of high school social categories is the axis

Table 6. The Underlying Structure of High School Social Categories

Class	Attitude/style	
	Tame	*Wild*
More capital	Popular kids Class officers	Jocks/Cheerleaders
Less capital	Ordinary citizens Eggheads ("nerds")	Hoods/Sluts Smokers, Burnouts

of personal qualities. The most salient kinds of "personal qualities," at least in high school, would be the native categories of "personality" — personal charm and charisma — and "looks." It is these that are thought to make people "popular" or not.[9] Both are indeed relevant, but they do not capture the more hidden social and cultural differentiators (like "class" on the left axis) that I am trying to get at here. A more careful consideration indicates that the "personal qualities" relevant, in conjunction with class, for producing not only the high school social categories but also things like "personality" and "looks" themselves is a kind of attitude/style related to "power" broadly conceived, and specifically in the high school context, to issues concerning submission to the system and its rules.[10] The poles of this axis are best summed up, for reasons that will become clear below, as "wild" versus "tame." The wild/tame distinction can refer to the question of submissiveness or resistance to authority, which is its most explicit "youth-culture" reference. But it carries other references as well: dress and demeanor, active sexuality, and more; I will come back to its wider range later.

Putting the two axes together, then, in table 6, we can see quite clearly how their intersection generates, like a grammar, the native social categories of the more or less generic American high school. (The categories within each box are not meant to be ranked, but are equivalents or historical variants of one another.) This is a classic fourfold table. It shows the way in which the main high school categories are produced out of the intersection of "class" differences (more/less "capital" of various kinds) and "attitude" differences (more/less submissive to power/authority; i.e., more/less "tame"). The four boxes represent the four possible combinations of these differences. Yet of course it is the very nature of culture from a Lévi-Straussian point of view, that its underlying structural axes disappear. What happens then is that the real differentiators—of class, and of relationships to power—are submerged within types/categories characterized by overtly physical and performable characteristics—looks, bodies, personality, style.

In moving back from the underlying structure to the public categories, a few caveats are in order. First, as Hervé Varenne (1982, 1983) in particular has stressed, the categories are defined in large part from the point of view of the people at the top: "nerds" and "hoods" and their related terms are pejorative labels that are projected on others from a position of would-be superiority.[11] Second, I repeat that the types represented in the boxes are precisely "types." Very few individual students fully fit the descriptions. But the social types are important in that they structure the symbolic universe within which everyone must operate, whether by conforming, by resisting, or—usually—some combination of the two. And finally, it must be acknowledged that the boundaries between the boxes are not hard and fast, and some types have a tendency to "bleed" into one another. This is not just a matter of saying that the students often evade or cross over the categories in practice, though that is certainly true and will be discussed in chapter 6. It is also a matter of saying that the cultural assumptions themselves do not always divide up so cleanly. In particular, the dominance of athletics in most American public high schools means that even the category of "popular guys" and "class officers" may include a significant component of athletic prowess.

The high school social system, like most systems, is thus never neat; but that does not mean—going wholly to the other extreme—that there is no system in place at all. At this point I want to look at a wide range of American high schools, from different parts of the country and from different periods of time, to show not only the extent to which the social categories are similar from school to school, but also the extent to which those categories partake of the structure just discussed, a structure in which the real underlying factors are class and (relationships to) power or, in the language of the table, capital and (relative) tameness.

High School Types across Time and Space

Like any good native, I start with the kids in the upper left-hand box (high capital/tame), the popular kids and class officer types. They are usually thought to be in this box by virtue of unique individual qualities of personality, charm, looks, and so on. Yet we can see how both high capital and tameness of style lurk beneath this category. Thus it is usually students with more capital—who have parents with more money or more education, or some other sort of sophisticated background—who are at the same time relatively compliant with authority who occupy this box. They tend to be the kids who are widely liked and/or admired (at least within certain circles), who generally have good (or good-enough) grades, and who occupy most of the class offices and seats on the student council. Different terms for the kids in this category reflect different aspects of their overall positionality. At the midwestern high school studied by Hollingshead in the 1940s, they were "the elites," a term that covers both their high capital and their high prestige in the system. Hollingshead emphasized the students' "leadership" but also their "conformity" (1949:22). At another midwestern high school, this one studied by C. Wayne Gordon in the 1950s, the kids in this category were "the big wheels," which presumably has to do with the idea that everything rotated around them, that they were (or thought they were) the center of the high school universe. Gordon's "big wheels" had a large component of athletic stardom, but he too made it clear that these students exhibited "conformity to variously approved patterns of behavior" (1957:22). Penelope Eckert's popular boys were actually called "jocks" (athletes, athletic stars) because the jock model was so dominant in the again midwestern high school she studied in the 1970s. Despite the term, however, it was possible for a guy to be very popular, to be a "jock" in that school, without being an athlete; his main characteristics were that he conformed to the "ideal of the squeaky-clean, all-American individual . . . [he] embodie[d] an attitude—an acceptance of the school and its institutions as an all-encompassing social context, and an unflagging enthusiasm and energy for working within those institutions" (1989:3).

In all of these cases, what is clear is what I am calling the "tameness" of the type in this category, the relative conformity, the willingness and even eagerness to work within the rules, as the means of achieving the highest prestige levels. Not surprisingly given the folk deemphasis of social class, the high capital that underlies these categories is often invisible in the terminology, although it was ambiguously present in Hollingshead's "elites," and also showed up in the "socies," short for "socialites," the term for the most popular kids in a high school, again in the Midwest, studied by Schwartz and Merten in the 1960s (1967, 1975: passim).

The upper right-hand box (high capital/wild) is occupied by the "jocks." These students appear to be here almost entirely because of athletic ability and "personality," but the situation is more complex than that. At least some of the jocks, the ones who become captains and stars, tend to come from higher-capital families; their leadership and stardom come as much—I would argue—from the self-confidence instilled by their backgrounds as from their athletic abilities. The box is also particularly open to upward mobility, with guys from working-class families and/or racial minorities who have the requisite physical skills being able to "make the team." But these boys would not necessarily be called "jocks," because jocks are not merely athletes but "stars," another kind of "popular guy."

Unlike the class officer/popular guy type, however, jocks are popular not because of their relative social tameness, but precisely because of their relative "wildness," their physicality and sexuality. Jocks' wildness is primarily reflected in their athletic strength, skills, and prowess, and in the case of more violent sports, their aggressive participation in that violence. But there is always also a connotation of heightened sexuality, as reflected in athletic uniforms/costumes, which usually exaggerate their masculine body forms, show a lot of flesh, or both. This sexuality is also partly embodied in the term *jock* itself. I am not sure of the historical derivation of the term, but at some point the "athletic supporter," the undergarment worn by athletes to protect/support their genitals, became known as a jockstrap, and since that time there is an inescapable sexual connotation to the very word, *jock*. Douglas Foley captured an even wider range of "wild" connotations in some of the terms for jocks at the Texas high school he studied in the 1970s: "studs" (which primarily has a sexual connotation), as well as "animals," "bulls," and "gorillas." Here wildness includes not only a "fearless" physicality in sports and a "cool" sexuality with girls but, as bulls or gorillas, an almost literal "wildness," in the sense of being untamable, undomesticated, uncontrollable (1990:52–53).

Moving to the lower left-hand box (less capital/tame), its central type is what I am calling the "ordinary citizens," who probably make up the majority of students at any standard U.S. high school. (They made up two-thirds of the student body at Hollingshead's Elmtown High [1949:221].) Those in this box tend to come from lower-capital families and are also relatively meek in personal style and behavior. At Elmtown High in the 1940s, they were called "the good kids." Hollingshead brought out their tameness: "They come to school, do their work, but do not distinguish themselves with glory or notoriety" (ibid.). He also indicated that they came mostly from middle- and lower-middle-class families (1949:222).

But in many schools there is no term for the "ordinary citizens." They are, as Hollingshead also said, "never this or never that" (1949:221); that is, they are not popular in either the class officer or the jock mode, but they are not oppositional like the hoods and greasers, about whom more in a moment. Eckert sometimes heard them called the "in-betweens" (1989:6); in the school Schwartz and Merten studied there was a kind of noncategory called "the others," which the authors also called "the conventionals" (1975:201). This box also contains what were called in the 1950s the "eggheads" or the "brain trust," and would today be called the "nerds" and "geeks."[12] These latter terms refer to very brainy but socially awkward boys, and here the terms refer to their "tameness" not only in the sense of school conformity, but in a kind of (projected) asexuality as well. The classic nerd is visualized through metonyms that say all mind and no body: "that kid . . . with the high water pants, the vinyl pencil holder in his shirt pocket, the tortoise shell glasses with the tape around the bridge" (Ikeda 1998:16).

Finally, there is the lower right-hand box (less capital/wild). These are the students who exhibit bad behavior, bad dress, and bad attitudes. Their position in this box, like the position of the jocks, appears to be based entirely on their behavior and attitudes, but in fact they are often from low-capital family backgrounds. Eckert captured both the class background and the "wild" style among the "burnouts" at the school she studied in the 1980s: "In the early 1980s, the stereotypic Belten High Burnout came from a working class home, enrolled primarily in general and vocational courses, smoked tobacco and pot, took chemicals, drank beer and hard liquor, skipped classes, and may have had occasional run-ins with the police" (Eckert 1989:3).

Other schools at other times had other terminologies for this set. At the school Hollingsworth studied in the 1940s they were called "the grubbies." The term called attention to their appearance ("they are not believed to be clean personally"), but they were also "trouble makers" who had "no interest in school affairs" (1949:221). In the 1950s and 1960s they were mostly called "hoods" or "greasers" (Schwartz and Merten 1975:200). *Hood* has gangster associations,[13] while *greaser* has pejorative ethnic connotations referring primarily to Italian or Hispanic Americans who were seen as using a lot of hair oil, or again being unwashed, or both. The terminology started to evolve with the counterculture in the 1970s, so that the oppositional types became defined by drug use (Eckert's "burnouts," Palonsky's "hempies") or the all-purpose word for weird-dressing (from the point of view of the dominant groups) countercultural types of that era, "freaks" (Varenne 1982, 1983:246ff.). Despite the evolution of the terminology, however, the general characteristics of the type in this box remain the same—"wild" in terms of both school opposition and (real or imagined) heightened sexuality; and modally lower- or working-class backgrounds.[14]

Each box also has a female counterpart of the male type. Among the popular kids in the upper left-hand box, the girls, like the boys, tend to come from high-capital families and to be respectful of parents and teachers. Here we have Schwartz and Merten's "socies" and Gordon's "Yearbook Queens" and their courts (Gordon 1957:22), but often the girls are simply "the popular girls." In the jock box, the female counterparts in many schools are the twirlers and cheerleaders (there were virtually no women's sports in the 1950s).[15] The twirlers and cheerleaders, like the (upper) male jocks, tend to come from higher-capital families; like male jocks they are popular in a "wild" style, especially in terms of body-revealing costumes and movements when they are performing their routines, but also a more generalized style of sexual attractiveness in dress and demeanor. Moving to the lower half of the table, both boxes are defined by relatively low capital, but again we have the wild/tame distinction. In the egghead/average citizen box, the female side consists to a great extent of the studious and/or mousy young women who are good citizens of the school, but who are seen as relatively asexual. In contrast, the female side of the "hoods" box contains those dreaded female counterparts of the hoods, the "sluts." "Sluts" as types are the virtual embodiments of sexual promiscuity; they are the negative type against which all "good girls" define themselves (Schwartz and Merten 1975, Canaan 1986).

Permutations of the Structure

Even though I am suggesting that most high schools over the past half century or more have had some version of this structure (see note 2), this does not mean that all high schools were or are alike. On the contrary, the character of different schools will vary enormously depending on which social type is the dominant type in the local school culture—or, in more contemporary jargon, which type "rules." Probably the most common configuration in the standard (that is, mostly white, working- to middle-class) American public high school is for the jock box to be very large and influential—for jocks to "rule" (see, e.g., Henry 1965, Eckert 1989, Foley 1990).

The rule of jocks (or of any single type) affects the character of all the other categories. Jocks may overflow the boundaries of their box in many ways—they may flood the class officer/popular student category, producing complex hybrids of conformity and wildness. The "jocking" of the whole upper layer of the structure in turn tends to exacerbate the differences between the jocks and the nerds, and to make nerd-baiting into a local sport. Indeed, the whole idea of "nerds" in the meek/weak (as opposed to "brainy") sense is almost certainly a jock invention, the jock view of nondominant men.

For a horrendous example of a jocks-rule configuration, I refer the reader to Bernard Lefkowitz's brilliant book, *Our Guys: The Glen Ridge Rape and the Secret Life of a Perfect Suburb* (1998). This is an account of the student culture behind the group sexual assault of a retarded girl at Glen Ridge High School in Glen Ridge, New Jersey, not far from Newark. Lefkowitz draws a chilling portrait of a school and a community in which violent, out-of-control behavior on the part of boys from "good" families was condoned and indeed encouraged in the name of the enormous importance of sports in the school, and a related, highly macho, construction of masculinity.

Lefkowitz also makes visible the impact of the rule of jocks on all the other social types. Cheerleader girls enacted the worst travesties of un-self-respecting femininity. They pandered to the jock boys at the personal level; in addition there were actual school rituals and events in which the official role of the girls was to cater to and celebrate the boys and their athletic prowess (even when the boys' teams were not winning very much, or when individual boys were not performing very well). To be outside this glorious world of jocks and cheerleaders was to be the lowest of the low. Boys in the band were not simply nerds but were called "band fags" (*fags* is one pejorative American term for homosexuals), not only by the students but by some of the parents as well (see also Foley 1990).

Other schools have other configurations. Working-class schools are not exempt from this structure, but the "hood" type may be much more prominent—as, for example, in the school described by Paul Willis in his classic *Learning to Labour* (1977).[16] Upper-class private schools also have the same structure, but the "popular kids" box is very large, and the schools would have outsiders believe that virtually all of their students are good looking, work hard academically, are deferential to authority, and go on to Harvard and Yale (see, e.g., Cookson and Persell 1985).

And finally there is Weequahic (and other very academically oriented schools like it) where some would argue that the nerd box was the strongest, though in fact the situation was rather more complicated (as no doubt it is in the other cases as well). Weequahic was about as different from jock-ruled Glen Ridge High as a school could be, and indeed it was the Glen Ridge book that finally made me realize Weequahic's distinctiveness. Schematically, one could say that at Weequahic the whole left side of the table was very strong—both the "class officer" box of "popular kids," and the "nerd" box of the studious, the shy, or the socially maladept. The "jock" box was very small, as was the space of the "hoods."

The strength of the whole left, or "tame," side of the table changed all the other values. For one thing, the nerds were not cut off and ridiculed, except perhaps by a handful of cheerleaders. In fact, at Weequahic there was no clear verbal category for these types; while the term *shmoe*, a Yiddish word roughly equivalent to nerd, cropped up once or twice in my interviews, it was not widely employed in high school social discourse. For another, the dominance of the "tame" side of the table made jockiness slightly ridiculous; sports were not very important at the school, and much of the outside world thought that the phrase "Weequahic athletics" was an oxymoron.[17] (I exaggerate, of course, and Weequahic was strong in a number of the "smaller" sports like swimming and track, but that was its reputation.) And finally the "hood" box had a distinctive quality in this context. Although there were a few genuine outlaws, most of the so-called hoods were not very hoody, and were hoods purely by stereotype—class and ethnic background; styles of dress, hair, and makeup—rather than by seriously oppositional behavior.

This basically structural analysis in turn provides us with another way of breaking through the question of the representativeness of Weequahic as an American high school. It allows us to place the school, despite its distinctive ethnic composition, squarely within the overall spectrum of American high schools, to see the ways in which it both fully participates in the structure and yet has a distinctive form. Many readers may suspect that the distinctive Weequahic configuration—the strength of the tame, the small role of jocks, and so on—is related to its largely Jewish population, and I would not necessarily disagree with that. But working with a structural framework in this context rather than with a notion of (race/class/ethnic distributional) "representativeness" allows us to see how this 83 percent Jewish school is just as "representative" as any other of a certain American (I am tempted to say all-American) way of organizing adolescent social life.

I began this chapter by arguing that high school social systems should be seen as attempts to push people into identity boxes, and to push identities, as it were, into people. I went on to argue further that these identity categories, which have been both extremely widespread and extremely durable in American high schools, must be deconstructed. They appear to be based on surface personal characteristics—looks, charm, athletic abilities—but in fact have an underlying structure in which "class" (as high or low "capital") and attitudes/styles related to power/authority ("wild" versus "tame") organize the system of available identities. But the operative word here is *available*. One of the reasons high school leaves such intense memory traces, I would suggest, is precisely because of the ways in which people do or do not fit into the system, the pleasure and pain of those fits and misfits, and the creativity of some of the alternatives. That is what we look at in the next chapter.

Project Journal 5: New York

[As a preamble to this section I should note that I lived in Manhattan from 1970 to 1976. On the one hand, I loved it and felt like it was the center of the universe. On the other hand, New York City almost went bankrupt in that period and the city was in very bad shape. The trip covered in these field notes was my first real stay in New York since that period.]

6/1/92 Arrived in NY, at Neal and Karin Goldman's* house in Park Slope. Another hair-raising driving experience—the experience of getting from LaGuardia to here via the Brooklyn Queens Expressway. My heart was pounding the whole time, I was sweating, my mouth went completely dry, like the time I landed in the helicopter in [a mountain village in Nepal]. LA was a piece of cake compared to this.

...... And NY is so incredibly decayed compared to anywhere else I've been on this trip. So much trash, the roads in such bad condition, the roads built for some entirely different civilization than the one that now inhabits the place.

...... Though people are busy here, they don't seem quite as hard to schedule as in LA, not quite so Hollywood.

6/2/92 My ethnography on [queue or] line behavior is that in NY everyone talks to everyone and that that is part of public culture. The talking however is primarily complaining, I now realize. You develop solidarity with your linemates by co-complaining about how slow it all is, and what the hell is that lady up front taking so long about, and why is the cashier so slow, etc. Out here [in Michigan] you really don't talk to people in public places at all—remember how uptight [a friend] used to get when I did that—and especially you don't complain. If you do, people either don't answer, like you couldn't possibly be talking to them and you must be a bag lady, or else they put you down for complaining—well she (the cashier) does seem awfully busy, or I think she (the lady who's taking ages) lost her checkbook, or something that excuses the others and makes you feel like a jerk. And then they turn away, like they definitely do not want to continue conversing. All of this goes along with the tolerance for

line-jumping here. In New York a line has social solidarity, and nobody toler-
ates anyone pushing in, like you could get killed, whereas here, though people
are mostly too polite to do it, if they did, nobody would do anything (except
think that you're a pushy ill-mannered person, probably from the East Coast
and/or Jewish).

...... Drove into the City from Brooklyn to interview [a classmate] last night. I
should take back my slander about the Upper West Side—it looked great! At
least West End Ave. did, cleaner and more elegant than I remembered. But it
really felt like home to me. And the ultimate triumph of New York success—I
found a parking place a block from her house.

...... [Interview with a woman married to a corporate executive.] She said
something that implied that she was affected by the '70s Counterculture. So
I said I was too, but it didn't seem to affect that many people in our class so
I had stopped asking about it. And she said oh yes, in fact I took off and lived
in Mexico for a year. I said why didn't you tell me that when you were telling
the story of your life? And she shrugged. I had the feeling—and she had said at
the beginning that she thought a lot about this interview beforehand—that she
wanted to provide me with some elevated and already-interpreted account of
her life, that is, interpreted along the lines that she thought I wanted. . . . So she
left out all the details of her actual life.

...... [Interview with a professional woman.] I never got to turn on the tape recorder, we started talking at top speed at the beginning, and then she served a
modest dinner (dressing bottle on the table, iceberg lettuce–tomato–shredded
carrot–cucumber salad like my mother used to make, prepared pasta/eggplant
heated up from Gristede's, a combination of Newark and Upper East Side), and
then we kept talking full speed, so there was never a moment where I could
officially turn on the machine—there was no beginning or end. So I'm on the
brain-download mode.

...... I said that I had repressed a lot about Weequahic, because I had really
wanted to flee from that background, although recently I changed my feelings
about that. She said the same was true of herself on both points, she said what
is there, some gene for nostalgia that kicks in when you're fifty? She said she
went to that famous Maple Ave. [grammar] School Reunion that everybody
talks about as some sort of epiphany of communitas and that she was depressed
about it for days afterward—how little people had changed, and how much she
herself reverted to the old culture when she was there. She had resolved before she went that she would not be nasty and cliquish, not just hang out with
the three people she had been friends with before, try to recognize everyone

as an equal human being, but she hadn't been there five minutes before she regressed to the old patterns.

...... I called Judith Pitman from Janet's place to confirm tomorrow and she cancelled. I wasn't terribly surprised—she didn't sound all that enthusiastic in the first place, and anyway there are always some cancellations and I've gotten philosophic about them.

6/3/92 Interview this morning with [a doctor] in Long Island. Arrived shaking like a leaf from contending with miles of Flatbush Ave. and the Belt Parkway and the Southern State. [As the reader may have guessed by now, I wound up with a driving phobia by the end of the fieldwork and have not gotten over it to this day.]

...... Arrived home to discover that Carol Cook's appointment had been cancelled by her sister, with the message that Carol did not want any further participation in the project. I had had a nice conversation with Carol on the phone and now wish desperately I had taken notes.

6/4/92 I went up to [a stockbroker's] office to meet to go out to dinner. I showed up in my best pink jeans and Barry, the broker, looked me over with a pained expression on his face and said, I've made reservations in a fancy restaurant, and I said I didn't bring a dress but I guess I could pop out and buy one. And I walked out onto Fifth Ave. and walked up to Saks and bought a little rayon frock for a mere $150, plus a pair of pantyhose for $6.50. I can't believe I did it. I don't think I've spent $150 for a dress, or even for a much more substantial wool suit for example, in my whole life. I wonder if I could charge it to the grant.

6/5/92 This morning I interviewed [a middle-class man] at a diner in Mineola— your standard glitzy NY-NJ diner. These diners are totally local institutions, with their own culture—10-page menus, oversized portions, multi-ethnic menu—there's nothing like them anywhere else in the country.

...... Now we all know the rumors, that [this classmate had been involved in some criminal activity earlier in his life], but I just couldn't get up the guts to ask him about it. . . . Even at the end, when he seemed to be giving me an opening, but not enough of one, I couldn't pop the question. He said, is that all you want to ask me? And I said, well is there anything I've left out or didn't cover? And he said, sort of cagily, well I don't know enough about the project to know. . . . But all I could get myself to say was, well if anything else comes up I'll get back to you, and he said fine. It was like I couldn't stand to ruin the rapport of the interview; if I told him at the end what I had known from the beginning it would make me seem terribly false throughout the preceding two hours. I guess I learned a lesson—maybe if I have a person [with some deep secret] like this I should really raise it up front, right at the beginning. I think that would actually work, and if the person got pissed off and threw me out, so be it. Otherwise presumably they would then talk freely about it. But if you save it to the end, you're in the position I was in, of redefining myself as having been utterly false for the whole past two hours. [I later confessed and apologized to him at a reunion.]

6/6/92 Took the subway back to Brooklyn, as I had come—I'm getting to be a real pro at [riding the subways again]. I find myself back in the New York mode of being in public streets and subways, being both totally alert and yet not looking at anything in particular, keeping a very blank face which does not register anything at all—disapproval, anxiety, interest, a kind of disappearing face. If it registers anything it is what Geertz called with respect to the Balinese "awayness."

...... I'm thinking to go out to [my cousin] Sheila [Tretter]'s* in Southampton for the weekend, which should be both pleasant (very pleasant) and which would also allow me to catch the Long Island classmates. And speaking of relatives, what would I have done without mine for this project?

6/7/92 [Interview with a businessman.] When we took a break from the interview, he took me for a ride on one of those four-wheel, overland vehicle, motorcycle type-things, and we went out to the shore of his property, which is on a cliff overlooking Long Island Sound, which was extremely lovely, and he's got a deck there, and we sat out there and completed the interview.

chapter 6

Weequahic

As I noted earlier, Weequahic High School was built in the 1930s. It is located on Chancellor Avenue in Newark, next to Chancellor Avenue School (elementary). It is a tan brick building of pretty much standard American institutional high school design. There are long corridors lined with lockers, with classrooms entered off the corridors. There is a gymnasium, an auditorium, and a lunchroom. There is a playing field on the other side of the elementary school, shared by the two schools. Physically, the only really distinctive feature of Weequahic High School is a mural over the entrance to the auditorium, front and center as one walks in the main door of the school. I do not remember specifically what is on that mural—I doubt if anyone ever looked at its content— but it is in the kind of colorful, allegorical, Diego Rivera–esque style that one associates with WPA art.[1]

In chapter 5 I looked at the high school social system as a system of identities that embody hidden assumptions about class and about relationships to authority. The analysis was relatively formal, a matter of dissecting the logic of the categories. Here I need to change the language somewhat, as I want to look at the ways in which real people related to those identities, whether by inhabiting them comfortably, by resisting their relevance to the self, or by doing other sorts of hybrid things in and around them.

One way to render this shift of focus is to recognize that the social categories are not only for purposes of labeling, "identifying" the self and others (he is popular, she is a bimbo cheerleader, she is a brain, I am a nobody), although that is one of their functions. They are also little packages of motivations and desires, fears and anxieties (I want to be popular, I want to be a star athlete, I want to make the twirling squad, I don't want to be seen as a nerd, I don't give a flying fuck what anybody thinks of me), as well as little packages of guidelines for fulfilling those desires (I must be nice to everybody, I must lose weight, I must acquire the latest styles, I must hide my brains, and so on). The categories, then, are both systems of classification and systems of desires, with related notions—virtually "rules"—about how to go about fulfilling those desires.

These packages of categories-as-classifications/desires/rules cannot be seen in isolation; they are parts of what I have elsewhere discussed as social and cultural "games." In that other context (Ortner 1996), where I was talking about games of power in the real world, I used the phrase "serious games." For high school, however, I will leave the term unmodified. There is no doubt that high school social games are played very intensely, and that both triumphs and failures are very strongly felt. And eventually I will get to some that were in fact highly consequential for real lives after high school. Indeed, the nature of the relationship between social success in high school and success in real life afterward is the subject of much debate. The "fall of the jock/rise of the nerd" narrative has fed the idea that there is no relationship between success in high school and afterward, but that is not quite true. What appears to be true is that, while successful people in high school will not necessarily be successful later, a great many people who are successful in the real world were in fact quite "big wheels" in high school (Keyes 1976).[2] Thus the slightly unreal world of high school status games, which I will not dignify with the adjective "serious," does trend into those more serious games of power and success in life later on.

But we are still at the level of the games as they are packed into the categories—what you need to do to be an X and not a Y—and not at the level of how real people in real times and places—in this case the Class of '58 of Weequahic High School—actually played them, felt about them, or resisted them. The forms of play—of conformity, nonconformity, and everything in between—are actually quite complex and various. In order to understand their variety, it is important to remember that the table of social categories involves the intersection of two different principles, a "class" principle (high and low capital) and a "personal qualities" principle (the "wild" versus "tame" style distinction, itself having several layers of meaning). Thus I will break up the discussion of modes of play into those two oppositions: the top versus the bottom layers (a sort of metaphoric class struggle), and the left versus the right columns (relationship to rules and to authority).

The Top of the Table: High-Capital Kids and Popularity

At one level, one can think of the four boxes of table 6 as involving four different games; and to some extent that is true. Each—the popular kids, the jocks, the ordinary citizens, and the hoods—involves its own rules, its own structures of feeling and disposition, its own boundaries of inclusion and exclusion. Yet at the same time we must recall that the table as a whole is grounded in the unequal distribution of capital, with the top half of the table being defined by coming from a relatively high-capital background, and the bottom half by coming from a relatively low-capital background. The fundamental inequality between high- and low-capital backgrounds, the fundamental division of the table into upper and lower halves, means that the four games do not have equal status and value. Specifically, the games of the top half of the table are hegemonic, and the others are defined in relation to them. Going further, one could say that there really is only one game— the game of being "popular"—although there are at least two variants of this, as discussed in chapter 5, the "class officer" mode and the "jock" mode. I will begin, then, with an account of how the Class of '58 played those two variants of the hegemonic game, and will then consider the ways in which people in the lower boxes positioned themselves—including various forms of evasion, rejection, and redefinition—in relation to the game of "popularity."

Doing Popularity I: Popular Kids/Class Officers

The name of the game here was to be well liked, and thus elected to many top offices. (One also had to do reasonably well in school, but one did not necessarily have to be regarded as one of the top geniuses.) One accomplished this popularity in part by having a warm personality, and also by being "friendly with everyone":

> *Lewis Friedland:* [from the field notes] He said that he didn't feel any social barriers between different groups. He himself was friendly with everyone. He was even friendly with the hoods, the guys who hung out in front of Sid's [the hot dog place across the street from the school].
> *Ralph Neiss:* "I felt especially in my senior year when I got elected to [high office in the Class] I was friendly with everybody in the class. I didn't

have any enemies, and although there were cliques we still managed to get along with people."

If anyone "ruled" the school it was this set of people. The set was fairly large. Class offices (president, vice president, treasurer, and secretary of the class, as well as membership on the class council) turned over every semester, so a significant number of people got to be a class officer or on the council at one point or another. In addition there was the student government organization, the OBA (Orange and Brown Association, named for the school colors), which also had several officers as well as a council, and which also turned over frequently.

The fact that all the offices turned over every semester meant that people who were playing this particular game were constantly running for some office or other, and were constantly either winning or losing something. Some kids were very good at this and identified very strongly with their own success:

> *Blanche Kaufman:* [from an account by Susan Wolkstein of a conversation she had with Blanche] "I remember we went to a reunion [and I saw] Blanche Kaufman, who to me was the epitome of what you should be in high school. She was a good student, she was [a class officer and head of the twirling/cheerleader squad]. And I remember taking her aside and saying to her, you know, Blanche, I wish you would answer this question, because it doesn't probably matter any more to you, and I'm very [curious]: Were you as happy in high school as we all thought you were? And she said to me, to tell you the truth, I really was."
>
> *Larry Kuperman:* "I had every success that you could want. I had athletic success . . . I was the captain of the [X] team. . . . I got a letter in [that sport] my freshman year in high school. . . . And I can remember walking around in my letter sweater, you know, freshman year as a big shot. . . . So I was the minor sport king, and also because I was [highly ranked academically], the coaches voted me top athlete in the class. . . . So that was my athletic career. And then academically obviously you know I did well. And politically I [held a major office], and socially I had a nice girlfriend."

Others took a more casual attitude toward playing this game, or at least presented themselves in that light. When I asked Joseph Finkel, a high-ranking class officer, how he got the idea of running for that office, he replied: "It was just sort of a pleasant undertaking to do, you know.

I wasn't driven, I wasn't possessed, but I just thought it would be a fun thing to do." In contrast, some kids worked very hard at climbing up from the lower ranks. In some cases it worked. David Barna talked about being at a disadvantage when he started Weequahic, because he was younger than the other boys and more physically underdeveloped. But he worked his way up to being elected to a high class office:

> "I had some problems with Weequahic because I was younger [than the rest of the class]. . . . But then I made the adjustment, I think I am OK. Physically I grew, you know what I mean, it was overall OK. . . . I mean I recognize the problems and limitation that I had. Overall I was active in the school [and was elected to various offices], I sort of made up for what I couldn't do in some areas [mostly athletics] in other areas [school politics]."

But one did not always win. Murray Barnett, who was clearly one of the popular kids and had earlier won a major election, talked about a subsequent loss:

> "I was president of the class/OBA association in one semester. [But] I lost the second half which sort of bothered me, to Larry Horowitz. . . . I do have a picture of when I was at assembly getting the torch or whatever they gave you, and then I got un-elected, I lost to Larry. I didn't get that final bit of glory."

Along these lines, I cannot resist inserting a non-Weequahic example here. Ralph Keyes's book *Is There Life after High School?* opens with a story of how President Gerald Ford never got over losing a high school election. Ford actually talked about it in his address to the nation on the occasion of his inauguration as president of the United States. The man who beat him, now an investment banker, was "absolutely amazed that this little incident would be any part of his mind" (Keyes 1976:17).

The students who won elections, even if they lost on some occasions, were among the most successful people in the school. Their elections to offices showed that they were well liked and popular, as did their various captaincies of teams, elections to head twirler/cheerleader, and so forth. This brings us to the jocks, who were in many cases not that clearly demarcated from the class officers.

Doing Popularity II: Athletes and Cheerleaders

The jock variant normally entails being successful in sports and related activities (twirling and cheerleading for the girls), being physically attractive, and being popular by virtue of athletic success and looks. Academic performance is normally secondary, though not completely brushed off.

The male jock style classically is very macho. At Weequahic, however, although a lot of boys participated in athletics, they did not for the most part act like classic jocks, that is, men who act dominant and arrogant by virtue of their bodies, their looks, and their athletic prowess. This kind of culture of jockdom simply did not exist at Weequahic, or if it was there it was very played down. In fact, many of the athletes operated more in the class officer/popular guys mode—reasonably serious about school, "friendly with everyone," modest ("tame") in personal style. We heard some of this from Larry Kuperman above. Another jock in the "modest" mode was Robert Gershon:

> "During the time I went to Chancellor Avenue School and Weequahic High School I was a sports jock. I played on the football team, basketball team, baseball team, and I was captain of a couple of those teams. I stayed away from the social scene to a great deal in high school and devoted my time to sports. I didn't date as heavily as some of the other kids in school."

Many of the African American men also played on the sports teams, and this seems to have been one of their few areas of extracurricular participation. This meant in turn that sports were among the few racial interfaces in the school; in most other contexts whites and Blacks had very little interaction. Al Walker, one of a small number of African American men in the class, remembered his sports activities:

> [from the field notes] He thought Weequahic was OK, those were pretty good times. He played football and remembered Herbert Graves [another African American classmate] from football, and he sort of took off on some nostalgia about all that, including a 96-yard touchdown return against Hillside, though we lost the game.

But if male athletes at Weequahic did not act like classic jocks, the games of some of the cheerleaders and twirlers were much closer to the classic games of cheerleaders elsewhere. What is distinctive about these games emerges in comparison with the games of the popular kids: where popular kids seek to be liked, jocks and cheerleaders as types often do not: they seek to be admired, even envied. They may be contemptuous of those they see as less well endowed with talent or looks than themselves, and they may make no attempt to hide this contempt. They do not seem to care if they are widely "liked," although it would probably upset them to find out that in at least some cases they are not.

Not all cheerleaders and twirlers at Weequahic played this game; some were (like some of the athletes) popular/class officer types, operating in the friendlier mode. Blanche Kaufman, mentioned earlier, was a twirler/cheerleader and eventually head of the squad, but she was widely liked and crossed over into the "class officer" box. Jackie Anapolsky was another extremely popular twirler/cheerleader, and while she never became a class officer, she "felt like I was in the nub of everything that happened." There were also "ordinary citizens" in this group who were simply pleased to have made one of the squads but did not let it go to their heads.

Some of the cheerleaders and twirlers, however, appeared to be playing the jock game in the classic arrogant way, and it is these individuals who have remained—possibly unfairly, and almost certainly out of proportion to the harm that they did—imprinted in many memories as forming one of the worst cliques at Weequahic, a clique, or at least a set, of rich, pretty, mindless, nasty young women. Here are a few comments about some of them:

> *Arleen Daitch:* [from the field notes] She says, do you remember Sylvia Zashin, she was the epitome of everything that was terrible about Weequahic, a completely empty, vacuous, bitchy person with money who was somehow admired and popular.
> *Marilyn Schwartz:* [from the field notes] In class, Sylvia would try to copy from her, she wanted to kill her.
> *Ellen Cahn:* [from the field notes] I asked if there was some crowd that seemed stuck up and that she felt excluded from and she reflected a minute, then said, well yeah, there was Judith Pitman and her crowd.
> *Harriet Kroll:* "I remember Judith Pitman. The twirlers/cheerleaders being the elite. . . . In some ways we might have envied the people like Judith and that crowd. [But] they weren't as smart as the rest of us.

They didn't do well academically, like the rest. And [they are] certainly not enviable any more. I can't imagine what happened to those kinds of people."

As with class officers, one had to try out/compete to be an athlete or a cheerleader or a twirler (and then beyond that, to become a captain of a team or the head cheerleader or head majorette). Making the team or squad was a major positive memory. Sherry Samuels described being a twirler as "a major memory of mine, because [getting in] was very competitive." Failing to make the team or the squad, in contrast, was another of those bad memories people carry around for years.

It is the competition to get in and stay in the various roles, positions, offices, teams, and so on of the upper half of the table that precisely sets off the upper-half boxes from everything else. This is to say that the categories of popularity are reproduced in practice, not only through styles of dress, looks, "personality," athletic skills, and so forth, but by actually formally engaging in tryouts, elections, and other competitions that are the very essence of playing the game. Most of the officer-type positions involved doing very little in the way of governing and leading; it was getting there and staying there that mattered.

The Lower Half of the Table: Low-Capital Kids and Resistance

I turn now to the lower half of table 6. In the last chapter I argued that the top versus bottom layers of the table represent—broadly—the difference between higher and lower capital. Not every student in the upper half was from a high-capital family, and not every student in the lower half was from a low-capital family, but there was a general tendency for this pattern to hold up at both levels. Thus the kids who would be classified as being in the lower boxes must be seen as excluded from popularity at least in part on grounds of class—of simply not coming from the right background of money, father's occupation, or for that matter the right race and/or ethnicity.

If there were two variants of the popularity game at the upper level, there were also two variants of the resistance game at the lower level: that of the ordinary citizens in the lower left-hand box, and that of the hoods and the (supposedly) bad girls in the lower right. Let me start with the hoods, whose working-class backgrounds were usually more clear-cut—that is, the class factor here is very visible, at least to an outside observer—and whose "resistance" is also more clear-cut: they tended to distance themselves from the high school popularity games more decisively.

Resistance I: The Hoods and Bad Girls

The hood "game," at least stereotypically, is the rejection of all the other games. There is a contempt for schoolwork and for the rules of the school; a rejection of the authority of teachers, and sometimes even the law; and a refusal to be judged by the style and performance standards of the hegemonic culture.

One of the ways in which this rejection of the school as a social system and a culture shows up is in a very low level of participation in school activities (clubs, committees, school newspaper, theater, etc.). Every student in the yearbook has a list of activities under his or her picture, and students who enacted a stereotypic hoody/oppositional style tend to have very few activities listed.[3] Of course there were others with few activities too, including shy kids who felt excluded or unwelcome, and poorer and/or working-class kids who went to work right after school and had no time for such activities. But if all low-activity kids were not hoods, most hoods did indeed tend not to participate in extracurricular activities.

There was one "real" group of hoods in the school. It seems that the group of guys (mostly from Jewish working-class backgrounds) who hung out at Sid's were actually into doing, and perhaps even dealing, drugs. I knew nothing about it at the time, and many of the people I interviewed knew nothing about it either. But enough people reported it with some certainty that I think it must have been true.[4] I was also told that virtually every guy involved in that scene (many of them were not members of the Class of '58) has died.

Beyond this group, the categories of hoods and sluts become much more complicated. Starting with the boys, it is likely that individuals who were really in trouble in one way or another—failing in school, in trouble with the law—had already dropped out by graduation. Thus the real hoods—and there probably were a few more like the druggies I did not know about—are mostly out of the study.

There was, however, a handful of guys, mostly from non-Jewish ethnic groups and/or working-class backgrounds, who performed a certain tough-guy style of appearance, dress, talk, smoking, and so on familiar to any American from fifties and neo-fifties youth movies and TV shows. They also tended to have their own social networks carried over from their grammar school neighborhoods, and not to get more than superficially friendly with the other kids in the school. (One effect of this is that they are the most poorly represented group in this study, though they are not totally absent.) They also tended to invest almost nothing in academic work, though they were not necessarily full-scale troublemakers. Thomas Toyas was one of these types:

"I was not involved with a group of friends in Weequahic. I had already developed a group of friends that I had known since [one of the nonelite elementary schools], and we sort of stayed together. And we didn't really bother with people outside that group. . . . It's unfortunate because . . . I think that if I would have developed a group of friends at Weequahic, I would have had a little more ambition to do better than I did. . . . [My friends were] a bunch of wise guys. I mean I was a wise guy. You know, I admit it. And I wasted my time in high school."

Joel Weiss was a similar case. Joel's father had abandoned the family, and he clearly felt that this played a role in his alienation and bad behavior in high school:

"As you think back on it now, of course, you had like residual anger which is what makes you do some of the stupid things that you did, which is probably why I was in and out of trouble in school all through high school. . . . As I look back on it I can see lots of mistakes we all made when we were growing up and there's lots of ways, when I got to that fork in the road, I wish I chose the other [better] one. But maybe I chose the ones I chose cause it's what I really [he laughed] wanted to do anyway. Who the hell knows."

But while the Class of '58 had a few hoody(-style) boys, alienated from and in trouble with school (or worse), there really were no comparable girls fulfilling the role of "sluts." In its dominant sense the term *slut* refers to sexual promiscuity, and Philip Roth, in *Portnoy's Complaint*, writes of a (supposedly fictional, but one never knows with Roth) non-Jewish, working-class girl in the neighboring town of Hillside whom his stand-in character visited with several other nervous Jewish boys for sex. But there was no one even remotely like that in the Class of '58 (indeed, the most sexually active group is rumored to have been among the twirlers and cheerleaders), and the promiscuity image seems to have been more a construction by parents, authorities, and movies, to the effect that if one dressed or otherwise behaved in a provocative way, people would *think* one was a slut.[5] This is not to say that nobody was having sex in the high school years; some were. But I will return to that when I consider the practices organized in relation to the wild/tame distinction.

In any event, the hoods enacted the first strategy of resistance to the game of popularity: They simply refused to play. One could say that they reversed the agency conferred by the power of high capital and rejected the system that tried to reject them.[6] The ordinary citizens, also from relatively low-capital backgrounds, constructed their "resistance" in different ways.

Resistance II: The Ordinary Citizens

Those who did not feel themselves to be in the "upper echelons" (as one classmate put it) of the school social system were in a position to feel excluded, a painful experience. Some people—more often, it seems, boys—blamed themselves for their exclusion:

> *Harvey Chatzklin:* "I felt I was always on the fringe. And I was a very shy guy anyway. Probably had I been different about [my working-class background], that kind of made me withdraw a bit more."
>
> *Hyman Cooperman:* "Well I wasn't a social person, I've never been a social person, but I felt the school was as good a school as I could go to in those days. But I never was the type of person to be a social person, [and] I was not an athletic person . . ." [all of which added up to why he was not "popular"].

Others—more often girls—were much more explicitly critical of the snobbery of some of the popular students, or simply of their greater wealth. Recall, among other things, the earlier caustic comments about cashmere sweaters and charm bracelets popular among the upper set. Recall too the strongly negative comments about some of the cheerleaders/twirlers. Here are some additional critical comments:

Maxine Schulaner: "But we didn't really have a chance to participate, we were really the outsiders. I don't think if we had made the effort we would have been included anyway. [SBO: You think even if you weren't working after school]? Yeah, I think had we wanted to. I think we really would have been considered outsiders even all through school."

Sondra Novick: "Elayne Braverman and I tried out for cheerleading and we were both—she was excellent—and didn't make it because there was the clique. . . . And we practiced, and we did our part. She was much better than I was. We both did those jumps and everything and we made the first elimination, but we never made it beyond that, and I think it was because we weren't part of the social thing."

Carol Cohen: "I was on the other side of the street [in class terms]. . . . Maybe eighteen was an awkward time, but I just found that these people felt they were better than you. That's why [when] I went back to the class reunion . . . [here she mimics one of the women at the reunion:] 'Oh, how are you?' [then back to her angry/caustic tone] She didn't talk to me for four years in high school; what are you talking to me now for?"

Despite an often lively critical sense of the nasty aspects of the system, however, it was the distinctive characteristic of "ordinary citizens" that, as this label implies, they wanted to remain involved in the social process. They may have hated the stereotyping of the categories, they may have hated the popularity games, but they wanted to participate. The trick, then, was to attempt to get away from measuring themselves against the popular kids and to shift their orientation toward other sources of satisfaction. This involved constructing a kind of alternative universe in which the very goal of popularity (and, to the extent that it was recognized, its underlying money) was criticized.

There were several variants of this strategy. One involved forming or participating in countergroups, whether intellectual/artistic or political, which implicitly or explicitly criticized the values of the dominant group. In the conformist 1950s at, one might say, conformist Weequahic, these were relatively small and few in number, though not totally absent. Some of the "eggheads," or honor students, among the ordinary citizens styled themselves as "intellectuals," and thus much more serious than the popular kids, even the smart ones, in the box above them. There was a sense, or an attempt to construct a sense, that being popular was actually rather shallow, and that being studious and intellectual was actually superior to (mere) popularity. Phyllis French-man talked, with some retrospective irony, about being in a sort of ele-vated culture group: "I was really just with this little group. . . . [I] re-member being in Ellen Schreiber's house all sitting around and reading and listening to music. . . . We thought we were the cat's meow." Carole Schwartz talked about founding a similar group with the involvement of one of the more bohemian Weequahic teachers:

> [from the fieldnotes] She said she only had one good teacher, Mrs. Nadel-son. She found her social studies/history class really challenging, and she approached [Mrs. N] and said that she wanted more study time. She founded the so-called Contemporary Club which met and did readings in philosophy, social studies, etc. Mrs. Nadelson really blew her mind, met with this club once a month in the evening at her house, took off her shoes, smoked, was a free spirit. Later Carole worked in Camp [X] and Mrs. Nadelson's son went there, and Mrs. N came and went skinny dipping. Carole said over and over that this woman, who was clearly out-side of all the conventions of the women/mothers we knew, was her first "mentor."[7]

There was also apparently a "Communist cell" at Weequahic. For obvious reasons in the fifties, this would have been very underground, and I learned virtually nothing about it. I was told about it by only one student, who said he joined it briefly "before reverting to his natu-ral conservatism." Both the artsy/intellectual groups and the politi-cally conscious group(s?) implied that the whole popularity game was shallow and superficial. Like the hoods, the students involved in these groups can be viewed as reversing the agency of exclusion and *choosing* not to play.

A second variant of not letting exclusion from the popularity game get one down was to be a very active citizen but in lower-visibility ac-tivities. From one point of view, this was a sort of B version of the games of the popular kids. In fact, some kids tried to use it as a launch-ing point for higher-level popularity, and a few succeeded: Remem-ber David Barna, above, who started out feeling inadequate because he was physically small, but overcame the handicap to become one of the election-winning "popular guys" in the class. Others, however, did not make it and reconciled themselves to remaining within the ranks of the ordinary citizens:

Saul Gabel: [from the fieldnotes] The major blow of his life seems to have been losing [a major] election. It was one of the first things he mentioned in the interview, and he came back to it again later. But he said he learned something from it . . . that whether he won or lost, the important thing is to remain a good and decent person. . . . It did depress him, however.

Yet most of the ordinary citizens playing this version of the game did not necessarily try for major offices. They simply involved themselves in a high level of participation in what might be called minor activities—for example, a high level of participation in activities surrounding athletics without necessarily being a cheerleader or twirler, or without being a first-team athlete. Guys could warm the benches of the major sports or participate in the minor sports. Girls could be in the color guard, the flag-bearers who marched out with the band during football games. One could be in the band. Or one could be among the "other" cheerleaders, who worked the basketball games in winter but not the much higher-visibility football games:

Maxine Schulaner: "I did the basketball games . . . I don't know why but they selected schmoes [nerds]. Because we weren't the popular [kids]. I don't know but I cheerleaded for basketball games. Don't ask me why, don't ask me how long, it's faded . . . it was nothing important, that's why you [her friend who was present at the interview] don't remember."

There were also many minor offices one could occupy if one had inclinations in this direction. Every homeroom and every class (e.g., Chemistry I) seems to have had a "chairman," for example. These petty offices were never mentioned in any interviews, and I was reminded of them only by looking through the yearbook and the lists of activities under people's pictures. In retrospect it seems clear that they simply represented more opportunities for getting involved as an active citizen of the school.

All of this may not seem very much like "resistance," but while many ordinary citizens had a very strong sense of critique of the popular kids, they also wanted to participate in and enjoy the pleasures of the social system as such. They thus redefined and revalued what these activities were all about. For the popular kids, running for offices and participating in high-visibility activities were all part of the endless quest for popularity. For the ordinary citizens, however, it was actually part of an essentially noninstrumental, non-self-promoting form of sociability. One man, very much an ordinary citizen, obviously took great pleasure in this lower-visibility, non-popularity-track mode of participation: "I enjoyed myself in high school. I was always involved in a lot of activities that sort of carried over to the present day. . . . My mother used to set me down every few years and say, 'What two activities are you giving up because you can't handle them all?' " And a woman, again not one of the "popular" types, said: "I remember I was in the choir and I liked that, we were all friendly in the choir. And then when we had our 4B Senior Hop [the fall precursor of the big event, the 4A Senior Prom] we were all on the committee and we all entertained. We took part in that and that was fun. I enjoyed doing all that." In these cases and many more, participation was not about popularity, but about pleasure and sociability.

In sum, there were at least three forms of resistance to/evasion of the dominant game: to reject the whole school "thing," with all its games—the "hoody" option; to play alternative games, intellectual/artistic/political, that redefined the main game as silly and shallow—one option of the ordinary citizens; or finally, the other option of the ordinary citizens, to play the game of school activism at a sort of B level (lower-visibility activities and offices) but in a way that defined school activism less as a path to popularity and more as a source of sociability and pleasure.

This last point actually signals a fourth mode of resisting/ignoring/evading the potential hurt of being outside the top group: the importance of friends. Friendship is hugely important in high school, and it came up in virtually every interview, with every category of student.[8] The true disaster for a student was friendlessness and social isolation:

> *Irving Davis:* "It took about two years in high school till I developed some kind of circle of friends. . . . But the first two years of high school were misery."
> *Linda Modell:* "If you talk to my older sister, she'll tell you her life was miserable. She hated high school. She had no friends."

In a variant of this, one girl from a lower-capital background talked about the pain of having her group of friends split up at Weequahic:

"I went to Madison Junior High and we came to Weequahic the second year of high school . . . the first year [we were there] they put us together in a homeroom, we were familiar with everybody. I remember I was devastated in our [junior] year, they broke us up and split us all up into different homerooms for our last two years of high school. . . . I remember it was very upsetting for me to be separated from all my friends at that point."

The importance of friendship is precisely why there is no simple correlation between having loved Weequahic and having been a super-successful person within its social game. For many people it was good friendships, even without great social success, that made for strong positive feelings, both at the time and later.[9]

> *Claire Friedlander:* [Despite commuting and entering Weequahic as a sophomore] "I must have made friends fairly quickly . . . I made very good friends and had a good time in high school."
>
> *William Rothbard:* "I really look back on [Weequahic] now as the greatest time in my life, because I have a lot of nostalgia for that time. . . . I was a shy guy, at Weequahic. I was quiet, [but] I had some friends."

Yet friends played different roles in the upper- and lower-capital levels of table 6. While socially successful people in the upper half of the table appreciated close friendships, their various successes put less weight on friendship as contributing to their being happy or unhappy in school. Among those in the lower half of the table, however, many felt that friendships were what saved the whole experience:

> *Janet Gold:* "I always felt very comfortable [at Weequahic]. I had a nice group of friends, I had a big group of friends, I was friendly with a lot of the guys also. Just as friends. I knew I wasn't in the clique that seemed to be the ones that everything was happening to. But that was OK because I was just happy with my group of friends."
>
> *Rochelle Loterstein:* [SBO: Did you feel there were snobby cliques and so on?] "Yeah. [SBO: But you didn't mind being excluded?] Well, we had our club, we had fun, and I was also in a sorority, so we had that and the [X] Club and so I was happy with my friends."[10]

Some students clearly recognized the class factors behind the cliques, and thought of friendship in terms of allowing them to ignore differences of money and class:

Lynn Ritz: "Oh, I think there were definite cliques. And I kind of found myself in the middle group and it was fine and they were great kids. We could all afford the same things."

Phyllis Brodsky: "I was conscious of the fact that where we lived, and we rented, and there were people that owned their houses. . . . But I had a lot of friends who had the same or less, and so it wasn't much of an issue."

Nancy Stein: "We had our own group of friends and everybody had a great deal more money than we did and they showed it off. [Nonetheless,] I remember having a wonderful time in school . . . I guess we had our own group of friends and it was fun."

Of course, class is not just a matter of money. We saw earlier that family disruption also tended to be associated with the lower-income families. One man had a very disrupted home life, and also had severe acne that was closely related to his situation at home. But his friends saved the day: "When I was in high school, when [my skin would break out badly], one thing I do know, my friends were supportive, which was something, and I don't know if you find that everywhere! . . . You know, they helped me, they didn't just back off."

Race was another form of low capital, and African American classmates were also likely to talk about how friendships helped them through. We heard William Smallwood much earlier talk about how Weequahic was so much better for him than Barringer not only because it was less overtly racist, but also because he made some good friends. And one woman talked about friendship as helping her through the trauma of integration within a majority-white school: "Having to deal with the colors and the grades and all, I really went through a lot, mentally. I did, really a lot. There was [a] tutor. [And] I had some friends that helped me along."

Again, all of this may not seem much like "resistance." Yet groups of friends not only buffered one from the slights of the system but often constituted sites for critiques of its categories and practices. For one thing, in another reversal of agency, one could resist the very idea that one was "excluded":

Judith Gordon: "I never felt I was excluded from anything. Yes there were cliques . . . but I didn't feel that I was excluded from one as opposed to another. I mean, it was my choice too, I chose to be with this group [of friends]."

Terry Alchek: "Well, I knew there were cliques but it didn't bother me, because I had my friends and I had my life and it just kind of rolled off my back. . . . I never felt that I wanted to be in that [group]. To tell you the truth. Because as long as you have your friends and you are enjoying what you're doing, [it doesn't matter]."

Similarly, friends could ironically invert the idea that unpopularity with the opposite sex was cause for social exclusion. Thus, one group of friends actually excluded girls who had too many dates. They formed "a 'Saturday night club'—all the girls who didn't date. If you had two dates you were out" (field notes). More generally, one could explicitly see one's group of friends as the antithesis of the snobbery of the in-group. Rita Osowitt recalled: "We had our own club. . . . Do you remember Fran Davidson? We were really close friends. . . . We would call Weequahic the Weequahic snobs . . . I guess in our own way we thought we were better than that group [of snobs]." Similarly, Carol Wiernik talked about how she and her best friend criticized the materialism of the in-group:

"Weequahic was a very materialistic group, and I didn't fit in, I knew I didn't fit in. And that was hard. And I remember, Faithe Platnick and I were good friends. . . . And lots of times we would sort of laugh, you know, the . . . cashmere sweaters that we didn't have, and the others had, and whatever. . . . Her thing [was], don't be "Weequahic-ish." . . . You don't want to be Weequahic-ish, that's not a good [attitude]."

I have been discussing the practices of the Class of '58 in high school as they were organized, roughly speaking, by "class." I have looked at the games of popularity among the relatively high-capital kids and the forms of resistance to and evasion of those games among the relatively low-capital kids. But we saw in chapter 5 that the social system of the high school is also organized by another opposition, one pertaining not to one's social background but to one's personal qualities. I labeled the poles of this opposition "wild" versus "tame," with the terms having at least two layers of meaning. The first and most overt refers to the young person's attitudes toward rules, authority, even power: in theory, the "tame" enact submission to authority and conformity to rules, while the "wild" enact the opposite. The second layer of meaning refers to sexuality: in theory, the "tame" enact conformity to the dominant norms of sexuality—heterosexuality and general sexual restraint appropriate to one's age and gender—while the "wild" enact both general lack of restraint and what one might call hyper-heterosexuality.

In the next section, then, I explore the practices of the Class of '58 with respect to this wild/tame opposition. Here it is not so much a question of pitting the two sides of the opposition against one another, as in the previous discussion centering on high versus low capital. Wild and tame do not represent a clearly ranked set of positions in the high school system of identities; instead they operate in a more complex interplay of attraction and repulsion. Indeed we will see this interplay not so much between different categories of students as within individual selves and identities. If high school was affectively powerful because of its social dynamics, it was also affectively powerful because of the "forcing" of identities, the pressing of people into categories—the idea with which I began this part of the book.

Identities I: The Wildness of the Tame

Although I sorted the social categories and their associated "games" into boxes and tried to show the degree to which people's real practices were structured by the fact that they were either playing the hegemonic game or reacting to it, I must also acknowledge a level of fluidity in the system that was not captured by the preceding discussion. I begin by noting that many people felt they did not fit into a single box. For example,

> [from the fieldnotes] I asked Ira how he would place his social position in high school and he thought a while and then said "mainstream." He wasn't among the big popular people (though that was my phrase, not his) though on the other hand he was friends with some of them. And he wasn't in the "intellectual elite" (that was his phrase) though again he was friendly with some of them. He emphasized the overlaps between the groups, which I guess is right.

Ira's comments reflect a very widespread tendency of people to resist being boxed into the categories or to be in a sense "assigned" to a particular game. This resistance often produced a range of hybrid social strategies as people played on the margins between categories, trying to elude any one stereotype. It also often produced a sense of a split self or of having a secret self—appearing one way in school but really being someone else, someone the other kids did not know about. I heard this again and again in the interviews.[11]

In this section I discuss the students who would have been classified as "tame"—the popular kids/class officers and the ordinary citizens. In both cases they are where they are precisely because they enact a general style of social conformity and sexual modesty. Yet there are many ways in which this tameness was a façade, and the student either harbored fantasies of rebellion against the type or actually (secretly) did something "wild." It is important to note however, that the rule-breaking, in fantasy or in fact, was often a source of confusion at best, and pain or shame at worst. Much of what follows is not a picture of a kind of exuberant breaking out from the constraints of the system. Rather it is a picture of people feeling trapped by the categories and the rules, breaking them anyway, and then—because they are, after all, "tame"—feeling bad or stupid or angry. This does not mean that the rule-breaking is irrelevant. Some of it may contain the seeds of changes that would emerge later. But it does mean that working against normative identities, as Foucault among others has insisted, is not easy.

The Popular Kids

While some classmates felt very comfortable with their high status in high school, others were secretly unhappy despite their social success. Several felt insecure, as if they did not really belong among the popular kids. In one case, a classmate from a relatively lower-capital family was well liked and elected to a high office in the class. He continued to feel, however, that others were looking down on him, and sustained a strong sense of resentment more common among the excluded. He kept it well under wraps in high school, but it came out very strongly in the interview. He asked with some sarcasm whether those classmates who went to fancy private colleges turned out any better than those, like himself, who went to local schools. In addition, as I wrote in my field notes: "Robert has very little nostalgia—he remembers the whole [high school] thing somewhat angrily, and said the reunion was boring as shit."

In a different vein, there is something about being a class officer or otherwise popular that presumes both a leadership orientation toward the school and an attitude of caring about it. This is also presumably part of what it means to be "friendly with everyone." In fact, however, several of the popular kids secretly viewed the high school (and indeed the whole community) with great ambivalence and could not wait to get out of there. Many of them went relatively far away to college (which was a function of their high capital as well) and many did not return to live in the area. A case in point was Allan Goldberg, who eventually became a lawyer in Florida:

> [from the field notes] Allan said he hung around with some of the faster crowds of guys, the Redskins and the Redmen [boys' clubs]. He put it in terms of not knowing what his identity was, and wanting to be everything, part of the faster crowd, but also part of the academic/successful crowd. . . . [He also] talked some more about how he had to get away from New Jersey when he was starting his career, and he put it this time in terms of not wanting to be "just another Jewish lawyer from NJ." It wasn't really an escape from being Jewish (à la [another classmate]) but it was the sense of [avoiding] being part of some standard type.

Allan was very good at playing the boundaries in Weequahic; on the one hand, he was popular and academically very successful; on the other hand, he successfully passed himself off as an ordinary guy. Harriet Kroll said, "The only thing that ever surprised me, as far as how bright he was, was Allan. Allan didn't let anybody know until it came down to push came to shove. He was so bright [but] he was just a good ole kid."

Though not a "class officer" type, Naomi Schwartz played the game rather similarly to Allan. For one thing, she said she tried to hide her academic abilities in order to seem to be a regular person rather than either a nerd or a snobbish "intellectual." She kept up her grades but also had a hoody-seeming boyfriend. And she said she too wanted to escape from New Jersey insofar as it signified a certain social type. "She said she wanted to get away from being a Jewish mink-coated suburban matron—wanting to be more [or other] than what was expected of one" (field notes).

Finally, there was Gloria Moscowitz, who acted out her rebellion against tameness quite overtly:

> [from the field notes] She had just had it with school, was tired of being a little girl. She had been an A student at [one of the top grammar schools] but in high school she got Cs, skipped school a lot, got tight black skirts and black ballet flats [shoes] and black stockings with seams up the back, and hung around with tough girls from [a working-class high school] and dated much older guys. . . . She was totally rebellious, just knew that this [bourgeois Weequahic] was not the life she wanted.

In short, many of the popular kids, expected to be paragons of upholding the rules and the identity types, really saw themselves as something else, something rebellious—dating or hanging out with some of the "wilder" citizens of the class and adopting certain dress or behavioral styles that allowed them to play the margins, or even cross them.

The Ordinary Citizens

I have already indicated that some of the ordinary citizens formed little clubs and societies for the pursuit of high culture and, to some extent, oppositional politics. While this does not appear very "wild," I note it here as a form of nonconformity, of students breaking out of the "ordinary citizen" type, questioning the prevailing values of the school and the culture. Some of these students, and this starts to become more visibly "wild," began going to Greenwich Village and attaching themselves to the fringes of the emerging bohemian/Beat subculture that was taking shape there. I will discuss this group more fully in the chapter on the sixties. Here, however, this proto-bohemian subset also connects with one more secret pattern of wildness among the tame.

Sex

One could not write a chapter on high school in the fifties without a discussion of sex. The era was famously repressive. The hegemonic ideology was that "nice girls didn't." Abortions were illegal. Homosexuality was totally off the charts.

Let me start with homosexuality, which was tabooed to the point that many people knew absolutely nothing about it:

> *Joseph Finkel:* "I remember that when I was a freshman in college, we were reading Plato's *Dialogues,* and all of a sudden there was talk about homosexuals and men [doing] this, and I was appalled, I'd never encountered this in my whole life."
>
> [*from the field notes on a group conversation*]: We all agreed that we simply didn't have the categories [at the time]. Even though Alan's friends knew he was [cross-dressing], they did not really focus it as "gay," he was not somehow sharply divided off from everyone else, they just thought he was fooling around.

To this day, there are no out lesbians in the Class of '58. Among the men, three classmates eventually came out as gay; one died of AIDS. The other two, Carl Ornstein and Peter Dvorin, were good friends in high school and were able to confide in each other about their secret desires and fears: "We had a little group and, you know, we were gay together. It was us against our families." But the secrecy made for a difficult time. As Carl said:

> "I don't think about high school very much. I think high school for me was difficult because of the duality in my life, because of my secret life and fear about that, and not understanding it and not knowing what to do with it, and learning about that side of me, the, you know, the gay side of me."

As to heterosex, again people talked about the repressiveness of the era. Fredda Kesselman went on about how oppressive the fifties were about sex. One of the reasons she went to [a relatively distant university] was to get "far away" from New Jersey and "this culture of vigilance" (field notes). There was, of course, the cardinal rule: girls were not supposed to "go all the way." Some, perhaps most, girls followed the rule:

> *Barbara Saltman:* [from the field notes] She said she did not screw around. She said Bobby left her for Sandi because she, Barbara, wasn't ready to screw and Sandi was.
>
> *Evelyn Cohen:* "I never had a relationship where I was that serious, the way a lot of my friends [did]. Those people were a little more seriously involved, emotionally and physically. No, I never had that, till college."

Both women were obviously aware that, while they were following the rules, other girls were not. And here there was a tacit modification of the cardinal rule: if you were going to "go all the way," it had to be within a "steady" relationship. The difference between a slut and a good girl was not so much that sluts had sex and good girls did not, although that was the ideal and the fiction, but that sluts were widely available, while good girls did it only in relationships: "She said she'd been 'doing it' since she was thirteen years old . . . but always within a relationship with a boyfriend" (field notes).

There was, in fact, a lot of sex going on in those repressive fifties, but it was highly secret, and often shameful at the time:

Susan Kleinman: "I had a really tough time in high school because I was going through all kinds of stuff. I guess no one knew I was running around with Neil. . . . I had to say I am sleeping with somebody. I'm fifteen years old. I'm leading an active sex life with [an older] boy."

Barbara Levy: [from the field notes] Somehow sex came up. She said that was a big thing in high school, that she did a lot of that, led a double life, dated a lot of older Italians but also the boys in the high school, a year or two older than us. Lots of sex, though she didn't "have intercourse" until the end of her junior year. She feels it messed up her sex life later, some guy made her do things she didn't want to do, but she found it hard to say no.

Judy Rosenberg: [from the field notes] She and Kenny started going steady in the middle of sophomore year. The sex just inched up further and further over time. Finally they "did it" senior year, in a parked car.[12]

Sexual intercourse in turn often led to the ultimate horror in the fifties, pregnancy.[13] Several of the girls of the Class of '58 were in fact "a little bit pregnant" at graduation. In that era, there were three possible choices: have the baby in secret and give it up for adoption (I know of one woman who did this, though not in the Class of '58); marry the father and have the baby, even if one got divorced almost immediately afterward (three cases in the Class of '58); or have an abortion (also three cases that I know of). Abortions, of course, were entirely illegal. It is thus presumably not an accident that the three cases I know of were all from high-capital families. Moreover, and presumably for the same reason, all managed to have semilegal or at least medically safe abortions. One of the women in the class was flown by her family to

Cuba for an abortion, though I do not know the details.[14] Here are two other stories:

> *Ina Rosen:* "I was going out with David Jentis, and I got pregnant, and he didn't want to get married, no way he wanted to get married. . . . So luckily I remembered, I have this very avant-garde aunt and she [had] said to me, I didn't even know what she was talking about, when I was like thirteen or fourteen, if you ever have any trouble, call me. . . . There was no hesitation in calling her. And she knew exactly what to do. And I got it done, thank God it was in a hospital."
>
> *Judy Grossman:* "I got knocked up in high school, and my parents arranged a semilegal abortion for me, by a real doctor in the local hospital. But I've always thought like I was the only one who had made this gruesome mistake, and it was like forever I was marked. And, just me, nobody else ever fucked up in the whole world, except for me."

The tone of these and some of the other quotes in this section brings us back to the point made earlier that secret forms of wildness among the officially "tame" were rarely comfortable or happy experiences. Except perhaps for what I called the proto-bohemians, who had a relatively self-conscious sense of doing something vaguely progressive, most of the rule-breaking, whether in mind or in body, was a kind of confused flailing against the system rather than a coherent move toward an alternative future. In retrospect, one can perhaps perceive the seeds of certain social and cultural changes (e.g., the sexual revolution of the sixties) in these various nonconformist moves, but at the time these were for many very difficult experiences.

AGENCY vs. STRUCTURE

Identities II: The Tameness of the Wild

I now flip the identity question over and look at the kids who were classified as in some sense "wild"—the jocks and cheerleader/twirlers in the top half of the table, and the hoods and "sluts" in the lower half. In both cases there is an assumption of an excessive physicality, or a kind of outlaw mentality, or both. Yet in fact we can find here the same dynamics we saw in the last section: the sense of an identity being forced on one and a secret desire for, or enactment of, its alternatives.

The Jocks/Cheerleaders

I have already indicated that jocks at Weequahic were not very jocky, but this was not a "secret" in the same sense as the other cases under discussion. Most of the men I knew who would be labeled jocks were not highly aggressive and macho, nor did they entirely neglect school-work in favor of sports. But this being Weequahic, they did not have to pretend (for the most part) to be tougher than they were.[15]

On the cheerleader/twirler side, however, there were several secret selves. Ellen Eisenberg said she regretted in retrospect having been a twirler (I am trying to mix up identities here, so she may have been a cheerleader; don't try to guess) because she realized too late that it labeled her as not being smart and not being a serious person. "She said first off that she always felt like a divided person, on the one hand a smart and good student, on the other hand a majorette wanting to be popular, doing a lot of dating, running with a 'fast' crowd. . . . [She said] she was smart too but people didn't know it" [from the field notes]. The fullest representation of this idea came from another cheer-leader/twirler. She felt she did what she had to do to be a high-energy cheerleader/twirler and an ebullient popular girl, but underneath all that was a serious intellectual and ethical person:

> "I lived a secret life, like my intellectual side. I loved reading, I had already read James Joyce's *Ulysses* and Virginia Woolf's *To the Lighthouse* [but] I never spoke to anybody who was more intellectual. I used to ask people to carry my [books home from the library]. . . . I think I was confused a great deal about where I belonged. I never fully fit in anywhere."

This girl was friendly with some of the most popular girls in the school, and some of them were thought of as very (in the jargon of the time) stuck-up. I did not know her very well in high school so I just assumed she was like her friends. In the course of the project, however, I kept hearing nice stories about her, about what a kind and generous and precisely not stuck-up person she had been. I told her this at the inter-view, and she replied, "My other life." I said my view of her had been entirely colored by the group of friends she hung out with. She replied: "That's what made me so miserable. Except that, I had this boyfriend named Tony D. You remember Tony D? He was six months ahead of

us. . . . And he was the opposite, he was the only one I really shared my
real self with."

In short, there were among the twirlers/cheerleaders women who
felt that they were forced by their roles to appear mindless and dumb,
or even forced in a more physical sense to participate in sexual relationships that upheld the "wildness" of their public identities. Secretly,
however, they were "tame"—smart, intellectual, artistically talented.

Hoods and Sluts

I said earlier that there were no real sluts in the Class of '58, if by sluts
we mean girls who "put out" (as the saying went) to all comers. Sluttiness was actually a complex idea. It was first and foremost a matter
of looks and style. It drew from certain dress styles that were popular among working-class girls. It involved wearing too much (from
the middle-class point of view) makeup; long, teased hair; a sheer
nylon blouse with a slip (covering the bra) visible through the nylon;
long, straight black skirts; black slip-on low-heeled shoes (flats); and
black nylon stockings with seams up the back. Such an appearance was
coded, by middle-class girls, as vaguely slutty, or at least "cheap" in the
several meanings of that term.

Yet in retrospect I think the style had little or nothing to do with
looking sexually provocative. On the contrary, it was meant to be
"feminine," even "ladylike," compared with the more bobby-soxer
style of the middle-class girls. This is to say that these supposedly wild
girls, most of them Catholic, were in fact quite tame, and perhaps
tamer—certainly better behaved sexually—than many of the middle-
class girls of the class. It is not so much that their tameness was a
"secret" identity; it was simply that the middle-class kids were too
busy reinforcing a particular system of identities, replacing class and
ethnicity with virtue and vice, to bother to read the codes of dress and
style correctly.

The boys, the so-called hoods, showed a similar though more inten-
tional dynamic. The hoody style—longish, highly styled (pompadours,
ducktails) and oiled hair; shirts opened just that extra button; boots
rather than shoes; the ever-present cigarette; and a certain scowling or
at least deadpan facial expression—was quite intentionally meant to
look "tough," "wild." And yet one sees, again mostly in retrospect, that

many of these boys had a hidden longing for the tame life. They may have looked "wild," succumbing to peer pressure to smoke or drink or be "wise guys" in school. Yet many seem to have secretly wished to be respectable and middle class.

No one in this category ever used the language of having had a "secret self," but it is interesting to note that people like Thomas Toyas, who talked about being a "wise guy" and wasting his high school years, or Joel Weiss, who talked about being in and out of trouble in school, nonetheless turned themselves around very quickly once they got out. Others could be named as well. Some of the hoody-seeming guys in high school went on to college (usually in commercial/accounting/business majors), but whether they did or not, most went on to respectable jobs, careers, or businesses. Again, then, there had clearly been a forcing of identities: It is almost as if these guys had been forced to play that hood role, at least publicly. If some of the "tame" kids wanted to be seen as "fast," some of the kids who enacted a certain kind of "fast" style secretly wanted to be respectable.

In this chapter I have tried to show how the system of identities and its underlying axes of differentiation played out in practice among the Class of '58. We have seen how top kids played at being popular through winning elections and high-visibility activities, while kids in the lower layer fashioned various critiques, in theory and practice, of the top layer. We have also seen how, if one looks at the wild/tame distinction of personal qualities, many people in tame categories had secret forms of wildness, while many people in wild categories were really quite tame. I also talked about the painfulness of many of these oppositional secrets/practices; it is not easy to buck the system or to work against the identity in which one finds oneself, in Foucault's term, "pinned." People did it, and indeed did it all the time, but not without various costs. These, I think, are among the real bases of the memory tattoos.

At this point, however, we are ready to leave the high school viewed primarily as a social system for the students. It was, after all, also (and indeed from the point of view of teachers and administrators, primarily) a place to teach students knowledge and skills and to prepare them for their futures, whatever those might be. In chapter 7 we turn to Weequahic as an educational institution with its many good points and its hidden biases, its own "secret self."

Project Journal 6: New Jersey

7/5/92   I thought I'd call Thad Roberts for help. Thad's a policeman in Newark. I called a work number someone had given me and reached some police office. . . . I enjoyed the telephone exchange, the guy was very cheerful and friendly, took my name and number and then said, "OK, Sherry [not Miss Ortner], I'll give him the message," and I said thanks a million, and he said "All right, hon." It's that little "hon" tag that I liked—warm, nice, no one would say that in the Midwest.

7/7/92   [Jack Washington was a working-class African American classmate who died young.] I called and made an appointment to see his mother. She was a nice old lady who seemed happy to have me come and see her—said she'd been sick and was just staying home anyway. When she gave me directions on the phone she said, do you know the Skinner Temple? And I said no, and she said, well it used to be Abraham Temple, and she couldn't see me smile, but of course it was Temple B'nai Abraham [to which my family belonged when I was growing up]. A flood of memories—of Rabbi [Joachim] Prinz's sermon on *Marjorie Morningstar,* of cutting Hebrew school with girlfriends and going to the bialystocker bakery and eating hot bialys.

7/8/92   [Certain rumors about a classmate that had seemed credible turned out to be false.] Still, if I weren't wired into these kinds of rumors, this project would be infinitely poorer. First of all some of them are true. And second of all, even if they're false, they provide me with some questions that I would never otherwise ask. And even when I don't ask, as with [another man], they provide me with a sense of what is not being said, as well as what is being said. It's what makes the whole thing ethnography, even more than going into physical sites, though that helps too—everything helps.

...... By the way [classmate] Jean Kalifon works part-time in [classmate] Nate Markowitz's office. He told me that, and then we ran into her on the way out. Isn't it amazing how many people [from the class] are still interconnected in how many different ways.

...... I can't describe the irrationality of the route that needed to be followed to get back onto the Garden State Parkway [near the old Weequahic neighborhood], but it involved crossing and recrossing it several times, and driving up one street and then having to make a virtual U-turn down another, and more. It's a product of trying to build a freeway into an existing urban conglomeration, and to sort of tuck it in, rather than having the luxury of laying it out according to its own rationality. When I finally got on, it turned out I was getting off one exit later.

...... Speaking of getting off one exit later, I'm struck too with how small New Jersey is—everything is right next to everything else, there are no spaces between places, and you begin in one place and are in the next place in the wink of an eye. As this observation suggests, the necessary "going away" that allowed me to do this New Jersey project was probably as much going to Michigan as going to Nepal.

7/9/92 [Staying at some cousins' house while they are away.] I've been meaning to enter this note about the empty wastebasket phenomenon. Wastebaskets in refined homes are not supposed to have any actual trash in them. I noticed that [one of my relatives] would always come and empty a wastebasket in which I had thrown, say, one tissue, and Nancy did the same thing in her place. I feel guilty about throwing waste into wastebaskets, and while I am allowing the one here to fill up since nobody is home, I know I must empty it before Nancy gets it back.

...... I went down to the Newark Police Department to meet with Thad Roberts today. First of all naturally I got lost on the spaghetti of Route 78 and wound up heading for the Holland Tunnel. But anyway I got there in one piece. Thad was on the one hand very welcoming but on the other hand he was in a funny way very defensive about being treated as a "subject" or a "connection" in any way. I asked if he would participate in my study and fill out the questionnaire, because he had such an interesting history, being the son of the first Black family on [one of the "better" streets of the neighborhood], his mother being the first Black [high-ranking official in the Board of Education], etc., and he acquiesced reluctantly, and kept making cracks about "here we are old friends and we haven't seen each other for 30 years and I thought she was coming down because she wanted to see me, but no, she wants to put me in a scientific experiment."

...... So there we were in the Director's office (I believe that's the actual Chief of Police), and there were people all around, and Thad had no qualms about everyone flowing in and out of the room and in and out of the conversation, or even just standing around and listening—it was more like Sherpa fieldwork than American.

...... When I left, the Puerto Rican guy at the parking lot calculated the time/rate in his head, and it was over the time for the $3 rate, but under the time for the $4 rate (and he actually asked me what time I came in, because it was not punched on the ticket), and he said well, just give me $3. So I said thanks, and he asked if I needed a receipt, and I said yes please, and he said should I write it up for more? And I said, no $3 is OK, and he said are you sure? Why don't I make it out for $4, and I had the feeling that he would view me as a total jerk if I refused again so I said OK. So I have this receipt for $4 but I am so deeply socialized that I know that I can't turn it in and will probably change it back.

...... I was late leaving the police station and there was a traffic tie-up on the ramp onto 78 (stalled car) and I was about 15 minutes late, and Janie Tanner [whom I was meeting] was pacing the sidewalk, and the Italian who owned the restaurant said they were about to send out an all-points-bulletin for me. Again, only in NJ/NY would the customer and the restaurateur engage each other in this kind of conversation, where the restaurant owner begins to worry about me too—some of my Midwestern friends would sooner die.

...... It's interesting how people pop the big one at the end [of an interview]. They don't know what I'm going to ask about, and they're sort of anxious, and then it turns out that the interview is sort of innocuous (tell me about your life since Weequahic) and I don't ask about their darkest secret (how could I?) and they want to tell it. They want somebody to know, some Foucauldian urge to confess which I incited but then failed to bring off. Confessus interruptus.

...... It's become clear that when people ask if I'm going to write about X [e.g., "are you going to write about people whose kids got into trouble?"], it means they specifically have some knot about it that they'd like to talk about, and I should pick up on this. I don't have the therapist's good training to answer every question with a question—if people ask about some pattern or other, I start nattering on (in generalizations) about the data, but I should just realize they want me to ask them about that pattern in their own case.

chapter 7

Tracks

Eventually, the intense emotions of high school, of winning and losing, of inclusion and exclusion, of inhabiting ill-fitting identities, come to an end. There is nothing ever again quite like high school. The emotional "tattoos" that it leaves, though real enough and enduring for many over a lifetime, nonetheless seem to congeal in a particular, and relatively limited, way in memory. Although certain situations (like reunions) can call them up in all their rich pain and pleasure, for the most part they operate primarily as what might be called baseline memories, against which later successes and failures are measured: I was a nothing in high school but look at (very successful) me now, or I was a big wheel in high school but (do not) look at (less successful) me now.

But there was another system of classification and practice in place in high school, this one related to its educational functions: the system of "tracks." In terms of controlling people's life chances, academic tracks were often much more pernicious over the long run than the social categories pertaining to popularity. Tracks were future-oriented: they basically took very young people, just starting out in high school at age thirteen or fourteen, and pegged them for either college or for an "unskilled" career (whether that be industrial labor or motherhood), before—one could say—the students even knew what was happening to them. This chapter is about the tracks system, about its relationship to various forms of social difference (class, race/ethnicity, gender), and about the college options (or not) toward which those tracks pointed.

I begin, however, with a general overview of Weequahic, now no longer as a social game, but specifically as an academic system.

Weequahic qua School

I have already indicated that Weequahic was thought to be a "good" school. This meant that it had a reputation for good teaching, for good test scores, and for sending relatively large numbers of students to college in general, a few to some of the top colleges in the country.

Let us start with the teaching. Although I did not interview any teachers for this project, I did have access to an existing interview with one teacher, Hannah Ginsberg Litzky,[1] who praised the school from a teacher's point of view. She saw the strength of the high school coming from good teachers, motivated students/families, and especially from a kind of powerful synergy between the two:

> The faculty was really extraordinary. And so was the student body. They were the children of highly motivated parents, upwardly mobile parents who wanted the best education for their children, and there was a kind of unusual chemistry going on there between faculty and students. When I meet students now, years and years later, they all go back to what a great school Weequahic was. There was a very strong attachment and inter-stimulation between faculty and students.[2]

Many classmates did indeed feel that they got an excellent education at Weequahic:

> *Anna Granger:* [SBO: How about the education?] "I thought it was very, very good."
> *Marie Chin:* [SBO: Did you feel Weequahic was a good school at the time?] "Yes. It was very good, yes. And everybody was geared toward academics and going to college."
> *Arthur Mayers:* "Educationally, socially, athletically, I mean it was just an outstanding high school with an outstanding group of teachers and faculty. . . . I think without it most of us probably would not have the opportunities we have had in our adult life."

Other students had more mixed memories of the quality of the school. Several remembered some truly dreadful teachers; some remembered overcrowded foreign-language classes where they never had a chance to speak; and several also remembered feeling very unprepared, especially with respect to critical writing, when they got to college. But some specific teachers stood out in their memories. Recall Carole Schwartz's discussion of the "free spirit," Mrs. Nadelson, in chapter 6. One of the African American women, Anna Granger, remembered Mrs. Steinholtz (her real name), "who was my shorthand teacher for a couple of years, she kind of took a liking to me and she helped me in my senior year, she encouraged me to take the civil servant's exam and she got a job for me that was waiting for me when I got out of high school." An unnamed teacher was recalled very fondly by Claire Adelsohn. Claire had quit one of the sororities because she thought the initiation rite was "incredibly stupid." The teacher came up to her in the hall and said, "I heard you dropped out of the sorority. Good for you, you're a nonconformist."

But without a doubt the teacher who wins the prize for leaving the highest number of lasting (positive) memories was Mrs. Sadie Rous (her real name). Mrs. Rous's classroom teaching had a powerful impact on many students:

> *Ellen Cohen:* [from the field notes] She said she remembered being in-spired by Mrs. Rous about [and here she stood up and threw her arms out] DEMOCRACY. Democracy meant rule of the majority but respect for the minority.
>
> *Perry Tucker:* "I was in love with Miss Rous. I thought she was great. . . . I think I was crazy about her because she was *rough*. She didn't take no stuff on her."
>
> *Roger Gordon:* "There was something magical about [Mrs. Rous]. She was a Socratic teacher, one of those teachers who gets the kids involved."[3]

But she is also remembered equally, if not more so, for the personal interest she took in her students beyond the classroom:

> *Robert Goldman:* "Strasny [another teacher] and Rous! They used to get me in the halls sometimes, both of them, and they're, uh, 'Why aren't you doing better?!' Because they knew I could go from an A student . . . what happened? All of a sudden I'm not [performing], something's wrong! Yeah, they used to get me in the hall, both of them, oh yeah."
>
> *Paul Abt:* Mrs. Rous "had me over to her house once to try to turn me around. That was the time when she said, you know, to come out of my shell. And she once pulled me up in front of the class and I remem-ber she berated me about what a lazy good-for-nothing I am. She says, 'This was a very good report you turned in, Paul. Did you do it last night?' and I said 'yes.' She said, 'Just think how good it would have been if you'd spent time and done research.' . . . As an educator, prob-ably of the two or three [best] teachers I ever had, she made the biggest mark on me."
>
> *Anita Schildkret:* "[Mrs. Rous] was a little scary but she loved us so much that I ended up really being in love with the woman. . . . I never felt that I was smart . . . but she was the first one who, so to speak, had faith in me. I thought she was nuts. But she put me into an honors his-

tory class and she assigned me things to read and it was kind of like you rise to the level. She had these expectations."[4]

But if many teachers are remembered as either excellent academic teachers or personally inspiring teachers or both, memories of the guidance counselors are almost uniformly negative:

Joyce Gershon: ". . . no college guidance whatsoever."

Betsy Uhrman: "I think what they weren't as aware of were bright kids who weren't being channeled in the right direction. . . . Judith Graifer, whose parents insisted she take a commercial track. This was a very bright person who was channeled, and no one was there saying, 'Don't do this to her.' "

Rosalyn Goldberg: "And the guidance department at Weequahic was not the greatest either! [They didn't think] to say, you really could be at a more academic school, and you belong there, and should be there."

While the people quoted above are mixed in terms of class background, the guidance counselors probably tended—no doubt with many exceptions—to do better with those "most likely to succeed": kids from high-capital families, kids with top grades, boys over girls, whites over blacks, and so on. Thus I never heard complaints from the people who went to the really top schools. On the other hand, some students had a strong sense that there was systematic social discrimination in the guidance they were given. Norman Huntley, an African American man, mentioned racial discrimination: "The guidance counselors were terrible. They put people, especially Black people, on the wrong track." Two other students felt there was class discrimination. Thelma Heller tied it to not having the money to go away to a prestigious or "exciting" school: "When I was preparing to go to college, counselors were not very helpful. I don't remember where I graduated in the Class [but it was quite high]. . . . And because I couldn't go away [to school] and do anything exciting they were totally and absolutely not helpful."

Lynda Beck's social class was indexed by her placement on the commercial track: ". . . that was something that bothered me about high school, with counselors I don't think they did a great job, especially for people who were in [the] business [track]." Lynda's complaint is ironic, since of course students on the commercial track were already pegged as those not going to college.

The guidance counselors were in the structural position of being the keepers of the "tracks"—the placement of students in different academic programs by virtue of their declared future intentions about, or assumed future capacities for, college. These tracks no doubt served certain pedagogic functions; as a teacher I know it is hard to teach a class that includes students with a wide range of abilities and motivation levels. On the whole, however, the tracks were quite pernicious. Thus, even if the guidance counselors were not uniformly incompetent at their jobs, they were at least structurally the villains of this story.

College Prep?

There were basically two official tracks at Weequahic: "college prep" and "commercial/secretarial." In the early decades of the twentieth century, fewer students went to high school altogether, although the number rose steadily over the first half of the century. In addition, there was much more segregation of schools by class: the upper class went to private schools, the middle class went to public schools, and the working class went to vocational schools.[5] After World War II, with the middle classing of the working class, there was a trend toward expanding the so-called comprehensive public high schools, putting the working and middle classes together in the same institutions. The tracks in turn seem to represent a recognition and a codification of the continuing, but now underground, class divisions in the schools.

At Weequahic, and I presume at most other schools with this kind of system, one had to "choose" a track fairly soon after entering the school. How that actually happened is rather hazy in the minds of my classmates, and nobody I interviewed had any specific memories about this. But we may tentatively reconstruct the process as follows. First of all, the guidance counselors played a critical role by administering tests. There were IQ tests that supposedly tested whether a student had the intellectual abilities necessary for college work. In addition, there were so-called career placement tests ("If you had spare time, would you rather fix an alarm clock, read a book, or tend to a sick person?"), which theoretically indicated what a student's talents and proclivities, other than "intelligence," might be. Armed with all these "scientific" results, the counselors must have proposed a track decision to a student who then was instructed to check with his or her parents. Or perhaps one's parents' desires and wishes were "obvious" and one knew intuitively what to choose (the Bourdieusian internalization of the possibilities and limits of one's class position).

Once one signed up for/was assigned to a particular track, the situation became very controlling. For one thing, it established a mind-set early on: one was or was not bound for college. For another, it created practical limitations by dictating a set of course requirements. If one took those courses and not others, it became difficult to change tracks later. Especially if one followed the commercial/secretarial track and later decided one wanted to go to college, it inevitably turned out that one did not have the right courses (languages, enough math and science) to make the switch. One was indeed "tracked."

> *Barbara Blecker:* "I even encourage my students [she is an art teacher today], I say, 'Look, you never know what life has in store for you, you are going to say you are never going to college as I did but I think you are going to go one day and you need your math.' I never had higher math . . . I never had biology, I never had a language . . . that is what put me off [from going to college] for six years."
>
> *Paula Holtzman:* "I was accepted at Rutgers but I had a math deficiency so they wanted me to take a year of math with no credit before I could matriculate. I was lazy, I didn't want to do that." [She never went to college.]
>
> *Helen Weisman:* [She went away to a state college.] "I hated it. It was the worst place in the world for me . . . [but] I didn't have the right courses to go to a lot of colleges. Because I'd taken the minimum of math, minimum science." [So she dropped out.]

The track system was based on a simple binary question: going to college or not? This in turn was ostensibly based on individual characteristics—"brains," "aptitude," "motivation," and so on—and there is no doubt that those played some role. But like everything else in this book that may seem to depend on personal characteristics alone, there are underlying and cross-cutting social factors. I begin with class.

The relationship of the tracking system to class at Weequahic was rather interesting. To begin with, a high percentage of the Class of '58 was in the college prep track (table 7). This, of course, is one of the things that is meant by saying that Weequahic was a "good school."

Table 7. The Class of '58 by Tracks (*N* = 292 known)

College prep, 220 (75%)
Commercial/secretarial, 70 (24%)
Both, 2 (1%)

The college prep (CP) track thus extended far down into the class structure and encompassed virtually all of the business/professional-class kids, virtually all of the middle-class kids, and some of the working-class kids as well. It appeared, in other words, highly inclusive. In a way, one could say that the numbers in table 7 replicate the "middle-classing" project of the period, the effort or desire or fantasy of making as many people as possible "middle class."[6]

But if the tracking system seemed to override class, it followed very closely—and indeed accentuated—the contours of race and ethnicity. It will be recalled that the race/ethnic distribution at Weequahic was 83 percent Jewish, 11 percent other ethnicities, and 6 percent African Americans. Table 8 shows the percentages of these groups on the two tracks. We can see that the numbers all run in the same directions as the representation of the groups in the Class of '58 as a whole, but all the numbers are exaggerated. The Jewish kids are overrepresented on the CP track, and the others are underrepresented, while the reverse is true for the commercial track.

Yet of course ethnicity and race are not unrelated to class. Within the high school social categories, and indeed within the prevailing thinking of large sectors of society, all African Americans and most white ethnics were seen as working/lower class. Yet in reality this was not true, and there were, in fact, families in these groups engaged in middle-classing projects of their own.[7] There were also evidently some among the much maligned guidance counselors who recognized this. Thus if one turns the race and ethnicity numbers around and looks at variations within the different groups, as in table 9, one gets a rather different picture. These numbers show that there was much more variation within each of the race/ethnic groups than people seem to have been aware of at the time: a substantial number of Jewish kids were not tracked for college, and significant percentages of non-Jewish kids, both Black and white, at least in terms of tracking were potentially college-bound.

Table 8. Tracks by Race and Ethnicity (*N* = 292)

College prep (*N* = 220)
  Jewish, 201 (91%)
  Other ethnicities (including 1 unknown), 14 (6%)
  African Americans, 5 (2%)
Commercial/secretarial track (*N* = 70)
  Jewish, 41 (59%)
  Other ethnicities, 18 (26%)
  African Americans, 11 (16%)
Both tracks (*N* = 2)
  Jewish, 2 (100%)

Nonetheless the systematic overrepresentation of the Jewish students on the academic track at Weequahic High School in the 1950s does require some comment before we go on. I will be brief here as there is a more extended discussion of Jewishness and "success" in chapter 9.

Cultural Capital

At issue here is what Bourdieu has called "cultural capital," a term that pertains mainly to education or to the valuing of education. The stereotype of (American) Jewry is, of course, that their culture places a very high value on education; this would account, among other things, for their overrepresentation on the college prep track at Weequahic. Although I do not have data on education levels among the parents of the Class of '58, we can deduce that those levels were in fact somewhat higher than among the other groups, in part because there were at least some degreed professionals among the Jewish parents (and none in the other groups), and in part because, in general, most of the Jewish families were further along in the middle-classing process than most of the families in the other groups.

Moreover, whether the parents were educated or not, it is clear from the interviews that most Jewish boys (if not girls) were encouraged to go to college, while this was less true for most members of other groups.

Table 9. Race/Ethnicity by Track (*N* = 292)

Jewish (*N* = 244)
   College prep, 201 (82%)
   Commercial, 41 (17%)
   Both, 2 (1%)
African Americans (*N* = 16)
   College prep, 5 (31%)
   Commercial, 11 (69%)
All others (*N* = 32)
   College prep, 14 (44%)
   Commercial, 18 (56%)

> *Sydney Burakof:* [His parents did not have much money. But] "I was an only child. If there was six in the family, who knows? But my parents were very loving and supportive. . . . They really wanted me to succeed and they pushed me. I mean not overly [so] and I have no resentment. It worked out."
>
> *Larry Uhrmann:* "I studied a lot because I needed to keep up. . . . I had terrific parents who were really supportive of me. I was not a great student. I was not good at it, but they were very good at making you feel good about yourself and I think that is part of a great deal of why I am what I have been able to be [a very successful businessman]."

Of course there were exceptions. Some Jewish classmates specifically noted in interviews that their parents did not share this value, or at any rate were very passive about whether the son went to college or not, and where:

> *Jerry Cohen:* "Actually, I guess the whole experience of growing up in Newark was pro-education, pro-culture, and my family really wasn't. They were hard working class, no one ever went to college, I was the first one on both sides."
>
> *Gary Horowitz:* "My parents didn't say, 'Well let's take you around to look at schools' . . . and I had a lot to do that sort of overwhelmed me and maybe if it would have been my children now I would have probably said, 'Let's sit back, see where you are. You need a tutor here, you need this there, we'll take care of this,' but that just didn't exist in those days."

Finally, a number of Jewish classmates who were children of immigrant parents noted that their parents simply did not know how the system worked and were unable to give their children the best advice about the importance of higher education. This kind of cultural know-how, this understanding of what it takes to succeed and how to go about getting what it takes, is, of course, another form of cultural capital, and children of immigrants often felt their parents were unable to provide it:

> *Yvette Weiss:* [from the field notes] Yvette emphasized the fact that her father was both an immigrant and deeply depressed about the loss of his family in the Holocaust. She felt her parents were relatively "unassimilated" and so were unable to give her good advice about, among other things, where to apply to college.

Exceptions aside, however, it is clear that most of the Jewish parents of the Class of '58 had the "high value on education" that has long been ascribed to Jewish people in general. In a later discussion I will join other scholars in arguing that all of this was a historically specific pattern, and not something rooted in some eternal "Jewish culture." Nonetheless, at Weequahic in the 1950s, Jewishness as such, embodying these educational values, was itself clearly a form of cultural capital. Thus in addition to Jewish parents pushing their kids onto the college prep track whether they were suited for it or not, one suspects that the guidance counselors too shared the stereotypes in question, and assigned more Jewish kids to the track than might otherwise have been indicated by all those "scientific" tests.

By the same token, and in keeping, no doubt, with other stereotypes, many classmates from other race/ethnic groups seem precisely to have been pushed off the college prep track, whether by their parents, the guidance counselors, or some combination of the two. If Jewishness as such represented high cultural capital, non-Jewishness and non-whiteness represented the opposite. Some classmates later managed to climb out of these stereotypes, and out of the practical and mental handicaps imposed by tracking, and we will hear from many of them as we go along. As the Class of '58 approached graduation, however, the tracks imposed a very powerful channeling effect on people's immediate futures. The next question is, what were the options?

College as a Cultural System

Within high school, the tracks to some extent organized social contact, if not actual relationships. One tended to be in many of the same classes with kids who were on the same track as oneself. It is no accident, for example, that the African American students whom the white and/or Jewish students knew best, whose names came up often in interviews with whites, were among the African Americans on the college prep track. It is also no accident that many of the friendships between Jewish girls and other white ethnic girls were among those all together on the commercial track.[8] But of course the point of the tracks was the future: bound for college or not? And if so, where? Here, then, we must look at the end point of all this tracking—the set of college options available to, and loaded with meaning by, the Class of '58.

If from the point of view of the official tracking system the question of going to college or not was a binary distinction, from the point of view of native/student categories it was actually more complicated. Like the high school social categories, which divided students up according to the intersections of various forms of capital, on the one hand, and personal qualities, on the other, so the available choices of colleges were similarly subject to finer distinctions and similarly organized by an underlying capital/personal qualities structure. As before, I begin from the set of native categories and then try to deduce their underlying logic.

There was first of all the distinction between those who went to "elite" schools and all the rest. The elite schools include the very competitive Ivies, big and little (all of which were all-male at the time), the so-called Seven Sisters and other private women's colleges, and other co-ed but private and highly ranked schools.

Then there was the critical question of whether one was able to go "away." There was a strongly felt distinction between people who "went away to school" and those who merely went to Rutgers Newark or any of the other local colleges and universities. In fact, the question of whether a school was educationally and socially elite was one variant of the more culturally salient category of "going away to school."[9]

Needless to say, going away was in large part a question of money. Either one's parents could afford to send one, or one had a stellar enough high school record to get a scholarship, or both. This means

Table 10. The Underlying Structure of College Choices

	Personal Qualities	
Class	More brains/motivation	Less brains/motivation
More capital	Away/top schools	Away/other schools
Less capital	Local schools	No college

that we can once again draw a table in which the left axis is the axis of "class" broadly conceived, with the table divided horizontally between higher versus lower family capital (see table 10).

The top axis of "personal qualities" in this case is at least in theory some combination of "brains" and "motivation." These replace the personal qualities that made one "popular" in various ways in the high school social system, but they still represent personal qualities that inhere in the individual, seemingly a matter of luck or random personal variation—some people just have it, some people do not. The intersection of capital, on the one hand, with brains/motivation, on the other, once again produces a little structure that organizes quite accurately (I daresay) the college possibilities as they were understood at the time.

Table 10 is in some ways a simple transformation of the system of high school social categories. It is a fairly simple step, and it would not be grossly inaccurate, to insert the old categories into these boxes. Class officers and "popular kids" (as well as some of the academically high performing but less popular nerds) generally went to top schools; jocks and cheerleaders from higher-capital families generally went away to school but to less elite (and in fact more jockish), institutions;[10] the hardworking but poorer students who filled the "average citizen" box in high school went to local colleges; and the "hoods," by virtue of attitude, and the others in that box, by virtue of low cultural (mostly race/ethnic) as well as low economic capital, tended not to go to college at all.

The boxes—like everything else in high school—were loaded with status implications. Going to a top school was, of course, the best and most prestigious thing to do because it combined "going away," which was a value in and of itself, with high-quality education leading ideally toward a lucrative future. Going to an "away" school, usually a state university, was also very highly valued, in part for the grown-up-ness of leaving home and entering into a new world of experience on one's own:

> *Norman Miller:* "When I was growing up as a child, I was never away from my parents, never went to summer camp, nothing. I was never out on my own. When it came time for me to go to college my parents didn't want me to go away to school [but] I said, 'I am going away, I've never been away from the house. It is time for me to go and learn how to be on my own.'"

In addition, as table 10 indicates, going away to school also usually signaled high family financial capital. Whereas a poorer but academically outstanding classmate might still go to a top school with the aid of a scholarship, only the wealthier classmates could go to an away school without being top students. Here are a few texts on the high social value of going away:

> *Cindy Kesselman:* [SBO: You didn't want to go to college?] "I didn't want to go the way I would have had to go. We didn't have a lot of money. You know, I wanted to go to Michigan, with a wardrobe, you know, the whole social experience. That's what I wanted. My parents couldn't afford that."
> *Barbara Max:* "I went to [Local] College. Which I hated. I wanted to be away and my parents just couldn't do it."

Ellen Menker had doting parents who knew their daughter's heart was set on going away to school. Even though they could not afford it, they scraped together what they could to send her away: "On top of it, for people that, my father was only a truck driver and my mother worked in [a clothing store], it was a very big thing for them to send away a daughter to [State U]. . . . I went away for a year."

If "going away to school" had an almost desperately high social value, going to a local school had very low status, and people still remember being made to feel small and low about it:

> *Howard Guttman:* [from the field notes] He was clearly self-conscious about having gone to [a local college]. He said when we were seniors someone asked him about where he was going to college and he said [Local U] and the person said "oh" and more or less turned away and he felt very put down. . . . [As a result of this experience,] he always

wanted his kids to be able to go to [college] wherever they wanted, and they did."

Gary Feilbogen: [Gary was still clearly smarting from the status issues involved in having gone to a local school] "I've always been curious about our graduating class because I always perceived it as a class of over-achievers, or a class or group of people whose parents wanted them to be overachievers. So, all I remember is, everybody wanting to go to Williams, Amherst, Hobart, or some jazzy little school like that. So, my curiosity is about what's happened to all those people that went to those places. . . . I'm not sure they ended up being anything other than they would've been than if they went to [Newark State]."

And finally, of course, not going to college at all, especially for boys, and especially for Jewish boys, was the lowest of the low.

Bernard Parness: "Since I didn't finish school my father didn't have anything to do with me, because in those days if you didn't finish college you're a nobody. My sister went to [a private women's college], and my brother went to [a private co-ed college]. I was the black sheep of the family."

But in introducing the point that not going to college was more of a status problem for boys in general, and Jewish boys in particular, we return to questions of difference lurking within the tracks. I have already discussed the relationship of the tracks to class and race/ethnicity. Now we must consider gender.

Gender Tracks

College prep and commercial/secretarial were the official tracks at Weequahic High School. There was, however, another, much less official, tracking system at Weequahic based on gender: we may say that there was a boy track and a girl track. This being the prefeminist fifties, issues of gender discrimination were if anything even more invisible than class, and the school seemed—at least to the unraised consciousnesses of the time—relatively gender-egalitarian. The teachers seemed about fifty-fifty male-female, possibly more female than male. Boys and girls were all together in the same institution and the same classes. They seemed equally represented in the clubs and committees and

Table 11. Tracks by Gender ($N = 292$)

College prep (known $N = 220$)
  Boys, 121 (55%)
  Girls, 99 (45%)
Commercial/secretarial track (known $N = 70$)
  Boys, 18 (26%)
  Girls, 52 (74%)
Both tracks (known $N = 2$)
  Girls, 2 (100%)

---

offices.[11] Many girls, like many boys, were very good students. Relations between boys and girls were largely friendly. Everything conspired (as the French like to say) to make it seem as if both sexes were proceeding in the same way toward the same future. But in the mid-fifties that was most definitely not true.

The first indication of this difference is the differential representation of girls and boys within the official tracks (table 11). It is worth remembering here that the overall sex ratio of the class was 48 percent boys, 52 percent girls. Looking at boys and girls on the tracks, then, we see how much they are skewed by gender. Boys were overrepresented on the college prep track, while girls were overrepresented on the commercial/secretarial track. The skewed numbers in turn index a deeper set of cultural ideas about gender.

The Boy Track

All boys were geared toward eventual work/careers, although the question of when and what kind obviously varied by class. Marriage and family were ultimately part of the future, but they were secondary. Girls, on the other hand, were destined for marriage; work was a secondary add-on, or a fallback, if necessary. This simple, and seemingly commonsensical, inversion of the relationship and valuation between work/career, on the one hand, and marriage, on the other, was the bottom-line difference between the boy track and the girl track in the fifties.

There were, of course, class, race, and ethnic differences within the gender tracks. On the one hand, as the imbalance between Jewish boys and other boys on the college prep track suggests, there were higher expectations for Jewish boys to go to college and lower expectations for non-Jewish boys. This does not mean that non-Jewish boys were not on the boy track, since they were still geared primarily toward working, making a good living, and successfully performing the role of breadwinner. But the expectations for them were clearly lower.

There were also class differences among the Jewish boys themselves. Thus although Jewish boys went to college at higher rates than other boys, and than all girls, and although I said earlier that Jewish rates of going to college seemed to "override class," nonetheless if one looks at and listens to class differences among Jewish boys, one can still see class at work. For one thing, high-capital Jewish boys went "away," many to "top schools," and poorer Jewish boys went to lower-status local colleges. The latter also usually involved continuing to live at home and/or working throughout the college years, making college for low-capital boys a continuation of the social and economic burdens of high school. As one classmate said, going to Rutgers Newark was just "more Weequahic."

We can also hear differences in terms of the ways college was integrated into the class fabric and class aspirations of the high- and low-capital families. Here class emerges as subtle differences of habitus and discourse. For high-capital boys, the expectation that they would go to college, and to a good college if possible, was so taken for granted that it hardly needed to be discussed:

> *Barry Harrison:* "My parents . . . simply assumed that I would go to college and go to a quality school."
>
> *Arthur Epstein:* "We were all gonna go to college, we were all in the top whatever [rank] in the class, we were all gonna go to university, we were all gonna be doctors, lawyers, or Indian chiefs. Y'know, that was our success track, there's no doubt about it. My folks didn't push me, but there was a certain unstated expectation, there's no question about that."

In many lower-capital Jewish families, on the other hand, the parental backing for college and for success through education was often much more explicit and, as it were, urgent:

> *Michael Feldman:* [Michael came from a poor family and also had very bad relations with his father.] "When I got out of high school, I wasn't

prepared for college, and I think my father died at that time, not that that would have mattered because he wasn't involved. But I knew I had to go to college. I was supposed to. Now, my mother was not very well educated. I think she went to the third or fourth grade, but she always talked about getting an education."

Jerome Kriegsfeld: [Jerome's father was a factory foreman.] "My father instilled the fact of go to college, make something of yourself, don't become like me. . . . It's a driving force, he was wasting his life. . . . He was an immigrant. There is an expectation, go to college, make yourself, don't wind up like me."

One could say that among high-capital families, the "value on education" had moved into the status of doxa, of unspoken, taken-for-granted assumptions, while among the poorer families it was still part of conscious, and almost desperate, strategies for escaping poverty and moving up the class ladder.

I have emphasized briefly here the variations within and inflections on the boy track, by ethnicity (with the strong advantage of Jewishness in that time and place), race (although whiteness alone, without Jewishness, would not make much difference for the Class of '58), and class (insofar as the non-Jewish boys, both white and African American, were mostly working class, and insofar as one could tease out class differences even among the Jewish boys). Yet in the long run all boys were on some version of the boy track. Although there were and are different ways of enacting this track, in the high school years the first cut was along the axis of whether one was bound for college or not. Most boys at Weequahic were. The girls were a different story.

The Girl Track

The "girl track" was almost entirely about marriage and motherhood. There was a strong ideal in the 1950s of marrying well and not having to work at all. There was also a realistic sense that many, even most, girls might "have to" work (there was virtually no idea that girls might actually want to have jobs and/or careers), but this was always supposed to be a secondary aspect of being a wife. It was seen as supplementing the husband's income if that was necessary to support the family, or it provided a fallback if for some highly unfortunate reason—non-marriage, disability, divorce, death—a husband was not in the picture supporting the family.

Like the boy track, the girl track was inflected by differences of class, race, and ethnicity. As with the boys, non-Jewish girls, both white and African American, were mostly not encouraged to go to college. But here the parallel with the Jewish-inflected boy track at Weequahic breaks down. Most Jewish boys, even at the working-class level, were encouraged to go to college, but the same was not true of the girls, and most working-class Jewish girls did not in fact go to college. Even more striking, a significant number of middle-class girls, almost entirely Jewish, also wound up not going. Finally, although many girls did go to college, they were encouraged to do so for very different reasons than those used for the boys. Let us explore some of these points in more detail.

We start with the working-class girls, whether Black, Jewish, or other white/ethnic, who for the most part received no encouragement to go to college.

> *Anna Granger* [African American]: "I don't remember that anyone ever said you should go to college, girls were either secretaries or nurses or cashiers or they got married."
>
> *Lynda Beck* [Jewish]: "In my family it was not encouraged that girls go to college. . . . It was expected that everyone got married or went out to work, secretary, that was the big thing. What were the choices we had?"
>
> *Mary Lou Papa* [Italian American]: "After high school, I announced to my father that I wanted to go to college, and he didn't agree with that at all. He said, what do you mean college, you get married and have a family."

In many cases, the parents did not even have to weigh in; many girls had already internalized the marriage ideal; it trickled down from the wider culture and was experienced as peer pressure from girlfriends or simply as a strong personal desire that pushed everything else out of the picture. The following statements are once again from working-class women of various race/ethnic backgrounds:

> *Lois Goldman:* "I was engaged, and somebody told me that [if I went to college] I had to pay back my scholarship if I didn't graduate . . . and in those days that [presumably the engagement] was a little bit more

important. I put my life aside—and I was happy, so. I'm not saying that I was really unhappy about the decision because I wasn't." [12]

Connie Cavallo: "I got married right after high school, maybe [one of the] one-third of the class that got married after high school. I was like, just turned nineteen. And I really got married, I thought, you know, he was so sweet and gentle. It was such a wonderful switch from my crazy upbringing. My parents just fought all the time. And he was just everything that I would want. I wanted so much to be a wife and mother. That's all I wanted."

Rona Klugman: "I guess after high school I was afraid to go away to school because I didn't want to be apart from [my boyfriend]. . . . So I started out at [Local U], had some flexibility, [but] then I got pregnant, got married to Bob, and I had, if I can remember this, when Nancy was born, one year [to go until] I finished."

But the story of never starting college or dropping out in the name of love and marriage was not entirely a working-class story. The following stories come from daughters of business/professional- or middle-class parents:

Linda Kirschner: "My senior year I was going out with Toby Lerner's cousin Nick Harrison from Hillside, and after I graduated we got engaged. And I really think I did that to serve two purposes. Number one was that I really wanted to get engaged; you know, everybody was getting engaged and I wanted to do that."

Rosalie Kurz: "When I was fifteen [I got involved] with [the guy she married]. I was a sophomore and from then on that was it. I still did well in school, I was in the college prep class, but when it came down to the end, he got accepted to medical school, he was going to [top-ranked Midwest U], and I wanted to get married, and I didn't see anything else but that."

Not all girls were discouraged from going to college, whether by parents or by internalized cultural girl-goals. However, going to college was never meant to undermine the ultimate girl track ideal of marriage and family first, career second (or never). Any alternative desires were quickly shut down:

Roberta Cohen: "I had said something to my father at one point about medical school, or something. And he told me after college I was on my own. . . . And if [my mother] had been a stronger person she would have encouraged me to do more."

Naomi Osowitt: "I wanted to be a ballet dancer, actually. That was my true love. And my father would say, 'You'll only wind up in the chorus. You'll never be a dancer.' "

Joan Bartash: "It was some time when we were seniors and I applied to one school. I knew I wanted to be a phys ed teacher. And at the same time I tried out for [a well-known show-dance company]. I wanted to be [in that company]. I made the [dance company] audition [but there was a lot of resistance]. It was all, 'nice Jewish girls don't do something like this.' And there was pressure from [her boyfriend], you know, 'if you do this I won't be able to see you.' And I just didn't have the guts to say, 'too bad. I'm doing it.' So I went to [college]. I went to [Local State and took a teaching degree]."

Later Joan had another opportunity for an unusual career. In this case she essentially shut herself down in the name of the girl track, which she called "the mold."

"By the end of my junior year [in college] I had won two gold medals in track and field. And here was another situation—the Olympic coach approached my parents and said, 'You know, she would be good on the team.' At that time there had been no Jewish people representing track and field except for [X]. So it was like, should I, shouldn't I, should I, shouldn't I. And [instead] I got married. It was like the mold won over. . . . And it was hard to know at the time. It would just seem to be so much pressure, get married, have children, get married, have children. And here I was already finishing college and everybody else that I knew was married and having babies."

In most cases, as in Joan's, the alternative nonstandard female career was shut down specifically in favor of teaching.

Lisa Goldberg: "My father was adamant about my becoming a teacher. . . . I remember when I was transferring I said, I think I'd like to go into business. And [my father] kept saying, well, what do you want to do? I was like, I don't know, but I think I want to be in business. He said, well, tell me what you're going to do, are you gonna get a job as a sales-lady in Saks, you going to work Thursday nights and Saturdays and get two weeks off vacation? I said no, I said there must be something more I could do! He said, right, tell me what it is and I'll pay for your education. So I didn't know what it was, so I went and became a teacher."

Arlene Cohen: "The question was, did I have to be a teacher? The answer was, yeah, you have a choice, you're a teacher or a nurse! So I guess it was a teacher, and all the decisions were out of my hands. It was never a question in my family, could you go into [the family] business, because, you know, women were not allowed."

The virtual fetishization of teaching as the only career for an educated woman was surely a function of its compatibility with the hegemony of wifehood/motherhood on the girl track. Thus, as with marriage itself, some girls "spontaneously" chose teaching without parental pressure, or spontaneously fell back into it after some other choice came to appear unrealistic:

Charlotte Fried: "I wanted to get out of New Jersey. No college guidance whatsoever, and this limitation of not spending a lot of money. So I decided—my father said I had to have a [implicitly female] career—that I had to go to school so I could have some kind of a career. So I decided I was going to be a speech therapist. Which, I have to tell you, I can't stand to do the same thing twice, was the most unlikely thing for me. . . . So I only applied to schools that had that program . . . I was a good kid. I did what they said and I went to [Away State U]. . . . And I took my teaching credits so that I could have a profession, make my father happy."

Harriet Perlstein: "And we had two choices: you were either a nurse or a teacher. I wanted to be an artist. I wanted to be a commercial artist. My uncle was a commercial artist. So the choice I made was art education. I put the two together."

But many girls could not picture themselves in those traditional female careers. At the same time no alternative pictures were available, and the girls were left with a kind of void of purpose, of agency:

Helena Wildstein: "I went to [Away State U] initially . . . I hated it. It was the worst place in the world for me. . . . But you know why I went, Sherry? . . . The only thing I knew I had to do was get out of the area, because all my parents wanted me to do was go to teacher's college, and I wasn't going to do that. . . . [But she didn't know what else she wanted, so] I dropped out."

Rose Stone: [SBO: Did your parents not encourage you to go to college?] "Oh, no, they did encourage me. I just didn't want to go. I don't know what I wanted to do, and I just didn't do it. . . . My parents were disappointed I didn't go. They really, really wanted me to go because . . . they wanted me to be a teacher. And it was not something I could ever see myself doing. And I guess that's the thing—I mean I couldn't see myself being a teacher and I didn't know what else I wanted to do and it just seemed like ridiculous to go on to school when I really didn't feel like it."

The girls in effect, then, marked time until the void could be filled by marriage and motherhood:

> *Toby Lerner:* "There was nothing, at that time, I didn't want to teach, there was nothing I wanted to be, so what was the point in going [to college]? I didn't want to *be* anything." [And so she got engaged.]
>
> *Lynn Marans:* "I started [going to college] but I didn't . . . I didn't know what I wanted to do. Then I went to [a technical training school], and I became a lab technician. And I was a lab technician for about a year and a half, and I found it just too depressing. So I went into secretarial work, and I became a private secretary to an advertising manager. And I worked there until I got married."

I should hasten to add that I am not disparaging getting married and having kids (I have done/am doing both myself). Nor am I disparaging women who make homemaking a choice, an act of agency. What I am criticizing is an era and a culture that nipped such choice and agency in the bud, that saw careers as antithetical to marriage and children, and set marriage and children as the default position even for women who had other skills, talents, and proclivities.

High school was enormously constraining. If there was ever, in Weber's phrase, an iron cage of social and cultural expectations, social and cultural categories, rules and regulations, all with seemingly dire consequences for their violation, this was it. Social violations made one an outcast, with the attendant feelings of shame, rage, inadequacy, and isolation that that involved. Academic violations—so it was threatened —ruined one's chances for future education, good jobs, and a happy and stable family life. Gender and sexual violations did the same. While success, social and academic, was imagined as a matter of individual effort and striving, and failure as a matter of individual failing, nonetheless the sense of a large and powerful system that stood over and above the individual and that did not tolerate much violation—what one student kept calling "the mold"—was felt equally deeply, though less articulately. Thus, even the kids in the most successful positions felt the weight of the system and hid their "secret selves."

If high school in general has this quality, high school in the fifties had it in spades. The era was famously conformist. The occasional infractions of some members of the Class of '58—girls putting on lipstick in the bathroom, students smoking cigarettes, dating "wrong" others, or cutting school once or twice—were taken so seriously as to be seen as virtually disrupting the order of the universe. One academically successful girl had all her grades lowered for one cycle of one semester for cutting school one day, destroying her chance to graduate in the top ten of the class. One academically successful boy was caught making prank phone calls and was barred forever from the Honor Society. Both of the students did go on to good schools and good careers, but were genuinely crushed at the time of the punishment.

High school ends, but some of its tracking and controlling mechanisms live on, for many people and for a long time to come. Yet the period right after high school is a kind of critical period in terms of whether people live out the destinies that were laid down for them or take their lives in different directions. Again this is probably true for kids moving into the post–high school period in general. But it was especially true for the Class of '58, insofar as their early post–high school lives intersected with the social movements of the Fifties (the Beats and so forth) and the Sixties (the counterculture, radical politics). These were times of enormous social and political ferment, in which other possible lives were at least imagined, and sometimes lived. In chapter 8 we will look at the Class of '58 in the decade or so after graduation.

Project Journal 7: New Jersey

[I was having trouble locating minority classmates or, if located, getting them to agree to talk to me. I decided to make a major effort on this trip to locate minority classmates and convince them to meet with me for an interview. I had some luck, but it took a lot of help. All the people mentioned below are African American classmates unless otherwise noted.]

7/9/92 I reached Joan Smith but we couldn't find a time. She said she's willing to participate. [Despite more calls we were never able to schedule anything.] I reached Maxine Jordan and she said she's not interested in participating.

7/11/92 Interview with Pearl Jones. . . . We went out and talked at a picnic table on a deck overlooking a nice backyard. . . . She was pleasant but reserved, a bit suspicious of signing the waiver, and after reading it saved it to the end of the interview, but then did sign it. She said, people can twist your words and use your name. In the end I said I hope you can trust me on this, and she said, well I didn't say anything that could cause a problem anyway.

7/13/92 David Wheeler* agreed to go around with me looking for some of the African American guys. . . . We located both Al Walker's house and Norman Huntley's house [I couldn't even find addresses for them], but nobody was home. David's wife had teased him before he left this morning, saying that here we were, him a genius and me a college professor, going off to look for people on a Monday who are probably off at work. It's true, and we all thought it was funny, and of course she was right. (She said she wants credit for helping with this project, dealing with all my phone calls, lending me David, etc.). . . . It's so great, I've got myself another wonderful helper. What would I do without all the generous people in this project?

...... [Later that evening.] First we got to the Huntley house. His father and a friend were home, but Norman had just stepped out. I never would have gotten in the door without David, but he's so nice and nonthreatening, and they invited us in.

David was great—he not only got me in the door, but really mediated the conversations—both the father and Norman would never I think have talked to me. I don't think the father would have invited me in without David, and then I wouldn't have been there when Norman got back. Further David was able to make all the right kinds of small talk to get the conversations going, both with the grownups and with Norman. I told him he was great for doing all this, and he said with a smile, well that's my job, isn't it?

...... We then went off to look for Al Walker. David had a great observation on what he and I must look like as we go up to people's houses—Jehovah's Witnesses. Perfect!

...... [Al's wife said Al might have gone to the Melody Bar, so we went there to look for him. One of the guys we met in the bar, Darius] did some long rap on how women shouldn't be president—they're too emotional, too illogical. For example, his wife wanted a fur coat, and he was in a bar one night and some guy walked in with a hot fur coat, really beautiful, worth about $300 dollars, but he had to get rid of it, and Darius offered him $50 and he took it. So he brought this coat home to his wife and it fit her absolutely perfectly, and she looked great, but then she says, does he have a different color? Similarly, his wife wanted an IBM Selectric typewriter and again Darius was able to get his hands on a hot typewriter, just what she wanted, and he brought it home, and she said, where's the manual? This was all told in a sort of hilarious way—they were funny stories, and Darius milked the humor in them all the way. What was funny was his incredulity—ANOTHER COLOR, THE MANUAL, can you BELIEVE it??? ...... Needless to say, none of this would have happened without David. I might have gone to the house, but the wife probably wouldn't have mentioned the Melody Bar [where we found Al eventually,] and anyway I almost certainly wouldn't have gone there alone, or if I did it's absolutely sure I wouldn't have sat there alone and waited for him to come in. In both cases the connection would literally not have been made.

What the Class of '58 Made

chapter 8

Counterlives

The book so far has been concerned with the ways in which the young Class of '58 was "constructed," how individuals were formed as diverse social and cultural subjects, as a result of their diverse backgrounds, but as a result too of the environment—the neighborhood, the high school, the historical moment—they shared. At this point the weight of the discussion tips over. The class has graduated from high school and is about to go out into the world. From here on out, the book is concerned with what the Class of '58 "made"—the lives they made for themselves and their families, and the ways in which those lives, individually and collectively, reproduced or transformed the larger culture.[1]

I think it is fair to say that graduation from high school represents a major moment of liberation for most young people, and it was certainly true for the Class of '58 of Weequahic High School. There would, of course, be new constraints, new limits. Yet to the extent that the Class left the hothouse high school social environment; to the extent that most, if not all, classmates actually left home as well; and to the extent that many left Newark and even New Jersey, there was a sense of breaking out into whole new worlds.

Many classmates went on to become "successful" in standard cultural ways—gaining college and higher degrees, marrying "well,"[2] having successful careers, making a lot of money. Most of the rest of the book will be devoted to them. In the present chapter, however, I am interested in a slightly different set of people, individuals who got caught up in various "alternative" movements, specifically the Beat movement of the fifties and the radical/counterculture movement of the sixties.[3] As a result, their lives took relatively unusual courses. They were not necessarily "unsuccessful" (although that often depends on who is making the judgment), but they in one way or another got off the success track relative to their own backgrounds, and relative to the expectations, high or low, that were placed on them.

"Getting off the success track" has several different meanings. On the one hand, it can mean embarking on a relatively self-destructive life course. For high-capital boys, who were expected to at least complete college, this would include not starting or finishing college. For girls, it would include early pregnancy. And for any student, it would include getting involved in drugs and/or other criminal activities leading to criminal convictions, messed-up careers, and in some cases even death. There are a number of cases like these in the Class of '58 but, since this book is not meant to be an exposé, I will not discuss them except in passing.[4]

But falling off the track can also go in the opposite direction. It can mean getting off the track of personal/individual ("selfish") success and pursuing a career that is to some degree in the service of others. It often means sacrificing the opportunity to make the kind of money one might have made if one had stayed on the standard success track. The set of people whom I will discuss in some detail in this chapter are thus for the most part people whose connection with the Beat and/or Sixties subcultures visibly moved them toward broader social concerns and broader political issues.

This chapter has three general themes. One is historical and concerns the ways in which the social movements the Class of '58 encountered in the decade or so after graduation changed some people's lives. For most of them, it sparked a desire to challenge injustices and/or help the unfortunate. These considerations link up with the second theme, which is to provide a broader overview of social activism and altruism among a group that might otherwise seem highly materialistic and self-involved. And finally, I begin here an argument that will carry through the remainder of this book, namely, that people's individual fates are best seen as tied to larger social movements.

Earlier Causes

Social activism in the Class of '58 did not start with the oppositional movements that emerged in the fifties and sixties. Before we get to that period we must briefly consider forms of activism rooted in earlier ideologies. One of these would be left-wing, communist or socialist, activities, and at least some of the Weequahic teachers seem to have been involved in these quite deeply. As far as I can tell, however, very few parents of the Class of '58 and no members of the Class itself went into left-wing politics in any significant way. One of the effects of this fact is that the politics of "class" will (ironically?) play very little role in the present chapter.

On the other hand, I must mention here the C58 classmates who went into "the helping professions"—the teachers, nurses, and social workers who give enormously of themselves to the young, the sick and dying, the poor, the traumatized. Commitments to these kinds of work also grew out of earlier ideologies of service, especially but not exclusively for women, and especially for a community that saw itself, as the Weequahic community generally did, as liberal. By the same token, many members of the Class do volunteer work for their specific religious, ethnic, or racial communities. At the very least many people dig into their pockets, sometimes quite deeply, to make financial contributions to agencies and causes that help others.

Finally, also growing out of earlier movements and ideologies, a significant number of (white/Jewish) members of the Class of '58 are actively involved in antiracism causes. I need to spend a bit of time on this group, as it is probably the single largest area of activism in the Class of '58. Some individuals have folded antiracism work into a larger career. Barry Rothenberg has done some civil rights work as a lawyer. Joel Goss, a doctor, was the coordinator of an outreach program at a hospital in an African American neighborhood. The outreach program mounted various free medical screening programs to serve the community, and also invited groups from the local schools to visit the hospital and contemplate careers in medicine and related fields. Janet Altman is a teacher who also works on race issues through a community group:

> JA: "When we lived near Seton Hall, the neighborhood we lived in was integrated. And we formed a neighborhood association. And we were involved in that for a while, and checking into steering, and all that sort of thing."
>
> SBO: "What is that?"
>
> JA: "Steering means when the realtor steers one couple away from the neighborhood, or one to the neighborhood. And, the feeling is, that in a lot of communities, it does go on, and it has gone on for years. Sometimes apparently the word is that there are separate books. And other times, it's more of, oh, I don't think you'd really like that neighborhood."

In addition to people who do antiracism work as part of their jobs or as part of a wider range of activist commitments (Janet is also active in her synagogue on behalf of various Jewish causes), there are two people in the Class of '58 who have devoted their entire lives and careers to working on behalf of minority communities. The first is Evelyn Eisenberg, who coordinates programs in New York City that give Black and Hispanic communities more involvement in their neighborhoods and more control over their schools. She has raised an enormous amount of money for community development; by her own accounting, more than thirty million dollars in twenty years. Her work also involves speaking to community groups and rallying them to involvement in community projects: "My work is always generated from my poetry. I stand up in front of four thousand people, and read a poem, and tell them, rebuild this neighborhood. . . . It's like a love affair. . . . I created a vegetable farm that produced eight thousand pounds of vegetables and restored an entire neighborhood." She particularly focuses on developing neighborhood schools: "I [also] created twenty-six small schools near the northwest corner of the Bronx; small mini-schools." At the time of the interview she had moved on to do the same thing in other communities, and then had been invited to head up a more official, city-based (but privately funded) project of the same sort in another city.

Lana Epstein has devoted her life to African American issues in a different way. Lana has a PhD in sociology and teaches a sociology course at the New School. But her full-time job for years has been as an administrator of a foundation that supports various African American cultural projects. She coordinated one of its subprograms, which supports research projects, conferences, and educational programs on African American history and culture. Most recently she has been heading a program that provides support to minority young people who are the first in their families to go to college. She has discovered a knack for fund-raising and has raised hundreds of thousands of dollars for this program. She is also currently writing a biography of a leading African American intellectual and activist.

White (as well as Black) involvement in antiracism activities began before the fifties and continues into the present. But the fifties also saw the birth of a new social and cultural movement, which came to be called the Beatnik, or Beat, movement and which offered other appeals for those dissatisfied with the status quo.[5]

The Other Fifties

The Class of '58 was in high school in the heart of the Fifties. There was very little in the way of collective forms of social and political critique within the school at the time. Both the political group(s?) and cultural/artistic groups were tiny and not very influential. Even what came to known as the "youth culture" of the Fifties was only just beginning to come into being. Elvis Presley hit the scene in 1956, rock 'n' roll music was beginning to take off, various movie stars evoked teenage crushes, and so on. Yet—one might say, amazingly—virtually none of this shows up in the interviews with the Class of '58 about the high school years, and it certainly does not form part of anyone's life story about their fates after high school. In reflecting on this odd absence in the interview material, it seems to me not that these features of fifties popular culture were unimportant, but that they were important in a very deep and doxic (inaccessible to conscious reflection) sort of way— for example, in the way in which almost everyone of that generation today responds quite viscerally to doo-wop music. The popular culture of "the Fifties" shaped what Raymond Williams has called "structures of feeling," but it is not apparently seen, at least in retrospect, as having provided life-changing ideas and practices that actually affected people's lives in long-term ways.

What do show up in the interviews are specific historical movements that combined alternative cultural forms with critical social messages and provided models for incorporating both into the real practices of life. There was first the Beat, or bohemian, subculture, concretely in nearby Greenwich Village and more abstractly in music (folk, political), in poetry and literature, and in intentionally shocking critical ideas about bourgeois American society. The Class of '58 graduated from high school just as the Beat subculture was becoming a significant alternative to staying on the track of a middle-class, individual achievement-oriented career.

A note about Greenwich Village. Much as it might have sounded this way so far, Weequahic was not a desert island. New York City was a short bus ride away. The 107 bus from the Weequahic neighborhood (immortalized by Philip Roth in *Portnoy's Complaint* by having Alexander Portnoy masturbate under his coat on that very bus) went to the Port Authority Bus Terminal, and still does, in less than an hour. Parents took kids to various New York museums, the Bronx Zoo, Radio City Music Hall. Older kids took the bus into the city on their own, some for relatively benign independent adventures—wandering about midtown or ice skating in Rockefeller Center—and some for slightly more daring excursions. Gary Goldman telescoped what must have been several years of Greenwich Village adventures: "You went to New York when you were twelve or thirteen years old and you went to [Greenwich] Village and drank beer and you did shit and you didn't realize it but you became street wise."[6]

Indeed, the Village had many attractions for these relatively unsophisticated kids from Newark. The Beat scene had been developing since the early fifties. Allen Ginsberg and his friends mainly hung out around Columbia University. They took drugs; they engaged in intense personal and (straight, homo-, and bi-) sexual relationships; but most of all—from the point of view of this becoming a "movement" —they wrote about it.[7] Moreover, they linked their alternative personal/sexual lifestyles with a larger critique of American society and culture. As Ginsberg wrote in one of his early poems, "Paterson":

> What do I want in these rooms papered with visions of money?
> How much can I make by cutting my hair? . . .
> What war [do] I enter, and for what a prize! the dead prick of
>   commonplace obsession . . . (1949; reprinted in Ginsberg 1996:12–13)

Or as he exploded later in "Howl":

> I saw the best minds of my generation . . .
> who were burned alive in their innocent flannel suits on Madison
>   Avenue amid blasts of leaden verse & the tanked-up clatter of the
>   iron regiments of fashion & the nitroglycerine shrieks of fairies of
>   advertising & the mustard gas of sinister intelligent editors, or were
>   run down by the drunken taxicabs of Absolute Reality, . . .
> What sphinx of cement and aluminum bashed open their skulls and
>   ate up their brains and imagination?

Moloch! Solitude! Filth! Ugliness! Ashcans and unobtainable
dollars! . . .
Moloch whose mind is pure machinery! Moloch whose blood is
running money! . . .
Moloch in whom I sit lonely! Moloch in whom I dream Angels! Crazy
in Moloch! Cocksucker in Moloch! Lacklove and manless in
Moloch! . . . (1955–56; reprinted in Ginsberg 1996:49–56)

These and hundreds of other poems and songs linking personal passion
and social critique, written and composed by many individuals who
were beginning to gravitate to New York City to join the scene,[8] were
read and sung in bars and cafés (including the West End Bar, still going
strong, near Columbia) that became known for providing platforms for
this kind of work. But it was Greenwich Village in particular, with its
cafés and street life open to all comers, that offered the Beat culture as
lifestyle—alternative sexualities; radical (in many senses) poetry, folk
music, and political song; cross-racial relationships; bohemian dress
styles; and other forbidden things—to a much wider range of young
people.

The Village was very much part of some classmates' fantasies. One
of the women of the class talked of admiring an older, rather bohemian neighbor when she was growing up: "I used to say, when people
asked me what I was going to do when I grew up, I used to say, 'I'm
gonna live in Greenwich Village.' Because she showed me a [bohemian]
world that I had no way of knowing existed." She later did drop out of
college and lived an alternative lifestyle in the Village for a while. She
described herself with some retrospective humor as having had "hair
down to my waist, living in a walkup in the Village," and being fixed up
with some clean-cut corporate type for a date that was a total disaster.

Another woman attended NYU and talked of the ways in which the
Village, and its cultural and political atmosphere, opened up her attitudes:

"It was really very interesting in the mid-sixties. . . . It was the Beat generation. I think of Ginsberg and Kerouac. . . . The reading, the theaters,
the literature. . . . I became very interested in reading avant-garde exis-
tential literature, poetry, art. And I think that probably prepared me to
become more involved with the women's movement, and to be very sym-

pathetic toward the Black movement. Reading all Black [writers]. I remember reading every Black author around."

Other classmates were attracted to the Village for its tolerance, even
its celebration, of homosexuality. As sophomores at a local university,
several C58 graduates, along with other college friends, began to make
frequent trips to some of the gay bars of the Village. Another man, in
an adjacent class, began frequenting Village gay bars in drag and other
costumes.

But for two men in the Class, the Beats' radical questioning of bourgeois American society literally changed their lives. The first was David
Schwartz, the son of a business/professional family:

"I started hanging out more in New York and not really with the kids in
the Class in the later part of my high school years. I never was really a
great student. I got into [Local U] and that's where I went. I wasn't a great
student there. I went through my junior year and at that time my parents
got a divorce and they moved [away] and I dropped out of college and
got an apartment in New York and started experimenting with smoking
pot and meeting other people. . . . There were a lot of people who were
pot smokers. They weren't hippies at the time, they were Beatniks."

Since David did not finish college, his father would not support him.

"I got a job working at an over-the-counter brokerage firm. I lied about
my age, because you had to be twenty-one to take the exam. I did well and
worked in there for a couple of years and at night I experimented with
taking drugs, mostly pot and maybe a little LSD. Then I left for Europe.
I was going to make a decision and go back to school because I had all
this guilt from when I was little. If you didn't finish college you'd be a
nobody. I didn't want to be a nobody, on the other hand I really didn't
want to go back to school. I was off on another tangent. I took a freighter
to Barcelona."

David read serious literature for the first time in his life on the ship:
"On the freighter they had this dormitory style room and they put me
in with this old Arab who was going back to Morocco. I was smoking
my joints on the boat and reading Dostoyevsky. I was going through
this intellectual period." Later he went to Ibiza, still doing drugs and

still reading some of the literature that defined the antibourgeois sub-culture(s) of the era:

> "I had been reading all these books—Philip Wylie, *Generation of Vipers*. I had this friend Marvin from [another town in] New Jersey, who was also an intellectual at that time and he was turning me on to all these books, and J. D. Salinger was one of my [heroes]."

David stayed in Europe for several years, married a European woman, and had a child. On the one hand, he continued to do (mostly soft) drugs, and these were a central part of his life for many years. On the other hand, he also began collecting certain kinds of antiques that he eventually brought back to the States with him. When he returned to the United States he worked in various countercultural enterprises, but also learned that the antiques he had been collecting had become extremely valuable. He still lives an off-beat life, on the one hand part of the bourgeoisie because of his antiques collection, on the other hand in many ways—I cannot think of a better word—untamed. From the point of view of his parents and/or some of the more conventional members of the Class of '58, he probably appears quite downwardly mobile. Yet that would assume that he was on the same track as everyone else, and simply did badly at it. Another explanation would be that, starting with his involvement with the Beats, he actually took a different track.

The other story goes in the opposite direction. Arthur Levine, the son of a poor and disrupted family, was in and out of trouble during high school. But in the later years of high school he started picking up on the cultural changes that were going on:

> "I actually started reading when I was about seventeen, and I remember exactly to this day what made me read, you know. Mel Jacobson [his real name] came up to me on the lawn outside of school one day, and we were seniors, and he said, 'You gotta read this book.' I said, 'What.' He hands me this book, it was [Jack Kerouac's] *On the Road*. And he said, 'You read this.' He said, 'You're really going to love this.' And I really never read anything other than newspapers. . . . So man, I read that and from that moment on I just [began to change]. . . . I wasn't consciously saying in my mind, 'hey, you're changing,' but I could see these things happening, and my attitudes around race and stuff started to change."

Artie started going in to the Village, and his politics became more and more critical:

> "When I was around sixteen or seventeen, I started going into Greenwich Village periodically with . . . some of the guys and, and then, you know, I would go [on my own]. And I started looking around and I started seeing a life that was different. It was like something happening out there. And I started seeing people standing on street corners with anti-A-bomb things, and I started going, 'wow, this is the right way.'"

He began to get more and more angry about a wide range of injustices, which he saw as all part and parcel of a single corrupt system:

> "I remember when [Governor] Faubus wouldn't let the [Black] kids in school in fucking Arkansas . . . and that's when I was beginning to get really angry about that stuff. And I remember I guess it was either our junior or senior year in high school, when they sent that fucking Sputnik up in the air. And suddenly America went apeshit, 'we're behind.' And I'm going like, Who cares? Who the fuck cares if we're behind them? We live the way we live, let them live the way they live. . . . That Sputnik thing I think is the beginning of me starting to realize. I mean, what the flying fuck is going on here? People are starving, people are hungry, people need housing, people are being treated unfairly, and what we're worried about [is] who's going to have satellites and bombs and stuff. . . . And I never really saw it as being distinct. I never really saw that there was a distinction between this Cold War mentality and racism. It all looked like it was part of a package, but that package just kept getting more and more full."

Artie did not go to college immediately after high school. He joined the army, and later he bounced around the country quite a bit, trying to figure out what to do with his life. Eventually, however, he did pull himself together and go to college. Moreover, he went on from there to law school and became an independent criminal lawyer. I quote below from a write-up about him in a local legal newsletter. First he defends his single-person practice: "I mean, the concept of being a wage slave, of dressing up for someone, of not being able to listen to Thelonious Monk in your office—why, it just doesn't appeal to me." Then he defends the practice of criminal law, on political grounds: "I gravitated to criminal law. I hate the government; I hate jails; I hate cops. I mean, individually I like them. I just hate the concept. To me the government is the largest criminal agency in the world. I have been around those who've been arrested, and I like the class of arrestees a lot better than the class of arrestors." He is just as passionately critical of the system today, and just as passionately committed to the practice of criminal law, as ever.

David's and Artie's stories illustrate three of the central themes of this chapter. The first is the major change in direction that some people's lives took in the years immediately after high school. David Schwartz, son of an upper-middle-class family, drops out of college, hooks up with the Beats, and embarks on an unorthodox lifestyle that continues to this day. Artie Levine, son of a family poor in many kinds of capital, does not immediately go to college, joins the army, moves restlessly back and forth across the country, yet eventually winds up with a law degree.

The second point to note is how these personal life changes essentially hitchhiked on the emergence of Beat culture in the 1950s. Both boys were clearly moved by the critique of mainstream culture as at least meaningless and at most hideously destructive. Yet they took this critique in two quite different directions. David started from a high-capital background but essentially dropped out of the rat race, seeking both meaning and livelihood anywhere but in the standard places.[9] Artie had all the makings of failure, but instead climbed back on the track enough to get a law degree.

And finally, Artie's case illustrates one important tendency of classmates whose lives were changed by the Beat culture and later the counterculture: he took up a life of political commitment and social service. As I said earlier, there were two ways to get off the track—downward, to self-destruction, or upward, to something transcending the quest for personal success. It is the latter that I focus on in this chapter. Now let us look at some cases from the sixties.

The Sixties

When did "the Sixties" begin? And what constitutes "the Sixties?" The Sixties included very importantly the Civil Rights movement and (later) the feminist movement, but these will be taken up in later chapters. For present purposes at least three other dimensions of that extraordinary era had life-changing impacts on members of the Class of '58: the Kennedy-era idealism that took most tangible form in the Peace Corps; the Vietnam War and the antiwar movement; and the counterculture of sex, drugs, rock 'n' roll, and alternative lifestyles of every sort.[10]

Let me start with the "sex, drugs, and rock 'n' roll." Like David Schwartz (who hooked up with the Beat subculture), Warren Ades came from a difficult family situation, and like David, he dropped out of college and moved to New York. The sixties drug scene was beginning to develop a kind of exuberant public culture that had not existed in the fifties, including psychedelic art and clothing, Eastern religious art and artifacts, specialized drug paraphernalia, and the like. "Head shops" and similar stores began to open up in both the West Village and the Lower East Side. Warren, whose college background had been in art, worked his way into this scene and wound up running "the first psychedelic boutique of any repute, Abracadabra, in New York City" — a tiny piece of the sixties revolution.

Of more lasting impact, no doubt, were the various social programs started in the Kennedy era. One of these was Head Start, a preschool learning program for poor kids. One woman in the Class of '58, a teacher, said she was inspired by Kennedy and went to work teaching in Head Start. And then there was the Peace Corps, probably the most visible of the social programs begun during the Kennedy administration. The Peace Corps, like Head Start, was designed with the dual purpose of doing good in the world and engaging American young people in the practice of social service.

Two men in the Class of '58 joined the Peace Corps in that era. Howard Isaacson got married shortly after college; he and his wife served in the Peace Corps in Africa. For both it was clearly a powerful experience, but it did not radically change the course of their lives. For Raymond Boyle it was a different story. Ray was from a lower-middle-class family that had suffered some disruption. He was not on the college prep track in high school and he did not know what he wanted to do when he graduated. He went to work for a while, and did not have any particular focus. But:

"Kennedy was trying to get people to go into the Peace Corps and Sargent Shriver, etc., and my mother suggested to me I try the Peace Corps, and

I said, 'They'll never admit me. I'm, you know, I'm just Joe . . .' and I *am*, in many ways, just Joe Average. I don't have a natural language ability. . . . And I went down, and I took the test, and I heard nothing from them. And of course, then Kennedy got assassinated, and the day Kennedy got assassinated, I had gone for my army physical . . . and I always figured that's why I was never drafted, because my physical was on the day he was shot and I always figured that there was so much chaos . . .'"

Eventually (and there are a lot of experiences in that "eventually," but I do not have the space to recount them here) he did go into the Peace Corps and was sent to the Philippines:

"It was the turning point of my life. That was the turning point of my life. They taught us how to teach English as a second language, and I lived with a family for two years. . . . I developed a friendship with Filipinos, and I think I learned so much about the people. It was funny because of course the Vietnam War was going on and occasionally I had to go to Manila on business, and I usually stayed with a Filipino family. And I remember there was a big rally in front of the American embassy and I had said I wanted to go and see what was happening. They didn't want me to go because I might get hurt, the Filipino family. And they would ask my opinion and I would start telling them something about the war, what I believed, and they said, 'Well, you're not an American, you're Peace Corps.'"[11]

His work in the Peace Corps in turn laid the groundwork for what he went on to do with the rest of his life: "After two years, I started the theater program at the college [in the Philippines]. The time of the Peace Corps is for two years, and after two years I decided that I had really found a shtick in life. I was meant to be a teacher. And so I opted for another year."

When Ray eventually came home, he translated the Peace Corps experience very directly into his life. He went to college (while working), finished up, and became a high school English teacher, and by all evidence a very dedicated one. Further, as he had founded a theater program at a school in the Philippines, so he also directs the drama program at the high school at which he teaches.

The Vietnam War was lurking in the background of Ray's story, but let me now turn to it more directly. Relatively speaking, the war as such had little direct impact on the Class of '58, perhaps because the

Weequahic community as a whole was relatively high capital. Forty-seven men (about one-third of the men) of the Class of '58 served in the military (including the reserves) during the Vietnam era, but only three, as far as I know, actually went to Vietnam: a doctor who served in a hospital; and two men who saw combat, one a helicopter pilot and the other a supply officer whose company was caught in several major battles.[12] No member of the Class, again as far as I know, was killed in the war.

The supply officer, Allen Schwartz, remained in the army after the war and eventually rose to the rank of lieutenant colonel. While he and I would no doubt disagree about the morality of the war, nonetheless I was struck by certain things in his interview that went against some of the stereotypes of masculinity in general, and military masculinity in particular. By the time of the interview he had retired from the military and was working in the private sector. He talked about the difference between the two, and especially about the ways the army fosters a less self-serving attitude in its members:

> [From the field notes] He said there's a big difference between corporations and the army. Corporations are cold, cut-throat, bottom-line operations. They feel no responsibility for the people who work for them. If there's a turndown, they simply fire people and you're out. In the army there's more concern about those under you, and he at any rate was always the kind of officer for whom the well-being of his men was his primary concern. He never was that focused on advancing his own career.

No doubt the military fosters a lot of bad attitudes as well. But Allen's experience as an officer established a kind of nurturing attitude about those below him in a hierarchy, and he has carried this attitude into his work in a corporation. Indeed, his experience in the military has fostered a critical attitude toward corporations for their heartless, bottom-line orientation.

If few members of the Class of '58 had direct contact with the Vietnam War, many more had contact with its reverberations back in the United States: the antiwar movement and the larger waves of radical activism that it set off. Quite a few classmates talked about having been involved in some antiwar activism. One man said: "I certainly was involved in the anti-Vietnam movement, and we were part of the Washington demonstration. It happened to be a very proud time of my life, as a matter of fact. . . . I wasn't going to this war, and that's all there was to it." This individual has continued to work on behalf of other liberal causes throughout his life; at one point he also called himself a "tree hugger."

For another classmate there was a more complex interaction between his experiences in the Sixties and the course his life eventually took. Jerry Eisenberg was in medical school when the demonstrations against the war and the government war machine became more frequent and more violent. He had started a residency in ObGyn, and he already felt inclined toward a more public service–oriented career:

> "After one year of residency I decided that I was interested in public health because I had helped to start a teen pregnancy clinic [he said later that 'none of the other residents were really interested in working with me on that'] and I took a year out to do a Masters in Public Health from Berkeley, California."

The year was 1968–69, a time of incredible public and political turmoil, especially in the Bay Area:

> "[It was the year of] the Free Speech Movement, Eldridge Cleaver, Patty Hearst, that was when Governor Reagan called out the troops to surround the campus and there was tear gas. Here I was, just a little older than the rest and I was in the School of Public Health. . . . I mean the [other] people were dressed in suits and ties [but] we in the Public Health Department were supposed to be . . . a little different. . . . That was a great year, I learned a lot in terms of public health and decided that when I went back that's what I would do."

When I asked Jerry about making this choice, as against the possibility of making a great deal more money in private medical practice as so many of the Class of '58 have done, he said:

> "I had always enjoyed the individual patient relationship [in private practice]. But working in public health there is a lot more that you get out of what you do. You can make many more dramatic things . . . happen for people who can't make things happen for themselves and you can do it on a larger scale. . . . It's more important to be recognized and remembered than to get rich . . . to leave some key programs behind."

While Raymond Boyle's Peace Corps experience translated directly into his subsequent career as a teacher, Jerry's story evinces a looser connection between the experiences of the sixties and the shape of his career later. Indeed, it seems fair to say that for many, the sixties did not so much put them on a particular track as rupture the seeming inevitability of the old tracks. For another example of this, let us look at one of the women of the Class, Leni Grossman. I will tell many more stories of transformations of women's lives in chapter 11. But Leni's story is specifically tied to the impact of the sixties; it is also, like many others in this context, about her life shifting in a more altruistic direction.

In the late 1960s Leni was married to a businessman and had two small children. She and her husband both had countercultural leanings, some of which dated back to the fifties. They both smoked marijuana from time to time and were also involved in the folk music scene. In the course of going to folk concerts, Leni connected with one particular European folk group and, despite having no experience, became the manager for their U.S. tours. The group would stay at her house, and there would be endless parties. While it was exciting, it also made her both more dissatisfied with her humdrum domestic life and more eager to get back to the kinds of things she had loved to do before she got married and had kids.

Eventually she got divorced. She had relationships with various dancers and artists. She traveled to Europe, very much a part of the sixties life. At the same time she still had her own dreams. She went back to school and got a Master's degree in Dance Education. She taught dance at various local schools and also did choreography for various community theaters. Eventually, as with the other people in this chapter, her work moved her into a career of public service. She discovered a calling for working with the elderly:

> "My cousin Linda . . . got a doctorate in gerontology and the creative arts. And in 1985 she was trying to establish a senior adult life story theater company that would be based on life stories. . . . So I said, 'That sounds like a wonderful idea, I'll help.' And then she got a call from an adult day care center in Jersey City. They were looking for somebody to do exercise aerobics with [the patients] in this day care center. And she explains it to me and I said, 'I never worked with adults. I don't know if I can do this. Well, I'll try.' . . . So I walked into this day care center and there are people in all kinds of different conditions. And once I started I knew that these were the people that I was going to work with for the rest of my life."

The opportunities for this kind of work continued to expand, and Leni herself began to have ideas for developing it further. She created a program called "At Home with the Arts" that involved visiting and working with Alzheimer patients in their homes. Her work has been written up in several local papers; in her own way, and in one small corner of the world, she has clearly made an enormous difference.

The Class of '58 graduated into a world in which various critiques of the dominant culture were taking shape and gathering steam—the Beats in the fifties and the counterculture/radical politics movement(s) in the sixties. Both subcultures criticized the political and economic violence of the dominant culture as well as the conventionality and repressiveness of bourgeois lifestyles of the times. Some members of the Class of '58 were caught up in one or the other of these movements, and their lives changed as a result.

The majority of the Class of '58 went off to pursue the American dream—money, upward mobility, a high-capital lifestyle. We shall see that many of them succeeded dramatically. Yet there is one important way in which their stories are continuous with those in this chapter: Their futures were tied up not only with their own personal strivings, but also with social movements on the larger stage of American history.

Project Journal 8: New Jersey

1/4/93 Somebody told me last night that Maxine Barish* just died. Funeral was yesterday. Cancer, they thought. Gosh, the person whose glasses I borrowed to find out whether I needed glasses in 6th grade.

1/6/93 Interview this morning with Barbara Saltman at the Millburn diner. . . . She has lupus, an autoimmune disease, and is really very ill, but keeps up the same spirit—talkative, funny, ironic. Unfortunately disaster struck—the batteries were dead and I've got no tape. How unprofessional can you get? I'm really miserable about it because she was a great talker—funny, dirty, and I kept thinking the whole time how great a transcript it was going to make.

...... [A wealthy woman] tried to cancel again but I wasn't here. She called back later and said she felt better so it was OK for me to come. [My cousin] said, don't let her jerk you around. That's exactly what she was doing.

1/8/93 [Classmate] Felix Decter is [classmate] Ezra Ertag's lawyer. Ezra said Felix is the best, the best. The amount of continuing interconnection between Weequahic people is astonishing. Julian Williams [another lawyer] told many such stories.

...... [Interview with a middle-class Jewish man.] His Italian friend Ed who owns the building he lives in dropped in. He was saying that Ed used to live downstairs in the building and you would never know how much money Ed has. He's a millionaire, but the outside of the house was very plain, even "low class," but inside it was all marble and fountains. He said, now the Jews would have all the fountains on the outside.

...... [Interview with middle-class woman.] I must say first she gave me the absolutely worst directions I have ever heard in my life. When I tried to write them down on the phone I knew I'd get lost, and I really did. I thought I'd joke with her that she got the award for worst directions of the project, but when I apologized for being a half hour late and said I got terribly lost, she said oh I thought I gave you such good directions. So I didn't make my little joke.

...... [Interview with a successful businessman who was rather hostile about this project.] He twice volunteered that "some people feel" — though it seemed clear that this agreed with his own feelings — that this project is kind of stupid — "What's the point of it all?" — all that money being spent, why didn't they put it into AIDS research, etc. A little passive aggression coming through. . . . It all feeds into my rather negative feelings about the project at the moment. I think I'm at that point in the whole thing where one is pissed off with everybody, the point where you have to get out of the village and take a field break.

chapter 9

Money

With this chapter I begin tracing the lives of the majority of the Class of '58 from graduation to the mid-1990s, with at least four questions in mind. The first is simply, What has become of these people? I pursue this question through various American interpretations of the idea of "success." The Class of '58 was on the whole "very successful," or certainly thinks of itself as such. How true is this? In what ways? For whom? And how did it come about?[1]

Second, I return to the question of "class." In part I ask the standard questions of the effects of class background: How and to what degree did "high-capital" or "low-capital" backgrounds inflect the later degrees of "success" of members of the Class of '58, specifically in terms of upward social mobility? At the same time, there is just so much one can do analytically with class as a social operator detached from the ethnic, racial, and gender categories with which it is always deeply intertwined, at least in the United States. Thus, as with several of the earlier chapters, this and the following chapters are organized not in the first instance by class divisions, but by ethnic, racial, and gender categories. Class questions are for the most part raised within, rather that outside of, those categories.

Third, I continue to look at the lives of the Class of '58 in relation to larger historical formations. Specifically, I continue an argument, begun in the last chapter, that what happened to the Class of '58 from graduation to the present can be understood only in terms of larger political transformations in the second half of the twentieth century. The relevant transformations have been brought about by what are now called "identity" movements: the upgrading of the Jews (which actually began earlier and was briefly discussed in relation to C58 parents moving to the Weequahic section in the first place); the Civil Rights and Black Power movements that rewrote both the social respect and capital opportunities for African Americans; and the women's/ feminist movement that both rewrote opportunities for women and reconfigured the relationships between the genders. This argument further motivates the organization of the following chapters in terms of ethnicity, race, and gender, now seen specifically as political "identities."

Finally, the adult lives of the Class of '58 span the entire second half of the twentieth century, moving across a period that recent scholarship sees as split by a major break: that between "classic" and "late" capitalism at the political-economic level, that between "modern" and "postmodern" culture at the cultural level. In this and the following chapters, I will be looking at changing patterns of class, lifestyle, and identity among the Class of '58 with the question of this theoretically massive social transformation (to be explained in more detail later) in mind.

Success

Success is, to dust off an old concept, a key symbol in American culture.[2] When I called people during the course of this project to say that I was doing a study of "what happened to the Class of '58," many immediately jumped to the question of "success" — who has become very wealthy or famous, who has gone downhill.

> *Carole Ades:* [from the field notes] And then of course [she mentioned] Bobby Jacobson, who has become internationally famous as an architect. In other words she was prompted, even before I raised my theme (as she called it) of "success," to start running off this litany of success stories.
>
> *Helen Tannenbaum:* [from the field notes] She launched on a whole big speech about how *incredibly successful* our whole class has been. How people have made incredible amounts of money and *really succeeded.* She said, now you [me, SBO], of course you're *successful* in your field, but you're not really *successful* in terms of, like you don't own a movie studio or something, I mean *monetarily.*

Like all key symbols, "success" has highly variable meanings in American culture. Probably the dominant meaning is, as Helen just said, making a lot of money. Other kinds of achievements (themselves rarely unrelated to financial success) may be significant as well: educational honors, professional fame (as in the case of Bobby Jacobson), and probably power (though the Class of '58 did not produce anybody obviously socially or politically powerful). By and large, however, the sentence "He is very successful" can be translated 99 percent of the time, with very little loss of meaning, as "He has made a lot of money."[3] As one woman, the wife of a successful businessman, put it: "Success is if [you are] financially successful. I think that's a component of it. I can't imagine being successful and not having some financial security or the ability to be flexible financially, to do things that you want to do." She added other things but came back again to money: "And success is also an intellectual thing . . . which is a minimum of college educated, and you still have some intellectual pursuits in your life. . . . And it's also having comfort financially. That's gotta be part of success, being able to pursue a lifestyle."

One can also signal gradations of monetary success:

Esther Cohen: "You know, my world has basically been people who have been *fairly successful,* . . . and I've gone from the world here of *successful people,* to the people in the Berkshires in their second homes who are *even more successful.*"

George Heller: [from the field notes] [His ex-wife's] father has been *very successful* and her brother is *very, very successful.*

Edie Bennett: "[My father] was *very, very successful,* we had a beautiful house, and everything was terrific."

Barbara Bauer: "She's *extremely successful.* I mean, she owns two apartments in New York and a house with an indoor swimming pool and she's off [the charts] financially, *very successful.*"

Of course, it is possible to talk about making money outright as well:

Marilyn Julian: "What you're going to find, I would say, probably a disproportionate number of people, of males, in our class became doctors, lawyers, architects, accountants, professionals, went that route to their success. I think that *they've done well, and they are either, anywhere from comfortable to wealthy.*"

Mark Ginsburg: [from the field notes] He is now semi-retired from the practice, which he said [in tones of some amazement] made a lot of money, repeat, a LOT of money.

Sydney Burakof: "What you call successful . . . I met my goal at maybe like thirty-five. I was a homeowner in two places. *I never thought I'd earn so much.*"

Morris Lerner: "I've been *successful financially* outside [his job], in real estate and stuff like that and stock market, which were hobbies. I have

190 New Jersey Dreaming

a very nice home in the hills, and I have a nice new Lexus coupe and I really can't ask for anything more."

Mostly, however, people do not like to talk about money as such; it is largely couched in the language of success and all its gradations. There are, at least for the Class of '58, at least two kinds of narratives contained within this "success = money" usage: that people started with a lot of capital in the first place and were therefore "tracked for success," or that people did not start with much but "beat the odds" and became successful (see also Harrington and Boardman 1997). The first is a deterministic narrative, although as we shall see it is modified to depend on "hard work" and what people make of their initial advantage; the second is the great American story of upward mobility. "Beating the odds" can, of course, go in the other direction too: people with a lot of capital who went downhill. This too is an important American story; its examples become moral lessons and/or personal nightmares that themselves underwrite the value of the dominant narrative.

Upward Mobility

With respect to questions of upward mobility, "class" appears as a ladder, with the ideology being that anyone with the right kinds of determination can climb it. It is a peculiarity of the Class of '58, however, that for virtually every group in this study, there had been a prior exclusion from the ladder of mobility on the basis of race, ethnicity, gender, or various combinations of the three. Thus I will ask not only how well or how poorly individuals have done, but how the groups to which they belong gained access to the ladder of mobility and the benefits of capitalism in the first place. One cannot be upwardly mobile if one is not even on the ladder.

In the American version of class—unlike, say, the English version— people are expected to at least try to beat the odds, to try to climb up out of lower-class origins and other disadvantages and do well. A disadvantaged background is, in this view, supposed to spur one to higher striving, not hold one back. In addition, within the local context of this study, the Weequahic education was thought to be so good that it was considered by at least some students to be a major resource in helping one beat the odds. Here is a text that combines all of these points. I was explaining to Marty Ziering that one of the assumptions of this study is that a lower-class background holds people back more than we notice. Marty disagreed quite strongly:

> MZ: "There are many doctors, lawyers, professional people that I guarantee in your study you will find in your final results that there are many top-notch people from other sections of town. [Marty and I went to Chancellor Avenue elementary school together, in the "best" part of the Weequahic neighborhood. His remarks about class are in terms of this geography.] Because I think that these people have the same IQs if not higher than people from our part of town. And there are very successful people [from] there."
>
> SBO: "I think they had the same IQs. I just wonder how much it affected them to start out with relatively less [capital], they had to work more [hours outside of school]."
>
> MZ: "I think they knew how to come out of the trenches. I mean I played football at Weequahic High School with many of the kids from the other part of town. And I know in at least a few instances where these people have done very well. And it just inspired them to go on. Of course, they came from a tougher area of the city than people who came from Chancellor Avenue but yet they went to Weequahic High School and got a solid education in high school, went on to college, and went on to get professional degrees."

In fact both of us were right, although for the Class of '58 at least, Marty was more right than I was. There is indeed a lot of upward mobility, and I will get to that in a moment, but let us look first at class drag. Reading Table 12 (the sample includes all race/ethnic groups and women as well as men; $N = 200$),[4] one can see in the bracketed percentages that, although many people with working class parents moved up the social ladder, they were less likely (50%) to move up into the PMC than people with middle class parents, who in turn were less likely (60%) to move up than children of the PMC itself (70%). Likewise, 9% of working class kids remained in the working class, while only .01% of children of higher class parents "fell" into the working class. Thus there was a certain tendency for differences of original privilege or lack of it to persist.

Moreover, I suspect that the class drag was somewhat stronger than it appears in the table. For example, all C58 professionals (doctors, law-

Table 12. Class Origins of the Class of '58 in Relation to Present Class Position (*N* = 200) [The percentages in brackets sum vertically; those without brackets sum horizontally.]

	Parents of the Class of '58		
The Class of '58	BPC[a] parents	Middle-class parents	Working-class parents
PMC[b] (known *N* = 120)	38 (32%) [70%]	54 (45%) [60%]	28 (23%) [50%]
Middle class (known *N* = 74)	16 (22%) [30%]	35 (47%) [39%]	23 (31%) [11%]
Working class (known *N* = 6)	—	1 (17%) [1%]	5 (83%) [9%]

[a] Business/professional class
[b] Professional/managerial class

yers, professors, etc.) are classed as Professional Middle Class or PMC. But some have pursued very high powered careers with great success, while others have remained at more modest levels of their fields. In reflecting on this more invisible form of difference (and degree of "mobility"), I found myself thinking back to Table 4 (page 40), showing the strong correlation between class background and family disruption while growing up. Most C58 informants who came from disrupted families felt a strong linkage between that background and their later levels of success. While I do not have the kind of fine grained data that would allow me to establish this correlation "objectively," if the informants are right there is a kind of invisible class drag that would in many cases make the difference between a high powered and a low powered version of the same career, or between being at the high end or the low end of the same class category.

But if there was both visible and invisible class drag in the system, there has obviously been an enormous amount of upward mobility. Reading the table in terms of the collective histories of each class (the unbracketed percentages), more than two-thirds of the present PMC have moved up from lower positions, a significant number of those—23 percent—even jumping two levels, from working class to PMC. And almost a third of the middle class is comprised of individuals who have risen up from the working class. From this point of view, then, the Class of '58 was indeed "very successful." More than half the known members of the class (105 people, or 53 percent) rose up above their origins. Moreover, the PMC has expanded enormously while the working class has almost entirely disappeared as a result of upward mobility.

The Success of Jewish Men

It may seem odd to look at Jewish men apart from Jewish women. Both of course benefited from the successful struggle against anti-Semitism and the general rise in status of Jews as a group since the Second World War. In addition, as wives of successful Jewish men, Jewish women have benefited materially and socially from their husbands' successes. Because of the feminist movement, however, women's (including Jewish women's) lives have followed a very different trajectory from men's in the decades since graduation. I thus discuss the men and their successes here and save the women for chapter 11.

There is no doubt that the Jewish men of the Class of '58 achieved a high level of success in terms defined by the "boy track" and as manifested by a high level of prestigious degrees, lucrative careers, or both.

For comparative purposes, I will start with the general rates of going to college. Since Weequahic was known as a good academic school, there was a widespread assumption that virtually all the students went on to college. As Ira Stern said, "We got the education, we had good standards, I think. I mean, 90 percent of the kids went to college, the best [colleges] in the country." In fact, only 63 percent of the class completed college.[5] But if this is lower than classmates' assumptions, it is still extremely high. As late as 1993, only 20.3 percent of the population in the United States finished college (*New York Times*, November 28, 1993, p. 30). In the 1950s the rate was about 13 percent (Barber 1957:394).[6]

But now let us break out men in general, and Jewish men in particular. Here the rates are dramatically higher (table 13). I have to note first that the numbers for Jewish men are much more reliable than for "all other men" because the latter category includes a large number of un-

Table 13. College Degree or Beyond by Race/Ethnicity and Gender
($N = 229$)

	Yes	No
Jewish men (known $N = 98$)	79 (81%)	19 (19%)
Jewish women (known $N = 103$)	76 (74%)	27 (26%)
All other men (known $N = 13$)	8 (62%)	5 (38%)
All other women (known $N = 15$)	5 (33%)	10 (67%)

Note: Averaging both genders, the rate of Jewish classmates completing college degrees is 78%; the rate of all others is 48%. This table includes people who went back and finished later.

knowns. That being said, the Jewish men went to college at a rate of 81 percent of knowns, compared with the other men, who went at a rate of 62 percent.

Not only did Jewish men get college degrees at much higher rates than all other groups, they also got advanced degrees at much higher rates. Of the eight non-Jewish men who got Bachelor's degrees, only two, or 25 percent, went on for higher degrees (one MA, one JD). Among the seventy-nine Jewish men with Bachelor's degrees, fifty-seven, or 72 percent, went on for higher degrees (seventeen Master's [including MA, MBA, MFA, MS], fifteen MDs, fourteen JDs, seven PhDs [including one MD/PhD], two DDSs, one CPA, and one DVM [Doctor of Veterinary Medicine]).

Again the numbers for the non-Jewish groups are very low, and there are many more unknowns among these groups. As a guess, however, I would say that if we had better numbers, they would only get worse, as the more successful people tend to be more visible; they tend to be known to other classmates, to come to reunions, and to come to the notice of the anthropologist. On the other hand, the Jewish numbers are reasonably reliable, and the rates of Jewish men both completing college and taking advanced degrees are very high by almost any measure.

But success cannot be entirely equated with degrees and/or with the practice of degreed professions. Some classmates are financially successful in business, with or without degrees. Some have top or high managerial positions in businesses, and others have top or high administrative positions in universities, social service agencies, and other parts of the service sector. If we look at the present professional/managerial class among Jewish men of the Class of '58, we find forty-seven men in the professions (accountants, architects, dentists, doctors, engineers, a journalist, a judge, lawyers, pharmacists, a school principal, professors, and a psychologist)—certainly the largest group; but there are also fourteen owners of businesses; seven men in top or high management positions in businesses or corporations; and four top or high administrators in the service sector.

Not every Jewish man in the Class of '58 is "successful" in terms of college degrees and/or money and/or prestige, but many more are than are not. The PMC outweighs the middle class among these men by a ratio of more than two to one. Of 103 Jewish men for whom I have reliable information, 72, or 70 percent, have made it into the professional/managerial class; 30, or 29 percent, are in the middle class, and only one is in the working class.[7]

All of this is perhaps not very surprising in the late twentieth century. It is fairly common knowledge that Jewish men tend to have high levels of education, to be highly represented in the professions, and to make a lot of money. This pattern has become so well established in recent decades that it seems unremarkable. Moreover, it is assumed that this kind of pattern is in some way related to distinctive characteristics of Jewish culture: the high value on education and hard work, the cultivation of high levels of ambition, perhaps something akin to greed in relation to money and material things.

There is a lot of debate in the ethnicity literature about the validity of these kinds of cultural explanations. One side attributes Jews' success to Jewish "culture"; the other side (see especially Steinberg 1981) claims that the Jews simply arrived in America with better skills (literacy, numeracy, mercantile skills, urban savvy, etc.) than most other immigrant groups, who were largely rural and unskilled. The Jews were thus able to move up the economic ladder faster; the "value on education" and the actual high rates of education followed rather than preceded this financial success.

Rather than favoring one explanation over the other, I see the two as being in a dialectical relationship. Cultural values can be very potent, and I think it is rather disingenuous to deny that there is something we can think of by now as Jewish culture that plays some role in the numbers we have just seen. But this needs to be qualified in two ways.

First, "Jewish culture" is not necessarily evenly distributed among all Jewish people, and even Jewish people who do share in its values may not have the resources to fully enact its supposedly success-producing characteristics. In other words, we must still ask questions about class differences among the Jews, and I will do that later in this chapter (gender too, for that matter, but not until chapter 11).

The second qualification involves insisting that "Jewish culture" itself has a history, that it has not existed in the same form since time immemorial, and that its emergence in the particular form that has made it a potent force in Jewish success in the late-twentieth-century United States needs to be understood as having been produced through real practices in real time and history. Steinberg may be right about the ways in which the early Jewish immigrants got their first leg up, although I have my doubts about his argument; somehow the vast numbers of illiterate and unsophisticated Jews from *shtetl*s (villages) seem to have disappeared from his account. Even if he is correct, however, this would not negate the cultural argument in the way he seems to think; rather it would be the beginning of a historical and dialectical account of how Jewish financial success through hard work and hard bargaining led to desires for social respectability and acceptance, especially through education. In other words, education in the modern sense might not have started as a primary value for Jewish immigrants, but one could trace the logic of its historical emergence.

I will not pursue this argument further, as I do not have the expertise on Jewish immigrant history to do so. But there is a third set of issues concerning the relationship between "Jewish culture" and "Jewish success." This argument would view the Jewish case as paralleling the cases of African Americans and women. Let us assume that the Jewish people had all the necessary cultural capital we have been discussing, however it may have evolved, yet were blocked from large-scale success in the first half of the century (and in some areas, until much later) by anti-Semitism. The increasing level of Jewish success since the 1950s and the degree to which anti-Semitism has by now greatly (though not entirely) receded have, I think, hidden its earlier prevalence and power, and have made the Jewish case seem different (more "cultural," less political) than the case of, say, African Americans. Of course there are important differences, but there is also an important parallel that I want to bring out. I will return to these points at the end of the chapter, after we examine how the success of Jewish men in the Class of '58 was itself inflected by class.

High-Capital Jewish Boys

The boys in the top of the table, the sons of high-capital families, were considered by many to have been "tracked for success." This had to do with both the financial capital and cultural capital of the families from which they started.

> *Joyce Feldman:* "On the whole, the boys with whom we graduated did very well, but they were programmed to succeed and achieve."
>
> *David Kurz:* [from the field notes] He remembers Chancellor [elementary school] kids [later in high school] as being on the success track, in two senses. On the one hand, they knew how to study, they worked hard, and they knew what they had to do. But on the other hand, if they didn't study, they knew the angles, what they needed to do to succeed anyway.[8]

A very large majority of the sons of high-capital families went on to high-capital careers and lifestyles, often greatly exceeding the level of wealth in their families of origin. Seventy-nine percent of the sons of business/professional families have themselves remained within the highest class level (what I am now calling the professional/managerial class). Joseph Stern expressed the sense of tremendous opportunity he felt starting out in life: "There was nothing closed to us. We had the opportunity to be lawyers, accountants, doctors, whatever we wanted to be. There were no limitations in any way, shape or form!"

Compared with the bootstrappers from whom we will hear below, there are fewer stories of "how I got to be where I am" among the men in this category. If they were "tracked for success," that tracking in a literal sense started back in high school. As Larry Wexlin said, "We were the college prep group, we took the college prep curriculum, you know what I'm saying? . . . That was our success track." Two other men talked about planning to be doctors while they were still in high school:

> *Arthur Fromkin:* "I had wanted to become a doctor, actually my father has always wanted me to be a doctor but they never pressured me into that. . . . I had on my own wanted to be a doctor."

Robert Schimmer: "I knew what I had to do, my life was planned. I decided
    I was going to be a doctor . . . so I knew I had to get [a degree] so I went
    to college. . . . [SBO: You felt you wanted to be a doctor even when you
    were in high school?] My father talked me into being a doctor, and,
    'what do you want to be an engineer for?' and that kind of thing. So I
    didn't really know what to be, what did I know, I was a kid. . . . My life
    was planned."

These last two comments are interesting not only because we can see
that the tracking toward a high-status career started early, but because
they both show a kind of confusion about the locus of agency in the
matter, which is, of course, how it feels when one is "tracked."

Being tracked for success by virtue of family capital did not mean
that one did not have to work hard to achieve that success. Most of the
successful people we are looking at would quite rightly resist the idea
that they just slid into their high-capital careers on the basis of their
family capital. Remember David Kurz saying the kids on the success
track "knew the angles" but also that they worked hard in high school.
Allan Rothstein was also seen as tracked for success, but as I wrote in
my field notes about both him and myself, "whatever wild things we
did we always kept our grades on track." Once people got into college,
the necessity for hard work became even stronger. As Larry Kuperman,
another high-capital classmate, said,

"Well, okay, so the problem was, Sherry, that I had been such a success
    in high school, that college was a problem. . . . The funny thing was, aca-
    demically, as hard as you worked, there were guys who either didn't work
    as hard—you never knew but they were stars. I struggled my freshman
    year, I probably had a B+ average my freshman year, you know there were
    guys with straight As and it was incredible."

And the need for hard work did not disappear when one finally moved
into one's profession:

[from the field notes] I asked Bernie how lawyers got so rich. Did they get
    a percentage or something? And he said no, it's simply that they charge
    so much per hour (I can't remember whether he said his firm charges
    $250 or $350 per hour), and they do put in a lot of hours. They work hard.

Yet, finally, not all men from high-capital families were "successful" in the sense of ending up in lucrative and/or high-prestige careers.

They did not necessarily self-destruct entirely (although some came close), but they were relatively downwardly mobile in comparison with their parents and siblings.

Downward Mobility

It is possible to read downward mobility in several ways. From the point of view of the dominant culture, it is essentially a matter of failure, or at least of falling far short of one's potential. In the cases we will look at here, "the dominant culture" comes in many voices. Sometimes it is in one's head: remember the woman I quoted early in the book who felt like a failure even when, to all appearances, she had done very well. In other cases one may feel that one has not "fallen," but rather has made a principled choice. Yet the dominant culture—in the voice of a spouse or a former high school classmate—will communicate that judgment of inadequacy or failure. Indeed, downward mobility is one of those areas around which high school memories and mind-sets may return to haunt the present in a particularly unpleasant way.

Marvin Schwarz was headed for law school but decided to seek a PhD in an academic field instead. From his point of view this was a principled choice based on better values:

"And the goal was to be a doctor or a lawyer. . . . But the framework is changed. I hadn't read Nietzsche at the time. I hadn't read a lot of people at the time. I hadn't studied anything. . . . When I gave up the idea of going to law school . . . and [decided] to choose going into academia . . . those are very different kinds of things. . . . And they meant that I was turning more and more I think away from the kind of values that informed my youth [which he had described earlier as being very competitive for grades] and defining myself [in terms of] new values."

Moreover, he chose to pursue a low-key and relatively unambitious approach to his academic career. His wife took him to task for his lack of ambition:

"One of the disagreements that my first wife and I had is that I didn't have what she thought of as goals, cause I kept saying that my life was what I was living at the time, and that was enough. I didn't have a goal of having to publish X number of books or articles or be a dean or president of a college or something like that, and that that wasn't terribly important. What was really important was enjoying what I was doing."

In a similar case, Michael Goldberg shifted his career choice in college from medicine to academic science. Moreover, he too chose a relatively low-key career.

"It seemed that most of the people [in his field] that were so dedicated to being successful put in a tremendous amount of time. For them it wasn't a hardship because most of them didn't have a great deal of other interests. I mean they did but still they didn't mind working ten or twelve hours a day, six or seven days a week. I didn't want to do it."

Michael in fact did a fair amount of public service in the 1970s and 1980s, working as a scientific consultant with a group in his community on environmental issues and helping to achieve several major victories. Yet the voice of judgment about downward mobility was overheard at a reunion, as one of the doctors in the Class of '58 came up to Michael and said, "Professor of [science]? What's the matter, you couldn't get into medical school?"

And finally there was Ira Rabstein, from whom much was expected. Ira came from a high-capital family, he was a class officer, and was something of a jock (in the double sense of being both a leader in athletics and a somewhat macho-style guy). Yet Ira never finished college and wound up as a waiter in a restaurant. Ira himself tries hard to count his blessings and hold the "failure" interpretation at bay. Yet his former stardom in high school makes him a particular target of judgment. Thus his "fall" was remarked on, with somewhat guilty pleasure, by Joel Lipman, a self-described former nerd. Joel rose from a very poor background and an unhappy high school experience to become the president of a successful corporation.

SBO: "Did you feel excluded in high school or . . ."
JL: "I felt that I was ugly, I was poor, I was fat. I recently met a gentleman waiting tables at [X restaurant]. And I always looked up to [him], he was in my homeroom for four years, and an athletic star and he was good looking and he had a convertible and the girls were always flocking around him and he was Mister Wonderful and the Most Likely to Succeed in This World."
SBO: (Laughs.)

JL: "And I met him and he was waiting tables! And, oh, 'Hi Joel,' he said. 'Well, what are you doing with your life?' And I said, 'I work up here in the X corporation.' I didn't want to flaunt anything. And he says, 'What do you mean?' So I said, 'Well, I'm the president of the corporation.' And he said 'Holy shit! You're the president!' . . . And it just, you know, struck a chord, and I remembered — not that I hold any grudges — but I didn't have any money [in high school] and I didn't have the social graces and I felt inferior."

Given dominant American values, the "downwardly mobile" are an endless source of fascination: a source of competitive pleasure for some, but also, I think, a source of great anxiety. For people just starting their careers, for people on tenuous incomes and/or in a tenuous economy, for parents worrying about their children's futures;[9] for all these people and more, the downwardly mobile provoke things like nagging from spouses, nasty comments from old classmates, and guilty pleasure from now-successful men who felt like nerds in high school. While I will continue to concentrate on the upwardly mobile and the relatively successful in this book, it is important to reflect on the ways in which images of relative unsuccess, and the anxieties they provoke, help sustain the dominant ideology in which people are measured against yardsticks of money and prestige.

Low-Capital Jewish Boys

We have already seen that Jewish boys went to and finished college at much higher rates than other boys. This is the case not only because virtually all Jewish boys from high-capital families went to college, but also because, overriding class, most Jewish boys from low-capital families went to and finished college, too (though it sometimes took them longer). Breaking the numbers down by class, 74 percent of sons of BPC parents, 81 percent of sons of middle-class parents, and 90 percent of sons of working-class parents completed college. It is interesting to note that the progression of numbers here tends to support one folk theory of class expressed by Marty Ziering earlier: that being at the low end actually drives people harder. Thus, at least among Jewish boys, the lower down on the ladder, the more likely the boy was to go to and complete college.

Once again, I will concentrate largely on success and upward mobility, here specifically on low-capital Jewish boys who got through college by going to local schools that were very cheap, usually living at home, and working their way through school. These, in other words, are the "bootstrapping stories" of the Class of '58, of which there are many. I will tell only a few of them here.

Neal Rosengold came from a poor family; his father was a "socialist" and—according to another classmate—was often out of work. Neal was very aware of the family's poverty: "We truly—well, you know, I don't want to sound deprived, but we lived in a tiny little apartment, my brother and I never had our own beds, we slept in a Castro convertible in the living room. . . . After Weequahic I just couldn't afford to go anywhere else, so I ended up at [Local U]." Neal went on to get a law degree and is today a successful lawyer.

Howard Guttman was one of eleven children, the first in his family to go to college: "My parents didn't have much wealth. They had to work very hard for what they had. I definitely wanted to go beyond that. . . . I basically put myself through college. I paid for most of my expenses." Howard took a degree in accounting, passed his CPA certification, and now co-owns a successful accounting practice.

Jerry Cohen's parents owned a little store. Jerry was the first in his family, on both sides, to go to college.

> "I didn't want to have what my parents and grandparents had, I wanted something better. . . . My parents were only able to pay for the first semester or two, so I played in bands and unloaded freight trains for the Newark Post Office. Made a lot of money, always had plenty of money in my pocket, but I worked my way through. And my grandparents would help me out once in a while, and so would my parents, but I really had to earn it."

Jerry took a Bachelor's and a Master's degree in education, and is now the principal of a middle school in a wealthy town in western New Jersey.

Billy Herman came from a poor and disrupted family and his parents were unable to help or advise him about college. But an uncle helped him fill out applications:

> "I just applied to schools all over the country although I had no money to go to them. It wasn't realistic. But I just knew I had to do something. And

I think I got into virtually no place. I didn't know what I was doing. . . . [But he went to various night and day college programs in the Newark area.] I think I graduated in about six years."

Billy went on to take a PhD in clinical social work and was a practicing social worker for many years.[10]

Arthur Mayers's father died when he was young, and his mother worked as a section manager in a discount store. They had, in his words, very little money when he was growing up. During senior year in high school,

> "the placement office had passed a notice around that Metropolitan Life had wanted some college trainees that would be willing to look at a college training program and work in New York City, so I applied. . . . It turned out to be something I really enjoyed. [Later] Linda and I had gotten married and we moved to [another town in New Jersey]. Traveled to Metropolitan Life in New York City every morning. Went to [Local U] in the evening in Newark, and did that for eight years."

Arthur went on to become the president of a major insurance corporation.

There are quite a few more bootstrapping stories like these in the Class of '58, but let me shift here to a slightly different group. The boys above were all highly motivated from the outset. They went directly to college, pursued their studies consistently until they finished, and in some cases went on for higher degrees. But there were some who did not know what they wanted. They either did not start college or started and dropped out, yet in the end they did go, or went back and finished later, providing even more bootstrapping stories.

For example, Erwin Feinstein came from a family that had started out middle class, but there was a major disruption: his father went out of business and wound up working in a butcher shop. Erwin went to a local college for a while but did not do well and was asked to leave. He took a job as a bank teller at relatively low pay, but eventually felt that he wanted more. He went back to school at night, while still working, and finished various degree programs—a Bachelor's in business administration from Pace, and a certificate in computer studies at NYU.

Bill Fierstein is another good example. Bill's family background, like Erwin's, was problematic. The family was poor in both financial and cultural capital: The parents fought a lot, and they were also immigrants who did not have the slightest idea about how the system worked. He started college but flunked out. He then went into the military, where they tested him, found that he had very high scores, and offered to send him to West Point, which he declined. When he got out of the army, he too enjoyed the counterculture for a while: "The sexual revolution of the sixties was interesting even though I was a little older than most of the kids. I was still getting some of the benefits of it, I guess." He also got a low-level job with a large corporation; both the company and the military paid parts of his tuition, and he went on to complete college while working full time.

On the whole, it is fair to say that the majority of Jewish boys of the Class of '58 did very well. They completed college at high rates and went on to successful careers. Boys who started with high capital mostly went on to surpass their parents. Boys who started with lower capital nonetheless did a lot of bootstrapping, of which they are justifiably proud. Apart from the feel-good effects of this discussion, however, what are the implications of emphasizing these high levels of upward mobility?

Mobility, Agency, and History

To talk about "class" is almost by definition to talk about determinism, constraint. That is why, in a sense, one raises it within the same mantra as race and gender; it is a form of social privilege or disadvantage that propels one forward or holds one back.

We have seen in earlier discussions that class can be very constraining, especially in the crucial early years when the family's class, in the form of various kinds of capital, exerts a strong influence over children's social placement in high school, their academic tracking, and the kinds of steering they get toward various kinds of colleges, or toward none at all. But then the story gets more complex. Even at the level of going to college, people begin to beat the odds. Poor but smart kids get scholarships. Rich but unmotivated kids "fall off the track" and do not go to college at all. After the college years things get even more complex. There is no doubt that people still get pushed around by class forces. But more and more, sometimes by intent and sometimes by accident, usually a mixture of the two, people become agents in ways that at least partially transcend the drag of their class of origin.

The large amount of mobility in the system raises several points. One is that I think it keeps alive, in a kind of perverse way, the hidden sense of class constraint. People may feel that they have risen up in the world, but they also retain a sense of where they came from and the ways in which that background still shapes certain aspects of their lives. A striking number of people quoted the adage to me, "You can take the person out of the class, but you can't take the class out of the person."[11] This hidden lower-class background within the seemingly higher-class person sometimes emerges in emotional student outbursts when I teach a course on class in the United States.

But more important for present purposes, the large amount of mobility raises once again the issue of agency. For the last several decades, Pierre Bourdieu (1978, 1990), Anthony Giddens (1979), Marshall Sahlins (1981), William H. Sewell Jr. (1992), myself (1995, 1996), Laura Ahearn (2001), and others have been developing theories that both take account of major structural constraints (like class) and at the same time recognize the role of real actors—their intentions, desires, fears, dreams; in short, their "agency"—in living within and/or against those constraints, and thus in both reproducing and/or transforming them.

If we dismiss claims of, and practices of, agency, we are left with a kind of class determinism that is both theoretically limited (to say the least) and simply wrong with respect to the data. Moreover, if we look back at the various fourfold tables in this book, we can see that they embody the cultural *recognition* of the necessary intersection of "capital" (the left axis) and some kind of personal agency (the top axis). Their ideological problem, and it is a large one, is that the top/agency dimension is culturally hegemonic, hiding and dominating the axis of capital, or resources. But if I have done my job so far, both sides should be equally clear. An emphasis on self-advancement without a sense of class constraints is not about "agency" as theorists use the concept; it is simply American cultural ideology about the unfettered individual and the payoff of personality, brains, and/or hard work. True agency is locked in a dialectic with capital, enabled or constrained by it, on the one hand, and reproducing or transforming it, on the other.

Thus far this derives from a fairly standard "practice theory" perspective (as articulated by Bourdieu, Giddens, etc., listed above), which resolves the structure versus agency debate by insisting on the dialectical relationship between the two. But there is still something missing: history in several senses. On the one hand, there is a vast array of larger historical processes—the shape and health of the economy at any given moment; the political hue of the federal government under a given administration; the "public culture" of TV, movies, music, and advertising which operates in a complex interplay with the economy and the polity—processes that shape and constrain the ways in which the structure/agency (here class drag/class mobility) dialectic plays itself out over time. Thus I have already contextualized the relative success of the parents of the Class of '58 in terms of the economic prosperity of the 1950s and 1960s, the federal policies (including especially the GI Bill) for boosting up large segments of the working class, and the general sense of optimism that was generated by winning the Second World War and by the federally boosted economic recovery that followed.

But there is another kind of historical process that is essential to an understanding of success: social movements that seek the advancement of particular groups. If the individual efforts ("agency") that produce success must be contextualized within hidden dimensions of capital, they must also be articulated with public, but sometimes forgotten, histories of social movements that created the opportunities to succeed, that created the very possibilities of playing the game of success at all. In the context of the present chapter highlighting a great deal of Jewish upward mobility, it is very important to point to the ways in which the Jewish community in a collective sense historically created conditions in the world that were favorable to the bootstrapping of Jewish individuals.[12]

It is hard to recapture a sense today of the virulence and the extensiveness of anti-Semitism in the first half of the twentieth century (Hollinger 1996). This was progressively broken down through varied collective efforts that can be only briefly sketched here. Unlike the later Civil Rights and women's movements, the breaking down of anti-Semitic barriers was not initially forwarded on a political level. Rather the collective project in its early stages operated primarily at the material and cultural levels. On the material level, there was the "model minority" strategy: put your head down, work hard, make money, enact the Protestant ethic. And in fact the Jews did this very well, such that many C58 parents, as discussed earlier in this book, were already successfully "middle-classing." Moreover, Jewish financial success, which had been recognized before but embedded in Shylock-type stereotypes, was at least partly revalorized through large-scale public philanthropy, like that of the Bamberger/Fulds.

On the cultural level, at least since the 1930s, there was the heavy Jewish presence in the culture industry—everything from the owners of the *New York Times* (Goldman 1991, Mann 1996), to Hollywood producers (Gabler 1988), to composers like Irving Berlin, to the inventors of the Barbie doll (Lieberman 1996, D. A. Segal 1999). Here again there was not a direct assault on the barriers that kept Jews out of many important educational, financial, and political institutions. Rather there was an essentially cultural attempt to blur the difference between Jews and "real" Americans. Jewish producers did not make Jewish movies, they made movies about a kind of undifferentiated "America" and about the power of the "American dream." The Jewish publishers of the *New York Times* certainly did not see themselves as publishing a Jewish newspaper, and in fact equated true news with utter social neutrality. Irving Berlin wrote songs like "White Christmas" and "Easter Parade" that became American classics; he also wrote "God Bless America," which nowadays is virtually replacing "The Star Spangled Banner" as the national anthem. And the Jewish inventors of the Barbie doll, that all-American blonde cheerleader who looks nothing like any Jewish girl I ever knew, were simply trying to find a successful formula for selling millions of toys, which indeed they did.

This was not quite a "social movement" in the contemporary sense. But it was nonetheless a kind of relentless campaign for material success, social respect, and what Karen Brodkin (1999) has called "whiteness"—a kind of merging of Jewishness and Americanness—that Jewish intellectuals, artists, entertainers, and writers pressed on many fronts.[13] The point is nicely captured in an article about Groucho Marx in which the author notes that Groucho would sometimes drop Yiddish words into his (not particularly Jewish) comic routines: "The interpolation of the Yiddish word is, in its comic way, as resonant a moment as the first clarinet slide in 'Rhapsody in Blue'—Jewish, bluish, and American, all at once" (Gopnik 2000:17).

It was this "movement" that was finally, just about the time the Class of '58 was growing up, allowing the Jews not only to succeed financially, but to be seen as legitimate players. It was also just about that time that the move to take on anti-Semitism directly finally took shape. It was in the generation between that of the parents of the Class of '58 and the Class of '58 itself that Jewish intellectuals and artists began to say, in effect, Jewish is cool (West 1990, Kleeblatt 1996, Brodkin 1999). The novels of Saul Bellow and Philip Roth and the films of Woody Allen began to bring Jewishness out of the closet, and to make of it an "identity" in the contemporary sense, that is, something that the group could publicly embrace and politically rally around.

Put in other words, we may think of all this as an early example of a certain kind of identity politics. Jewish parents, and certainly Jewish grandparents, felt poor and fearful, vulnerable to anti-Semitism, and socially inferior. But the Weequahic "strategy"—the combination of economic mobility and ethnic assertiveness—produced at its most successful a very self-confident Jewish identity. Jewish kids had been taught in Hebrew school that the Jews were oppressed and persecuted throughout history, yet this seemed utterly unreal in the Weequahic section, where the Jews were numerically and socially dominant, and where many families were now economically comfortable.[14] One effect of this was to make many C58 classmates quite self-confident about being Jewish—just as good as anybody else, and maybe better. As one classmate said, "When I went to college, to me someone who wasn't Jewish wasn't as good as me." One woman talked about the election of the homecoming queen at her university: "And I looked at these people, and these were WASP-y America. And I said, they're not even pretty!" And finally, one woman who went to a fancy private college said:

> "[Despite the fact that I met all these upper-class types] I didn't feel inferior! I got such a sense, growing up [in the Weequahic section], of being absolutely 'okay.' I mean, we were the top of the heap in the Weequahic section and so the idea of [being] inferior, [that] I should be self-conscious, never occurred to me. I mean, we just sort of sailed through life thinking, 'of course!'"

Needless to say, some of this was quite unrealistic. Anti-Semitism was still prevalent in many areas of life: most colleges and universities still had quotas, most major corporations would not hire known Jews (and corporate America is still the least Jewish-populated part of the economy), most country clubs refused to have Jewish members, Richard Nixon thought that much of the opposition that brought him down was a Jewish conspiracy, and so on and so forth. Nonetheless, as with other identity movements to be discussed later, there was a significant shift in the discourse, and in some areas in the practices, concerning both public perceptions of Jews (the beginnings of Brodkin's shift to "whiteness") and Jewish self-perceptions.

Much of this history *as political history* has been erased, so that the Jewish case of high rates of mobility is easily cast as an exceptional case, grounded entirely in specific traits of "Jewish culture" and realized entirely through the agency of individuals. Moreover, because the various strands of the movement that broke down at least some of the anti-Semitism and got the Jews at least partly admitted to the game of success happened so much earlier and took a slightly different form from the more recent social movements, there is again a tendency to separate the history of Jewish success from the more recent, and less fully realized at this point, histories of other groups. Yet I would argue strongly that the parallels are very important, and indeed this was the point of the brilliantly organized "Too Jewish?" exhibit (Kleeblatt 1996, D. A. Segal 1999), the whole point of which was to put the Jewish case into effective parallel with more contemporary liberation movements. The point is important not only to undermine Jewish exceptionalism (and unfettered agency) arguments, but to argue that the seeming lesser success of other groups within the Class of '58 cohort is at least partly an effect of sheer timing. Which brings us, after the next Project Journal, to the non-Jewish minorities in the Class, and their careers since high school.

Project Journal 9: Children of the Class of '58, New Jersey

[Preamble: I had originally intended to make this a multigenerational study, but then became absorbed in the Class of '58 itself. When I reached the psychological moment described at the end of the last chapter's project journal—"where you have to get out of the village" —I went back to the idea of bringing the next generation into the project. I spent several months interviewing children of the Class of '58, though when it came to writing this book, the C58 itself took up all the space after all, and the kids are not included. I nonetheless include two chunks of field journals from the interviews with the kids, both because those interviews were all part of the same fieldwork project, and because they often made me rethink my readings of their parents.

After some initial experimentation, interviews with children of the Class of '58 were confined to young adults at the age where they were starting jobs and/or families. While there were some younger kids among the children of the Class of '58, the average age of C58 kids in the early 1990s was the mid-twenties (technically Generation X), and these were the young people I focused on.]

4/21/93 I guess the big decision of the trip was to start something with the kids of '58. Leonard kept saying, you ought to interview my son Sandy, he's the future. So finally I thought, yeah, time to do something new and different. So I drew up the questionnaire. Now let's see what happens.

8/13/93 Reading the kid questionnaires: One has a definite sense with many of these questionnaires that the kids treat them as if they were writing an essay exam. Sometimes you see this in the way they blow hot air without actually saying anything substantial ("the world is definitely different today than it was for my parents; things have really changed"); sometimes you see it in the writing conventions ("thus in conclusion" etc.).

A lot of expressions of sheer confusion—life is tough, it's hard to make decisions, the world is complex, the world is confusing, etc. Hard to know if this is just youth, or people do feel more confused (and disillusioned) by the world. Parents in turn are seen as having lived in a world of limited and clear-cut choices, for better and for worse. Over and over we hear that they [we] lived in a "simpler" world. Also safer. Lots of fear now, by contrast. Also, a lot of AIDS awareness.

8/18/93 [Interview with a middle-class, married daughter of working-class parents.] We got on the subject of women working, and I said well a lot of people noted that times are different in that both parents need to work, but I had the feeling that women would want to work anyway, even if they didn't have to. And she said yeah, but not for any of the reasons I would have thought. I would have said boredom at being home with the kids, and the satisfactions of your own career. But she said it's because no one respects homemaking any more, so you have to work "for respect," and she added "for self-respect," meaning I gathered that the external gaze has now been internalized. But it was clear that she thought that staying home with the kids would be quite satisfying—at one point she said something like what could be bad about being home with your children? [It may or may not be relevant that she didn't have any children yet.]

...... [Interview with middle-class, unmarried daughter of middle-class parents.] It was a little tricky when I picked her up at the house. I didn't want to stay and chat with the parents [her father was my classmate], and in fact I guess—on reflection—I didn't really want to be seen by the daughter as affiliated with the parents at all. It was all very awkward. I'll have to do better than that, especially with parents whom I haven't interviewed at the point where I'm interviewing their kid.

...... [same woman] She asked me "what I thought of her essay" on the questionnaire. I thought that was fascinating—that she had a certain amount of ego invested in it, it was not just a throwaway, and also—as I wrote in some earlier notes—that she felt it was being evaluated. I had it in front of me (good strategy by the way) and reread it and it had all this stuff about how scary the world was, and I said, well we all read about this, but how much does it affect our lives. . . . And she challenged me, well don't you feel that way? Or even, why don't you feel that way? And I had to think a minute, and I said, well first of all I'm probably just a relatively optimistic personality. But second I think we're protected by class from most of those things. The chances are, the percentages are, that most of that violence won't happen to us. And I think that sort of sank in.

...... [same woman] When I asked if any of her siblings had ever verged on "getting off the track," she thought about it for a while and then said—totally astonishingly—her older brother, the PhD, the college professor. And what she meant by that was that her brother was a terrible grind and totally antisocial and a complete nerd, and as far as she was concerned, while the brother might look successful, and is trying now to act like a normal person, he is still a failure as a human being. Questions about siblings seem to be very productive. [Among other things,] they give you a real different view of "success"—obviously all us parents think that the PhD/professor son is perfect, the pinnacle of success. But clearly there's a different possible view of the matter.

8/19/93 [Interview with an about-to-be-married young man, son of PMC parents.] He was one of the few people who wrote on his questionnaire that the world hasn't changed much, except that everything has been speeded up and rendered more visible and immediate by "technology"—fast media. He came back to this theme a lot in the interview—he really thinks this is the key thing about the world today. One of the things I've been thinking about is how people can talk about the world being so different from their parents', yet the class reproduction is virtually perfect, they are for the most part totally reproducing their parents' lifestyles and values.

8/20/93 [Interview with an unmarried graduate student, the son of a PMC family.] He said he thought the one thing that was really different nowadays was the possibility of random violence, the fact that there are so many guns around. I said, well and AIDS, and he said, yeah but that's different, you get AIDS because of something you do, whereas with getting shot it just happens to you. I was thinking about that after he had said he avoids any active political participation with groups of any kind. And I was thinking, if violence is the biggest problem today, it's something that you can't in effect organize against. It's a naturalistic category, and it's "random," so how can you have a politics against it? [On further reflection, one could have a right-wing, law-and-order position, but this was not his political inclination either.]

...... [Because this child of the Class of '58 was a graduate student:] One thing I realized about most of the people I'm interviewing is that they're basically the age of my graduate students. They only look exotic because they're the Weequahic kids—otherwise I'm literally surrounded by exactly this cohort of people every day.

8/22/93 On the way to my interviews today, I saw a bumper sticker—"I'm not religious, I just love the Lord." I thought it was interesting—there's a whole bunch of labels that people disclaim—I'm not a feminist, I'm not into politics, I'm not religious. These are all very negative words, always suggesting some kind of fanaticism, even if the person has views and/or practices that are clearly religious, or feminist, or political.

chapter 10

Happiness

I focused the last chapter on Jewish boys, both high and low capital, in part because Jewish students in general and Jewish boys in particular "did better" than most of the other groups in the class. They went to and completed college in higher numbers, they went on to advanced degrees in higher numbers, and they wound up in what we would now call the professional-managerial class in higher numbers. Large numbers of them enacted one of the key scenarios of American culture: succeed through hard work, personal effort, and the achievement of respected credentials that in turn produce high incomes.

I also focused on Jewish boys because they represented the continuation of an argument begun earlier, to the effect that the relative success of particular groups must be seen as only in part a function of their "cultural values," though this is not to be dismissed entirely; it is also a function of their political histories in the United States, and particularly their relationship to the social movements for the advancement of those groups. I argued that the relatively greater success of Jewish boys in the Class of '58 was at least in part an effect of the fact that the Jewish community, through a variety of strategies, had already opened many doors for the advancement of Jewish individuals, and in fact can be seen as the first of the so-called identity movements. I want to argue in this and the next chapter that later identity movements—for African Americans and for women—have similar effects.

In order to see this, I want to look at what I think of as box 4 in the College Choices table (table 10, p. 152; table 14, p. 217, the category of "zero college" students). As we have seen, this box contains some Jewish students and virtually all of the African American and other ethnic students. Not all of them were "working class"—a few of the Jewish students, other ethnics, and African Americans were in fact middle class or even higher—but the majority were from the lowest class level based on father's occupation and/or other kinds of (lack of) capital.

Before I get to the numbers, however, I must briefly address a more general question: whether it is correct or fair to assume that everyone (or, at least in that era, every man) was trying to "succeed" along the lines I have largely assumed thus far. The people in box 4, it will be recalled, were defined within the local cultural framework by the intersection of low capital and "low brains/motivation." Focusing on motivation for a moment, I argued earlier, and still tend to assume, that the imputation of low motivation or ambition is ideological—projected particularly on non-Jewish people (in a context like that of Weequahic), and/or working-class people, and/or women by stereotype rather than reality.

Yet there is a body of social science literature that reports that the working class(es) in particular do indeed tend to have different attitudes toward upward striving than the middle classes (Bourdieu 1984, Rapp 1982, Vanneman and Cannon 1987, Stewart et. al. n.d.). These attitudes may take a variety of forms: there may be a kind of culture of contentment with what one has, or an inability to imagine alternatives, or a critique of upward striving as putting on airs or as tearing one away from kin and community.

The idea that many people/groups in the United States do not buy into the mobility game is quite widespread in the popular imagination as well. Thus when I have presented pieces of this project as talks, I have frequently encountered the comment from the floor to the effect that all this emphasis on success and mobility seems very culturally and regionally specific (I suppose they mean Jewish), that the commenters came from working-class or solidly middle-class families that felt they had their own quite satisfactory identities and lifestyles. Their families might have liked to have had more money, more resources, but this was not the same thing as harboring ambitions to rise up the class ladder. In addition, so the argument went, the groups they came from often cherished cultural identities, as well as ties of kinship and community, which they feared would be attenuated, even lost, if they pursued the kinds of things necessary for personal career advancement, and they looked down on people who would sacrifice those things for "success."

At one level this picture does seems to characterize a good many of the non-Jewish and/or working-class families at Weequahic in the fifties. We see it first in the college numbers: the percentage of non-Jewish classmates going on to college is half (or less, depending on the category) of that of the Jewish kids. We also hear it in parental attitudes about college versus work after high school: for most of the working-class kids, Black and white, there was a strong push to get to work and begin earning some money. We will hear it as well later in this chapter, as many people define "success" less as getting rich and famous, and more as having good friends and a good family life.

Yet two points need to be made here. First, I think the picture is greatly overgeneralized. In this culture of capitalism and consumption, advertising alone makes it unlikely that every individual buys into the limitations of their low social position. Even in families in which the prevailing attitude is relative satisfaction with a low-capital but so-cially rich lifestyle, there is often the "different" child who wants to go (away) to college—once again, college tends to be the big marker—and who thereby takes the first step on the mobility escalator.[1] This figure (or specter) of the child who escapes from a low-capital (and low-ambition) background "to pursue his/her dreams" is as much a clas-sic American story as the downwardly mobile child of a high-capital family. Along these lines, it is worth remembering that 31 percent of the African American members of C58 and 44 percent of the "other ethnic" (mostly working-class) members were on the college prep track in high school. They may not have made it to college right away, or even at all, but the numbers suggest that the ambition to do so was not wholly absent.

Second, although many C58 classmates may have started out in fami-lies that did not encourage upward striving, an impressive number somehow got past that background and went on to do quite well. Some did not start college right after high school, but went later and fin-ished, and even went on for higher degrees. Some pursued a career to a high level of success without going to or finishing college. Often these various flowerings of ambition followed some kind of personal eye-opening experience. But for many, to return to my ongoing argu-ment, the critical factor was an intersection between an individual's life course and one or another of the important identity movements of the sixties and seventies.

Given these points, then, I will continue to focus on the more suc-cessful and upwardly mobile individuals, even among "low-capital" groups that are supposedly less focused on it themselves. At the same time I do not wish to dismiss as sour grapes or false consciousness the notion that many people resist upward striving because of a strong valuation of culture and community. The discourse and practices of community, like the discourse and practices of friendship discussed

earlier, represent important critiques and counterweights to the individualism of hegemonic American culture. We shall see, however, that
some version of a discourse of the importance of relationships remains
important for virtually *all* members of the Class of '58. It is, to be sure,
differently inflected among higher- and lower-capital people, but it is
clearly very significant for all. *No one* seems to think that making a
lot of money and leading an upscale lifestyle is satisfactory if important relationships are allowed to slide. Thus, after I explore the relative
degrees of success in the more conventional sense among the groups
who did not start college after high school, or started and dropped out
("box 4"), I will return to this discourse and its implications.

Zero College

I am interested in both the comparative numbers of those not going
to college and the comparative numbers of those returning later and
completing a degree. Not starting at all tended to represent the kind
of low-encouragement background discussed above. Starting but not
finishing often represented personal problems and/or stressful family
backgrounds. But returning to college and finishing later often followed some kind of "liberation," some kind of fairly radical change of
perspective, often associated with one or another identity movement
that both authorized and encouraged its members to try to move beyond the conventions and limitations they started with.

   I do this again by ethnic groups, for reasons explained earlier. And
while my numbers for the non-Jewish groups are smaller, and therefore
less reliable, than those for their Jewish classmates, we can at least get
a tentative picture (table 14). Since I spent a great deal of time on the
Jewish students in chapter 9, I will say relatively little about them here.
The Jewish students obviously had a much lower rate of not starting
college than the others; this is simply the obverse of what we learned in
the last chapter. However, two things are worth noting here. First, as I
always feel it necessary to break down stereotypes and attack homoge-
nization, it is worth noting that there *were* Jewish kids who did not go
to college. Some were dropouts from higher-capital families, but many
were from low-capital, working-class families. Second, we must look
at the gender ratios: of the sixty Jewish classmates who did not go to

Table 14. Zero College by Race/Ethnicity (*N* = 235; both genders)

Race/Ethnicity	Did not originally go to college[a]	Returned and finished later[b]
Jews (known *N* = 201)	60 (30%)	19/60 (32%)
African Americans (known *N* = 13)	11 (85%)	5/11 (45%)
Other ethnicities (known *N* = 21)	12 (57%)	1/12 (8%)

[a] This includes any kind of post–high school program or institution.
[b] This includes all kinds of certification, from two-year degrees and up.

college, thirty-six, or sixty percent, were girls, while only twenty-four or 40 percent, were boys. The gender asymmetry will run through all the other groups as well, and we will look at that as an issue in its own right in the next chapter.

Finally, the 32 percent rate of Jewish zero-college kids returning and completing a degree later is midway between the African American rate of 45 percent and the rate among the other ethnic groups of 8 percent. The latter two groups present a strong contrast, and in the course of this chapter I will consider why this might be the case, in relation to the issue of identity movements discussed earlier. Briefly, I will suggest that many African American classmates were able to capitalize on the Civil Rights/Black Power movements that developed into a mass movement a few years after the Class of '58 finished high school, and thus members of that group began to move onto and climb up the ladder. The non-Jewish other ethnics, on the other hand, never had such a movement (indeed, they were not really a group, unless one defines them religiously—mostly Catholic—and even then the point still holds; they never had a movement), and their numbers are actually the worst in the class. I will start with the African American students.

African American Classmates

The African Americans in the Class of '58 started out with the worst odds in the class. Recall the discussion of their "immigrant" status and the culture shock that went with it. Recall the racism, which may have been less overt at Weequahic than, according to William Smallwood's or Amiri Baraka's experience, at Barringer, but which was still certainly

present in the system. Socially, it largely took the form of exclusion
and racial separation. Academically, the majority (69 percent) of African Americans were on the non–college prep track and, according to at
least one classmate, were given bad guidance concerning college when
the time came for that. Only two African American classmates started
some kind of degree program right after high school.[2] And four of the
nineteen are already known to be dead.

Let us pause for a moment and look more closely at the mortality
rate of African Americans in the Class of '58. There were only nineteen
African Americans in the class. Of these, I have information on only
thirteen, or 68 percent. Of these in turn, four, or 31 percent, are known
to have died. This compares with twenty persons deceased, or 9 percent, among (known) white/Jewish classmates. The extremely high
mortality rate for African Americans is clearly something (negatively)
distinctive to the group, differentiating them from all others regardless
of class.[3]

Yet it is difficult not to see Black mortality as related as much to
class as to race, especially in that era. Many of the Black families were
(relatively) poor, displaced, or both. The individuals who died did not
for the most part die of the kinds of things that seem "typical" of
poor ghetto Blacks today—physical violence and drugs—things that
seem specific to the ghetto situation. Rather, they died of things that
they shared with other poor and displaced people: poor working conditions, poor health care, and poor nutrition. George Quincy was a
Newark policeman; he died of pneumonia. Agnes Lane was a minister;
she died of a heart attack while preaching one Sunday. Charles Tucker
died of brain cancer. John Koonce was burned badly in a work accident
in a chemical plant. It is not clear what he died of eventually; some have
said drugs, but his mother denied it and said that he was just never the
same after the accident.

But the bad odds did not stop many African Americans in the Class
from trying to move up, one way or another. Again, there were several ways of moving up. Although gender issues in a broad sense are
considered in the next chapter, here I will keep the men and women
together in order to look at them through the lenses of race and class.
At least one of the women married well (to a man who himself took a
college degree) and moved up the ladder in the approved 1950s manner for women.[4] One of the women (now deceased) became a minister.

One of the men (now deceased) became a policeman, which within the range of traditional African American class possibilities in that era was considered a middle-class status.[5]

In addition, five African American classmates went back to school and took one or another degree. This is a dramatic ratio (five out of eleven, or 45 percent), in fact the highest among the zero-college students. Before speculating on the factors that went into it, let me tell some of their stories here. Pearl Smith works as a nurse in Newark:

> "From high school I was interested in nursing. And I went to a nursing school up in upstate New York. . . . I didn't like it very well, so I [came back and] went into keypunching. And I studied that, I worked there for about, oh, five years. And then [at] Western Electric, at that time there was a big lay-off. . . . And then I went back into nursing, really went to school. . . . First I studied [for] an LPN [Licensed Practical Nurse]. . . . "Manpower" [a job-training program] at the time was opening a program where they'd pay you to go to school, to work. So that was two years for LPN school. So I graduated, and I started working as an LPN. And once I got into the hospital facilities, I decided I wanted to go on. And I went on! And I received a grant from one of the hospitals, that I could work, and go to school. . . . And they just sent me to school full time. For registered nursing, I received that [degree], and an Associate degree."

Herbert Graves is the assistant manager of a large retail store:

> [from the field notes] He didn't go to college [right after high school]. He was working as a cabinetmaker. He then signed up for the army for four years, and kept re-upping. He enjoyed being in the service. . . . After finishing twenty years, he retired, went to community college, did a two-year degree in marketing. He [said he] was very scared at first—"If you haven't done math for twenty years you feel like you can't do it"—but he did well, got a lot of job offers because of his GPA, and also [he said] being a minority.

Finally, Perry Lucas holds three degrees (BA, MBA, and JD) and is a vice president of a major corporation. Perry went into the marines right after high school, but there he realized that there was a big difference in favor of the guys who had college degrees:

> "You're in an environment where you have college graduates, some have gone to college, some high school, some just grammar school. And all of a

sudden you're fending for yourself [for] the first time. And immediately, I learned that education was a necessity, not a luxury."

Perry enjoyed the service, traveled a lot, but eventually was very ready to get out.

"And then I decided I definitely wanted to go back to school. And I was more geared for school. When I say more geared, I [had] better insight, I knew more what I wanted to do, and I also became very independent, from the point [that] I didn't want anyone to do it for me."

He would work for a while, then take a year off and go to school full time. It was the late 1960s:

"Life was good, jobs were plentiful, I got out of college, I didn't know what I'm gonna do. Had a BA in economics, what do you do with a BA in economics? And people were searching to hire you, and I got four job offers. First day!"

He continued the pattern of working and schooling, eventually winding up with an MBA and a law degree, facilitating his rise to the high position he holds today.[6]

The African American classmates who have moved up are proud of their achievements and see them as the result of their personal efforts, which indeed they are. At the same time, I would, as with the Jewish men in chapter 9, look at other factors as well. The first is class. Perhaps the first thing to be said is that probably all the African American families that moved into the Weequahic neighborhood in that era were middle-classing to some degree. But some families were clearly still more "working class" than others, and the difference does seem to have made a difference. Thus of the five students who went back and finished degrees, four came from families that were recognizably further along toward middle-class status. Pearl Smith's father was a skilled worker who later opened his own business, and her stepmother was a nurse. Al Walker's father had owned his own small business in another city, and then owned a tiny enterprise in Newark. Herbert Graves's father was a government clerk. But the clearest case was Perry Lucas's family. Perry's father was a skilled craftsman, and his mother was a teacher. And while his parents did not take going to college for granted in the same way that many Jewish boys' parents did, it was at least an option: "My father had a rule in the house that upon graduation, you must do one of three things. You must go to college, get a job, or go in service. One of those three. And you had until Monday. There was no finding yourself."

But in addition to class factors, I again introduce the question of the relationship between individual success and the impact of a social movement aimed at improving the opportunities for this group. The Civil Rights movement was just getting started while the Class of '58 was in high school, and became both bigger and more militant in the succeeding decades. There is little doubt that, even though none of my African American classmates was actively involved, the cultural and material transformations set in motion by the movement had an impact on them. Indeed, one can hear at least fragments of it in some of their interviews. Pearl Smith mentioned taking advantage of the Manpower program, one of the major programs for job training or retraining for minorities established in the wake of the Civil Rights/Black Power movements. Herbert Graves was explicitly aware that, in addition to his good GPA, affirmative action hiring programs for minorities facilitated his getting a good job. Perry Lucas seemed to imply the same thing when he exclaimed that people were "searching for you" and that he had four job offers his first day on the market.

A note should be added here about timing. The Civil Rights movement was still fairly small in 1958. It enlarged and gained momentum enormously over the next five or six years: 1963 was the year of the March on Washington for Peace and Freedom, when Martin Luther King Jr. made his "I have a dream" speech.[7] Thus, if African American classmates went right into secure working-class jobs, as did, for example, William Smallwood and John Koonce, then they tended to settle into those jobs and be unavailable for some of the benefits that became available in the 1960s as a result of the movement. The people who did take advantage of those benefits were available to do so at least in part because they did not get locked into such a job. Perry Lucas, Herbert Graves, Al Walker, and Norman Huntley all went into military service right out of high school, and came out at the time that new benefits and opportunities for minorities were becoming available. For different reasons, Pearl Smith also was in a position to take advantage of some of these programs because of timing: she had dropped out of

222 New Jersey Dreaming

nursing school, was in a seemingly secure industrial job and might not have done anything else, but then—one has to say in this case, fortunately—she got laid off.

Again, to emphasize class advantages and/or the ways in which a social movement opened certain doors is not to negate the individual effort of those who achieved some personal success. Undoubtedly both the Civil Rights movement and, later, black nationalism created opportunities that did not exist before, and also changed the cultural climate in major ways. Without these things, there would have been much less possibility of individuals moving up. Yet at the same time, just as people like C58 parents had to seize the postwar economic "boom" and make it work for them, so here African American individuals had to capitalize on these political processes and their effects, and make those things work for them as well. Movements articulate demands and goals, and ideally even produce real programs and resources, but without the practices of ordinary people who work to realize those goals in their own lives, movements and their effects can evaporate.

Let us look now at the "other ethnic" students in the Class of '58, the non-Jewish, non–African American classmates. Without claiming in any hard sense that they "prove" this point about the relationship between personal advancement and larger social movements, we shall see that they present a somewhat negative case in contrast to both the Jewish men in the last chapter and the African Americans just discussed.

Non-Jewish, Non–African American Ethnic Classmates

I must caution once again that the numbers here are not as good as those for the other groups. Of thirty-five members of the Class of '58 who belong to other ethnic groups, I have data on twenty-one, or 60 percent, which is the lowest of the three race/ethnic categories. But here I need to break this already small group down even further. Although "non-Jewish" tended to be equated with "working class" at Weequahic, in fact, several of the "other ethnic" classmates were from higher-capital backgrounds. One of the boys in this category came from a professional background; he went straight to and through college to a bachelor's degree. Two of the girls in the category came from middle-class backgrounds, and both of them went straight to and through college to bachelor's degrees as well. If we take them out of the pool, the "other ethnicity" factor recedes, and the group is quite clearly "working class."

If we redo the numbers without these three people, they get worse. The "working-class" sample size drops to eighteen, while the percentage of those who never started college rises to 78 percent, close to that of the African Americans. How to explain the poor college numbers for this group, which seemed, at least because of racial privilege, to have had better odds than their African American classmates? White working-class members of C58 tended to point to various factors intrinsic to their own situations that would have held them back: ethnic cultural values (e.g., patriarchal Catholicism—we will hear this from some of the girls), material necessity (the parents could not afford it), the kind of negative class culture discussed earlier (it simply was not expected or encouraged), or family disruption. Ted Nero's story combines several of these points:

> "I always kind of knew that my parents could not afford to send me to college. Which may have been a reason I really never tried to achieve any heights, you know, academically . . . I really think it's probably a lack of interest on my parents' part. They were so wrapped up in their own problems, they didn't have the time to instill values into us, my sister and I."

These kinds of factors are important in understanding why so many children of working-class families did not start college, but I also want to call attention to the low rate of returning to college later, compared not only with Jewish kids, but with the African American classmates as well. It is here that the absence of some kind of identity movement perhaps had an effect. Of course, with these small numbers one can only speculate. But I would also note that the working class in this era had almost the opposite of an identity movement: they had the labor movement.

I in no way wish to undercut the importance of the labor movement. Even if it did not achieve its more radical goals, it raised significant questions about the morality of capitalism itself. At the same time it brought better pay, better working conditions, and greatly increased security to the working class, softening some of the most tangible aspects of their exploitation.

The working-class parents of the Class of '58 were already the benefi-
ciaries of these achievements of the labor movement.[8] But by that very
token the labor movement would not have promoted the kind of upward mobility at issue here, and in fact would have worked in quite the
opposite direction. In its radical form, it was not about advancing individuals or groups but about organizing against capitalism as a whole.
Even in its liberal form it was about getting better wages, benefits, and
working conditions for workers, thus making working-class positionality and identity more comfortable and the sense of group membership stronger.

Moreover, in conjunction with all this, the era when the Class of
'58 was in high school was very prosperous, the working class was
doing well, and people in traditional working-class occupations could
buy some of the trappings of middle-class life—houses, cars—without
actually climbing onto the class escalator or putting their kids on that
escalator by sending them to college. Any anti–upward mobility values
that might have been operating would have been reinforced by these
material factors.

In the end, given the extraordinary expansion of the economy in
general and the middle class in particular in this era, most of the
C58 sons of working-class parents would eventually move up into the
middle class anyway. In addition to the people already mentioned, two
men listed occupations that would have required some kind of degree,
which evidently launched them into solid careers. Others got entry-
level white-collar jobs (which in those days could often be had without a college diploma) and then moved up the ladder of promotions;
and others went into small businesses. Yet the highest degree attained
among "other ethnic men" is, as far as I know, a Master's degree, and
the case of this one man actually strengthens the general argument
here, because he is the individual discussed earlier who went into the
Peace Corps and thus rode another kind of "social movement."

In any event, most of the men in this group did rise up, but much
more modestly than those in the other groups. Some of the women did
better, as we shall see in chapter 11, either by marrying men who themselves made it up into the professional/managerial class or, in one case,
by a rather spectacular career trajectory of her own.

At this point we must return to the success question. Does everyone
want to move up the class ladder? Is "success" in America only a mat-

ter of money and prestigious occupations? The answer, as one might imagine, is ambivalent. We turn, then, to the second major meaning of "success" that emerged in the course of this project.

Success II: Happiness

I have focused in this chapter on those who started out with relatively low odds—the African American and "other ethnic" members of the Class of '58, most of whom were also working class—and considered how they fared in the great game of "success." I have continued to use the idea of success in its dominant meaning—that is, as money, prestige, and other kinds of capital.

But of course, as the saying goes, money isn't everything. There is another major translation of "success" that is quite different; it is something like "happiness" or "satisfaction." When I asked people directly how *they* would define success (as opposed to listening for phrases on the order of "he is very successful"), they almost always said something like "being happy with who you are or what you have." This was an extraordinarily widespread answer,[9] coming from people all across the economic spectrum. Here, for example, is an answer from a wealthy woman. She was married to a very successful lawyer and lived in a huge and expensively decorated house in a very high-class neighborhood. Nonetheless, her answer was completely couched in terms of "happiness" with nonmonetary aspects of life:

> "I think to be successful you have to have personal happiness, I think that comes first. Happiness with yourself, happiness with your family, and I think that's very important. Have people to love and people who love you too, that's very important. And I think to do work that you feel satisfied [with] is very important to success. And if it provides you with your needs, I think that's very important."

A man in the middle of the spectrum said:

> "I think the secret to life is not success, the secret is happiness. I want [my kids] to be happy. I've been very successful, I've been busted, I've come from humble beginnings, I've lived like a king and a prince and I guess I am somewhere in between right now. Well you know it is not money and success, it is happiness that is the key."

And finally, a woman in a fairly low-capital position said:

> "I would say, [success is] being what you want, having what you want, and being satisfied with what you have. If you're satisfied with that, then you are successful. . . . So I find I am successful, because there's people that don't have what I have. And, I'm talking about happiness, the independence."

As I wrote in my field notes on another occasion:

> She [another high-capital woman] said that success is being happy with what you do. The consistency and almost verbatim repetition of this answer is getting kind of scary. This is the fourth or fifth person who answered in almost identical words. I feel like I've tapped into some kind of cultural tape.

"Happiness" in this context is, I would argue, something like "friendship" in high school. It is a value in itself, to be desired with or without money, and indeed obtainable with or without money. And as with friendship, it is at least potentially a critical discourse, something that allows one to stand apart from the success = money game and question the values at the heart of that game. Here again I will divide the discussion between high- and low-capital people.

High-Capital Happiness

I start with the "high-capital" people, those about whom others would probably say, "He/she is very successful" in its dominant money-meaning. Some of these people have become enormously materialistic in their outlook, and it is clear that the quality of their homes, their cars, their children's schools, and so on is very important to them. Some of these people, moreover, are quite snobbish about those who have done less well. One woman, herself in the high-capital set, was quite critical of these snobbish people:

> "I also see so much of the change of some of these people that I know very well. It will be interesting when you interview them how important material success has become to [some] men . . . to the point where I don't know who these people are, some of them, people I've known for so long. I want to say to them, 'Hey, remember where you came from.'

It's not enough [money, things], I hear it from several, they want more, more, more."

Without denying the evident materialism of some of the very successful high-capital C58 classmates, at the same time I found a quite widespread reflective attitude about money and things, and about the importance of not letting them take first place in one's life. For some, it had to do with getting older and wiser:

> *Laurence Cohen:* "I think it has to do with quality of life. Finding your own peace, peace within yourself, your environment, your family, and all that kind of stuff. [SBO: But it changes with life stage? I think earlier on you need to get the money to feel really comfortable?] I think once you've got the money then you can . . . be content. Well, not everybody can. [But] then you sort of take a look around and say, you know, 'Well, now I got the money. And I got this. Now what have I got?' "
> *Barbara Max:* [SBO: How do you feel about factors like money and professional status in the idea of success?] "I thought it was more important before I was involved in it personally. [She is married to a successful professional man.] Once you're in it, then other things become more important. Because I see people around me who have all that, and they're not happy."

What is important in these comments is the *relative* value of money versus other things. It is not that money does not matter; the key is that it alone cannot make one "happy."

In elaborating on the question of happiness, people stressed a variety of things. Since many of these people had risen up from humbler beginnings, there is often an emphasis in their statements on the pleasure of achievement. Although "achievement" itself usually translates into money, the point seems to be that the effort and the success of reaching one's goals were just as important as the monetary reward:

> *Marie Romero:* "[How would I define success?] Um, feeling good about yourself . . . feeling good with your own personal accomplishments."
> *Russell Horowitz:* [from the field notes] After the tape was turned off, he defined success as "self-fulfillment, achieving what you set out to do."
> *Beverly Rothman:* "Success to me is if you're happy wherever you are and whatever you have. . . . I feel very successful. I feel, personally, that I have done a hell of a job, given my circumstances. Coming from where

I come from, and I'm the tops in my field [sales]. . . . I didn't ever plan to be president. I . . . lived out all my dreams. That's success to me."

Closely related to the pride/pleasure of having achieved one's goals is the pleasure of having the kind of work one enjoys. Again, such work is generally lucrative, and so the discourse of happiness is not totally opposed to the discourse of money; and yet there is a sense that enjoying one's work is a distinct value:

> *Jackie Low:* [SBO: How would you define success, personally?] "Well I guess it's when you're happy at what you're doing."
> *Gary Sharenow:* "What is success? You've got to make a good living, and you've got to enjoy what you're doing, to some extent, you don't have to love it, but you can't hate it."
> *Robert Vernick:* "Success is having the freedom to do what I want to do, being able to control my own destiny in terms of spending my day, my working day, to be able to spend it in a way that's interesting and satisfying to me."

But more than anything the issue of "happiness" is tied up with the quality of one's personal relationships. Virtually all the people who talked about being happy because of their personal achievements, or because of enjoying their work, went on to say something about the importance of good family relationships. Beverly Rothman, for instance, went on to say, "I brought up wonderful children, I have a beautiful family, I'm successful." Robert Vernick went on to say that money allows him to "treat the people I'm close to fairly and honestly, treat my family with love and respect." [10] Jackie Low coupled "being happy with what you're doing" with "[being] able to provide for your family." And Gary Sharenow added, "You've got to have a good relationship with a [spouse]." [11] Here are more comments along those lines:

> *Sam Finn:* [SBO: How would you rate yourself in terms of some kind of success scale, nowadays?] "You mean financially, or? [SBO: Well, I don't know . . . whatever scale you want to use.] Well, what with the recession, I'm not doing as well as I did three years ago. . . . But as to my relationships with people, I'm really lucky; I have these great kids and my wife and my friends. I'm lucky that way."
> *Bernard Rous:* "I have a friend of mine who was a judge here, and who has recently resigned from the job because it's so lousy now. And he

said, he knows why I'm successful and why I'm happy, and it's because practicing law is the seventh-place priority in my life, instead of being number one. Well, I practice and I go home! I don't want to take this stuff home with me. And I have to give [my wife] Phyllis credit for that, too, the two of us sat down, worked out a goal. And I said I was not going to be a 'Gee, I wish I was with my kids more when they grew up' father."

Again, nobody in this high-capital group said that success = money is unimportant. Indeed, it is my strong impression that most of the high-capital people I spoke to could not imagine being "happy" without it. They simply said that success = money is not enough for happiness, and that good relationships, usually with family, must be part of the picture.

Lower-Capital Happiness

I turn here to people who would be considered less "successful" in the money sense than the people in the previous section. There are many similarities between their views and those of the higher-capital people. People talked about the pleasure of achieving life goals even if these were relatively modest. (For example, one woman, who makes a modest middle-class salary, said that she feels as successful as one of the extremely wealthy lawyers in the class, because "it depends on your own goals.") People talked about the importance of enjoying one's work. (For example, one woman defined success as "doing or achieving what you want, or liking what you're doing, and feeling good about it.") And many talked about the importance of having a good family life. But there is a small but important shift of emphasis in these responses. High-capital people said that success-as-money isn't enough; lower-capital people came closer to saying that success-as-money does not matter. High-capital people said that one needs more than monetary success for happiness; lower-capital people came closer to saying that happiness, rather than money, *is* success.

Even when lower-capital people seemed to be saying the same things as the higher-capital people, there was a persistent, if subtle, downgrading of money as the basis of success. For one thing, what counts as adequate wealth was, if mentioned at all, recast as something usually called "comfortable."

William Terry: "My job is not a real high-paying job but I'm very comfortable in my job. I more or less get to do what I want to do. . . . So I
consider myself fortunate, maybe not successful, fortunate, I have no
problem with that. I'm comfortable in everything I do. My home life
is very comfortable."

Judith Mann: "Financially, I wouldn't say we are wealthy but we are comfortable, we have a nice home, it took us a long time to get there, it
took a lot of years of struggle. But I think in general the way our life is
going I call that being successful."

Carol Cook: "I was brought up by this father who says, 'I'm the richest
person on earth because I have all of you [his family] in my life!' . . . So
[being rich is] not part of my definition [of success], but it's certainly
nice to be comfortable."

As Carol's comments suggest, the most important source of success
= happiness is one's family. But here family is not *added on* to money
as a source of happiness; it is presented virtually as an alternative to
money. Here are some more comments along these lines:

William Terry: [SBO: How would you define success?] "Now that depends
because [even though I don't make a lot of money] I really think that
I'm successful, especially when it comes down to my relationship with
my family, my relationship with my children."

Judith Mann: [SBO: How would you define success?] "Not totally financial, just being in a happy home, raising children and your life just
going normally. We have had a good marriage together and our children have grown up to be adjusted, happy people."

Irving Resnick: "Even though I may not have much money, success is
having a good life, good children, watching them grow up, money
doesn't mean that much to me as long as I'm happy. This year we
are celebrating [several major family milestones]. We have a lot to be
happy about."

In a sense, all of these statements represent an implicit critique of
an excessive valuation of money and of an equation of money and success. Others develop the point in different, and more pointed, ways.
For example, one man made a point of contrasting his relative lack of
financial success with his success in instilling good ethics and values
in his children:

Malcolm Schwartz: "Financially I'm not a great success. But I think, hopefully, I've tried to instill some things in my kids. I don't think that if anyone sits around the table however many years from now when I've passed away and say he was a bastard and so on, I don't think that will happen. So I think I'm successful that way."

One woman denied the equation of success with money entirely, and emphasized both her relationship with her children and her many long-term friendships:

Judith Gordon: "I don't have monetary things but I kind of think that my life has been successful. . . . I have my kids. And I'm very successful in my friendships. . . . So that's success. It has nothing to do with money or employment or where you are in the business world—I don't think."

And finally, another woman recounted a conversation in which her own lack of focus on wealth contrasts with a more materialist interlocutor:

"We are invited to a birthday party Saturday night, 'Come as someone you would like to [be reincarnated as].' . . . So I brought that problem into work one day, . . . and we were talking about it, and someone said, 'Well, first of all, you want to be rich, right?' I said, you know, I hadn't thought of that . . . because it's not the primary thing."

Of course, money never disappears entirely:

Judith Stang: "Success is being happy with yourself and liking yourself. I don't think of [success] as monetary but I will say that if there is no money it is not very happy."

And in another conversation, William Terry poked fun at himself for downgrading money so much:

[from the field notes] Somebody just down the street from him won a zillion dollars in the lottery. And when I talked to him, he was laughing, he said, "You know, I said to you the other day that money doesn't count." He said, "What was I talking about?!"

All in all, however, it seems fair to say that low-capital people are much more likely to downgrade the relative importance of money, to make a much stronger equation between success and personal happiness, especially through friends and family, and to implicitly criticize the dominant materialism of the culture.

False Consciousness?

There are, of course, a variety of possible readings of these texts. One possibility is that the only "true" texts are those that acknowledge that success really means money in American culture, that money is the bottom line, and that all this talk about happiness and fulfillment is just a kind of "therapy-speak" that has taken over the culture (Bellah et al., 1996). People have been encouraged by advertising, schooling-ideology, and other things to translate social realities into personal feeling-states, and thus to misrecognize their own lack of privilege and its sources.

One body of evidence in support of this point is the extent to which one can hear people more or less consciously adjusting or adapting to a lower level of financial success than they may have hoped for or imagined themselves achieving earlier in life. I noted earlier that there was an age factor even for high-capital people, who may have achieved high financial success but then began to look around in later years and ask what they had left behind. We hear something similar from low-capital people, but it is more in terms of giving up earlier fantasies:

> *Gerald Fisher:* [SBO: How would you define success?] "I've defined it different ways in different times in my life. I've been driven in terms of success, whatever that is, and maybe I also have a quality in me that I have to feel like I've been [financially] successful. . . . [But] I can say that success means [now] having loving relationships and putting a lot into those relationships."
>
> *Steven de Leon:* [SBO: Some people don't want to meet with me, you know, there are people who . . . feel like where they got to now isn't enough.] "Well, I'll tell you, maybe ten years ago I would have felt that way, but you know, it changes. I don't feel as successful as I would have wanted to be, or certainly not as rich as I would have liked to be. But every once in a while [my spouse] has to call to my attention, and put things in perspective. You know, we do live in a lovely apartment in a good neighborhood, and we have wonderful friends, we have wonderful family, we have health which is extremely important."
>
> *Ronni Greenberg:* "I guess I used to define success as living in a big house

and having a lot of money and a big car and all that. Now I think I would
define success as being happy in what you do and doing the best you
can . . . being honest with yourself and everyone around you, healthy,
and just, I think happiness is success."

At one level these passages convey a strong sense of Bourdieu's arguments, already noted several times, to the effect that people internalize
external limits as personal desires, or more precisely denial of desires,
that they adjust their sense of what they want to what is in fact possible,
and that what is possible must moreover be recognized as an effect of
the economics of capitalism and its construction of the social field of
classes.

In different ways, both Bellah's points about the expansion of ther-
apy-discourse and Bourdieu's points about internalizing the inevitable
represent pessimistic and/or cynical takes on the possibilities of count-
erdiscourses and counterpractices. In the case of Bellah's arguments,
the assumption is that the widespread triumph of therapeutic discourse represents a triumph of the private individual over the individual who participates in civil society. This is, of course, partly true,
but I want to note here how much the people we have been hearing
from in this chapter, in all their "feeling-talk," emphasize the importance of relationships—with spouses, friends, and children. This may
not fulfill the functions of the public-minded citizen that Bellah et al.
had in mind, but it also does not represent the kind of total selfish individualism that Bellah rightly fears.

Let me push this point a little further by returning to the high school
social categories discussed in chapter 5. I argued there that insofar as
people thought everything was accomplished by "personal qualities"
(charisma, brains, natural abilities, and so on), there was a false consciousness in not recognizing the left side of the table, the role of class
in people's high school careers. But I also found that people placed
enormous value on friendships, and often consciously used friendships
to step back from and criticize the entire structure. This suggested that
the top of the table, the focus on "personal qualities," was doubly ideological, hiding not just the impact of class, but also the enormous value
of social relationships and the fulfillment they provide.

My point here is similar. People's talk about success in terms of
happiness-in-relationships rather than money has precisely the same

double quality. At one level it may serve some defensive psychological function—sour grapes for the lower-capital people, presenting one-self as a "good person" for the higher-capital people. But at another level there seems to be a genuine sense of critique, of seeing the single-minded pursuit of money as to some extent antithetical to human values of relationship, love, and caring.

The same points apply, mutatis mutandis, to Bourdieu's position. Without going into a detailed critique of his texts, which would take us far beyond the space possibilities of this book, I think it is fair to say that Bourdieu sees relationships as themselves a form of capital. In many cases they are. But I am arguing that they also operate in counterpoint to capital (as much of the popular culture indeed recognizes: "can't buy me lo-ove"), as well as operating in counterpoint to the individualism at the top of the table (looks, charisma, brains, etc.)[12] To the extent that—as I have tried to argue—"American culture" is not just capitalism, but the intersection of capitalism and individualism, then the critique of American culture must critique the structure as a whole. The discourse of success as happiness, which includes but goes beyond money, like the practices of friendship and of service/activism discussed earlier, represents another "everyday form" of such a critique.

Project Journal 10: Children of the Class of '58
(LA and Other Far-flung Places, Including New Jersey)

9/12/93 [Interview with son of middle-class parents.] He noted [as a change from his parents' generation] the openness about things. How he had knocked up a girl when he was a freshman at [college]. How he thought it never happened in his mom's time and she wouldn't be understanding about it, but when he talked to her she was very understanding. She said it was common, but much more under wraps.

...... [Interview with the son of a professional/managerial class family.] What a character! A largely (though not entirely) humorless person, with strong and often left-field views on just about everything. . . . He was pretty obsessive about everything—very intense and really slightly nuts. But even him, even him, I just liked him, felt touched to look into the lives of these twenty-somethings and try to see the future.

9/13/93 [Interview with the son of professional parents.] Both he and [another young man I interviewed, the son of working-class parents] talked a lot about their parents, in such nice good warm ways. While some of that may be because they know I know their parents and this is for the record, I don't really think it's true in most cases. I'm amazed at the number of people who think the world of their parents—including [a close friend], who described his father as the nicest man on the planet. A lot of parents are obviously doing a good job.

9/15/93 I haven't written much about the pleasure of being back in LA. First of all Nancy [Lutkehaus,* with whom I was staying] is near the beach in Santa Monica and we have gone walking over there several times—it's just incredible to be near the ocean like this. There's a beautiful park up on the bluffs overlooking the ocean that we walked through, and after you stop noticing (a) the physical beauty of the place, and (b) all the thin, running, skating, pulse-taking beautiful people, then you begin to notice (c) all the homeless people under those amazing palm trees.

9/15/93 [Interview with the son of middle-class parents.] He said in California people are very flaky, people only call you when they need you, back east your friends will always be there. He said there's a definite difference between friends you grew up with since the age of 6 and friends you meet late in life. When you're young you actually grow with people, you grow together. On the other hand he's glad he's not in NJ any more, it's so limited. But if he ends up wealthy, he'll build a place back east so he can spend time there.

He also said he doesn't like the women out here [in California], they're just not like the ones back home. . . . He said you know, back east you complain that the women are too JAPpy [Jewish American Princess-y] and all that, but now he misses them.

11/6/93 [In Boston/Cambridge.] Somewhere along the line I realized that many of these kids are framing the interviews within the frame of college admission or job interviews. [One male graduate student] had said to me that he had been asked one of my questions on his college interviews (I think it was the one about who were your role models), and then I realized also that [an undergraduate woman] was waiting for my questions, rather than conversing, in very much an interviewee pose. And at the end, she said "I hope that was useful for you," and I said oh yes, that was great, I really enjoyed it, it's so interesting to hear your perspective, and she said "Oh I like interviews, I enjoyed my college interviews too." Now this is something nobody has talked about, what kinds of frames informants bring to the interview event. This goes along with the observation that they fill out the questionnaires like exams—a bunch of short answers and an essay question.

6/12/94 [Back in NJ. Interview with the daughter of a working-class Jewish man.] She asked me shyly after the tape was turned off how her father was viewed in high school. Yikes, I didn't want to say that her father was viewed as a terminal nerd and people teased him mercilessly. I also didn't want to lie in some grossly outright way. So I searched my brain and remembered dimly that though people teased Lenny he was always tolerant and benign and didn't (visibly) get angry. So I said he was thought of as "a very nice guy." And the daughter just glowed and said yes, he's the best, he'd give you the shirt off his back, he's such a good and giving person. I guess I said the right thing.

6/15/94 [Interview with daughter of professional parents, at their house. I was impressed with the young woman as very smart and self-possessed. Afterwards her parents invited me to stay for dinner, which I did.] Nothing special that I recall about the conversation, except it was interesting to see how the daughter, who had previously been a whole person in the context of the interview, was now reduced to being their child, having to fight for a voice at the dinner table (which in fact she complained about on the tape), etc.

...... Went down to Holmdel to interview [the son of a classmate] working at Bell Labs/AT&T. He had said on the phone that it was an amazing building, a humongous building, "not like a normal building," and he was right. In fact it was a masterpiece of modern architecture by Eero Saarinen and it was absolutely stunning. Outside it was an enormous (the perimeter is about a mile) box of black glass, but the interior lobbies and walkways and atriums and God knows what were just breathtaking. In fact, when I got inside I took out my camera immediately and began taking pictures of the lobby, and the security man and the receptionist converged on me and I had to leave my camera at the front desk. Turns out that this particular facility is devoted to R&D of new products and also there is a certain amount of classified government work done there so obviously security is very tight. I had a visitor badge in bright red that said I could only be in the building with an escort.

6/15/94 [This young man] said corporations like AT&T were really changing (in terms of informality of dress and general norms of interaction, time management, etc.). Maybe insurance and investment banking corporations are still very buttoned up, but in a place like this, or many others, they look at models like Microsoft and see how well that philosophy is working. I asked if [he thought] this betokened some real change in capitalism, and he sort of said yes, it means these companies care more about their workers than making a profit. [I must have looked skeptical.] Then he modified his point a bit and said or at least they discovered they can make just as much money being good to their workers as not. In any event, it does mean something, there's a different sort of discipline (in the Foucauldian sense) at work here. I think Paul Rabinow has written something about this.

7/11/94 [After an interview with a son of a professional/managerial-class family, who compared himself a lot with his brother.] I have a sense of siblings as providing one of the key images of social right and wrong, justice and injustice, in American life. Your sibling is always the path you might have taken, or could have, or were deprived of, or don't want to be, etc. I'm not being very articulate here, but the sibling is so close, it could have been you, in a way that is not true of parents or anybody else. So the sibling's success or failure or differentness or privilege or whatever leaves a very big mark on people's hearts and imaginations.

chapter 11

Liberation

One of the things that struck me in the course of writing this book was how hard it was to class-ify women consistently. They simply had a different relationship to the class structure than the men. For the generation of the parents of C58 it was (relatively) simple—the mothers were all classified according to the occupations of their husbands, unless there was no husband present. This may itself have been an injustice to some of the mothers, but that was largely invisible.

There was in a sense a lack of correlation between women's class status and what women actually did. Women might work outside the home, sometimes in relatively high (e.g., managerial) positions, but this had nothing to do with their "success," which, to rehearse the girl track once again, was almost entirely tied to marriage:

> *Marlene Bank:* "Getting married was still, that was your success. . . . I have a cousin who is a musician and a producer, and a lot of the things he did, he never made money at. And his father was a businessman and he and his father lock horns a lot. . . . And my cousin Eddie says to me, he says, he said, 'My father doesn't look at you that way.' He said, 'You are successful because you married Michael. You did what you were supposed to do. You married and you married someone who was successful. That was all that could be wanted of a girl. So you achieved it. You did the right thing.'"

Single women, whether never married or divorced and never remarried, were very problematic figures in the culture. Their work or career may have made them autonomous class agents, in the sense that what they did would have a direct relationship to their success (as money/ status). But it also confounded the gender categories, leaving them open to negative stereotypes.

All of this began to change in the course of the adult lives of the women of the Class of '58. Although they began in the 1950s under the regime of the girl track, in the course of their lives many of them managed to get off it, or rework it, so that they show an occupational and marital profile much different from that of their mothers. At issue, centrally, is the question of becoming "class agents," of being allowed to play the class game in one's own right rather than through the proxy of a husband. This does not necessarily mean being single, though singleness may make *some* things easier. But many married women managed to make the transition too, and for them it meant a reconfiguration of their relationship to their families, and of their families to them.

These are some of the issues of this chapter. We begin by going back to that critical turning point, college (and if so, what kind) or not.

Women and Higher Education

We have already seen that the rates of going to college, or not, for the Class of '58 were heavily skewed by class and race/ethnicity. Class alone created a significant advantage or disadvantage, but this was both compounded and complicated further when race/ethnicity was added into the equation. Thus we saw in table 13 (p. 194) that Jewish classmates received BAS or higher degrees at a rate of 78 percent, while members of other race/ethnic groups, virtually all of whom were working class, received BAS or higher degrees at a rate of 48 percent.

But now let us break things down further by gender. Looking at table 15, one is struck first by the ways in which practice falls in line with ideology. The left column ("more brains/motivation) is ideologically "male," and in fact men predominate; the right column ("less brains/motivation) is ideologically "female," and in fact women predominate. Overall, however, more boys than girls went to college: 69 percent of boys versus 57 percent of girls. This differential is similar across both classes. Thus among the high-capital students, boys represented 54 percent of the total going to college, and girls 46 percent; among the lower-capital students, boys represented 27 percent, and girls 22 percent.

I have already indicated that the general level of Weequahic students going to college was relatively high compared with the rest of the nation. I do not have comparable figures broken down by gender. I do have figures taken from a different perspective that tell us something about the differentials between boys and girls *in college* in that era. Thus according to the *Statistical Abstracts of the United States* for 1962 (table 147, p. 116), college-enrolled students showed a ratio of 63 per-

Table 15. Types of College Education by Class and Gender (*N* = 214)

	More brains/motivation	*Less brains/motivation*
More capital	Away/top schools[a] (*N* = 18) Boys, 13 (72%) Girls, 5 (28%)	Away/less prestigious schools[b] (*N* = 39) Boys, 18 (46%) Girls, 21 (54%)
Less capital	Local schools[c] (*N* = 78) Boys, 43 (55%) Girls, 35 (45%)	No college (*N* = 79) Boys, 33 (42%) Girls, 46 (58%)
Average	Boys 64% Girls 37%	Boys 44% Girls 56%

Note: This table includes only people who went through college without a break, straight from high school.

[a] All private, including Antioch College, Bryn Mawr College, Columbia University, Cornell University, Hamilton College, Princeton University, Skidmore College, Tufts University, and Williams College.

[b] Mostly state universities, including Penn State, the University of Michigan, the University of Vermont, the University of Buffalo, Rutgers (New Brunswick), Douglass College, and Trenton State. There were also some private universities (e.g., Syracuse) in this category, and there are some ambiguous cases, for example, NYU. Although most of the kids who went to NYU lived at home and commuted from Newark, students seemed to feel that going there was almost as good as "going away," as it was private and also exposed the students to a wider and more diverse world. I thus classified it as an "away" school.

[c] All within commuter distance, including Rutgers Newark, Seton Hall University, Upsala College, Fairleigh Dickinson University, Newark State Teacher's College (now Keane College), Montclair State Teacher's College, Newark College of Engineering, and Jersey City State College. Again there is an ambiguous case: Pratt Institute of Technology, in Brooklyn. Although when Barry Goldstein went there he lived "away," he characterized the school as a "working-class school" and I have followed his lead and classified it with the "local schools."

cent males and 37 percent females. Another table (168, p. 131) of college *graduates* by sex shows a ratio of 66 percent boys and 34 percent girls.[1] If we compare these (and they are not, again, perfectly comparable) with the Weequahic figures, we see that the Weequahic boys went to college at close to the rate of boys in college at that time (69 percent), but Weequahic girls went to college at a significantly higher rate than girls in college at that time (57 percent).

The higher rate of Weequahic girls going to college may relate in part to the Jewish factor discussed earlier, but also in good part to the strong middle-classing efforts of many of the parents of the Class of '58.[2] This middle-classing push, which evidently included relatively higher rates of educating daughters, comes through very clearly in the comments of Rhoda Rosenberg:

> "My parents thought it was very important that I be educated. There was never a question of whether I was going to college or not. Never. . . . But my parents' idea of the reason for my education [SBO: was to get a better husband?] No. [No?] was to have something to fall back on if 'God forbid' something happened to my husband. So that I didn't have to go to work in a retail store, like my mother did. . . . My mother knew if I had an education that if 'God forbid' I needed to, I could earn a living in a very respectable way. That was the purpose."

As my little interjections suggest, I suspected that there may have been other things going on as well. Insofar as the Jews were middle-classing, and insofar as Jewish boys were going to college in great numbers, I suspect that at least some Jewish parents must have been thinking that colleges were good marriage markets for their daughters, although nobody ever said such a thing. At the same time Rhoda's comments specifically put her parents' thinking in class terms: there is a point of distinction between the kind of jobs working-class girls might take (working "in a retail store, like my mother did") and the kind of "respectable" job a girl could get (in the 'God forbid' situation) if she had a college degree.

Another way to look at the interaction of class with women's education is to directly correlate the girls' parents' class with girls' attainment of college degrees. Very simply put, the higher the parents' class, the more and higher the degrees (table 16).

Any way one looks at it, class has a significant impact on gender patterns of education, in terms of whether or not the girls went to college; the rates at which they went compared with boys, or compared with national numbers; the kinds of schools they attended; and the level of degrees they obtained. Yet class is working on a system of gender norms that operate on their own logic and with their own force. Thus more boys than girls went to college overall, more boys went to the kinds of colleges associated with more brains/ambition, and more boys than girls took higher degrees overall, particularly degrees that pro-

Table 16. Girls' Degrees by Parents' Class (N = 103)

Business/professional–class parents (N = 26)
  Advanced degrees, 16 (3 PhDs, 1 JD, 12 Masters [MA, MPA]) (62%)
  Bachelors, 7 (27%)
  No degrees, 3 (12%)
Middle-class parents (N = 45)
  Advanced degrees, 13 (1 PhD, 12 Masters) (29%)
  Bachelors, 13 (29%)
  Technical degrees, 4 (2 Associates, 2 RNs) (9%)
  No degrees, 15 (33%)
Working-class parents (N = 32)
  Advanced degrees, 8 (1 JD, 7 Masters) (25%)
  Bachelors, 8 (25%)
  Technical degrees, 2 (1 Associate, 1 RN) (6%)
  No degrees, 14 (44%)

Note: This table includes girls who went back and finished later.

duced high incomes and prestige. (Whereas most of the girls' higher degrees are at the Master's level, most of the boys' higher degrees were professional degrees, especially MDs, JDs, and PhDs.)

But, as noted earlier, levels of education for girls did not predict "success" as strongly as they did for boys, since college degrees did not have the same relationship to subsequent life patterns for girls as they did for boys. Thus, for example, every boy—literally 100 percent—who went to a "top" school went on to a higher professional degree and in most cases a very lucrative career. Among the five girls who went to top schools, however, only three went on to higher degrees and/or full-time careers; the others married successful men and became home-makers (see table 17). Or, looking at the other end of the spectrum, a significant number of girls who did not go to or finish college nonetheless married men who did very well professionally and/or financially. These women are, from the standard cultural perspective of the time, at least as "successful" as the women PhDs and JDs.

But what counts as "success" for women today? The question has been rendered enormously complicated by the intervening feminist movement, which challenged virtually all the old norms and values of the prevailing gender system: the taboo on singlehood and on alter-

Table 17. Lucrative/Prestigious Post-Bachelors Degrees
by Type of College and Gender (*N* = 152)

Top schools
    Men, 13/13 (100%)
    Women, 3/5 (60%)
	Away schools
	    Men, 14/18 (78%)
	    Women, 14/20 (70%)

Local schools
    Men, 23/43 (53%)
    Women, 12/35 (34%)
	Zero college, returned later
	    Men, 5/9 (56%)
	    Women, 5/9 (56%)

native sexualities; the taboo on abortion and divorce; the taboo on women working outside the home, especially after marriage and even more especially after children; the notion that men should earn more than women; and so on. Yet the feminist movement did not come out of nowhere. It represented a codification and intensification of ideas and practices that were already happening out there in the lives of real women, including the women of the Class of '58.

Class of '58 Women and the Feminist Movement

Betty Friedan's *The Feminine Mystique* was published in 1963, five years after the Class of '58 graduated from high school. Friedan argued that fifties married women, isolated in the suburbs and enacting the ideal role of the nonworking housewife, were quietly going crazy. Friedan's book has been criticized for a variety of problems, including especially its bourgeois bias, which ignores, among other things, the large number of women who were in fact working (Meyerowitz 1994). Although for many purposes these criticisms are justified, Friedan's arguments fit the mostly middle-class Class of '58 very well.

In fact, the discontent and frustration of many women in the Class of '58 began even earlier, at the point at which girls were sorted into the college possibilities just discussed. The problem seems to have been particularly acute among girls from high-capital families who went away, but not to top schools. Lower-capital girls were often unhappy about not going away to college or not going to college at all, but the gender factor here was often (though not always) less visible than simply the low capital of the family. For high-capital girls, on the other hand, there was no explanation other than gender itself—especially if they were good students—for not being sent to top schools.

Thus several girls who went to away-but-not-top schools looked resentfully at brothers who went to higher-status schools or otherwise received a greater parental investment in their education:

> *Beth Rosenblatt:* "So to start out, we [she and her brother] were very encouraged [to go to college]. We were very—my brother was encouraged more than I was, I found. . . . I really didn't want to go to [X] college, [away but not very prestigious]. But it was a question of, you know, the summer before I was ready to [apply] to college, my parents said, 'You know, we can't send your brother to law school and you to private college at the same time.' I was resentful of that and I still am, because I felt that I was the one who was probably the better student. There was no question that I was. . . . I really wanted to go to Mount Holyoke or Vassar or some place like that and, you know, to have been cut off at the pass. I think my mother really thought that would finish me off. She'd never see me again. Maybe she was right."

> *Phyllis Brodsky:* "You know, it always seemed when push came to shove, and there was a choice to be made, [my brother] got whatever was chosen. He got a brand-new [sports] car, and I was driving an old '55 Pontiac. . . . Whatever it was it was a leftover something and that was it. . . . And I mentioned before when he graduated from high school, he went to a more prestigious college than I went to."

This woman—a practicing social worker, married with children, and no raving feminist—went on to say wryly, "These men, just because they have a dick, they think they walk on water."

But one did not need to have a privileged brother to resent being tracked away from the better schools:

> *Irene Ziering:* "I went to [away-but-not-top U] for all the wrong reasons, because I heard you could really have a nice time there! . . . I mean my parents really didn't know. They wanted me to go to college . . . but they had absolutely no background or knowledge about it. And the guidance department at Weequahic was not the greatest either! [They didn't think] to say, you really could be at a more academic school, and you belong there, and should be there. So that's where I ended up."

> *Marilyn Greenwald:* "I deeply resent the fact that I didn't apply to better schools. I should have. No one told me I had a brain, ever. Ever. . . . I

was told, meet the bright young man, get married, live and be well and have children."

Beyond the question of which college one went to, there was the question of what college was preparing a girl for. Here there was tremendous pressure to stay within the narrow range of female occupations. Indeed there is a whiff of the idea that parents did not send bright daughters to top schools not only because sons received the greater investment, but because daughters might get excessively ambitious. This seems to be Beth Rosenblatt's implication: "I think my mother thought [Mount Holyoke or Vassar] would finish me off. She'd never see me again. Maybe she was right." It is quite clearly the implication of one father refusing to support his daughter going to graduate school who said she was "pricing herself out of the [marriage] market."

But most of the women of the Class of '58 did what they were supposed to do. After college came marriage. I know of six women (and no men) in the class who did not marry, though I have no data on their reasons and cannot say much about them. The rest duly married, and most had children.[3] Some of these marriages were happy; some were unhappy but the women stayed with them anyway, holding them together from a sense of obligation, duty, traditional moral judgments, and so on. None of the latter complained to me about their husbands outright, but there were telling comments:

> *Ruth Zieper:* [SBO: How long are you married now?] "Thirty years. [SBO: Congratulations.] Yeah, thirty years . . . and . . . it wasn't always easy. I don't think life is always easy."
>
> *Carol Wiernik:* [SBO: So how long you married now?] "Next month will be twenty-nine years. [SBO: Wow!]. Long time. It's not been an easy marriage. I mistrust anybody who tells you that marriage is easy."

But quite a few women in the Class of '58 found themselves in intolerable situations in their marriages and chose divorce or had it chosen for them. Most of these divorces took place in the 1960s and 1970s, and while one could say the women were taking courage from the feminist movement, one could say as well, with Betty Friedan, that the feminist movement was feeding on the mounting discontent of ordinary women like those of the Class of '58.[4]

Table 18. Divorce Rates by Ethnicity

Jews (*N* = 210)	All others (*N* = 28)
Married, never divorced, 131 (62%)	Married, never divorced, 16 (57%)
Ever divorced, 74 (35%)	Ever divorced, 11 (39%)
Single, never married, 5 (2%)	Single, never married, 1 (4%)

Divorce

A few general notes on divorce in the Class of '58. The rate of durability of marriage for the Class of '58 is approximately 60 percent; that is, 60 percent of those who married are still married to their original spouses. I am including in this figure two long-term gay male partnerships. Reciprocally, and after subtracting the small number of never-marrieds, the divorce rate for the Class of '58 is approximately 37 percent. The divorce rate of the birth cohort of which the Class of '58 was a part was, of course, lower than today's rate. However, the Class of '58's 37 percent is below even that lower rate.[5]

One might think that this is related to the heavy Jewish weighting of Weequahic High School, since stereotypically Jewish people are supposed to be stronger on "family values," but this does not appear to be a major factor. According to my numbers, there is relatively little difference in divorce rates between Jews and non-Jews in the Class of '58. Sixty-two percent of Jews and 57 percent of non-Jews are still married (as of the year 2000) to their original spouses (see table 18). There are, however, significant differences by class. At least in the C58 generation, the more successful end of the class has been significantly more likely to stay married than the rest—a 27 percent divorce rate for the professional/managerial class versus a 44 percent divorce rate for everybody else (table 19).

And then there is gender. Men and women got divorced at about equal rates. Yet women were much more likely to talk spontaneously about their divorces in interviews, and in this sense it appears to be more of a "women's issue," which is how I will address it here.[6]

As discussed by the women, the causes of these divorces varied. In quite a few cases the husband left. In many other cases the women themselves fled the marriage. In most cases both parties played a role,

Table 19. Divorce Rates by Class and Gender

	Married, never divorced	Ever divorced	Single, never married
Professional/managerial class (*N* = 133)			
Men (*N* = 72)	52 (72%)	20 (28%)	0
Women (*N* = 61)	45 (74%)	16 (26%)	1 (2%)
Total/Average	97 (73%)	36 (27%)	1 (1%)
All others (*N* = 91)			
Men (*N* = 38)	22 (58%)	16 (42%)	0
Women (*N* = 53)	24 (45%)	24 (45%)	5 (9%)
Total/Average	46 (51%)	40 (44%)	5 (5%)

and it is not particularly useful to try to place the blame. But however it came about, the women I want to discuss here took the divorce as, at the very least, a manifestation of a degree of agency and empowerment that they did not know they had, and at most as an opportunity to develop their own independence. Without in any way glorifying divorce, which is always difficult and problematic for all concerned, I will thus look at many of these divorces as breaking out of "the girl track," and as representing a change in patterns of practice for many women in the Class of '58 that resonated with the emerging women's movement.

I present a rather large number of these stories because the structures and textures of feeling involved go a long way toward making the case that these women viewed themselves as "breaking out." The reader may immediately think that many of the women's stories are reconstructed in light of the intervening women's movement, and to some extent that is true. But I am also suggesting that the women of the Class of '58 (along, of course, with millions of other women) made the movement as much as the movement made them. Their discontents went into making what we came to know as feminism, while at the same time the emerging feminist movement gave them a language, an authorization, and to some extent a solution for their discontents.

I have organized the stories according to the woman's (husband's) class position at about the time of the divorce. Echoes of class position can be heard in a variety of ways in the stories. At the same time there is an overarching theme of personal liberation that comes through across the class differences. I start with some stories from the PMC:

> *Sherry Kleinman:* "For many years I lived as a doctor's wife. And totally lost whatever self-esteem I had. Had none. I was a good mother but that's all I did, I raised my kids. I cared about material things, and just wanted more, more, more. . . . And I never really analyzed our marriage, too. [She laughed.] [But] I found out he was having an affair. It was extremely traumatic. It was horrible. It never ever occurred to me to leave him. I just would have totally fallen apart. What could I do? I mean I couldn't. Finally I created a situation where he left. . . . And during that separation period I thought about how I could live my life."
>
> *Carol Ginsburg:* "We had on the surface a good marriage, because I kept my mouth shut. It was like the good girl, everything's fine, I never told anybody everything wasn't fine. . . . So, I wrote the saddest poems, you know, all suicidal. . . . I started going to a therapist. . . . I started telling the therapist about all this stuff. So she said to me one time, listen here, which was a real turning point for me, she said, if you want to live with a gun at your head? if you do, let's do that! Let's get down and do that. But it was the first time where I saw, that I had put myself into a situation where I [had chosen] to live that way. And I started owning responsibility for needing to be needed more than I needed to be autonomous. And that was the real change."
>
> *Susan Rosenfeld:* [Susan dropped out of school after her first child was born, had a second child, and then began thinking of going back to school.] "I was complaining about [her husband] Fred because I am getting all this pressure, 'You are going to school, what kind of a mother are you.' I said, 'What are you talking about, he could go to school and get his degree. He is finished, he can go to school and get his graduate degree and I can't get my undergraduate degree? Fuck you.' I said, 'What are you telling me, I am a bad mother? I don't give a shit.' [SBO: Where was this pressure coming from?] Everybody and anybody, they would say, 'You have these two children and you are going to school?' I don't know what they are talking about, I don't understand it. . . . Everybody was saying, 'What's your hurry, you are so young. Stay home only with your children.' What do you mean stay home only with my kids, I would be completely out of my mind, I stay home two days with those kids and I can't make a sentence the third day; forget it. How much was I away, it wasn't forty or fifty hours a week like mothers do now, I was taking a few classes a week, big deal."

Some stories from the middle class:

Joan Bartash: "I couldn't handle this lifestyle . . . and be serious about what I wanted to do. When I needed to paint there were two kids, you know, running around. It was like this whole artistic part of me which had basically never been reinforced over the years, I was struggling to hold on to. Every time I felt a glimmer of it, it was sort of knocked down by something that was stronger. A lot of it has to do with the 'mold' that I thought, you know, we were all supposed to be part of. . . . And what happened between 1968 and, like the fall of '77 when I started to teach, for the next three years was that it was just a process of [her husband] Louis and I dissolving whatever we had had."

Davita Reingold: "We were married like five days after I graduated from college. . . . I was teaching high school. And, I didn't want to teach, and I didn't want to be married. I didn't want to be anything I was supposed to be. . . . It was pre- the women's movement. . . . And it was devastating, I mean this was the first divorce [in her family]. . . . But I knew if I didn't do something, then I was going to kill myself. Because that's how serious it was. It was either, I got to find another way, because their way is not my way, or I don't want to be here. And I went in [to her family doctor] very, very depressed. [The doctor sent her to a psychiatrist.] And I saw her twice a week for six months. At the end of the six months she had me put on antidepressants for a period of time and one day I said to her, 'You know, I don't take those pills anymore.' . . . And I said, 'And I've gotten a job in New York and can't come back here anymore.' . . . But, what I got there was the permission, and the empowerment to be what I had to be."

And some from the working class:

Helene Kessler: "I mean, it took me years to get out of that marriage. I was in therapy, I was enraged, I couldn't get up, I was in a state of rage. . . . And then they look at me like I'm a jerk because I said I'm gonna [split with him and] get a job. I'm like, oh, that never occurred to me, get a job? [We both laughed.] Um, it took me years to get out of that. To decide to get out of it."

Rose Stone: "He lost his job, and then I went back to work full time and, from that point on everything went sour. When he finally got the type of job he wanted, I was working full time, I couldn't afford to leave because he wasn't making enough, it was not as much as he was making at the other job, and it really tore us apart. [SBO: He couldn't handle your working, or . . . ?] No, he was very upset with me working, I think because his mother always worked, and probably couldn't go to things that they had in schools. . . . He was more concerned I was going to take away [time] from him than the children. And all of a sudden of course—I mean I went from my father to him—all of a sudden [at work] I felt "I'm being judged [for myself]—not Charlie's mother, Nancy's mother, Eddie's wife," and I liked it, and I'm sure I changed from that and he didn't like the change."

The women who told these stories, and there are more, come from across the whole class spectrum. In some cases they initiated the divorce and in others they did not. Some of them went on to major careers and others did not. But what the stories have in common is a sense of the desperate need to break out of the girl track. Those of the women who had children all, as far as I know, continued to raise their children;[7] some but not all of them remarried. But the terms were clearly different. They did these things not as an unthinking glide down the girl track but on the terms of their own hard-won self-awareness.

Finally, we need to connect these divorce numbers back to the question of "success." It will probably not surprise the reader to learn that there is some correlation between levels of divorce for women in the Class of '58 and levels of success in the career sense. Homemakers, which we may take as the most "traditional" category, had virtually no divorces (although that may be tautological); women in "traditional" female careers had a divorce rate of 32 percent, close to the average for women in the Class of '58 as a whole (36 percent); and women in nontraditional careers had the highest divorce rate in the class: 50 percent. But this only says that there is more to divorce than simply getting out of bad marriages. There is the question of women doing something with their lives that they would not have been able to do under the old regime. We turn then to what the women of the Class of '58, divorced or not, actually did with their lives in the world of work, jobs, careers.

Careers

Table 20 shows the occupations of the women of the Class of '58 today, organized in terms of traditional versus nontraditional patterns for women. As the categories of traditional and nontraditional are not

Table 20. Present Occupations of Women of the Class of '58 ($N = 119$)

Homemakers, 14 (12%)

Traditional female careers, 69 (58%)
   Traditional professions, 32 (27%)[a]
   Traditional jobs, 37 (31%)[b]

Nontraditional female careers, 33 (28%)[c]

Unemployed, 3 (3%)

---

[a] 12 teachers, 5 nurses [including 1 RN/MSW]; 2 speech/language pathologists; 1 each: crisis intervention counseling, director of learning resources, learning center coordinator, learning consultant, librarian, [social] program director, psychiatric social worker, school psychologist, social worker, supervisor of teachers.
[b] 2 each: legal secretary, office manager, real estate sales, teacher's aide; 1 each: administrative assistant, administrative coordinator, bookkeeper/office manager, accounting systems specialist, administrator/sales, auto theft claims, bookkeeper, chiropractic insurance, clerk/administrator, clerk/typist, concierge, credit manager, data entry, makeup artist, medical assistant, medical receptionist, medical lab technician, medical secretary, part-time preschool aide, pharmacy technician, polygraph administrator, public insurance adjuster, retail sales representative, secretary, senior collections representative, senior credit administrator, telephone operator, travel agent.
[c] 5 owners of own businesses; 2 each: attorney, corporate executive; 1 each: adolescent psychologist (PhD), artist/writer, assistant executive vice president, corporate manager, director of treatment center, foreign service officer, free-lance journalist, free-lance movement therapist, graduate student, independent consultant on public school reform, insurance actuary, management consultant, ordained minister, paralegal, clinical psychologist, public relations consultant, real estate broker, senior foundation officer, self-employed (music and entertainment), self-employed festival organizer, software engineer, supervisor of consumer affairs agency, university administrator, university librarian, university professor.

totally self-evident, and because the range of what these women are doing is quite interesting, I list the actual occupations in notes accompanying the table.

The most obvious things about the table are the drop in the proportion of homemakers and the concomitant rise in the proportion of women working outside the home. There are only fourteen homemakers out of a total of 119 women, or 12 percent. This is a huge drop from the parental generation, where the rate of homemakers was lower than expected but still around 52 percent. Subtracting the 3 percent of

Table 21. Class of '58 Women's Occupations Today by Type of Postsecondary Education (N = 106)

Away/top schools (N = 5)
  Homemakers, 2 (40%)
  Traditional female
    careers, 1 (20%)
  Nontraditional careers, 2 (40%)
	Away/not top schools (N = 20)
	  Homemakers, 2 (10%)
	  Traditional female
	    careers, 9 (45%)
	  Nontraditional careers, 9 (45%)

Local schools (N = 35 + 9 who
returned and finished later = 44)
  Homemakers, 6 (14%)
  Traditional female
    careers, 23 (52%)
  Nontraditional careers, 13 (30%)
  Unemployed, 2 (5%)
	Zero college (N = 37)
	  Homemakers, 5 (14%)
	  Traditional female
	    careers, 28 (76%)
	  Nontraditional careers, 4 (11%)

unemployed women, 85 percent of the women of the Class of '58 work outside the home. Some may have stopped briefly while the children were small, but many did not even do that. The level of women working full time, regardless of occupation, implicitly undermines the girl track in the same way that the rise in the divorce rate does. It is not necessarily "feminist," but it involves women voting, as it were, with their feet.

But now let us put these categories back into the context of class origins, as I have done with the men. In order to see this, I will put the numbers back into the college boxes, since those may stand in reasonably well (though not, of course, perfectly) for class background (table 21).

A few notes on this table. First, homemakers: I have already noted the huge drop in the number and percentage of homemakers between the generation of the mothers of the Class of '58 and the Class of '58 itself. But while homemakers are scattered all over the table, it is still the case that high-capital women (those in the top of the table) are homemakers at an average (across the boxes) rate of 30 percent, or more than twice the average rate of low-capital women, which is 14 percent across the boxes. The size of the group of what one classmate called "ladies of leisure" is shrinking, but there is still a distinct class difference in who gets to enjoy that kind of leisure.

With respect to working women, we can also see several patterns. First, there is the question of whether the women are doing traditional women's work (both jobs and professions). Here we see that the rates of women in traditional women's work rise in inverse proportion to the class/college ladder, from the lowest rate, among women who went to top colleges, to the highest rate, among women who did not go to college at all.

Turning the point around, we can also ask about women who took up nontraditional careers. In many cases, they moved into fields or positions that had traditionally been dominated by men—law (but no medicine yet); high-level positions in corporations, social service agencies, and universities; consultancies and small business ownership in their own names; and so forth. In addition, whatever the nature of the work, they represent women moving into careers with ladders of increasing success, and then succeeding in moving up those ladders. In either case, these women have become class agents in their own right. And here once again, there is a class background correlation: the percentages of women in nontraditional careers increase as one goes up the ladder of class background.

Yet having pointed out the boost- or drag-factor of class background, it is time to turn to the other side of the great American coin, "beating the odds." How *did* some women get past the idea that women were not class agents in their own right? How did they get on the class ladder in the first place, and how did they rise up? Let us look more closely at their stories.

Succeeding in Nontraditional Careers

Unlike many men's stories of success, the women's stories are always played out against a backdrop of marriage and family. I have had some men narrate their entire career to me without ever mentioning their marriage(s) or the birth of their child(ren). I had to go back and ask them where in the narrative these fit in. But, single women aside, no woman's success narrative, at least in the Class of '58, could be told without reference to marriage—either breaking it up, keeping it together, or doing it right the next time around.

Many of the divorce stories we heard earlier were preludes to successful nontraditional careers. Joan Bartash has had some success with her painting. Sherry Kleinman opened a successful retail business. Davita Reingold worked her way up through several jobs in the entertainment industry, and finally opened her own talent agency. Carol Ginsburg became a senior official in her city government. Two women whose stories I did not include went on to take law degrees and to practice law.

But a woman did not have to get a divorce to succeed. A kind of intermediate strategy for women who had some ambitions but did not want them to interfere with their marriages was to wait until the kids were grown up and the husband's career was well established, so as not to rock any boats. Thus, for example, Karen Goldberg had been very active in college:

> [from the field notes] She went to Away State and did well but realized she was not (in her word) "brilliant." [But] she started various clubs and projects, and realized that she was an innovator, a starter, somebody who comes in and starts things or changes things in a new way.

After college she taught school for a while and also got married, had kids, and stopped teaching. When the kids were grown she went back to teaching, but she had a hankering for something different:

> [from the field notes] She currently has her own public relations business, mostly doing public relations work for [the small city she lives in]. . . . Her work is going very well. [Her city] recently won first prize in the state of Connecticut for its public relations work. "To tell you the truth," she said with a self-conscious laugh, "I'm feeling very successful."

Paula Friendlander also waited until late in her family cycle to start on a nontraditional career, though her story involves much more stress and strain than Karen's:

> [from the field notes] She got married early, they had a baby immediately, it was a big mistake, and she split with the baby. She went back and lived with her mother, and she and her mother both worked, on complementary schedules, so that one took care of the baby while the other worked and vice versa. Her father had died suddenly when she was fourteen, and things were rough. . . . Four years or so later she took a vacation . . . and met her present husband, to whom she has been married for twenty-five years. He was a recently divorced businessman. After they were married,

she moved to his house with her son and his two kids. They never had any kids together. The early years were rough, there were times when all of them were in therapy. She had started college but dropped out, because of her family finances. Eventually—much later—she decided to go back to school and did well, and then went on to a PhD.

Paula's story is a kind of mixture of old and new girl tracks. She started out in difficult circumstances, both poor and saddled with an early baby—that is, doubly penalized by class and gender. Then she married a relatively wealthy man and her class circumstances improved, but her domestic situation remained "rough." Finally, however—I assume when the kids were finally grown up—she picked herself up and went back to school, finishing her Bachelor's degree and pushing all the way on to a PhD.

But some women just could not wait that long, and yet at the same time did not want to disrupt their marriages. These, then, are the stories of women who tried to pull off that still very difficult feat for women today, "having it all." I know of three cases in which the women have risen to impressive levels of success while at the same time holding together their marriages and raising their children. These stories are worth telling in some detail, for they are object lessons in at least some women's ability to become class agents while maintaining important relationships.

Thelma Heller, first, came from quite a poor background and went to a local college. She was a brilliant student who received a national grant for research in political science as an undergraduate. But she also met her future husband in college and when they became engaged, "That's when I realized that marriage and academic research weren't going to mix." Her professor tried to persuade her that she and her husband could both go on to graduate school together. "But I think part of me yearned for a conventional life. . . . I wanted what everyone else wanted, I wanted a calm life with a husband and children . . . I was really a product of the times." She got married, had two kids, nursed two elderly parents, and was teaching school but not really happy about it. But again she decided she did not want to rock the boat of her marriage: "And I mean my husband is actively the most terrific guy in the world and I think he's the one who encouraged me in all the things I did later but in those early years . . . I consciously made a choice that I would

have to take a back seat if this was going to work." At some point, however, she decided the marriage could take it, and with her husband's
encouragement and support, she went back to school for a law degree:

> "And that's what I did. Stuart was eight and Patsy was ten and I started
> law school. The first year was a riot. It was like learning a foreign lan-
> guage. . . . And I went in with this terrible fear that I was not going to
> be able to do this, and I did it, and I did it immodestly very well. And
> my kids will tell you I drove them nuts because I studied harder in law
> school than I did in college. You know, leave me alone I've got to learn
> this. Perfection was what I was looking for and I got it. I graduated with
> a straight A average, first in the class, that kind of thing because I needed
> to see that, I just needed to see that."

She joined a local law firm and rose quickly to the level of partner,
all the while keeping together what she still describes as a very happy
family.

Rosalie Borkowsky, next, was the daughter of an electrician. Rosalie
went to Local U on scholarships and did so well that they encouraged
her to begin taking graduate courses while she was still an undergraduate. By her junior year she had essentially moved on to graduate-level
research. But she had met her future husband in high school, and that
relationship continued while they were both in college. They got married right after she graduated from college (1962).

> SBO: "So when did you have your child?"
> RB: "Sixty-eight . . . But not until I really had a five-year plan. That I
> had to make sure with Nick that we had our own home, and that we
> were financially secure. And that I could continue to work and have a
> family."
> SBO: "Did your husband share [in the domestic work]? I mean was he
> [. . .]?"
> RB: "Receptive. Extremely."
> SBO: "So you got a prize [husband], early on . . ."
> RB: "You know, I really did."

Rosalie worked first as an adoption consultant, but she was also doing
pioneering research on adoption patterns and was one of a group of
people involved in changing New Jersey laws and policies about this
issue. She founded the state Association of Adoption Consultants, is
a national spokesperson for the International Adoption Society, and

has now opened her own "Rosalie Borkowsky Adoption Counseling Center."

Finally, there is the case of Sharon Lordi. Sharon's is in some ways the most impressive story of all. At least Thelma and Rosalie had the cultural capital of Jewish ethnicity, even if they were from working-class backgrounds. Sharon, on the other hand was from a non-Jewish, working-class family, and was actively discouraged from going to college or having any sort of independent career. She went to work right out of high school, and then:

> "I got married, after we were out of school for four years I was married, and I had my son two years later. I always worked. I worked in between my son and my daughter, and I continued going to school, when my daughter was less than four years old, I went back to work full time. And I worked for a small manufacturing company. That company went out of business, and I went with the supervisor who opened his own. He had difficulties, he joined someone else, I went with him, and each time the company got bigger, and my position grew."

The company turned over again. Sharon was unhappy with her place in the new company and decided she was going to leave. But she had a talk with the new president of the company:

> "The President liked what he heard, and [said] we're going to create a position for you, you can't leave. Within two months . . . things just started happening, and I got a number of promotions, I became the assistant to the vice president, and I was then asked to transfer to Florida. For two and a half years I lived in Florida, I commuted, every Monday I went down to Florida, every Friday I came back home to my family."

Sharon was keenly aware of the value of her husband's support:

> "My husband is enormously supportive of my position. I really would not have been able to do what I did without him. For two and a half years we lived apart, we only lived together on weekends, and, actually we made the most of weekends, and went to our apartment every weekend, in New York."

Sharon rose to the level of comptroller of the company.

> "And, after two and a half years I was transferred back here. It was my decision, to be with my family, and I was promoted to director of store

operations. So this is really a success story. I truly feel that I earned every promotion that I received with [this corporation], but I'm also very grateful for being given the opportunity, you know it's an opportunity that many people don't get in a lifetime. So, here I am. Here I am, yeah."

Like African American men, C58 women of all races, ethnicities, and classes were raised under a certain cultural regime which dictated that they were excluded from direct participation in the game of "success," the game of rising up the class ladder through their own efforts. I have called this cultural regime the girl track. The way to success for the women of this Class was twofold: First, it involved subverting the girl track as such by questioning the ideal of the perfect wife, and either getting divorced or reconstructing their marriages. And second, it involved becoming class agents—finding ways to gain access to the game of class, and pursuing "success" by their own efforts. We may see this combination as a third variety of American "success": success as liberation.

I have looked at the ways in which women's capacity to achieve success was facilitated or hampered by class origins. As with men, there was a significant amount of class "boost" or class "drag" on women's chances of success, in terms of both higher education and of moving into high-income, high-prestige careers. Yet I have tried to balance this point with an emphasis on the commonalities of women's experience, especially within the family (relationships with/obligations to parents, husbands, and children). This has been a kind of tightrope act of writing: women share common experiences BUT these are subverted by class; class differences have an enormous impact BUT women ultimately share large areas of experience and structures of feeling.

Finally, there has been the question of the relationship between the life patterns of the women of the Class of '58 and the feminist movement that began to gather significant force in the early 1970s. A handful of women in the Class participated actively in the feminist movement. Several mentioned marching on Washington, doing volunteer work, or making donations to feminist organizations. It is probably fair to say, however, that most did not get directly involved. Even among those who broke out of the girl track in some way—getting divorced, and/or going to work, and/or having a career—there is little indication that the movement played a role in their thinking. It seems more accurate to say that the women of the Class of '58 who made these kinds of moves were the Friedanesque vanguard—discontented, restless, pushing on doors without knowing what was on the other side. They were not, for the most part, practicing "feminism," they were practicing what was to become, in the course of their lives, feminism.

And now we come to the final chapter. I have been looking at a set of 304 people over the course of the second half of the twentieth century. I have tracked changes in their lives over time, relating those changes both to the class/race/gender circumstances in which they started and to the larger historical contexts in which they took place, all with an eye to understanding the "success" of the Class of '58. The Class was, for the most part, "very successful." But what does this mean in the larger scheme of things? What difference do the lives of 304 people who started out in a small neighborhood in Newark, New Jersey, make to the world we inhabit in the new millennium? That is the question for the final chapter.

Project Journal 11: Endgame

8/22/93 [A classmate married to a wealthy professional man] had called Roberta Cohen about the reunion, and Roberta expressed a sense of being hurt that she was not going to be interviewed. I knew there was going to be some of that, but what can I do? [As I explained in my letter to classmates at the beginning of this book, many people did not realize and/or believe that the interviewees were pretty randomly selected, not in the scientific sense but in the accidental sense.]

9/20/93 Bryna Eisenfeld talked to Mitzi De Hagara about the reunion. Mitzi asked "if any of the popular kids are coming." These categories never die.

10/10/93 I don't think I've complained much in these notes about the difficulty of combining fieldwork with real life. It's so much better to close out all your affairs and get on a plane and go away for a year. Here life goes on; the fieldwork is added on without subtracting anything else.

...... The actual 35th reunion was today. I had a reasonably nice time, hung out with the Willises* and the Koonces* and didn't do too much in an ethnographic mode except take pictures. I'm tired and can't get up the energy to write much, but I really didn't observe much either. It's definitely time to get out of the field.

...... A bunch of people went back to [a classmate's house] afterward. . . . The whole thing was . . . highly, what, tribalized. It's like a New Guinea clan getting together, everyone sits all bunched up and in physical contact with one another (Knauft 1985), and there's a lot of Durkheimian collective effervescence, just sheer heady giddy high spirits emanating from the sheer fact of being together. I did feel like they were all my brothers and sisters.

10/11/93 I'm reminded that I've been thinking some time I should get in touch with Rosalyn Goldberg, and reassure her that her confidences, the extreme intimacy of our interview, would not be abused. You may recall [reminding myself] she talked [a lot] about high school sex. . . . So I took her aside at the reunion yesterday and said that I hoped she wasn't uncomfortable about our interview but I wanted to assure her that her confidence was protected. And she said, I don't even remember what I said. So that was a relief. I have a picture of all these people festering after the interview, feeling seduced and abandoned.

11/18/93 I can't wait to stop collecting data. I'm drowning in it.

5/6/95 The amount of Weequahic self-historicizing, by the way, is unbelievable. [My brother] Mel* showed me something he received called "Born at the Beth," in which for a donation of a mere Xty dollars, you get some certificate and join the club of those born at the Beth Israel Hospital (which of course you already joined by being born there—maybe you get a secret decoder ring as well). For this you get other future mailings, as well as being inscribed on a "wall of life" which will be installed in the lobby. Can you believe it? My *landsmen* sure know how to raise funds.

10/26/98 Yesterday was the 40th(!) reunion of the Class of '58 in a hotel in Morristown. . . . Everyone of course drove me crazy about the book not being finished. It is terrible, really. I wore a badge saying "No the book is not finished yet."

2/28/00 I gave a talk at the [National Humanities] Center about this project. The big news from that event was that Barbara Harris* showed up. Barbara Harris is a professor of medieval English history, who teaches at the University of North Carolina and also has been heading the Women's Studies Program there. Her main claim to fame for my purposes, however, is that she turns out to be the daughter of [the Class of '58's most famous and beloved teacher] Mrs. Rous [see chapter 7]. Barbara graduated from Weequahic H.S. in 1959. We are everywhere.

7/18/01 Trying to finish the book. Calling people to get final bits of data. Vast numbers of people have moved and it has been hard to track down many of them. I thought the children of the Class of '58 were bad; their addresses and phone numbers have a shelf-life of about 6 months. But my classmates are almost as bad. I had this brainstorm about how much people move. It is a rite of passage, and not just metaphorically. They move every time there is some change in their lives. People move for new jobs, or to look for jobs; they move when they get married, when they have kids, when they get divorced, when the kids leave home, when they retire. They may not go far but they just keep moving. Meanwhile the phone company keeps changing area codes so that even people in the same place at the same phone can't be reached without further tracking.

7/18/01 I'm also having second thoughts about following up this study with a study of the children of the Class of '58. The kids were fascinating but there are a lot of problems. For one thing I now have a list of a huge number of them. For another, if I'm having trouble keeping track of the Class of '58, imagine how much harder it would be to keep track of the kids. Finally, they constitute even less of a community than the Class of '58 and I really think I don't want to do another interview-based, talking-heads project. So I'm trying to think of something more conventionally ethnographic, more place-based, if not actually in a single site. I'm thinking to do something about show business, in which a number of the children of the Class of '58 were (trying to be) involved. That would also allow me to get back to a more cultural perspective, compared to the heavy sociological bent of this book. But as they say in LA, I'm not ready "to commit."

chapter 12

Late Capitalism

In chapters 8–11 I looked at how the Class of '58 fared in life. I had originally planned to break up the Class by class and compare how the "high-capital" kids and the "low-capital" kids did, in order to see the degree of class "drag" on their later lives, and also the different structures of discourse and feeling in which their different experiences were framed and embedded. For reasons that I explained earlier, however, the discussion turned out to be virtually unwritable in that form, since people do not for the most part live class in America as socially naked actors, but via other, more salient, identities. Moreover, to look at both class drag and class mobility abstracted from these other identities is to get locked into a kind of simplistic structure/agency binary—either people's life chances were held back (or facilitated) by the effects of class, or people by their own individual efforts (or failures thereof) managed to pull themselves up or drop down.

This binary is real enough, and I have, of course, used it throughout this book; but used "nakedly," it ignores not only the identities through which people function as class subjects but also the histories of those identities. The last several decades of so-called identity politics have forced us to recognize the ways in which "agency" itself is constrained by collective forms of oppression and facilitated by collective forms of liberation. Thus I shifted my strategy and broke up the Class of '58 into identity groups, discussing their class projects and class fates within those categories. The categories may have seemed odd—Jewish men, other ethnicities, African Americans, and women—but they were more or less dictated by the historical existence of social movements that addressed the specific situations of those categories: the early Jewish move toward financial success and social acceptance via a Protestant-style work ethic and cultural "Americanization" (not purely directed at men, of course, but leaving many aspects of women's situations unreconstructed); the labor movement and its relationship to the members of other ethnicities in the Class, who were mostly from working-class families; the later movements for African Americans' and women's liberation. To ignore the ways in which personal agency and one's fate in the mobility game are tied to larger group histories like these is to fall into American individualism of the most ideological sort.

The identity politics of the last several decades have also been important in enlarging our sense of the forms of inequality. Within a classic Marxist reading, the base of all inequality is class inequality, and other forms—race, gender—will in a sense get fixed when class itself is dissolved by the revolution. Even within a kind of bourgeois American common sense, the only real source of structural difference and inequality in America is money. If women, African Americans, and other groups did not do as well in the game of class, this was because—so the thinking went—women and Blacks simply did not have the right kinds of brains and ambition to succeed. Identity politics, on the other hand, has insisted on the distinctiveness of these different forms of inequality, and on the fact that class is only one among several forms.[1] Thus the mantra that took shape in the seventies: race, class, and gender.

The problem was, however, that class tended to keep dropping out of the picture. There are cultural and historical reasons for this, and I touched upon them in the course of earlier chapters (see also Ortner 1996). But the fact that class kept dropping out was what pushed me to do this project and write this book—to "bring class back in." Yet if the identity politics people, both scholars and activists, kept losing class, the "bringing class back in" people tended to be relatively classic Marxists who either opposed or ignored the importance of identity politics, and who also opposed or ignored the turn to culture and discourse that has so enriched our ideas about social life in general and class in particular.[2] I still consider myself to have been inspired by Marx's brilliant critical analysis of capitalism, but I also identify, both intellectually and politically, with the important work of such identity movements as feminism and racial liberation. Further, I am deeply intellectually committed to the cultural/discursive turn; that is, to the move to understand the ways in which class, like all identities, is socially and historically constructed and reconstructed out of the much more amorphous maldistributions of resources and other forms of capital in ordinary social life. In life there is continuity, flow, messy blendings. Discourse imposes categories and boundaries, and invests them with meaning and value, for better and, very often, for worse.

In practice, then, I have looked at class in a variety of ways. I have coded and located people within would-be objective class categories, always with a sense of discomfort about the coding itself, always with a sense of uncertainty about where to draw the lines and who should go in what box. The anthropologist in me was uncomfortable with this process, but it seemed to be one of the necessary "objectivist" moments that Bourdieu talks about in his theory of practice.[3] It was necessary in part to get a picture of where the Class of '58 started within the larger U.S. scheme of things, and it will also be necessary in this chapter when I return—in another objectivist moment—to that larger American scheme of class and culture and ask how it has changed and what role the Class of '58 played in changing it.

But I have also looked at class very much as a cultural object, in a wide variety of ways: I discussed the discourse of invisibility of class; the difference between several two-part and three-part models, both native and theoretical, of class; the ways in which class as capital intersects with cultural notions of individual charisma, brains, and so forth in producing the cultural schemes of popularity in high school, and of status rankings of colleges; I discussed discourses of "success" as money, as happiness, and as liberation. And, of course, I looked at class as it is refracted through individual intentions and desires: class projects, class anxieties, class resentments.

The book as a whole has been biased toward looking primarily at the upward mobility of the Class of '58. A few comments on this emphasis are in order. First, the emphasis on upward mobility is simply historically accurate. The Class was part of a highly successful age cohort nationwide. In addition, the emphasis on upward mobility is ethnographically real; that is, it is clearly a central part of "the native point of view." As I have emphasized throughout the book, the notion that one should and could be "successful" was very much a part of the worldview of many, probably most, members of the Class of '58. In their case it coincided with a historical era of real opportunity, but what is interesting about the "American Dream" of upward mobility is that it seems to live on even when opportunities shrink.

Second, while I share in the Marxist critique of capitalism, I also have a very strong sense that one must make the prior critique of who gets to enact its practices, climb its ladders, and seek to enjoy its benefits in the first place. The Class of '58 was largely composed of the children and grandchildren of immigrants—Jews who were just beginning to get a toehold in the American system, first- and second-generation offspring of other ethnic groups, African Americans almost entirely up from the South, and women in all those groups. None of these were, in the first instance, seen as legitimate players in the hegemonic game of success in America. The Jews were further along than the other groups, but even for them many doors were still closed, and their financial success was still often seen as somewhat unclean, emerging from greed and shady practices rather than the supposedly honest money of white America. Thus although I have emphasized (though again, not disproportionately in relation to the real history of C58) success and mobility, I essentially made a decision to pitch my political critique at the level of questions of access to the system, rather than critiquing the evils of the system as a whole. That would be a different book.

But now let us go back to the Class of '58 with a few final questions. The world of 2003 is very different from the world of the fifties. It is a commonplace in the discourse of contemporary social theory that the late twentieth century saw a major set of interlocked shifts in the social, economic, and cultural order of the world, a set of shifts that have been dubbed "late capitalism" and its cultural correlate, "postmodernism." In what sense can we say that the lives we have looked at, the real practices of the Class of '58, played a role—as they must have— in those enormous transformations?

The Class of '58 and the Making of Late Capitalism

"Late capitalism" is, like all the other attempts to grasp the shape of the world economy in the late twentieth century and the early twenty-first, a cultural construction, in this case a theoretical construction.[4] One of the most influential attempts to theorize it was that of Fredric Jameson, who actually said little about late capitalism's characteristics as a social-political-economic system. Rather, he used it largely as a jumping-off point for his discussion of "postmodernism," a radically new set/style of cultural forms and associated forms of consciousness that he considered to be the "cultural logic" of late capitalism (Jameson 1984; see also Harvey 1989). Other scholars have attempted to describe more fully the sociology of late capitalist economies, and to link these with the kinds of cultural transformations Jameson discussed. Scott Lash and John Urry's *The End of Organized Capitalism* (1987) offers a fourteen-point description of the key changes in the capitalist order in the second half of the twentieth century, including globalization, changes in the productive organization of capitalism and of the American class structure, the emergence of new social movements (feminism, environmentalism, and so on), and the emergence of postmodern culture. Similarly, Alan Wolfe's *America at Century's End* (1991) offers a seventeen-point list of changes (I'll say more about the trope of the list below),[5] which include most of the above as well as several points related to changes in family configurations that are missing from Lash and Urry. Most recently, Jean and John Comaroff have discussed, under the rubric of "millennial capitalism" (2001), a configuration of factors that centers on globalization, the decline of the possibility of class politics in the Marxist sense, the hyperemphasis on ethnic identities, and an upsurge of magical and millennial thinking about economy and society.

The Class of 1958 of Weequahic High School is in many ways not very "late" in its participation in, and practices of, capitalism. Its members are for the most part, to adapt a phrase from Paul Rabinow (1991), "resolutely modern." Yet the transformations of economy, society, and culture that now come under the rubric of late capitalism did not come from nowhere, and their seeds must be found in part in the lives and practices of the preceding generation(s). Or, to turn the point around, when the Class of '58 lived their lives and practiced their values as they understood them, they were making something that extended beyond their own individual successes or unsuccesses. They were, I would argue, contributing to the beginnings of late capitalism.

It is worth repeating that late capitalism includes a wide range of social, economic, political, and cultural changes, not all of them obviously or directly related to one another. Different authors make different elements central—many emphasize "globalization," others focus on technological changes, and so forth. Moreover, different authors weave the various changes together in different ways, producing different narratives of causality and different pictures of the world we inhabit today. While I am persuaded that the present world is in many ways very different from that of the mid-twentieth century, I have not been captivated by any single narrative of how we got here, by any magic word that supposedly captures or organizes all the changes (e.g., *globalization*), or by any single picture of how everything hangs together. In the following discussion of the ways in which the Class of '58 participated in the making of late capitalism, then, I will stick with the eclecticism signaled by listing a variety of changes. In keeping with the theme of this book, however, I will also give special emphasis to transformations in the U.S. class structure, something that often gets lost among other, seemingly sexier, issues.

Let me start small, with some contributions that were made by specific individual members of the Class of '58. Taken alone, they would seem idiosyncratic; yet we can see in retrospect how they fit into the larger picture of late capitalist transformations. Here, then, the first list: (1) Technological changes are, as noted, central to many theories of late capitalism. Most of these changes are electronic and communicational—the computer, the fax, the Internet (Castells 1996). In addition, however, and often ignored by nonfeminist scholars, are the development and expansion of radically new reproductive technologies (Ginsburg and Rapp 1995, Franklin 1997, Rapp 1999), with radical effects on both family experience and family law. And here is the C58 example: One man confessed, with some intensity, that he and his wife had availed themselves of a controversial new reproductive technology in order to have their child. (2) "Globalization" is, for most theorists of late capitalism, one of the central transformations of the new era. The Class of '58 has had very little direct participation in the global economy. Again, however, there is one key story. Larry Goldman had built up a successful business in New Jersey the old-fashioned way—working his way up from being a salesman for another company; leaving and starting his own company; and succeeding through hard work, smart entrepreneurialism, and careful management. He recently sold his company to a Japanese corporation for a sizable sum of money. I like to see the sale of Larry's very modern business to Japanese buyers as one individual handoff from modern to late capitalism, from the local to the global economy.[6] (3) The emergence of "postmodern" cultural forms has been seen as another of the central transformations of late capitalism. I noted a moment ago that one would be hard-put to see the Class of '58 as participating in postmodernism. Yet once again there is a key individual story. Most scholars would agree that the original usage of the term, and the original site of the emergence of a self-consciously postmodern aesthetic, was in architecture.

Postmodern architecture broke with the austere and hyperrational aesthetics of architectural modernism (Gropius's famous Bauhaus dictum that "form follows function," which gave us the glass-and-steel box) and began producing much more complex, playful, and "wild" architectural forms. Within the United States, in turn, one of the architectural firms that has been credited with being in the forefront of this development is a firm called Jackson, Jentis and Rogers [a pseudonym] of New York City. The "Jentis" of the firm name is none other than C58's own Martin Jentis, son of one of the teachers at Weequahic High School, class officer, and all-around popular person. Martin's work, which has been nationally recognized and enormously influential, thus represents an even clearer moment of handoff from the cultural world in which the Class of '58 grew up to the world in which we live now, from modernism to postmodernism.

These are individual cases, yet each finds its place in larger patterns that represent major changes in the world. Indeed "finds its place" is perhaps too passive a phrase for what these individual acts and careers represent. For how else do patterns take shape except by the individual and cumulative acts and practices of real historical subjects, even if those subjects had other intentions entirely?

Beyond individual acts and careers, however, we have also seen broader changes in the Class of '58, changes that place the Class as a whole relatively clearly on the path to the present configurations of social life. I mention two of these briefly, as they have already been discussed at length. (1) The rise in the divorce rate, which is part of the shift to postmodern family patterns (e.g., the "recombinant family" discussed in Stacey 1990): The Class of '58 was obviously moving the rate up. The parents of the Class of '58 probably had something like a 5 percent divorce rate, or perhaps a little higher if one includes a number of fathers who deserted the families without divorce. The Class of '58 by contrast has a 37 percent rate, low for its age cohort, but nonetheless more than seven times higher than that of the parents, and well on the way to the 50 percent rate of today.[7] (2) The appropriation of the benefits of the new social movements: Although few members of the class actively participated in these movements, many individuals were able to capitalize on the gains of both the Civil Rights/Black Power and feminist movements. This in turn produced significant upward mobility for many of the African Americans in the Class, an enormous influx of C58 women into the workforce (doubling the rate of the collective mothers of C58), and a significant number of those women moving into nontraditional occupations. These patterns in turn fit into nationwide transformations that have permanently changed the face of the economy, now more diverse in terms of race, ethnicity, and gender, with many more people having access to the ladders of success. And finally, (3) the transformation of the American class structure, and specifically the tremendous growth—and also the changing characteristics—of a new privileged class, the so-called professional/managerial class, or PMC: Insofar as the Class of '58 collectively embodies and reflects a major piece of the making of late capitalism, I would argue that it was primarily at the level of participating in this particular class transformation. If the rise of women and minorities changed the face of the class structure, the extraordinary upward mobility of the Class of '58, and the nationwide cohort of which it was a part, changed its shape. We need to explore this set of transformations in more detail.

The Growth of the PMC

Much of the earlier literature on late capitalism was concerned precisely with changes in the social and economic formations of the advanced capitalist nations, including changes in production, class structures, and class politics. Yet the idea of late capitalism quickly moved in two different directions: into postmodernism ("the cultural logic of late capitalism"), on the one hand, and into "globalization" (the accelerated transnational "flows" not only of capital but of people, images, and ideologies [Appadurai 1996, Hannerz 1996]), on the other. Both of these issues are enormously important, and I will return to globalization in particular later in the chapter. But I resist the tendency to let class get lost, once again, in the shuffle. Here, then, I pull together some of the class transformations that have been noted as—once again—a less visible dimension of late capitalism and look at the ways in which the Class of '58 participated in those changes.

Let us return to Lash and Urry's *The End of Organized Capitalism* (1987). One of their key points concerns the enormous growth of the professional/managerial class (which they call a "service class"), and the impact this has had in undermining the traditional shape of capitalism in the West: "The continued expansion of the number of white-collar workers and particularly of a distinctive service class (of managers, professionals, educators, scientists, etc.) which is an effect of organized capitalism, becomes an increasingly significant element which then disorganizes modern capitalism" (1987:5).

The class of managers and professionals has been growing since the late nineteenth century. Its importance has been increasingly recognized (e.g., Walker 1979), and its significance endlessly debated. It has been given various names—the Ehrenreichs' "professional-managerial class," or PMC (1979); Galbraith's "new class" (1984); Lash and Urry's "service class" or "service sector" (1987); Eder's "new middle class" (1993); and others. In each formulation it has a somewhat different significance and includes somewhat different categories of occupation. Differences aside, however, it is essentially what it sounds like, a class (or more accurately a category) comprising people who are neither owners nor workers, but rather professionals and managers who in a sense operate the system, via specialized knowledge and various forms of power and authority derived therefrom. One could think of them as a Foucauldian class, a class that derives its wealth not from ownership of the means of production but from the knowledge/power on which production rests.

Michael Lind (1995a, 1995b) has gone further and merged this class with the owners of the means of production, the wealthiest and most powerful people in society, treating the two groups as a single powerful "overclass."[8] I have already noted the differences between a two-tier model (here, overclass/everybody else) and a three-tier model (some variant of upper/middle/lower) of class in America. Both can help make sense of the system in different ways and in different contexts. I have mostly bowed to the folk usage of a three-tier model, but whichever model one chooses, it is clear that the Class of '58 has contributed to the enormous growth of the PMC, and has participated actively in the transformations Lash and Urry, Lind, and others have described. The whole occupational chart of the Class of '58 and their spouses is reproduced in appendix 4, but in table 22 we can see, in schematic form, the large shifts in the numbers from the generation of the parents of the Class of '58 to the Class itself.

As we can see, the PMC of the Class of '58 has more than doubled in relation to its parents' generation. But there are changes further down

Table 22. Class Configurations of Class of '58 Parents and the Class of '58 Itself

	Parents of the Class of '58[a] (known N = 207)	The Class of '58 (known N = 241)
PMC [BPC]	55 (27%)	139 (58%)
Middle class	92 (44%)	91 (38%)
Working class	60 (29%)	11 (5%)

[a] The specific distribution of occupations of the parents of the Class of '58 is attached to table 2.

in the profile as well. Whereas among the parents there was still a substantial middle class (indeed it was the largest class in the group) and a substantial working class, the middle class is now proportionally smaller (in fact smaller than the PMC), and the traditional working class has virtually disappeared. The shrinkage of the traditional working class in the Western nations is another hallmark of late capitalism: There is a "decline in the absolute and relative size of the core working class, that is, of manual laborers in manufacturing industry, as [Western] economies are de-industrialized" (Lash and Urry 1987:5), and as industrial labor is outsourced to the Third World.

How did this growth of the PMC and shrinkage of the working class come about—not merely for the Class of '58 of Weequahic High School but for the nation as a whole? That is, to say the least, a large question, and part of the answer would involve a major macropolitical-economic analysis, including analysis of corporate, national, and global economic policies (see, e.g., Comaroff and Comaroff 2001, Storper 2001). At the same time, as I once again maintain, we must still ask about the role of real, on-the-ground social and economic actors. At this level, to write of the "growth" of the service sector is to use a misleading organic metaphor. A class does not "grow" by itself. People act as class agents, working or not, succeeding or not. For the Class of '58 and similar cases across the nation, large numbers of people were upwardly mobile, producing at the microlevel the enormous "growth" of the PMC.

A final word here on the Jewish factor in the high rates of upward mobility for the Class of '58. As I discussed earlier, there is a tendency in both the popular imagination and in some of the scholarly literature to attribute high rates of Jewish success to Jewish cultural patterns: the value on education, the instilling of Jewish children with the ambition and the drive to succeed. Yet I would argue that this kind of pressure/encouragement on the children, traditionally on the boys but now to a greater extent on both sexes, has as much to do with more general immigrant dreams and fears, hopes and desires. Despite the emphasis on globalization, Lash and Urry and other theorists of late capitalism have little to say about the continuing role of immigration and ethnicity in the transformations of the capitalist order. But here is one place where the Jewishness of Weequahic—not because it is Jewish but because it embodies a certain kind of driven immigrant culture that can be seen in many groups—may add something important to the late capitalism narrative. Immigrants may "flow" into a country from elsewhere, but when they stop they move into a class structure, and the consequences of this must be followed in much the way I have followed the Class of '58.

Returning to the professional-managerial class, the PMC of late capitalism is not only greatly enlarged, it is also different from the old business-professional class (as I called it) of the parental generation. For one thing it has a different occupational composition: whereas for C58 parents business was the largest sector of the BPC, for the Class of '58 it is one of the smaller sectors, and the new PMC, which occupies the same class space, is dominated precisely by professionals (again see appendix 4). Partly related to that shift, in turn, is a shift in strategies of social reproduction for this group, which is behaving increasingly like the Old Money, Old Upper Classes of WASP America. These classes relied on institutional mechanisms—trust funds, college legacy policies, clubs, and old boy networks—to ensure that their children received the benefits of their class membership (Aldrich 1988, Marcus 1992). The old middle class, on the other hand, as Barbara Ehrenreich in particular has argued (1979, 1989), was classically achievement based, and lay great stress on parental practices in bringing up the kinds of children who would have the right kinds and amounts of ambition, brains, talents, and so forth to "make it." But the new PMC, at least according to a riveting piece by Michael Lind (1995a), is no longer that traditional middle class. While it still has some of the old emphasis on parenting for ambition and brains, it has also appropriated the institutional mechanisms that the old upper classes relied on, especially trust funds and college legacies. The new PMC is thus increasingly turning itself into a castelike formation analogous to the old upper class.

The Class of '58 mirrors this transformation in every respect. Nearly 60 percent of the Class are now in high-income and/or high-prestige professional/managerial positions. Although I have not been able to write about family wealth management strategies here, C58 as parents have availed themselves of all the strategies just noted for passing on wealth and cultural capital: endowing their children with trust funds, sending them to private schools and then, as legacies, to the colleges whose gates the Class of '58 "crashed" (Christopher 1989) in the first place.

But this is, of course, a double edged point. On the one hand, the Class of '58 mostly did very well for itself, and those who pulled themselves up by hard work and dedication have a right to be proud of what they have accomplished. On the other hand, in doing so they have joined in another late capitalist transformation, the process of inadvertently changing the shape of the U.S. class structure, to the often severe disadvantage of those who have not been able to achieve the same kinds of success. Where the class structure of the country after the Second World War had the shape of a top—fatter in the middle and thinner at the top and bottom (like that of the C58 parents, only more exaggerated)—it now has the shape of an hourglass— skinny in the middle and fat at the top and bottom. What we are seeing in the class numbers of C58 today is mostly the "fat top." The fat bottom is invisible because so many classmates have moved up. But it is "out there," both locally—new immigrant labor—and globally—the outsourcing of industrial labor to Third World nations.

Put in other words, the gap on the national level between the PMC and everyone else is quite wide, and getting wider. Moreover, the situation has been getting worse for several decades. Michael Lind went so far as to talk of the "Brazilification" of America, in which there is a growing gap between an increasingly rich and powerful overclass and a range of "everyone else," who are either struggling to make ends meet or have virtually given up. Ulrich Beck (2000) similarly wrote of "the Brazilification of the West." Virtually all economists and economic sociologists agree: Approximately since the 1970s, the rich have been getting richer and the poor have been getting poorer (Morris and Western 1999, Keister and Moller 2000). At this point, according to a recent piece in the New York Times, "the level of inequality [in the United States] is higher than in any other industrialized nation" (Stille 2001).

This is not to blame the Class of '58 for its ambition and its success. It is simply to say that, as we think of large and seemingly impersonal processes like globalization, deindustrialization, postmodernism, or—in this case—large-scale redistributions of wealth and power, we must remember that they do not come solely from the actions of corporations, banks, policy organs, and culture industries; they also, and equally importantly, come from the ordinary practices of real people pursuing the good life as they understand it.

Moreover, the successful members of the Class of '58 did not entirely turn their backs on those who were less fortunate. For the most part they practiced a liberal politics that was consistent with their commitment to capitalism, on the one hand, and to democratic social ideals, on the other. In particular, quite a few members of the Class, both white and African American, put time, effort, money, and caring into problems surrounding race (in part, of course, always a surrogate for class), and I want to return to that issue one more time here.

Race Again

One would have to say that the race situation for the Class of '58 today has shown modest improvement. Several African American members of the Class have been successful in a variety of ways: relatively high educational levels, good jobs/careers, marriages to successful spouses, and—looking down the road—children on their way to even higher levels of success. I discussed this at length earlier (except for the kids, who are beyond the scope of this book) and will not go over it again. But two issues remain. The first is whether one can say that there have been analogous improvements in the white community when it comes to racism. We know that there were many liberal members of the Class, themselves children of liberal parents, committed to working on these issues (one woman heads an organization that focuses on early childhood education against racism, another works with a community group to fight "steering"), but what about those who did not come from more enlightened families? While I did not pursue this issue in detail, several classmates did volunteer stories of responding to the changed racial climate and moving beyond a prejudiced family background. Here is one:

> *Ralph Lee:* "When my father was in the department, you know, in the police department in Newark, he was exposed to the [criminals]. And it wasn't the upper crust. So his attitude towards African Americans, Blacks, was not what mine was. Because my exposure wasn't to that. And you know he used these words, 'nigger this, nigger that.' All over the place. And up to a certain age, I heard this, I lived with it. It became part of my life. And I did at one time develop an attitude. You know, my manner was pretty much a reflection of his. Well, after a certain point, I did not believe what he had said any more, because it wasn't what I was experiencing. And after I got married, I told him, I refused to allow him to say 'nigger' in my house. I didn't want that word. I didn't like that word. I just don't use it. I don't allow my kids to use it. Of course they don't feel that way."

This is not to say that all is well in New Jersey concerning race; far from it. One man talked about returning to the old Weequahic neighborhood, which is now mostly Black and poor:

> *Robert Weinstein:* "We went back to New Jersey, I was with my [teenage] kid. So we went out with my friends. . . . We were riding through Newark. And everybody in the car was going, 'fucking niggers this, fucking niggers that, look what they did to Newark, blah blah blah . . .' My kid's like, you can see him, he's getting more and more part of the upholstery in the back. Pretty soon I'm not even going to see him, he's going to shrink into the trunk. . . . He's grown up [where] . . . race isn't. . . . He's never heard people talk like this before."

This little vignette goes in several directions: on the one hand, the old racism is thankfully completely alien to at least some members of the next generation (in this case, Robert's son); on the other hand, it is unfortunately still rampant in other quarters; and finally, to come full circle, Newark in general, and Weequahic High School in particular, are still areas in which racism is a major problem. In the years after the Class of '58 graduated the neighborhood underwent a radical racial shift. Increasing numbers of African American families moved in and white families fled (frightened, many said, by realtors). The Newark riot took place in 1967. While a number of '58 graduates devoted serious efforts not only to fighting racism but to materially and politically working on ameliorating African American poverty, most of this work was not directed at the racial situation in Newark, in the Weequahic neighborhood (except for the doctor running the outreach program from Beth Israel Hospital), or in Weequahic High School. It was as if there had been two Weequahic High Schools, one white, Jewish, middle class, and academically strong—and surviving only in nostalgia—and then suddenly a different school: Black, poor, socially troubled, academically weak, and very much physically and socially still there.

The Newark school system overall is in serious trouble today, and has recently been taken over by the state. But with respect to Weequahic in particular, several 1950s graduates, successful professional men, finally woke up and decided to do something about/for the school. Harold Braff* ('52) and Sheldon Bross* ('55), among others, joined some more recent African American graduates of the school in founding a new Weequahic High School Alumni Association, one that bridges the old Jewish Weequahic and the new African American Weequahic. The goals are described on the front of the first newsletter:

—To recapture the spirit and memories of Weequahic High School that were so meaningful to many of us.
—To transcend the generational and cultural differences spanning seven decades from 1932 to the present by bringing together our graduates, teachers, administrators and friends for reunions and special events.
—To remember and honor those Weequahic High School graduates and staff who have made important contributions to the school and our larger community.
—To utilize the resources of our alumni to support the current students at Weequahic High School through scholarships, tutoring, mentoring, job opportunities and cultural events.

The Weequahic Alumni Association has already raised money for college scholarships for a number of top-ranked seniors graduating in the last several Classes at the school. Its officers have also organized several all-alumni reunions in the Newark area, reunions that have been much more racially integrated than the Class reunions, which by definition mirror the racial composition of the school at given points in time. The newsletter is upbeat and optimistic.

The new Alumni Association is not going to solve all the problems of race in the school and the neighborhood, much less in larger arenas. But it does represent a continuation, in a very fitting site, of the kind of antiracist, antipoverty, and pro-civil rights work that many members of the Class of '58 have done for years. I conclude with it here because I think it is worthy, and hopefully effective, in and of itself. I conclude with it as well to counter the strong materialistic image of the Class of '58 that has come through at times, not wholly unjustifiably, in this book. And finally I conclude with it as a ray of hope in what feels, at the moment, like a world with a very dismal future. The horrendous events of September 11 took place only six months ago. India and Pakistan are threatening each other with nuclear war (again). Israel and Palestinians are locked in mortal combat (again).

The main point of this book has been the simple, yet very complex, idea that history makes people, but people make history. We have watched the Class of '58 being constructed as diverse (young) subjects under particular social, cultural, and historical conditions. We have watched them move out in the world and succeed or not, as a function of their backgrounds, motivation, and hard work, but also by "piggybacking"—often without even realizing it—on powerful social movements. And we have seen finally that, while for the most part they succeeded in making at least "comfortable" lives for themselves and their families, they also became—invisibly to themselves—actors in vast social transformations with literally unimaginable chains of consequences. This is not the place to attempt to link the bombing of the World Trade Center or violence in the Middle East to the growing chasm between the haves and have-nots in America. But as one classmate said, linking American racism and the launch of Sputnik in the 1950s, "they are all part of one package and that package keeps getting larger." Yet if one focuses one's ethnographic lens closely, one can at least see good people—like many members of the Class of '58—trying to combat social evils in whatever little corners of the world they inhabit.

Appendix 1. Finding People

JUDY EPSTEIN ROTHBARD

I first learned of Project Weequahic while having dinner with Sherry in 1990 during my son's freshman year at the University of Michigan. At that time she was able to contact approximately 100 of my classmates (out of 304). I knew the whereabouts of (or could easily find through the grapevine) another 25 and offered to send her their addresses after I returned home.

The following year, while looking through a friend's thirtieth reunion booklet (Weequahic Class of '60), I noticed about five or six names that were the same as those of my classmates, and thus was born the first of my hypotheses: I assumed these people were younger siblings. When this proved to be true, I became intrigued by the search that would re-create my teenage years and eagerly accepted Sherry's offer of a job as a research assistant.

While the Internet seemed the most expedient vehicle for locating the missing (and it did ultimately yield a number of people), it was useless when looking for common names like Weiss, Grossman, Katz, Goldberg, etc.[1] After exhausting my-word-of mouth leads ("his sister lives in Maplewood," "her uncle owns the cleaning store in Livingston"), which did lead me to find those in question, I began to call people in Essex and Union Counties (à la cold-canvassing telemarketers) on the assumption that since a large number were known to live in those suburbs, an even larger number were likely to be found there. I contacted two local newspapers with blurbs about an upcoming reunion and then felt obliged to call the six people who eagerly responded with their addresses and tell them no reunion was currently being planned.

After this I had to think "larger." I called Weequahic High School to see if there was a list of colleges attended by graduates or any other way I could track down missing classmates. Luckily, I reached a secretary who had been at the school for more than thirty years and knew everything that went on in the building as only an "old-timer" would. She told me about the graduation list on file at the Board of Education that contained full names, addresses, age at graduation, and names of parents. My next lucky break came in a phone call to the secretary of the superintendent, who seemed

1. [SBO: This was the early 1990s, before sites like Classmates.com existed. I have recently found some very long-lost people through Classmates.com.]

intrigued by my duties as "head of the research department for Dr. Ortner" and happily sent me the list in question. This became the key to locating the majority of the missing. By taking the age in June 1958 (e.g., seventeen years, eight months) I came up with a birthdate, and with a full name and a date of birth, for a nominal fee (five dollars in New Jersey) one could contact the Division of Motor Vehicles of the state and get the address of any resident. I continued this in other states using notes from previous reunion committees, assuming that people stayed in the same state they went to as young adults embarking on a career. This proved largely to be true. California was the only state where I could not do this because a recently passed law prohibits such searches after the stalking and killing of an actress whose murderer found her address by running a search of her license plate number. Many of our former classmates are rumored to be living on the West Coast, and judging by the large number we found in California, the rumor is probably true, but we have no way to locate them.

After finding one of our male classmates through the Division of Motor Vehicles of a neighboring state, I mentioned a rumor that one of the women in our class was supposed to be living in the same county and even working in the same field as he did. He said that while there was a professional list, it consisted of more than three thousand names, and without a last (married) name, she would be very difficult to find. I mentioned that her first name had an unusual spelling, and by the next day he had located and spoken to the person in question and called me back with her address. Another rumor that one of our classmates had appeared on the *Johnny Carson Show* failed to produce that person's address but did get me an invitation to a taping of the *Jay Leno Show* the next time I was in California.

A wedding announcement in a local paper of a bride from Marietta, Georgia, led me to one of our missing classmates. I remembered that this bride's grandmother and our classmate's mother were partners in a local boutique while we were growing up in Newark. In a phone call to the parents in Georgia I learned that our classmate had died three years earlier.

Having exhausted this strategy it was back to the Board of Education list, this time to the parents column and the assumption that if they were still alive, they constituted the exodus from Newark in the late '60s. I further assumed that they resided in either the nearby suburbs, "down the shore" (as we call the New Jersey shore), or on the east coast of Florida in Dade, Broward, or Palm Beach Counties. These efforts also eventually resulted in a good yield. As an aside I must comment on my conversations with the parents, which ranged from lengthy talks about the old neighborhood ending with them happily telling me how to contact their children, to complete skepticism and distrust and agreeing only to take my phone number and have their son or daughter call me if they were interested. In one case I received a callback in five minutes from a classmate who had lost touch with everyone, settled out of state after college graduation in 1962, and had wanted to go to a reunion all these years but did not know whom to contact—he hoped someday someone would find him.

One of my chief frustrations through the more than one year that I conducted these searches was the number of missing women, most of whom I was sure had taken their husbands' last names. I contacted the Hall of Records to see if I could look up marriages in Essex County in the 1960s, but the Catch-22 was that these records are inaccessible without the groom's name. I did find a number of female classmates whose married names I had not known when I read the obituary of a parent in the *Jewish News*.

At this point I had accounted for nearly 80 percent of our classmates, almost all of them Jewish. My success rate with the African American population was running about 15 percent and going nowhere. I found one person through the Division of Motor Vehicles, another through a random call to someone in the Oranges who told me her sister lived in the home where they grew up in Newark, and a third by calling his mother—a lead I got from my second contact. Shortly after this it came to me that perhaps some of this segment of our class or their families never left the city. Once I began to explore that possibility I quickly located ten more of our classmates. Again, the women dominated the unknown list because I did not know their married names.

My last major foray was to the Mormon church in Short Hills, where I spent days poring over the death rolls, checking Social Security numbers beginning with 135–158 (those originating in New Jersey) against my list of names and birthdates. Unfortunately, I found some of our classmates listed. I did contact the Social Security Office in Washington, D.C., and sent preprinted postage-paid cards with a request to send them on to the remainder of the missing. But even though they do this in some instances, they declined for the purpose of academic research.

At the conclusion of my search more than 90 percent of the Class of '58, living and dead, had been found, although some of the found got lost again in the course of the study, so the unknown list remains higher than 10 percent.

Appendix 2. In Memoriam

Twenty-four members of the Class of '58 are known to have died. They are listed below. Table 23 breaks down the class's mortality rates by race/ethnicity and gender.

Maxine Barish Halem (1992)
Ellen Brodsky Goff (1995)
Herbert Childs (1988)
Janet Ehrenkranz
  Schneider-Stoddard (1999)
Sondra Farber Isaac (1979)
Rosalyn Fein (1987)
Martin Henick (1998)
Mel Jacobson (1959)
Michael Kampf (2003)
Saul Kaplan (2002)
Alan Keselman (1994)
Sanford Kleiman (1995)
Alpha Lane Jr. (1992)

Susan Mann Yaffee (1991)
Harvey Marans (1991)
Ellen Reingold Bernstein (2002)
Betsy Rosenberg Krichman (1988)
Elaine Rosenblum Stepner (2002)
Carol Sassiver Kaelin
  (date unknown)
Barbara Silberman Sloan (1983)
Georgieanna Smallwood Terry
  (1983 or 1984)
Rufus Smith (1986)
Leonard Stone (date unknown)
Ira Tanner (1995)

Table 23. Mortality Rates by Race/Ethnicity and Gender

African American (known N = 13/19, or 68%)
  Men 3; Women 1
  Total 4 (or 31% of knowns)

Jewish (known N = 220/249, or 88%)
  Men 9; Women 11
  Total 20 (or 9% of knowns)

All others, including 1 unknown ethnicity
(known N = 28/37, or 76%)
  Total 0

Appendix 3. Lost Classmates

I count as lost anyone for whom I do not have a current address and for whom there is no definite information (although sometimes there are rumors). Some of these people were actually spotted or contacted at one point or another, but no information was collected and they cannot be found now. Here is the present list of forty-four, by gender:

WOMEN
Irene Beck
Phyllis Bernstein
Rose Cherny
Blanche Cooperman
Joyce Figueroa
Thelma Friedland
Merle Fruchterman
Mary Lou Gandy
Tamara Gordon
Geraldine Granger Lustenberger
Cindy Greenstein
Helaine Hoffman
Marguerite Huntley
Joan Edna Jordan
Roberta Kaduck
Joan Kleinman
Patricia Kozuszko
Harriet Lerner
Gloria Loterstein
Paula Lozinsky
Margot Miller
Agnes Smith Coleman
Jean Sona
Janet Spain
Despina Toyas
Sandra Vice Fink
Davita Zieper

MEN
Robert Bennett
Jerome Bressler
Joseph Demboski
Robert Ellis
Arthur Feinstein
Bernard Goldberg
Thomas Gonzales
John Graves
Hyman Kusnetz
Robert Lowyns
Saul Markowitz
Edward Parness
Neil Resnick
Ronald Rosenberg
Ralph Rothman
Jon Tester
William Walker Jr.

Appendix 4. The Class of '58 Today

The following table shows the full set of occupations of the Class of '58 and of their spouses, if known. Each individual is "classed" by his or her own occupation if single, or by the occupation of the spouse with the higher-status position, if married. Generally, men did not marry women of higher occupational status, but women often married higher men. In these cases, I had to revert to the old pattern of classifying a woman, even if she had her own occupation, according to the occupation of her husband.

For some women I had information on their own occupations but none on their marital status and/or husband's occupations. If these women were in professional/managerial occupations, the lack of marital data did not matter as the husband's occupation could not pull the wife's standing up any further. However, if the women were not in PMC occupations and I had no marital data, I had to classify them as unknown, because a woman with a seemingly lower-level occupation might still be pulled up by a husband in a higher-level occupation if I had that information.

Deceased members of the Class are included if the full set of relevant occupational data was available.

Key

P = Professional/managerial class (PMC); M = Middle Class; W = Working class; N = Never worked; U = Unknown

Marital Statuses:

All are spelled out, except for "divorced/never remarried," which is shown as [div].

Summary of the Class Profile of the Class of '58 Today
(known *N* = 241)

Professional/Managerial Class (*N* = 139, or 58% of knowns)
    76 men, 63 women
Middle Class (*N* = 91, or 38% of knowns)
    41 men, 50 women
Working Class (*N* = 11, or 5% of knowns)
    5 men, 6 women
Never worked (*N* = 3, or 1% of knowns)
    3 men
Unknown (*N* = 60, or 20% of total C58)
    21 men, 39 women

Table 24. Class Profile of the Class of '58 Today

Code Number	Class	Gender	Occupation	Spouse's Occupation
258	P	F	?	Physician
61	P	F	Actuary for large insurance company	Professor
112	P	F	Attorney	Attorney
227	P	F	Attorney	[div]
191	P	F	Auto theft claims	CPA
205	P	F	Clerk/administrator	Electrical design engineer
186	P	F	Corporate executive	CPA
211	P	F	Crisis intervention counselor	President of distribution company
87	P	F	Director of learning resources	Attorney
106	P	F	Director of social service center	Apparel importer
157	P	F	Director of social service program	Physician
289	P	F	Disabled	CPA
297	P	F	Education consultant	[div]
28	P	F	Foreign service officer	Physician
232	P	F	Free-lance journalist	Finance, large corporation
38	P	F	Homemaker	Attorney
172	P	F	Homemaker	Commercial real estate
189	P	F	Homemaker	Corporate VP and creative director
29	P	F	Homemaker	Dentist
7	P	F	Homemaker	Franchise owner
236	P	F	Homemaker	Owner of large company
120	P	F	Homemaker	Pharmacist (own store)
30	P	F	Homemaker	Physician
58	P	F	Homemaker	Produce broker
246	P	F	Homemaker	Research physicist
178	P	F	Homemaker	TV director
154	P	F	Homemaker/tax preparer	Civil engineer
214	P	F	Homemaker/volunteer	VP and attorney of international corporation
310	P	F	Homemaker/volunteer	CPA
156	P	F	Learning center coordinator	[div]

Table 24. Continued

Code Number	Class	Gender	Occupation	Spouse's Occupation
276	P	F	Management consultant (EdD)	[single]
206	P	F	Medical lab technician	VP of large insurance company
55	P	F	Movement therapist	Industrial sales engineer
70	P	F	Own advertising agency	Accountant and business partner
88	P	F	Own educational consulting company	Retailer
166	P	F	Owns real estate agency	Real estate sales
204	P	F	Professor	Professor
140	P	F	Program officer, foundation	Financial adviser
203	P	F	Psychiatric social worker	President of large company
257	P	F	Psychologist	Business
150	P	F	Psychologist	Sales manager
295	P	F	Psychologist (PhD)	Business
228	P	F	Public insurance adjuster	Business
84	P	F	Public relations consultant	Professor
41	P	F	RN/licensed social worker	Physician
182	P	F	RN/homemaker	Physician
245	P	F	Real estate broker	CPA
93	P	F	Real estate sales	Pharmacist
210	P	F	Real estate sales & development	Physician
98	P	F	Sales representative	CPA
293	P	F	School librarian, antiques dealer	Attorney
264	P	F	Speech/language pathologist	Chemist/lab supervisor
302	P	F	Speech/language pathologist	Corporate executive
162	P	F	Teacher	Chemical engineer
188	P	F	Teacher	Consulting psychologist
60	P	F	Teacher, program coordinator	Engineer
161	P	F	Temp; administration and sales	Business (securities)

Table 24. Continued

Code Number	Class	Gender	Occupation	Spouse's Occupation
45	P	F	Tutor	VP securities company
256	P	F	University librarian	Physician
237	P	F	VP, large corporation	Self-employed retailer
169	P	F	Own business	Research chemist
122	P	F	Software engineer	Physician
225	P	F	Teacher, restaurants owner	Co-owns restaurants with wife
124	P	M	Architect	Homemaker
252	P	M	Architect	Marketing and public relations
248	P	M	Art dealer	[div]
95	P	M	Attorney	Attorney
288	P	M	Attorney	College administrator
306	P	M	Attorney	Director of large social program
275	P	M	Attorney	Director of nursery school
259	P	M	Attorney	Homemaker
304	P	M	Attorney	Legal secretary
184	P	M	Attorney	Teacher, chair of department
229	P	M	Attorney	[div]
234	P	M	Attorney	Midwife
26	P	M	CPA	Systems analyst
40	P	M	CPA, partner in firm	Homemaker
301	P	M	CPA, owner of R&D company	Homemaker
148	P	M	Chief financial officer	Homemaker
2	P	M	Civil engineer, president of company	Director of nursery school
196	P	M	Commercial real estate	Homemaker
134	P	M	Corporate executive	Management
89	P	M	Corporate executive	Homemaker
251	P	M	Corporate president	Writer
23	P	M	Dentist	Homemaker
146	P	M	Dentist	Homemaker
287	P	M	Director, management info. systems	Clerical
92	P	M	Electronics engineer	Homemaker

Table 24. Continued

Code Number	Class	Gender	Occupation	Spouse's Occupation
113	P	M	Engineering mgr	Director of personnel
238	P	M	Exec. dir., social service agency	Management, insurance
19	P	M	Exec. VP, care facility	Medical secretary
135	P	M	Finance, large corporation	Teacher
241	P	M	Freelance writer	Book illustrator
175	P	M	International business	?
299	P	M	International trading company	Works for municipality
170	P	M	Investment banker	Systems engineer
77	P	M	Judge/businessman	?
202	P	M	Manufacturing engineer	?
44	P	M	Mechanical engineer	Municipal planner
294	P	M	Owns legal processing firm	Works in husband's business
243	P	M	Partner in accounting firm	Teacher
303	P	M	Pharmacist	Homemaker
309	P	M	Pharmacist	Research librarian
51	P	M	Pharmacist	[div]
56	P	M	Physician	?
74	P	M	Physician	?
305	P	M	Physician	?
46	P	M	Physician	Banker
52	P	M	Physician	Clinical social worker
117	P	M	Physician	Homemaker
59	P	M	Physician	Homemaker, volunteer
274	P	M	Physician	Homemaker, works in husband's office
267	P	M	Physician	Legal administrator
90	P	M	Physician	Nurse
102	P	M	Physician	Owns gift shop
8	P	M	Physician	Psychiatric nurse
200	P	M	Physician	[div]
10	P	M	Physician and PhD	Librarian
39	P	M	Pres. & CEO of large service company	?
142	P	M	Pres. of large business	Homemaker
5	P	M	Principal	Teacher

Table 24. Continued

Code Number	Class	Gender	Occupation	Spouse's Occupation
231	P	M	Produce broker	Homemaker
116	P	M	Professor	Director of educational program
247	P	M	Professor	Early childhood education
260	P	M	Professor	Sales and manager
1	P	M	Professor and MD	Computer consultant
109	P	M	Professor, administrator	?
111	P	M	Professor, artist	Art therapist
212	P	M	Psychologist/publisher	Audiologist
82	P	M	Public health director, MD	Training coordinator
79	P	M	Real estate development	PhD researcher
235	P	M	Securities broker	Photographer
104	P	M	Senior VP of large corporation	?
253	P	M	Stockbroker	Community service
190	P	M	Stockbroker	Travel agent
62	P	M	Tax consulting service	Teacher
66	P	M	VP, large company	Admin. asst.
81	P	M	VP, insurance company	?
96	P	M	VP, real estate company	Manager, real estate office
165	M	F	Accounting systems specialist	[single]
9	M	F	Admin. asst. advertising	[div]
42	M	F	Admin. coordinator	[div]
226	M	F	Administrator at university	Management consultant
195	M	F	Asst. exec. VP, social service agency	[div]
105	M	F	Bookkeeper/office manager	Sales/advertising
73	M	F	Clerk/typist, data entry	Teacher
215	M	F	Clothing decorator	General manager for local company
180	M	F	Co-owns consulting company	Co-owns with wife
194	M	F	Co-owns entertainment company	Co-owns with wife
286	M	F	Credit manager	Policeman
244	M	F	Festival organizer	[div]

Table 24. Continued

Code Number	Class	Gender	Occupation	Spouse's Occupation
284	M	F	Homemaker	Sales manager
68	M	F	Homemaker	Tax accountant
65	M	F	Homemaker	[div]
127	M	F	Homemaker	[div]
163	M	F	Learning consultant for school	[single]
171	M	F	Legal secretary	Office manager
4	M	F	Legal secretary	Sales manager
133	M	F	Legal secretary	[div]
72	M	F	Librarian	Industrial designer
49	M	F	Librarian	[single]
173	M	F	Makeup artist	General contractor
218	M	F	Medical assistant	Legal sales
11	M	F	Medical secretary	Director of special services
197	M	F	Manager for computer company	[div]
22	M	F	Office manager	Admin. asst. to sales manager
31	M	F	Office manager	[single]
222	M	F	Office manager	[widowed]
261	M	F	Ordained minister	Musician
223	M	F	Paralegal	Psychiatric nurse
3	M	F	Polygraph administrator	Owns security company
177	M	F	RN	Butcher
34	M	F	RN	Owns gas station
12	M	F	RN	[div]
130	M	F	Real estate sales	[div]
201	M	F	Secretary	[div]
250	M	F	Social worker, fund raiser	[disabled]
75	M	F	Senior collection rep.	[div]
86	M	F	Senior credit administrator	[div]
282	M	F	Supervisor of teachers	[div]
167	M	F	Supervisor, state agency	[single]
35	M	F	Teacher	Floral consultant
141	M	F	Teacher	Management specialist
217	M	F	Teacher	Sales
153	M	F	Teacher	[single]
239	M	F	Teacher	[widowed]

Table 24. Continued

Code Number	Class	Gender	Occupation	Spouse's Occupation
85	M	F	Travel agent	Health care
209	M	F	Tutor	[div]
97	M	F	Medical receptionist	Sales
249	M	M	"Writer" but has "day jobs"	Secretary
136	M	M	Accountant, self-employed	[div]
168	M	M	Actor, partner in small business	Composer, musical director
19	M	M	Associate cantor	Speech and language pathologist
147	M	M	Asst. manager, supermarket	Teacher
230	M	M	Asst. auto center manager	Secretary
50	M	M	Business manager & personal trainer	?
143	M	M	Camera man	[div]
292	M	M	Chairman, consulting company	Works in husband's business
155	M	M	Data processing	Homemaker
37	M	M	Detective, Newark Police	?
16	M	M	Director of small company	?
101	M	M	Guidance counselor/cantor	Teacher, guidance counselor
14	M	M	Insurance adjustor	Self-employed collector
33	M	M	Labor relations manager	Homemaker
278	M	M	Novelty business	Helps in business
25	M	M	Owns small business	?
151	M	M	Owns small business	Exec. secretary
144	M	M	Owns small business	Partner in business
187	M	M	Owns small business	Teacher
298	M	M	Owns small business	[div]
32	M	M	Owns small business	Secretary
78	M	M	Partner in restaurant supply company	RN/homemaker
255	M	M	Quality control	RN
20	M	M	Real estate	[div]
198	M	M	Sales	Advertising manager
152	M	M	Sales (building related)	Homemaker
159	M	M	Sales manager	Head of accounting department

Table 24. Continued

Code Number	Class	Gender	Occupation	Spouse's Occupation
192	M	M	Sales rep.	Purchasing agent for building company
266	M	M	Salesman	Systems analyst, insurance company
307	M	M	School administrator	Legal secretary
115	M	M	Section manager, financial company	Secretary
119	M	M	Self-employed	Office supervisor
220	M	M	Self-employed/sales	Homemaker
254	M	M	Service merchandiser?	?
296	M	M	Songwriter	[div]
118	M	M	Stores supervision	RN
131	M	M	Subscription sales manager	Marketing
125	M	M	Teacher	Teacher
208	M	M	Works for department store	?
219	M	M	Self-employed	?
138	W	F	Clerical	[single]
221	W	F	Data entry	[widowed]
94	W	F	Hotel worker	?
15	W	F	Insurance asst.	Warehouseman
270	W	F	Teacher's aide	Electrician
6	W	F	Part-time preschool	Custodian
300	W	M	Chemical worker	Homemaker
160	W	M	Drug counselor	?
262	W	M	Factory Work	[div]
27	W	M	Furniture refinisher	?
28	W	M	Truck driver	Secretary
128	N	M	Died young	
64	N	M	Disabled/unemployed	?
213	N	M	Disabled/unemployed	[div]
21	U	F		
36	U	F		
47	U	F		
48	U	F		

Table 24. Continued

Code Number	Class	Gender	Occupation	Spouse's Occupation
63	U	F		
67	U	F		
76	U	F		
83	U	F		
103	U	F		
107	U	F		
110	U	F		
114	U	F		
121	U	F		
123	U	F		
126	U	F		
129	U	F		
132	U	F		
145	U	F		
149	U	F		
164	U	F		
174	U	F		
176	U	F		
181	U	F		
193	U	F		
242	U	F		
263	U	F		
268	U	F		
269	U	F		
272	U	F		
279	U	F		
283	U	F		
308	U	F		
17	U	F	Bookkeeper	?
271	U	F	Cooking demonstrator	?
137	U	F	Paralegal	?
290	U	F	Pharmacy technician	?
80	U	F	Teacher	?
280	U	F	Teacher's aide	?
265	U	F	Telephone operator	?
13	U	M		
18	U	M		
24	U	M		

Table 24. Continued

Code Number	Class	Gender	Occupation	Spouse's Occupation
53	U	M		
54	U	M		
57	U	M		
71	U	M		
91	U	M		
99	U	M		
108	U	M		
139	U	M		
158	U	M		
183	U	M		
185	U	M		
216	U	M		
224	U	M		
233	U	M		
240	U	M		
277	U	M		
281	U	M		
291	U	M		

Notes

1. Introduction

1 Actually only 303 members of the class marched. One woman had completed her credits and left school early, but I include her in the Class and in this study.

2 For some early examples, see Warner and Lunt 1941, Goldschmidt 1950, Powdermaker 1951, *American Anthropologist* 1955.

3 Nonetheless, there is a growing body of ethnographic work on New Jersey, which has become something of a laboratory for the study of U.S. social and cultural phenomena. See Roth 1959 and his many later ethnographic novels, Halle 1985, McGuire 1988, Moffatt 1989, Behling 1991, Newman 1993, Cousins 1994, Lyons 1994, Kaplan 1998 (fiction), and Lefkowitz 1998 (journalism/ethnography). For a selection of New Jersey–based films, see Peerce 1969, Sayles 1982, 1991, and Rudolph 1991, not to mention *The Sopranos* series on television.

4 Many people could not wait to get out of there: *Enid Bauer* [from the field notes]: She said she has no great nostalgia for Weequahic High School and the neighborhood. She had a good time there, and got a great education, but it was a small and narrow place and she got out. *John Chopin* [from the field notes]: John was contacted by another classmate, who said he was very cool, very "aloof," uninterested in making a connection. He said he hated Newark, couldn't wait to get away. *Susan Goff* [from the field notes]: She said she felt like she was "escaping" from New Jersey. She swore she would never accept a job there later in her career. On the other hand, it is worth remembering that nearly 60 percent of the Class of '58 still lives in New Jersey.

5 In the fall of 1958 (the next graduating class after the one in this study) the entire senior class took the National Merit Examinations while allegedly only a select handful of students at other schools took the exams. "The test score achieved or exceeded by 98 percent of the Weequahic pupils was reached by only 93 percent on the national level" (*Newark Evening News*, January 18, 1959).

6 His agent actually calls him an ethnographer in *The Counterlife* (1988).

7 Recent fieldwork in the Weequahic section includes Todd Behling's senior thesis (1991) on a black church in the neighborhood, with excellent data on the resentment of the Jewish flight, and Linwood Cousins's

ethnography (1994) of the high school, including both the internal social patterns and problems and the relationship between the school and the community.

8　At the time there were graduations in both January and June. January graduations were later eliminated.

9　Most interviews were taped, but some were not, and these were reproduced as accurately as possible in my field notes. In addition there are field notes about the encounter and about the interview. In excerpts from interview transcripts, direct quotes are enclosed in quotation marks. Where field notes rather than interview transcripts are quoted, this is always indicated by a bracketed note.

10　See, e.g., Connerton 1989, Boyarin 1994, Antze and Lambek 1996.

11　Thus, too, I do not attend much to questions of "narrative," though these are very important. See Ginsburg 1989, Ochs and Capps 1996.

12　One African American woman lives with her mother at her original address in Newark. It is not clear, however, whether she lived there continuously or returned when her mother became infirm.

13　In later years, one woman officially converted from Judaism. Two men told me they had renounced Judaism, although they did not officially convert to something else.

14　The question of the place of the middle class(es) in class theory is itself contested. Marx recognized—historically and/or ethnographically— the presence of various "middle strata," but they played little role in his theory of the dynamics of capitalism. It has long been argued, however, that the middle class is central to some of the unexpected ways in which capitalism has evolved. See, for example, Mills 1951, Poulantzas 1975, Walker 1979, Bourdieu 1984, Vanneman and Cannon 1987, Wacquant 1991, and Eder 1993.

15　Twelve more people died in the course of the project, for a total of twenty-four people now (February 2002) known to be deceased in the Class of '58. The list of their names is in appendix 2.

16　The current list of lost people is in appendix 3. (These are only the people who have never been located at all. I do not include people I once found and collected data from, whether questionnaires or interviews, but who have now disappeared from the classmate-finding radar.) As the sociologists would predict, various known indicators (grammar school attended, race/ethnicity) suggest that the lost classmates are disproportionately from the lower end of the class spectrum. Although this would bias the study toward the high end if I were relying totally on statistics, I still have plenty of voices from the lower end to draw on for ethnographic purposes.

17 At some points I thought of the project in terms of the American "road book" literary genre. It would take me too far afield to reflect on the relationships between this project and those books, some of which I love (e.g., Tom Wolfe's *The Electric Kool-Aid Acid Test*), and some of which I have much more mixed feelings about (e.g., Baudrillard's *America*). The "project journals" interspersed between the chapters in this book are in part meant to capture some of the on-the-roadness of this project.

18 Despite this, I decided early on not to organize the book simply as a series of life histories. Having read Medved and Wallechinsky's study of the Class of '65 of Beverly Hills High School (1976; see also Wallechinsky 1986), which is organized in that way, I found that while many of the individual stories they collected were interesting, the presentation in terms of one story after another was simply too undigested. One virtually had to have been a member of that Class to stay interested in the individual stories unconnected to some larger historical narrative.

19 This book is short on discussions of public culture—film, television, and so on—and I regret it. But the emphasis on the interviews tended to preclude it, especially since, as I discuss later, people themselves rarely mentioned public culture as an influence on their lives. Of course I could have brought it into the argument myself, but the book would have been twice as long. It is worth thinking about how hard it is to combine textual, public culture interpretation, on the one hand, and ethnographic and/or interview-based material, on the other, in a context where one has not made media an explicit focus of the project.

20 In quite a few of the interviews with male classmates in their homes, their wives made a point of being present. People did not always ask whether it was alright for a spouse to be present; if they did, I always said it was completely up to them, and if they didn't, I made no comment. When I interviewed grown children of the Class of '58, we can add to the list: college dormitories, college campuses, my own faculty offices, and lunchrooms and offices of large corporations.

21 I have written more about this in "Fieldwork in the Post-Community" (1997).

22 The only writer who, in my opinion, really pulls off the feat of getting virtually uninterpreted interviews to "speak for themselves" is Studs Terkel.

23 I have discussed something I called "documentary ethnography" in a spin-off article from this book; see Ortner 2002a.

24 The general theoretical framework behind this structure of inquiry and exposition is so-called practice theory, which I mostly leave implicit in

the course of the book. See Bourdieu 1978, 1990, Giddens 1979, Sahlins 1981, Sewell 1992, 1999, Ortner 1996, 1999a, Holland et al. 1998, Holland and Lave 2001.

25   For an older example of a highly reflective "native anthropologist," see Myerhoff 1978.

26   Thanks to Alison Baker for the transcript of her 1998 interview with me.

27   I am aware that some (many?) anthropologists keep distinct personal "field journals" apart from the official field notes. I could never do this as it all seemed to run together.

2. Reading Class

This chapter is an extensively revised version of Ortner 2002b.

1   On the multiple long-term effects of growing up during the Great Depression, see the classic: Elder 1974. Elder's book also has some affinities with this book insofar as it concerns the relationships between large-scale events and the individual lives of a particular historical cohort.

2   The GI Bill is the popular name for the Serviceman's Readjustment Act of 1944, which "provided employment and education allowances and home, farm, and business loans for millions of World War II veterans." (See "GI Bill" in Microsoft's Encarta.)

3   David Potter's *People of Plenty,* questionably arguing that American national character was shaped by abundance, was published in this period, in 1955.

4   Many classmates talked about how hard their fathers worked when they were growing up. About half the mothers in the class worked outside the home as well. And many classmates themselves worked from a very young age. I had to skip these stories in the interest of space.

5   See the classic "What Really Happened to Rosie the Riveter?" (Tobias and Anderson 1974).

6   The book was published in 1969, but it describes "Alexander Portnoy's" childhood and youth in the fifties.

7   A number of students had immigrant parents who were felt to be highly problematic, verging on dysfunctional, and I went back and forth on whether to include immigrant parents as a category with these other kinds of disrupted families. In the end I did so only on a case-by-case basis; that is, if an immigrant parent was actually clinically depressed (long illness), or if the parents were said to have fought all the time

(high conflict). But I did not include cases where the parents were simply said not to have understood their children's lives because they were immigrants. That problem was not restricted to immigrant parents.

8   Ironically, one person denied social divisions at Weequahic precisely because of his own poverty: "[from the field notes] He said he was not conscious of social divisions in high school. He was too busy working in his father's store." Another man said that class differences didn't matter in the younger years of the Class of '58 because kids didn't know about class differences. This is echoed by Amiri Baraka concerning race; Baraka writes about very strong memories of mixed race groups when he was a kid, but then children learned the pernicious views of the grownups and friendships divided by race (1997:9).

9   The phrase is a variant of the title of Katherine Newman's book on middle-class downward mobility, *Declining Fortunes* (1993).

10   Think too of the Roth character from the Weequahic section dating the rich suburban girl in *Goodbye, Columbus* (1995).

11   One is reminded here of the fetishistic quality attributed by Carolyn Steedman to her mother's desire for a certain coat, in Steedman's working-class memoir (1986).

12   In addition to Sennett and Cobb, James Scott 1990 has an excellent discussion of the role of shame and humiliation in relations of power and inequality.

3. Drawing Boundaries

1   For a comprehensive historical overview, see Helmreich 1999.

2   In contrast, see the old classic, *Life Is with People* (Zborowski and Herzog 1952), and the more recent classic, *Number Our Days* (Myerhoff 1978).

3   In terms of official congregational affiliations, the Jews of Weequahic were probably split between Orthodox congregations (which were much less fundamentalist than many of them are today) and Conservative (or middle-of-the-road) congregations. There was, as far as I know, no Reform congregation in the neighborhood; Reform Judaism, with services in English and other liberal changes, was too religiously radical for the local mores.

4   There are obviously issues of generational transition and generational friction running throughout this book, and especially in these early chapters as we look at the Class of '58 against the background of their parents. Once again I have had to make some representational choices

and have chosen not to consider this issue systematically. On the other hand, see Ortner 1998b for a fuller discussion of generational relations between the Class of '58 and their children.

5   It also seems to be the case that many parents did not talk about the Holocaust, at least in front of the children. Although I do not have detailed data on this point, my sense is that many Jewish parents were trying to protect their children from this awful knowledge and allow them to be "normal" and "just like everybody else."

6   People who did not live in the Weequahic district had to pull strings to get into the high school. The most common strategy was to claim that one wanted to study Hebrew, which was available at no other school in the city. In Marilyn's case, it was political strings: "The mayor [of Newark], what the hell was his name, Carlin, lived around the corner from us and my father used to play pinochle or something with him, and that's how my brother [and then I] got into Weequahic."

7   Zionist ideology among Jews was very strong at that time. The creation of a Jewish state was the ultimate form of both physical security and normalization of Jewishness. The state of Israel was created in 1948, during the childhood of the Class of '58.

8   It was not common for girls to be Bat Mitzvahed at that time, although they were sent to Hebrew school along with the boys.

9   This pattern could be seen in Boston, Detroit, Chicago, and Los Angeles (A. I. Gordon 1959). Gordon discussed the WASP flight phenomenon in general, and specifically noted the Newark situation in the fifties: "Certain neighborhoods in the Essex county suburbs of Newark (N.J.) are spoken of by city officials as 'Little Israel' " (1959:171). In fact, this is still going on in other parts of the country. One can see it very clearly in Florida, where the Jews have been moving up the east coast from an earlier concentration around Miami. They have taken over formerly WASP areas along the Atlantic coast, while the WASPs have withdrawn to their own enclaves, especially on the west, or gulf, coast.

10 Barry Sommer, a very activist Zionist who has spent a great deal of time in Israel, told the following funny story, which must have been from the kind of area that Candy came from. He was sitting in on some interviews at an immigration absorption center in Israel: "I never forgot this one woman who said, 'I came [from] the United States because I came from a terrible place, it was anti-Semitic, it was a terrible area.' And I was waiting to hear that she came from Arkansas or someplace like that. She went on to talk about how her neighbors hated her and all of that and how she was so happy to be in Israel. And she came from New Jersey."

11 See the 1911 map of "different nationalities" in Newark in Cunning-
    ham 1988: 204–5. At that point the Jews had not yet moved into
    the Weequahic section, which is shown on the left side of the map
    unmarked for specific nationalities, and was presumably still native
    whites.

12 To be fair, Michael's parents later turned around on the subject: "And
    my parents went to visit one of my father's uncles and his wife. And
    they said, 'So what do you want to do? Disown your son? . . . He's still
    part of our family. And you can't do that.' And so they turned around,
    and to the level that they could accept it, they did, which is pretty,
    pretty high on the scale of things. He got the piano! . . . They're married
    twenty-four, twenty-five years [now]."

13 Emmett Till was a fourteen-year-old African American boy from Chi-
    cago who was beaten and killed while visiting relatives in the South
    in 1955.

14 Of course this is not a new story for the Jews; the question of policing
    the boundaries of Jewishness against wrong alliances threads its way
    through the entire Old Testament. See Leach 1969, Douglas 1970.

15 Even non-Jewish girls sometimes seemed exotic to Jewish girls: Carol
    Wiernik asked me if I remembered one of the non-Jewish girls, Pat
    O'Grady, who was very athletic. She said, laughing at herself, that she
    thought at the time it was because Pat was a Gentile.

4. Dealing with Boundaries

1 For an excellent overview of African American history in Newark, see
   Cousins 1994; see also Jackson and Jackson 1972.

2 This is, of course, what Marx called "false consciousness." But Bourdieu's point is that such false consciousness is not primarily the effect
   of the culture of dominant groups being imposed on mystified masses.
   Rather it is the outcome of a series of ordinary, everyday practices
   within a larger structure of inequality, their everydayness, their rou-
   tineness, making it all the more impossible to see clearly the structures
   of constraint and mystification.

3 As far as I can tell (and there are several unknowns) only one African
   American individual in the Class of '58—Peter Lucas—was born and
   raised in Newark, his parents apparently having moved there (from
   Ohio, not the South) before he was born. He and several older brothers
   went to Weequahic, suggesting a significantly longer-term adaptation
   to the area and the school than for virtually any other African Ameri-

can student in the class. Peter has become highly successful by any set of standards; he completed several advanced degrees and holds a very high level job in a major corporation. No doubt many things fed into his success, but in the context of the present discussion, I throw in at least the suggestion that he was the one person in the group who did not have the handicap of having transferred in from elsewhere.

4 Eckert (1989) reported that working-class kids at "Belten High" very commonly maintained ties with their childhood friends outside the high school.

5. American High Schools

1 One could also do a list of movies about the hell of high school. They come in all genres, including comedies, dramas, and horror films. Of the latter, the most terrifying is probably Brian de Palma's *Carrie* (1976).

2 The first three decades of the twentieth century saw a spectacular democratization and enlargement of high schools. Previously, secondary schooling was limited to a small elite. But in this era compulsory attendance ages were raised, and laws against child labor sent more working-class children to school. "By the early 1930's, 60% of America's youth of high-school age were in school" (Fass 1977:211). For an excellent overview of the development and transformation of public education, including high schools, from the mid-nineteenth through the early twentieth centuries, see Ueda 1987.

   Some version of the *pre-1950s* system of social categories can be read between the lines in Fass 1977 for the 1920s; the Vonnegut quote used earlier refers to *the 1930s* (Vonnegut was Class of '40). For *the 1940s,* see Warner et al. 1944, Hollingshead 1949, and C. W. Gordon 1957. For the *fifties and later,* see Parsons 1959, J. S. Coleman 1961, Henry 1965, Palonsky 1975, Schwartz and Merten 1967, 1975, Varenne 1982, 1983, Canaan 1986, Eckert 1989, Foley 1990, Chang 1992, Bettie 2000. There is also a large literature on "youth culture" that partially overlaps with high school studies. I especially want to mention here William Graebner's outstanding *Coming of Age in Buffalo: Youth and Authority in the Postwar Era* (1990).

3 Key works on "the Fifties" as a distinct era include Baritz 1982, Jezer 1982, Hine 1986, O'Neill 1986, Graebner 1990, Halberstam 1993, Samuelson 1995.

4 On 1950s youth culture in particular, see Graebner 1990, Lipsitz 1990, Breines 1992, Grover 1997.

5   On 1950s consumerism, see Jezer 1982, Hine 1986, May 1989, Lipsitz
     1990.

6   It is interesting that looks did not come up much in the interviews;
     this is one of the few examples.

7   I have argued elsewhere (Ortner 2002c) that this intersection of class
     and individual qualities is nothing other than the deep structure of
     hegemonic "American culture." On "American culture," very variably
     conceived, see Potter 1955, Warner 1962, Spradley and Rynkiewich 1975,
     Varenne 1986, Reynolds and Norman 1988, Plotnicov 1990, Bellah et al.
     1996, Trencher 2000.

8   The classic work on this intersection in EuroAmerican culture is Aber-
     crombie et al. 1986.

9   Warren Susman has written a classic article on the shift in American
     notions of selfhood from the importance of "character" to the impor-
     tance of "personality." He places this shift in the early decades of the
     twentieth century and links it especially to the growth of a culture of
     consumerism over a culture of productivism. The idea of personality,
     emphasizing social magnetism by virtue of charm and style, contrasts
     with the idea of character, emphasizing self-discipline and moral rec-
     titude (Susman 1984).

10 I have argued elsewhere (Ortner 2002c) that both personality and
     looks, which seem to Americans to come simply from the luck of the
     draw, have an enormous class component. On the other hand, they can
     never be reduced to class, and to the extent that they are independently
     emergent, they are thought potentially to work against class. Good per-
     sonality and looks are assumed to help a person potentially beat a bad
     class background, and they probably do in many cases.

11 Michael Peletz (personal communication) suggested that the terms
     for the people on the top, from the point of view of those in the bot-
     tom categories, may be equally pejorative: brown-nose, suckup, goody-
     goody, etc. But those are the voices that are rarely heard.

12 I suspect that this category crystallized out from among the "average
     citizens" largely in the 1950s as a result of the Sputnik boost of brainy
     science boys. But I have no data on this one way or the other.

13 Loïc Wacquant tells me that "hoods" as a label for the alienated tough
     guys in the high schools derives from the word "neighborhood" and
     has links to the idea of gangs, which are usually neighborhood based.
     This has been true in recent years, but I think the term in the 1950s de-
     rived from "hoodlums," a term for gangsters in the older, "mob" sense.

14 During the countercultural era (late 1960s–early 1970s), the druggies
     and freaks also contained a significant element of middle-class drop-

outs. Nonetheless the type itself remained linked to a working-class and/or African American oppositional style. Indeed that was part of its attraction for middle-class kids.

15   It would be interesting to see what the growth of female sports has done to the system. This point has come up in discussion after talks, and some have suggested that it does not change the overall structure very much. On the other hand, a recent *Newsweek* article (June 3, 2002) on "gamma girls" argues that women's sports have created a whole new female niche in the high school social system of strong and confident young women who do not fit into the old popular/nonpopular binary.

16   Also inner-city schools; see Cousins 1994.

17   In *Portnoy's Complaint* (1967:56), Philip Roth quotes the famous cheer:

> Ikey, Mikey, Jake and Sam,
> We're the boys who eat no ham,
> We play football, we play soccer,
> We keep matzos in our locker.

The origins of the cheer are unknown. It could have been coined by non-Jews ridiculing Weequahic athletics, or it could have been coined by the famously self-ironizing Jews themselves. Thanks to "P.R." for a timely response to my query about where he had quoted the cheer.

6. Weequahic

1   The WPA, or Works Progress Administration, had a well-known program for supporting unemployed artists. According to the Weequahic alumni newsletter of Fall 2004, the mural was painted by one Michael Lenson in 1939 with WPA funds.

2   This little book, written for a popular audience, takes many people who have become successful in the real world and looks back at their careers in high school (rather than the standard academic social science strategy of seeing whether success in high school predicts success in the future). I was fascinated to learn that, for example, Jesse Jackson was president of the student body of his school, and that such diverse characters as Warren Beatty, Hugh Hefner, Philip Roth, and John Updike were all on their respective student councils (Keyes 1976:43). In other words, not all successful people in the world rose up out of geekdom.

3   There was a tradition among the yearbook staff that no individual should have a complete blank under his or her picture. Thus, if a stu-

dent had no activities at all, the phrase "service club" was inserted under the picture. In retrospect, this was an ironic choice of phrase.

4 For example, Jayne Epstein said, "My cousin, who's sixty-something, talks about when he went to Weequahic, and there were drugs. I said, oh, were there drugs when I went to Weequahic? I knew nothing!"

5 I was told that one girl, who was not in the class but hung out with a lot of Class of '58 people, verged on sluttiness: [from the field notes] "It turned out that she was screwing a lot of people in high school, evidently in a pretty out front, who-cares sort of way." But the person who told me this also quickly said, by way of excusing her behavior, that she had had a rough childhood with an abusive father.

6 This, of course, is what Paul Willis described so well for the "lads" of the working-class school he studied (1977). Willis's point was that while one could admire the agency and the resistance involved, it ultimately worked to the disadvantage of the boys who took that course, and sent them back into low-level working-class jobs.

7 There were no more bohemian/countercultural spaces than these at Weequahic in the 1950s. For example, while there was a drama club, it did not become the place where the more "artsy" kids congregated.

8 Many of the friendships of the Class of '58 began much earlier in life and have continued up until the present. See Ortner 1997, "Fieldwork in the Post-Community," for more on the impressive continuity of many friendships. This is part of what the idea of "post-community" is about.

9 See Crain 2000:39: "In America, the relationship that exists only for its own sake, the relationship outside of institutions, the relationship whose impermanence is the guarantee of its intensity . . . in America, that relationship is same-sex friendship."

10 Going steady with a member of the opposite sex could also serve this same function of allowing one to ignore the games of popularity. Dorothy Wallin for instance, said: "I met Dave in my sophomore year [in Weequahic]. I met my girlfriend Sheila the first day of ninth grade at the Annex. . . . She met her [future] husband the following year. And so we didn't need other people." And Rosalie Borkowsky said, "The nice thing about Weequahic, of course, is that I met my husband, who really, I think, made it bearable for me, and was a source of support."

11 Julie Bettie (2000) makes a useful distinction between the "class of origin" and the "class of performance" of the students at the high school she studied in California. Some performed an identity that was at odds with their identity of origin.

12 This and the previous two examples all involved inappropriate, basi-

cally working- or lower-class and/or non-Jewish men. Thus there is a double rebellion here, both the sex itself and the choice of partners.

13   In the prudish 1950s, even pregnancy *in a married woman* was something to be kept out of sight. Thus two women in the class told stories of having been teachers as young married women, but there were rules in place to the effect that pregnant women had to resign after the third month of pregnancy. When they got pregnant the schools forced them to resign, or at least tried to—one of them successfully hid the pregnancy till the end of the school year.

14   At last report, she is writing a movie script about her experience.

15   Contrast with this statement from *American High,* a "reality" TV show that aired briefly on Fox TV in September 2000: "Like, on the outside, I'm this, like, captain of lacrosse, captain of soccer, like, this jock, and that's how people see me, but on the inside I just got like a lot of love going through me" (*New Yorker,* August 21 and 28 [one issue], 2000, 169).

7. Tracks

1   This is Allen Ginsberg's aunt mentioned earlier. (Transcript of interview with Mrs. Litzky dated 11/19/86, in "The Golden Age of Weequahic," archive, New York Public Library.)

2   Ibid., 12.

3   Mrs. Rous was later recognized for her contributions to the school and the community (Gilliland 1968). Thanks to Barbara Rous Harris for the clipping.

4   I later met Mrs. Rous's daughter, Barbara Rous Harris (Weequahic '59), now a professor of medieval history and women's studies at the University of North Carolina, Chapel Hill. Barbara told me that Mrs. Rous had severe asthma and died quite young.

5   On prewar high school patterns—percentage of the population attending, relationship of different kinds of high schools to social class—see Warner et al. 1944, Fass 1977, Ueda 1987, Graebner 1990.

6   In fact, however, there were tracks within tracks. There were so-called advanced classes—Advanced History, Advanced Math, and so on—for the academically elite among the college prep students.

7   See, for example, the *Autobiography of Leroi Jones* (Baraka 1997).

8   This did not always work. Jewish girls on the commercial track may still have felt superior to non-Jewish and African American girls. As one Jewish woman on the commercial track said, "I wasn't friends out-

side of school with the people that I had classes with, because we came from very different lives."

9 One person put it in terms of going to a "sleepaway school," on the analogy with going to a "sleepaway camp." Going or not being able to go to sleepaway summer camp was itself invoked in some people's stories as a marker of privilege or poverty.

10 These were mostly state universities. The reason I say they were "jockish" is that I have a very clear memory of the way I described them at the time to the guidance counselors, saying (initially) that I wanted to go to "some place with a big campus, and football teams."

11 It is only in retrospect that one notices that girls never occupied the top offices.

12 Lois's parents also were not encouraging her: "I didn't [take the] college [prep] course, because I wanted to be a teacher. My mother didn't feel that I was teacher material because I was very emotional, and she said I would take everything home with me and I would aggravate myself so she says, 'nah.' And in those days we listened to our mothers and we did what we were told."

8. Counterlives

1 On the constructed/made distinction, see Ortner 1996.

2 Although issues of family life are discussed briefly here, a broader discussion of adult family patterns among the Class of '58 will be reserved for another publication.

3 For sustained work on the relationship between individual lives and social movements, see Stewart 1994, 2000, Stewart et al. 1998.

4 People with major problems often (though not always) disappeared from the Weequahic networks and even from the most assiduous search efforts of the anthropologist and her person-finder. Indeed, I and other classmates assume that many of the forty or so unfindable members of the Class are in one way or another in this position. Among the "found," four men and one woman (all white/Jewish) are known to have been charged with criminal activities. Two Jewish men and one African American man are said to have died of drugs.

5 The race issues of the earlier era blended briefly into the Beat subculture, but the relationship was edgy. Eventually black activists like LeRoi Jones/Amiri Baraka dissociated themselves from the Beat subculture. See Baraka 1997.

6 At that time the drinking age in New York was eighteen and the drink-

ing age in New Jersey was twenty-one. It is doubtful that Gary was served beer at twelve or thirteen, but you never know.

7　For a comprehensive biography of Ginsberg, see Schumacher 1992.

8　And later, of course, San Francisco.

9　Except for that stint in a brokerage firm!

10　I am focusing in this chapter on those classmates who got involved in one way or another in these movements. Many classmates, however, made a point of saying some version of (as one man put it) "I stayed away from all that stuff."

11　Based on the response of the Filipino family, I am assuming his position was antiwar, but it is not clear.

12　I heard about the helicopter pilot secondhand. He dropped out of contact with the Class of '58, and although he was eventually located in a distant state, his telephone number is unlisted and I never spoke to him.

9. Money

1　This book as a whole focuses primarily on people's careers in the world of work and money, and not on people's lives in families. Although I have a fair amount of family data, the book was already quite long without it. I hope to write about the family material in other contexts—at the very least in an article or two, or at most as the early chapters for a book on the children of the Class of '58.

2　See Ortner 1973 on "key symbols" in ethnographic writing.

3　I use the male pronoun intentionally; I will come back to women later.

4　I have a larger N for present occupations/class positions of classmates (see chapter 12), but I do not have a class background for all of them. Hence the discrepancy between those numbers and these.

5　Not counting those who went back and finished later.

6　Barber quotes another author who says the rate is "one in eight" for 1952.

7　As always, these classifications are somewhat imprecise. In particular, some who are classified by occupation as middle class are clearly in quite low-pay and/or low-income situations, and if one were classifying by income they would probably be in the low rather than the middle category.

8　For example, he remembers some girl pinning her notes for a test to a nearby bulletin board in the classroom, where she could see them when she was taking the test.

9   See Ortner 1998b on parents' anxieties about Generation X.

10   At the time of the interview he was no longer practicing and had shifted to a home business in desktop publishing of publications related to his earlier field.

11   One Jewish man from a working-class, disrupted-family background married and lived for some time in one of the wealthier Jewish suburbs in the area. But he said he always felt uncomfortable there, and after he and his wife got divorced he moved to a much more blue-collar town. Even though he was very Jewish-identified, and even though this was a mostly not-Jewish town, he said he was much happier there.

12   Only one classmate, Howard Guttman, spontaneously referred to his Jewish parentage as having played a role in his success: "There are many factors that got me to where I am today. I think one of the basic things is, especially Jewish parentage. We have lots of obstacles that other peoples don't have. And we have to depend basically on ourselves to get where we are and to jump some of the hurdles that people put in our way. And it's an accomplishment. When you do it, you get more energy to go to the next hurdle." A few other classmates said that they felt their Jewish background gave them a boost in various ways, but this was generally in response to a query on my part.

13   Brodkin's book (1999) is a must-read for anyone trying to understand the history and dynamics of Jewish acceptance, and ultimately influence, in the United States.

14   It also seems to be the case that many Jewish parents did not talk about the Holocaust, at least in front of the children. One classmate remembered that the woman who shortened her clothes had a concentration camp number tattooed on her arm, which the classmate's mother mentioned in hushed tones. Other than this anecdote, however, the data here are very scanty. My own sense is that many Jewish parents very much wanted a fresh start here in the United States, for themselves and their children.

10. Happiness

1   Indeed, the very individual who asks this question at an academic talk is probably a person with this sort of history.

2   Training and ordination as a minister, training and certification as a policeman.

3   The full mortality information for the Class of '58 is in appendix 2.

4   She is now in the process of going back to school herself and getting a degree.

5   Insofar as there is a separate African American class structure (Hannerz 1969, Bell 1983), it has been changing over the last several decades, and I am not sure how a policeman would be classified now.

6   Not every African American classmate with a college degree was able to move up the ladder. This, of course, is true for any group, but given the bad odds I discussed earlier, it is probably significantly more of a problem for African Americans; two of the men with degrees are thus unemployed.

7   Martin Luther King Jr. was flanked by two clergymen, a rabbi and a priest, when he led the march. The rabbi, Joachim Prinz, was the leader of one of the major Weequahic Jewish congregations, Temple B'nai Abraham.

8   Surely some of the parents of the Class of '58 who were industrial or dock workers were unionized, but no one ever mentioned unions in their interviews. This silence may have been an effect of the McCarthyism of the 1950s.

9   Americans in the 1950s and 1960s tended to think of themselves as relatively "happy" in general. See the fascinating "happiness report" by Norman Bradburn and David Caplovitz (1965). One wonders how the study would shape up in less prosperous times.

10   There was also a whiff of money-as-power in his comments. He spoke of how money allowed him "to influence the people around me in a positive way." Apart from this—and surprisingly, perhaps—the connection between money and power was rarely made.

11   He and several others also mentioned the importance of good health.

12   This means bringing back at least some of Durkheim, minus the functionalism that has caused him to be so discredited. Durkheim believed in the force of relationships as such in the social process, and that is what is at issue here.

11. Liberation

1   A thousand thanks to Abigail Stewart and David Winter for directing me to this source of statistical information, and more generally for patiently answering many of my questions about the mysteries of statistics.

2   I am avoiding breaking out "Jewish women" as I am avoiding breaking out the other race/ethnic groups among women for reasons discussed

earlier, namely, that I will be concerned to look at the impact of the women's movement in general on the women of the Class of '58. There is, however, a small but valuable body of anthropological literature on ordinary, middle-class, Jewish women (see especially Prell 1990, 1996; see also Lieberman 1996 and D. A. Segal 1999). There is also a body of relevant fiction on Jewish women in the 1950s, most especially Herman Wouk's *Marjorie Morningstar*, which captures the ways even feisty and independent young Jewish women of the era caved in to the girl track in the end. There is an even larger body of literature on orthodox Jewish women, but that is not relevant to the project at hand.

3 One hundred ninety-six known members of the Class of '58 produced 434 children, or the classic 2.2 children. The number of children per classmate ranged from 0 to 5, but the vast majority had 2 or 3. Three hundred ninety-eight of these children were produced the old-fashioned way, while 36 were acquired by other means—stepchildren acquired through marriage, adoptions (including some of stepchildren), and surrogacy.

4 The key body of work linking women's lives and careers with the impact of the feminist movement has been that of Abigail Stewart (see 1994 and further cited sources in that piece).

5 Thomas Fricke found the relevant source and helped me interpret this number, and I am deeply grateful. The interpretation is based on the chart on p. 23 of Andrew Cherlin's *Marriage, Divorce, Remarriage* (1992). The Class of '58 mostly got married between 1958 (right out of high school) and 1970. According to Cherlin's chart, the divorce rate for that marriage cohort averages about 42 or 43 percent.

6 Only one man talked spontaneously—and very bitterly—about his divorce. Other men mentioned divorce but either passed over it quickly or became visibly uncomfortable and said they did not wish to talk about it.

7 I heard of one case where the husband, who came from a wealthy family, initiated and won a custody suit, and barred the wife from contact with the children. I have no further information on this, but it was extremely unusual at the time (it still is, though a bit less so); virtually all other divorced C58 mothers, as far as I know, retained custody of their children.

12. Late Capitalism

1   Again, the pathbreaking work on this was Laclau and Mouffe 1985.
2   On "bringing class back in," see, for example, many of the contributors to McNall et al. 1991; see also Wright 1985.
3   Bourdieu (1978, 1990) discusses the importance of a dialectic, rather than an opposition, between objectivist modes of analysis, that is, of looking at structures and patterns of social life and cultural thought that may not be visible to actors, and "phenomenological" modes of analysis, in which one tries to understand things "from the actor's point of view." Obviously this entire book shares that point of view.
4   The phrase was originally coined by Ernst Mandel (1978).
5   Taylor 1997 also notes the proliferation of lists in works that attempt to get a grip on the range of social and cultural transformations under way.
6   Many have argued with some justice that globalization, including foreign investments in or purchases of U.S. businesses, has been going on much longer than late capitalism. Yet it is clear that it is central, as a concept and a practice, to the idea of late capitalism in a way in which it was not central to classic capitalism.
7   Weiss (2000) specifically argued that the rising divorce rate starts with the C58 generation. See also McLeod 1990.
8   Lind emphasizes race and ethnicity more than the other theorists, and actually calls this overclass "The *White* Overclass" (Lind 1995). Lind's overclass includes both WASPs and, for the first time that I have seen, Jews, clearly referring to people like Henry Kissinger, Alan Greenspan, and 2000 Democratic vice presidential nominee Joe Lieberman. The Weequahic case fits his point as well.

Works Cited

Books and Articles

Abercrombie, Nicholas, Stephen Hill, and Bryan S. Turner. 1986. *Sovereign Individuals of Capitalism*. London: Allen and Unwin.

Ahearn, Laura. 2001. "Language and Agency." *Annual Review of Anthropology* 30: 109–37.

Alba, Richard D. 1990. *Ethnic Identity: The Transformation of White America*. New Haven: Yale University Press.

Aldrich, Nelson W. Jr. 1988. *Old Money: The Mythology of America's Upper Class*. New York: Alfred A. Knopf.

Althusser, Louis. 1971. "Ideology and Ideological State Apparatuses," 127–86. In his *Lenin and Philosophy*. New York: Monthly Review Press.

American Anthropologist. 1955. [Untitled special issue on American culture.] Volume 56, number 6, part 1, December.

Antze, Paul, and Michael Lambek. 1996. *Tense Past: Cultural Essays in Trauma and Memory*. New York: Routledge.

Appadurai, Arjun. 1996. *Modernity at Large: Cultural Dimensions of Globalization*. Minneapolis: University of Minnesota Press.

Applebome, Peter. 1999. "Two Words behind the Massacre." *New York Times*, May 2, 1.

Aronowitz, Stanley. 1991. *The Politics of Identity: Class, Culture, Social Movements*. New York: Routledge.

Avineri, Shlomo. 1968. *The Social and Political Thought of Karl Marx*. Cambridge: Cambridge University Press.

Baraka, Amiri. 1997 (1984). *The Autobiography of Leroi Jones*. Reprint. Chicago: Lawrence Hill Books.

Barber, Bernard. 1957. *Social Stratification: A Comparative Analysis of Structure and Process*. New York: Harper, Brace and World.

Baritz, Loren. 1982. *The Good Life: The Meaning of Success for the American Middle Class*. New York: Harper and Row.

Baudrillard, Jean. 1988a. *America*. Trans. Chris Turner. London: Verso.
———. 1988b. *Selected Writings*. Ed. Mark Poster. Stanford: Stanford University Press.

Beauvoir, Simone de. 1970 (1949). *The Second Sex*. Trans. H. M. Parshley. New York: Alfred A. Knopf.

Beck, Ulrich. 2000. *The Brave New World of Work.* Trans. P. Camiller. Cambridge: Polity Press.

Behling, Todd. 1991. "Stress and Response in a Middle Class Urban Church." Honors thesis, University of Michigan.

Bell, Michael J. 1983. *The World from Brown's Lounge: An Ethnography of Black Middle-Class Play.* Urbana: University of Illinois Press.

Bellah, Robert N., Richard Madsen, William M. Sullivan, Ann Swidler, and Steven M. Tipton. 1996 (1985). *Habits of the Heart: Individualism and Commitment in American Life.* Berkeley: University of California Press.

Bendix, Reinhard, and Seymour Martin Lipset, eds. 1967. *Class, Status, and Power: A Reader in Social Stratification.* 2d ed. London: Routledge.

Bettie, Julie. 2000. "Women without Class: Chicas, Cholas, Trash and the Presence/Absence of Class Identity." *Signs* 26 (1): 1–35.

Birmingham, Stephan. 1967. *"Our Crowd": The Great Jewish Families of New York.* New York: Harper and Row.

Biskind, Peter. 1983. *Seeing Is Believing: How Hollywood Taught Us to Stop Worrying and Love the Fifties.* New York: Henry Holt.

Bolte, Charles G., and Louis Harris. 1947. *Our Negro Veterans.* New York: Public Affairs Committee, Inc.

Bourdieu, Pierre. 1978. *Outline of a Theory of Practice.* Trans. R. Nice. Cambridge: Cambridge University Press.

———. 1984. *Distinction: A Social Critique of the Judgement of Taste.* Trans. R. Nice. Cambridge: Harvard University Press.

———. 1990. *The Logic of Practice.* Trans. R. Nice. Stanford: Stanford University Press.

Boyarin, Jonathan, ed. 1994. *Remapping Memory: The Politics of TimeSpace.* Minneapolis: University of Minnesota Press.

Bradburn, Norman M., and David Caplovitz. 1965. *Report on Happiness: A Pilot Study of Behavior Related to Mental Health.* Chicago: Aldine.

Breines, Wini. 1992. *Young, White, and Miserable: Growing Up Female in the Fifties.* Boston: Beacon Press.

Brettell, Caroline B. 1993. *When They Read What We Write: The Politics of Ethnography.* Westport, Conn.: Bergin and Garvey.

Brodkin, Karen [as Karen Brodkin Sacks]. 1989. "Toward a Unified Theory of Class, Race, and Gender." *American Ethnologist* 16 (3): 534–50.

———. 1999. *How Jews Became White Folks and What That Says about Race in America.* New Brunswick: Rutgers University Press.

Burnett, Jacquetta Hill. 1975. "Ceremony, Rites, and Economy in the Student System of an American High School." In *The Nacirema: Readings on American Culture*, ed. J. P. Spradley and M. A. Rynkiewich, 43–54. Boston: Little, Brown.

Calhoun, Craig, ed. 1994. *Social Theory and the Politics of Identity*. Cambridge, Mass.: Blackwell.

Canaan, Joyce. 1986. "Why a 'Slut' Is a 'Slut': Cautionary Tales of Middle-Class Teenage Girls' Morality." In *Symbolizing America*, ed. H. Varenne, 184–208. Lincoln: University of Nebraska Press.

Castells, Manuel. 1996. *The Rise of the Network Society*. Cambridge, Mass.: Blackwell.

Chang, Heewon. 1992. *Adolescent Life and Ethos: An Ethnography of a US High School*. London: Falmer Press.

Cherlin, Andrew J. 1992. *Marriage, Divorce, Remarriage*. Cambridge, Mass.: Harvard University Press.

Christopher, Robert C. 1989. *Crashing the Gates: The De-WASPing of America's Power Elite*. New York: Simon and Schuster.

Clifford, James, and George Marcus, eds. 1986. *Writing Culture: The Poetics and Politics of Ethnography*. Berkeley: University of California Press.

Cohen, Jean 1982. *Class and Civil Society: The Limits of Marxian Critical Theory*. Amherst: University of Massachussetts Press.

Coleman, James S. 1961. *The Adolescent Society: The Social Life of the Teenager and Its Impact on Education*. New York: Free Press.

Coleman, R. P., and Lee Rainwater. 1978. *Social Standing in America*. New York: Basic Books.

Comaroff, Jean, and John L. Comaroff. 2001. "Millennial Capitalism: First Thoughts on a Second Coming." In *Millennial Capitalism and the Culture of Neoliberalism*, ed. J. and J. L. Comaroff, 1–56. Durham: Duke University Press.

Connerton, Paul. 1989. *How Societies Remember*. Cambridge: Cambridge University Press.

Cookson, Peter W. Jr., and Caroline Hodges Persell. 1985. *Preparing for Power: America's Elite Boarding Schools*. New York: Basic Books.

Cousins, Linwood H. 1994. "Community High: The Complexity of Race and Social Class in a Black Urban High School." Ph.D. diss., University of Michigan, Ann Arbor.

Crain, Caleb. 2000. "The Ties That Bound in America." *New York Times Book Review*. December 17, 39.

Cunningham, John T. 1988. *Newark*. Newark: New Jersey Historical Society.

DeMott, Benjamin. 1990. *The Imperial Middle: Why Americans Can't Think Straight about Class*. New York: William Morrow.

————. 1991. "In Hollywood, Class Doesn't Put Up Much of a Struggle."
  New York Times, Arts and Leisure section, January 20, 1, 22.

Denby, David. 1999. "High School Confidential." *New Yorker,* May 31,
  94–98.

Dirks, Nicholas B., Geoff Eley, and Sherry B. Ortner. 1994. Introduction to
  Culture/Power/History, 3–46. Princeton: Princeton University Press.

Douglas, Mary. 1970. *Natural Symbols: Explorations in Cosmology.* New
  York: Pantheon Books.

Duncan, Greg J., Timothy M. Smeeding, and Willard Rogers. 1992. "The
  Incredible Shrinking Middle Class." *American Demographics* 14 (May):
  34–38.

Eckert, Penelope. 1989. *Jocks and Burnouts: Social Categories and Identity in
  the High School.* New York: Teachers College Press.

Eder, Klaus. 1993. *The New Politics of Class: Social Movements and Cultural
  Dynamics in Advanced Societies.* London: Sage.

Ehrenreich, Barbara. 1983. *The Hearts of Men: American Dreams and the
  Flight from Commitment.* Garden City, N.Y.: Anchor Press/Doubleday.

————. 1989. *Fear of Falling: The Inner Life of the Middle Class.* New York:
  Pantheon Books.

Ehrenreich, Barbara, and John Ehrenreich. 1979 (1977). "The Professional-
  Managerial Class." Reprinted in *Between Labour and Capital,* ed. Pat
  Walker, 5–45. Hassocks, Sussex: Harvester Press.

Eisler, Benita. 1983. *Class Act: America's Last Dirty Secret.* New York:
  Franklin Watts.

Elder, Glen H. Jr. 1974. *Children of the Great Depression: Social Change in Life
  Experience.* Chicago: University of Chicago Press.

Fass, Paula. 1977. *The Damned and the Beautiful: American Youth in the 1920s.*
  New York: Oxford University Press.

Fisher, Michael M. J. 1986. "Ethnicity and the Post-modern Arts of Memory." In *Writing Culture: The Poetics and Politics of Ethnography,* ed. J. Clifford and G. Marcus, 194–233. Berkeley: University of California Press.

Foley, Douglas E. 1990. *Learning Capitalist Culture: Deep in the Heart of
  Tejas.* Philadelphia: University of Pennsylvania Press.

Foucault, Michel. 1982. "The Subject and Power." In *Michel Foucault: Beyond Structuralism and Hermeneutics,* ed. H. L. Dreyfus and P. Rabinow,
  208–26. Chicago: University of Chicago Press.

Franklin, Sarah. 1997. *Embodied Progress: A Cultural Account of Assisted
  Conception.* London: Routledge.

Friedan, Betty. 1963. *The Feminine Mystique.* New York: Norton.

Fussell, Paul. 1983. *Class: A Guide through the American Status System.* New
  York: Ballantine Books.

Gabbard, Glen O., and Krin Gabbard. 1999. *Psychiatry and the Cinema.* 2d ed. Washington, D.C.: American Psychiatric Press.

Gabler, Neal. 1988. *An Empire of Their Own: How the Jews Invented Hollywood.* New York: Anchor/Doubleday.

Galbraith, John Kenneth. 1984 (1958). *The Affluent Society.* New York: New American Library.

Gates, Anita. 1998. "Yes, America Has a Class System. See 'Frasier.'" *New York Times*, April 19, 35, 43.

Giddens, Anthony. 1973. *The Class Structure of the Advanced Societies.* London: Hutchinson.

———. 1979. *Central Problems in Social Theory: Action, Structure, and Contradiction in Social Analysis.* Berkeley: University of California Press.

Gilliland, Paula. 1968. "Success Key: You Can't Fool the Students." *Newark Star Ledger,* June 23.

Ginsberg, Allen. 1996. *Selected Poems, 1947-1995.* New York: HarperCollins.

Ginsburg, Faye. 1989. *Contested Lives: The Abortion Debate in an American Community.* Berkeley: University of California Press.

Ginsburg, Faye, and Rayna Rapp, eds. 1995. *Conceiving the New World Order.* Berkeley: University of California Press.

Goldman, Ari L. 1991. "The *Times* and Judaism." In his *The Search for God at Harvard,* 151–67. New York: Ballantine Books.

Goldschmidt, Walter. 1950. "Social Class in America: A Critical Review." *American Anthropologist* 52 (4, part 1): 483-98.

Gopnik, Adam. 2000. "Talking Man: A New Biography Looks at Groucho's Inner Life." *New Yorker,* April 17, 112-20.

Gordon, Albert I. 1959. *Jews in Suburbia.* Boston: Beacon Press.

Gordon, C. Wayne. 1957. *The Social System of the High School: A Study in the Sociology of Adolescence.* Glencoe, Ill.: Free Press.

Graebner, William. 1990. *Coming of Age in Buffalo: Youth and Authority in the Postwar Era.* Philadelphia: Temple University Press.

Gregory, Steven. 1998. *Black Corona: Race and the Politics of Place in an Urban Community.* Princeton: Princeton University Press.

Grover, Kathryn. 1997. *Teenage New Jersey, 1941-1975.* Newark: New Jersey Historical Society.

Gupta, Akhil, and James Ferguson, eds. 1997. *Anthropological Locations: Boundaries and Grounds of a Field Science.* Berkeley: University of California Press.

Halberstam, David. 1993. *The Fifties.* New York: Fawcett Columbine.

Hale, Nathan G. Jr. 1995. *The Rise and Crisis of Psychoanalysis in the United*

States: Freud and the Americans, 1917–1985. New York: Oxford University Press.

Hall, Stuart. 1989. "Ethnicity: Identity and Difference." *Radical America* 23 (4): 9–21.

Halle, David. 1985. *America's Working Man: Work, Home, and Politics among Blue Collar Property Owners.* Chicago: University of Chicago Press.

Hannerz, Ulf. 1969. *Soulside: Inquiries into Ghetto Culture and Community.* New York: Columbia University Press.

———. 1996. *Transnational Connections: Culture, People, Places.* London: Routledge.

Harrington, Charles C., and Susan K. Boardman. 1997. *Paths to Success: Beating the Odds in American Society.* Cambridge: Harvard University Press.

Hartsock, Nancy. 1990. "Rethinking Modernism: Minority vs. Majority Theories." In *The Nature and Context of Minority Discourse,* ed. A. R. JanMohamed and D. Lloyd, 17–36. New York: Oxford University Press.

Harvey, David. 1989. *The Condition of Postmodernity: An Enquiry into the Origins of Cultural Change.* Oxford: Blackwell.

Hayden, Tom. 1988. *Reunion: A Memoir.* New York: Random House.

Helmreich, William B. 1999. *The Enduring Community: The Jews of Newark and Metrowest.* New Brunswick: Transaction Publishers.

Henry, Jules. 1965 (1963). "Rome High School and Its Students." In *Culture against Man,* 182–282. New York: Vintage Books.

Herman, Ellen. 1995. *The Romance of American Psychology: Political Culture in the Age of Experts.* Berkeley: University of California Press.

Hine, Thomas. 1986. *Populuxe.* New York: MJF Books.

Holland, Dorothy, and Jean Lave, eds. 2001. *History in Person: Enduring Struggles, Contentious Practices, Intimate Identities.* Santa Fe, N.M.: School of American Research Press.

Holland, Dorothy, Debra Skinner, William Lachicotte Jr., and Carole Cain. 1998. *Identity and Agency in Cultural Worlds.* Cambridge, Mass.: Harvard University Press.

Hollinger, David A. 1996. Science, Jews, and Secular Culture. Princeton: Princeton University Press.

Hollingshead, August B. 1949. *Elmtown's Youth: The Impact of Social Classes on Adolescents.* New York: John Wiley and Sons.

hooks, bell. 2000. *Where We Stand: Class Matters.* New York: Routledge.

Howe, Neil, and Bill Strauss. 1993. *13th Gen: Abort, Retry, Ignore, Fail?* New York: Vintage Books.

Huff, Darrell. 1954. *How to Lie with Statistics.* New York: Norton.

Ikeda, Keiko. 1998. *A Room Full of Mirrors: High School Reunions in Middle America.* Stanford: Stanford University Press.

Illick, Joseph E. 1989. *At Liberty: The Story of a Community and a Generation.* Knoxville: University of Tennessee Press.

Jackman, Mary, and Robert W. Jackman. 1983. *Class Awareness in the United States.* Berkeley: University of California Press.

Jackson, K. T., and B. B. Jackson. 1972. "The Black Experience in Newark: The Growth of the Ghetto, 1870–1970." In *New Jersey since 1860: New Findings and Interpretations,* ed. W. C. Wright, 36–59. Trenton: New Jersey Historical Commission.

Jameson, Fredric. 1984. "Postmodernism, or the Cultural Logic of Late Capitalism." *New Left Review* 146: 53–92.

———. 1996. "Actually Existing Marxism." In *Marxism beyond Marxism,* ed. Saree Makdisi et al., 14–54. New York: Routledge.

Jezer, Marty. 1982. *The Dark Ages: Life in the United States, 1945–1960.* Boston: South End Press.

Jones, Hettie. 1990. *How I Came to Be Hettie Jones.* New York: Grove Press.

Joyce, Patrick, ed. 1995. *Class.* Oxford: Oxford University Press.

Kaplan, James. 1998. *Two Guys from Verona.* New York: Grove Press.

Katz, Donald R. 1992. *Home Fires: An Intimate Portrait of One Middle-Class Family in Postwar America.* New York: HarperCollins.

Keister, Lisa A., and Stephanie Moller. 2000. "Wealth Inequality in the United States." *Annual Review of Sociology* 26: 63–81.

Kelley, Robin D. G. 1997. *Yo' Mama's Disfunktional: Fighting the Culture Wars in Urban America.* Boston: Beacon Press.

Keniston, Kenneth. 1968. *Young Radicals.* New York: Harcourt, Brace and World.

Keyes, Ralph. 1976. *Is There Life after High School?* Boston: Little, Brown.

Kleeblatt, Norman L. 1996. " 'Passing' into Multiculturalism." In his *Too Jewish: Challenging Traditional Identities,* 3–38. New York: The Jewish Museum, and New Brunswick: Rutgers University Press.

Knauft, Bruce. 1985. *Good Company and Violence: Sorcery and Social Action in a Lowland New Guinea Society.* Berkeley: University of California Press.

Kraft, Herbert C. 1986. *The Lenape: Archaeology, History and Ethnography.* Newark: New Jersey Historical Society.

Laclau, Ernesto, and Chantal Mouffe. 1985. *Hegemony and Socialist Strategy: Towards a Radical Democratic Politics.* Trans. W. Moore and P. Cammack. London: Verso.

Lamont, Michèle, and Marcel Fournier, eds. 1992. *Cultivating Differences: Symbolic Boundaries and the Making of Inequality.* Chicago: University of Chicago Press.

Lash, Scott, and John Urry. 1987. *The End of Organized Capitalism*. Madison: University of Wisconsin Press.

Leach, Edmund. 1969. "The Legitimacy of Solomon." In his *Genesis as Myth and Other Essays*, 25–83. London: Jonathan Cape.

Lefkowitz, Bernard. 1998. *Our Guys: The Glen Ridge Rape and the Secret Life of the Perfect Suburb*. New York: Vintage Books.

Levine, Joe. 1996. "The Long Way Home." *University of Chicago Magazine* 88 (3): 22–27.

Lévi-Strauss, Claude. 1966. *The Savage Mind*. Chicago: University of Chicago Press.

———. 1970. *The Raw and the Cooked: Introduction to a Science of Mythology*. Trans. J. Weightman and D. Weightman. Harmondsworth, Middlesex, England: Penguin.

Lewis, Michael. 1978. *The Culture of Inequality*. Amherst: University of Massachusetts Press.

Lieberman, Rhonda. 1996. "Jewish Barbie." In *Too Jewish? Challenging Traditional Identities*, ed. N. L. Kleeblatt, 108–14. New York: The Jewish Museum, and New Brunswick: Rutgers University Press.

Lind, Michael. 1995. *The Next American Nation: The New Nationalism and the Fourth American Revolution*. New York: Free Press.

Lipset, Seymour Martin, and Reinhard Bendix. 1957. *Social Mobility in Industrial Society*. Berkeley: University of California Press.

Lipsitz, George. 1990. *Time Passages: Collective Memory and American Popular Culture*. Minneapolis: University of Minnesota Press.

Lynd, Robert, and Helen Merrell Lynd. 1957. *Middletown: A Study of Contemporary American Culture*. 1929. New York: Harcourt Brace Jovanovich.

Lyons, Paul. 1994. *Class of '66: Living in Suburban America*. Philadelphia: Temple University Press.

Lyotard, Jean-François. 1984. *The Postmodern Condition*. Minneapolis: University of Minnesota Press.

Mandel, Ernest. 1978 (1972). *Late Capitalism*. Trans. J. De Bres. London: Verso.

Mankekar, Purnima. 1999. *Screening Culture, Viewing Politics: An Ethnography of Television, Womanhood and Nation in Postcolonial India*. Durham: Duke University Press.

Mann, Cynthia. 1996. "[*New York*] *Times* Celebrates Centennial; Editors Debate Jewish Influence." *Jewish Monthly*, December–January, 14–37.

Marable, Manning. 1983. *How Capitalism Undeveloped Black America: Problems in Race, Political Economy, and Society*. Boston: South End Press.

Marcus, George E. 1998. *Ethnography through Thick and Thin*. Princeton: Princeton University Press.

———, ed. 1999. *Critical Anthropology Now: Unexpected Contexts, Shifting Constituencies, Changing Agendas*. Santa Fe, N.M.: School of American Research Press.

Marcus, George E., with Peter Dobkin Hall. 1992. *Lives in Trust: The Fortunes of Dynastic Families in Late Twentieth-Century America*. Boulder: Westview Press.

Marx, Karl. 1965 (1867). *The Communist Manifesto*. New York: Washington Square Press.

May, Lary. 1989. *Recasting America: Culture and Politics in the Age of the Cold War*. Chicago: University of Chicago Press.

McDonough, John. 1990. "Class Picture: At Its 25th Reunion, a Close-up of a High School Class—and a Generation." *Chicago Tribune Magazine*, November 11, 14–18.

McGuire, Meredith B. 1988. *Ritual Healing in Suburban America*. New Brunswick: Rutgers University Press.

McLeod, Ramon G. 1990. "World War II Babies Set Family Trends." *San Francisco Chronicle*, May 9, A2.

McMurrer, Daniel P., and Isabel V. Sawhill. 1998. *Getting Ahead: Economic and Social Mobility in America*. Washington, D.C.: Urban Institute Press.

McNall, Scott, R. Levine, and R. Fantasia, eds. 1991. *Bringing Class Back In: Contemporary and Historical Perspectives*. Boulder: Westview Press.

Medved, Michael, and David Wallechinsky. 1976. *What Really Happened to the Class of '65?* New York: Random House.

Menand, Louis. 1997. "The Irony and the Ecstasy: Philip Roth and the Jewish Atlantis." *New Yorker*, May 19, 88–94.

Messerschmidt, Donald A., ed. 1981. *Anthropologists at Home in North America: Methods and Issues in the Study of One's Own Society*. New York: Cambridge University Press.

Metalious, Grace. 1999 (1956). *Peyton Place*. Boston: Northeastern University Press.

Meyerowitz, Joanne. 1994. "Beyond the Feminine Mystique: A Reassessment of Postwar Mass Culture, 1946–1958." In her *Not June Cleaver: Women and Gender in Postwar America*, 1–16. Philadelphia: Temple University Press.

Mills, C. Wright. 1951. *White Collar: The American Middle Classes*. New York: Oxford University Press.

———. 1956. *The Power Elite*. London: Oxford University Press.

Moffatt, Michael. 1989. *Coming of Age in New Jersey: College and American Culture*. New Brunswick: Rutgers University Press.

———. 1992. "Ethnographic Writing about American Culture." *Annual Review of Anthropology* 21: 205–27.

Mohanty, S. P. 1989. "Us and Them: On the Philosophical Bases of Political Criticism." *Yale Journal of Criticism* 2 (2): 1–31.

Morris, Martina, and Bruce Western. 1999. "Inequality in Earnings at the Close of the 20th Century." *Annual Review of Sociology* 25: 623–57.

Myerhoff, Barbara. 1978. *Number Our Days.* New York: Touchstone/Simon and Schuster.

Narayan, Kirin. 1993. "How Native Is a 'Native' Anthropologist?" *American Anthropologist* 95: 671–86.

Newark Evening News. 1959a. "Weequahic Rated Tops." January 18.

———. 1959b. "School Honors." January 21.

Newman, Katherine S. 1988. *Falling from Grace: The Experience of Downward Mobility in the American Middle Class.* New York: Free Press.

———. 1993. *Declining Fortunes: The Withering of the American Dream.* New York: Basic Books.

Ochs, Elinor, and Lisa Capps. 1996. "Narrating the Self." *Annual Review of Anthropology* 25: 19–43.

O'Neill, William L. 1986. *American High: The Years of Confidence, 1945–1960.* New York: Free Press.

Ortner, Sherry B. 1973. "On Key Symbols." *American Anthropologist* 75: 1338–46.

———. 1991. "Reading America: Preliminary Notes on Class and Culture." In *Recapturing Anthropology: Working in the Present*, ed. Richard G. Fox, 163–90. Advanced Seminar Series. Santa Fe, N.M.: School of American Research Press.

———. 1993. "Ethnography among the Newark: The Class of '58 of Weequahic High School." *Michigan Quarterly Review* 32 (3): 410–29. Reprinted in *Naturalizing Power*, ed. C. Delaney and S. Yanagisako. Stanford: Stanford University Press, 1995.

———. 1995. "Resistance and the Problem of Ethnographic Refusal." *Comparative Studies in Society and History* 37 (1): 173–93.

———. 1996. "Making Gender: Toward a Feminist, Minority, Postcolonial, Subaltern, etc., Theory of Practice." In *Making Gender: The Politics and Erotics of Culture*, 1–20. Boston: Beacon Press.

———. 1997. "Fieldwork in the Post-Community." *Anthropology and Humanism* 27 (1): 61–80.

———. 1998a. "Identities: The Hidden Life of Class." *Journal of Anthropological Research* 54 (1): 1–17.

———. 1998b. "Generation X: Anthropology in a Media-Saturated World." *Cultural Anthropology* 13 (3): 414–40.

————. 1999. *Life and Death on Mount Everest: Sherpas and Himalayan Mountaineering*. Princeton: Princeton University Press.

————. 2000. "Some Futures of Anthropology." *American Ethnologist* 26 (4): 984–91.

————. 2002a. "The Death and Rebirth of Anthropology." *Ethnos* 67 (1): 7–8.

————. 2002b. "Subjects and Capital: A Fragment of a Documentary Ethnography." *Ethnos* 67 (1): 9–32.

————. 2002c. "Burned like a Tattoo: High School Social Categories and 'American Culture.'" *Ethnography* 3 (2): 115–48.

Owen, David. 2000. "Taking Humor Seriously: George Meyer, the Funniest Man behind the Funniest Show on TV." *New Yorker*, March 13, 64–75.

Palonsky, Stuart B. 1975. "Hempies and Squeaks, Truckers and Cruisers—A Participant Observer Study in a City High School." *Educational Administration Quarterly* 11 (2): 86–103.

Parker, Richard. 1972. *The Myth of the Middle Class: Notes on Affluence and Equality*. New York: Harper and Row.

Parsons, Talcott. 1959. "The School Class as a Social System: Some of Its Functions in American Society." *Harvard Educational Review* 29 (4): 297–318.

Pateman, Carol. 1988. *The Sexual Contract*. Stanford: Stanford University Press.

Plotnicov, Leonard, ed. 1990. *American Culture: Essays on the Familiar and Unfamiliar*. Pittsburgh: University of Pittsburgh Press.

Potter, David Morris. 1955. *People of Plenty: Economic Abundance and the American Character*. Chicago: University of Chicago Press.

Poulantzas, Nicos. 1975. *Classes in Contemporary Capitalism*. London: NLB.

Powdermaker, Hortense. 1951. *Hollywood the Dream Factory: An Anthropologist Looks at the Movie Makers*. Boston: Little, Brown.

Prell, Riv-Ellen. 1990. "Rage and Representation: Jewish Gender Stereotypes in American Culture." In *Uncertain Terms: Negotiating Gender in American Culture*, ed. Faye Ginsburg and Anna Lowenhaupt Tsing, 248–68. Boston: Beacon Press.

————. 1996. "Why Jewish Princesses Don't Sweat: Desire and Consumption in Postwar American Jewish Culture." In N. L. Kleeblatt, *Too Jewish: Challenging Traditional Identities*, 74–92. New York: The Jewish Museum, New Brunswick: Rutgers University Press.

Quindlen, Anna. 2001. "Watching the World Go By." *Newsweek*, February 26, 74.

Rabinow, Paul. 1991. "For Hire: Resolutely Late Modern." In *Recapturing*

Anthropology: Working in the Present, ed. R. Fox, 59–72. Santa Fe, N.M.: School of American Research Press.

Rabkin, Leslie Y. 1998. *The Celluloid Couch*. Lanham, Md.: Scarecrow Press.

Rapp, Rayna. 1982. "Family and Class in Contemporary America: Notes toward an Understanding of Ideology." In *Rethinking the Family: Some Feminist Questions*, ed. B. Thorne and M. Yalom, 168–87. New York: Longman.

———. 1999. *Testing Women, Testing the Fetus: The Social Impact of Amniocentesis in America*. New York: Routledge.

Reynolds, Charles H., and Ralph V. Norman, eds. 1988. *Community in America: The Challenge of Habits of the Heart*. Berkeley: University of California Press.

Rieder, Jonathan. 1985. *Canarsie: The Jews and Italians of Brooklyn against Liberalism*. Cambridge, Mass.: Harvard University Press.

Ross, Andrew. 1989. "Containing Culture in the Cold War." In his *No Respect: Intellectuals and Popular Culture*, 42–64. New York: Routledge.

Roth, Philip. 1959. *Goodbye, Columbus and Five Short Stories*. New York: Modern Library.

———. 1967. *Portnoy's Complaint*. New York: Random House.

———. 1987. "My Life as a Boy." *New York Times Book Review*, October 18, 1.

———. 1988. *The Counterlife*. New York: Penguin.

———. 1993. *Operation Shylock*. New York: Simon and Schuster.

———. 1997. *American Pastoral*. Boston: Houghton Mifflin.

———. 2000. Interview on *Fresh Air*. National Public Radio, May 8.

Sahlins, Marshall. 1981. *Historical Metaphors and Mythical Realities*. Ann Arbor: University of Michigan Press.

Samuelson, Robert J. 1995. *The Good Life and Its Discontents: The American Dream in the Age of Entitlement, 1945–1995*. New York: Times Books/Random House.

Sanjek, Roger. 1990. *Fieldnotes: The Makings of Anthropology*. Ithaca: Cornell University Press.

Sartre, Jean-Paul. 1956. *Being and Nothingness: An Essay on Phenomenological Ontology*. Trans. Hazel E. Barnes. New York: Philosophical Library.

———. 1963. *Search for a Method*. Trans. H. E. Barnes. New York: Alfred A. Knopf.

Sawhill, Isabel V. 1999. "Still the Land of Opportunity?" *Public Interest* (Spring): 3–17.

Scase, Richard. 1992. *Class*. Minneapolis: University of Minnesota Press.

Schneider, Barbara, and David Stevenson. 1999. *The Ambitious Genera-*

tion: *America's Teenagers, Motivated but Directionless.* New Haven: Yale University Press.

Schumacher, Michael. 1992. *Dharma Lion: A Critical Biography of Allen Ginsberg.* New York: St. Martin's Press.

Schwartz, Gary, and Don Merten. 1967. "The Language of Adolescence: An Anthropological Approach to the Youth Culture." *American Journal of Sociology* 72 (5): 453–68.

———. 1975. "Social Identity and Expressive Symbols." In *The Nacirema: Readings on American Culture,* ed. J. Spradley and M. Rynkiewich, 195–211. Boston: Little, Brown.

Scott, James. 1990. *Domination and the Arts of Resistance: Hidden Transcripts.* New Haven: Yale University Press.

Scott, Joan. 1988. "On Language, Gender, and Working-Class History." In her *Gender and the Politics of History,* 53–67. New York: Columbia University Press.

Segal, Daniel A. 1998. "The Hypervisible and the Masked: Some Thoughts on the Mutual Embeddedness of 'Race' and 'Class' in the United States Now." In *Democracy and Ethnography: Constructing Identities in Multicultural Liberal States,* ed. C. J. Greenhouse with R. Kheshti, 50–60. Albany: State University of New York Press.

———. 1999. "Can You Tell a Jew When You See One? Or Thoughts on Meeting Barbra/Barbie at the Museum." *Judaism* 48 (2): 234–41.

Segal, Troy. 1992. "The [L.A.] Riots: 'Just as Much about Class as about Race.'" *Business Week,* May 18, 47.

Sennett, Richard, and Jonathan Cobb. 1972. *The Hidden Injuries of Class.* New York: Vintage Books.

Sewell, William H. Jr. 1992. "A Theory of Structure: Duality, Agency, and Transformation." *American Journal of Sociology* 98 (1): 1–29.

———. 1996. "Three Temporalities: Toward an Eventful Sociology." In *The Historic Turn in the Human Sciences,* ed. T. McDonald, 245–80. Ann Arbor: University of Michigan Press.

———. 1999. "A Theory of the Event: Reflections on Marshall Sahlins' 'Possible Theory of History.'" Unpublished manuscript.

Shapiro, Isaac, and Robert Greenstein. 1999. "The Widening Income Gulf." September 4. Washington, D.C.: Center on Budget and Policy Priorities.

Shapiro, Svi. 1999. "The Littleton Tragedy." *Tikkun* 14 (4): 13–14, 62.

Sklare, Marshall, and Joseph Greenblum. 1967. *Jewish Identity on the Suburban Frontier: A Study of Group Survival in the Open Society.* New York: Basic Books.

Spradley, James P., and Michael A. Rynkiewich, eds. 1975. *The Nacirema: Readings on American Culture*. Boston: Little, Brown.

Stacey, Judith. 1990. *Brave New Families: Stories of Domestic Upheaval in Late Twentieth Century America*. New York: Basic Books.

Statistical Abstract of the United States 1962. 83d annual edition. Prepared under the direction of Edwin D. Goldfield. Washington, D.C.: U.S. Government Printing Office.

Stedman Jones, Gareth. 1983. *Languages of Class: Studies in English Working-Class History, 1832-1982*. Cambridge: Cambridge University Press.

Steedman, Carolyn Kay. 1986. *Landscape for a Good Woman: A Story of Two Lives*. New Brunswick: Rutgers University Press.

Steinberg, Stephen. 1981. *The Ethnic Myth: Race, Ethnicity, and Class in America*. New York: Atheneum.

Stewart, Abigail J. 1994. "The Women's Movement and Women's Lives: Linking Individual Development and Social Events." In *Exploring Identity and Gender: The Narrative Study of Lives*, ed. A. Lieblich and R. Josselson, 230-50. Thousand Oaks, Calif.: Sage.

———. 2000. "Uses of the Past: Toward a Psychology of Generations." Henry B. Russel Lecture. Ann Arbor: University of Michigan. Unpublished manuscript.

Stewart, Abigail J., I. H., Settles, and N. J. G. Winter. 1998. "Women and the Social Movements of the 1960s: Activists, Engaged Observers, and Nonparticipants." *Political Psychology* 19 (1): 63-94.

Stewart, Abigail J., D. G. Winter, D. Henderson-King, and E. Henderson-King. n.d. "Staying and Leaving Home: The Impact of Close Encounters with the Fifties on Midwestern Families." Unpublished manuscript.

Stille, Alexander. 2001. "Grounded by an Income Gap." On-line at New York Times.com. December 15.

Storper, Michael. 2001. "Lived Effects of the Contemporary Economy: Globalization, Inequality, and Consumer Society." In *Millennial Capitalism and the Culture of Neoliberalism*, ed. J. Comaroff and J. L. Comaroff, 88-125. Durham: Duke University Press.

Strathern, Marilyn. 1992. *Reproducing the Future: Anthropology, Kinship, and the New Reproductive Technologies*. London: Routledge.

Surowiecki, James. 2000. "The Box That Launched a Thousand Ships." *New Yorker*, December 11, 46.

Susman, Warren I. 1984 (1973). " 'Personality' and the Making of Twentieth Century Culture." In *Culture as History: The Transformation of American Society in the 20th Century*, 271-86. New York: Pantheon Books.

Taylor, Timothy D. 1997. *Global Pop: World Music, World Markets*. New York: Routledge.

Terkel, Studs. 1974. *Working: People Talk about What They Do All Day and How They Feel about What They Do*. New York: Pantheon Books.

Thernstrom, Stephan. 1964. *Poverty and Progress*. New York: Atheneum.

Thompson, E. P. 1966. *The Making of the English Working Class*. New York: Vintage.

Tobias, Sheila, and Lisa Anderson. 1974. "What Really Happened to Rosie the Riveter? Demobilization and the Female Labor Force, 1944–47." *Module* 9: 1–36. New York: MSS Modular Publications.

Trencher, Susan R. 2000. *Mirrored Images: American Anthropology and American Culture, 1960–1980*. Westport, Conn.: Bergin and Garvey.

Ueda, Reed. 1987. *Avenues to Adulthood: The Origins of the High School and Social Mobility in an American Suburb*. Cambridge: Cambridge University Press.

Vanneman, Reeve, and Lynn Weber Cannon. 1987. *The American Perception of Class*. Philadelphia: Temple University Press.

Varenne, Hervé. 1982. "Jocks and Freaks: The Symbolic Structure of the Expression of Social Interaction among American Senior High School Students." In *Doing the Ethnography of Schooling*, ed. G. Spindler, 210–35. New York: Holt, Rinehart and Winston.

———. 1983. *American School Language: Culturally Patterned Conflicts in a Suburban High School*. New York: Irvington Publishers.

———, ed. 1986. *Symbolizing America*. Lincoln: University of Nebraska Press.

Wacquant, Loïc. 1991. "Making Class: The Middle Class(es) in Social Theory and Social Structure." In *Bringing Class Back In: Contemporary and Historical Perspectives*, ed. S. McNall, R. Levine, and R. Fantasia, 39–64. Boulder: Westview Press.

Walker, Pat, ed. 1979. *Between Labour and Capital*. Sussex, England: Harvester Press.

Wallechinsky, David. 1986. *Class Reunion '65: Tales of an American Generation*. New York: Viking/Penguin.

Walzer, Michael. 1996. "Minority Rites." *Dissent* (Summer): 53–55.

Warner, W. Lloyd. 1962 (1953). *American Life: Dream and Reality*. Chicago: University of Chicago Press.

Warner, W. Lloyd, Robert J. Havighurst, and Martin B. Loeb. 1944. *Who Shall Be Educated? The Challenge of Unequal Opportunities*. New York: Harper and Brothers.

Warner, W. L., and P. S. Lunt. 1941. *The Social Life of a Modern Community*. Volume 1 of the Yankee City series. New Haven: Yale University Press.

Weiss, Jessica. 2000. *To Have and to Hold: Marriage, the Baby Boom, and Social Change.* Chicago: University of Chicago Press.

West, Cornel. 1990. "The New Cultural Politics of Difference." *October* 53: 93–109.

Willis, Paul. 1977. *Learning to Labor: How Working Class Kids Get Working Class Jobs.* New York: Columbia University Press.

Winter, David G. n.d. "Education, Race, and the American Dream: The Life and Death of Midwest High School." Unpublished manuscript.

Wolfe, Alan. 1991. *America at Century's End.* Berkeley: University of California Press.

Wolfe, Tom. 1968. *The Electric Kool-Aid Acid Test.* New York: Bantam Books.

Wouk, Herman. 1955. *Marjorie Morningstar.* Garden City, N.Y.: Doubleday and Company.

Wright, Erik Olin. 1985. *Classes.* London: Verso.

Yanagisako, Sylvia J. n.d. "Culture and Capital: Producing Italian Family Capitalism." Unpublished manuscript.

Zborowski, Mark, and B. G. Herzog. 1952. *Life Is with People: The Jewish Little-Town of Eastern Europe.* New York: International Universities Press.

Films

Apted, Michael (filmmaker). 1985. *Twenty-eight Up* (videorecording). Granada Television, Manchester, England.

———. 1992. *Thirty-five Up.* Samuel Goldwyn Films/Granada Television.

———. 1998. *Forty-two Up.* BBC/Granada Television.

Burns, Ken (filmmaker). 1990. *The Civil War* (videorecording series). American Documentaries, Inc.

Dante, Joe, et al. (directors). 1987. *Amazon Women on the Moon.* Universal Pictures.

DePalma, Brian (director). 1976. *Carrie.* MGM.

Gilbert, Craig (producer), Alan Raymond and Susan Raymond (filmmakers). 1973. *An American Family* (twelve-part videorecording series). WNET/13.

Mann, Anthony (director). 1955. *The Man from Laramie.* Columbia Pictures.

Peerce, Larry (director). 1969. *Goodbye, Columbus.* Willow Tree/Paramount.

Rapper, Irving (director). 1958. *Marjorie Morningstar.* Beachwold/Warner Bros.

Ray, Nicholas (director). 1955. *Rebel without a Cause.* Warner Bros.

Robbins, Tim (director). 1999. *The Cradle Will Rock.* Touchstone/Buena Vista Pictures.

Rudolph, Alan (director). 1991. *Mortal Thoughts.* Columbia Pictures.

Sayles, John (director). 1982. *Baby It's You.* Double Play/Paramount.

——. 1991. *City of Hope.* Esperanza/Samuel Goldwyn Company.

Stevens, George (director). 1956. *Giant.* Warner Bros.

Wilcox, Fred M. (director). 1956. *Forbidden Planet.* MGM.

Wiseman, Frederick (filmmaker). 1969. *High School.* Zipporah Films.

Index

Sherry B. Ortner is Distinguished Professor of Anthropology at the University of California, Los Angeles. Her previous books include *Life and Death on Mt. Everest: Sherpas and Himalayan Mountaineering* (1999), *The Fate of "Culture": Geertz and Beyond* (1999), and *Making Gender: The Politics and Erotics of Culture* (1996).

Library of Congress has cataloged the hardcover edition as follows:
Ortner, Sherry B.
New Jersey dreaming : capital, culture, and the class of '58 /
Sherry B. Ortner.
p. cm.
Includes bibliographical references and index.
ISBN 0-8223-3108-X (cloth : alk. paper)
1. Social mobility—United States—Case studies.   2. High school
graduates—New Jersey—Newark—Social conditions.   3. High school
graduates—New Jersey—Newark—Economic conditions.   4. Weequahic
High School (Newark, N.J.). Class of 1958.   I. Title.
HN90.S65O77   2003
305.5'13'0973—dc21   2002155153

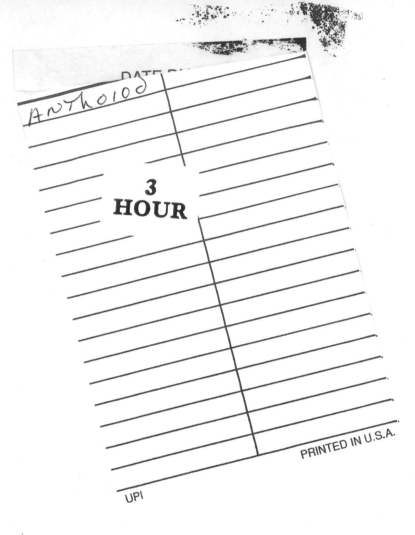

DATE D...

ANTHOLOG

**3
HOUR**

PRINTED IN U.S.A.

UPI